POWER
AND
PowerPC

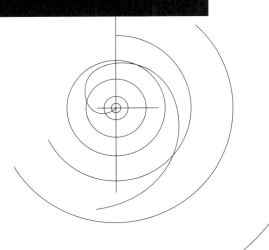

POWER

AND

PowerPC

Shlomo Weiss

James E. Smith

Morgan Kaufmann Publishers, Inc.

San Francisco, California

Executive Editor: Bruce M. Spatz
Production Manager: Yonie Overton
Assistant Editor: Douglas Sery
Production Coordinator: Julie Pabst
Copyeditor: Fran Taylor
Proofreader: Gary Morris
Cover & Text Design: Carron Design
Composition: Ed Sznyter, Babel Press
Printer: R.R. Donnelley & Sons

Editorial Offices:

Morgan Kaufmann Publishers, Inc.
340 Pine Street, Sixth Floor
San Francisco, CA 94104

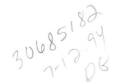

To our wives, Adina and Jerrie,
and to our children, Meytal and Roni
and Barbara, Carolyn, and Jimmy

FOREWORD

By Michael Slater
President, MicroDesign Resources
Publisher and Editorial Director, *Microprocessor Report*

This book, which provides an exceptionally complete view of the POWER and PowerPC architectures, comes at a fortuitous time. After years of evolution, PowerPC is rising to a position of great importance among microprocessor architectures.

In the past 15 years, a new style of computer architecture, called RISC (for reduced instruction set computer), has emerged. While Intel's x86 architecture, which is quite the opposite of RISC, still dominates microprocessor shipments for general-purpose computers, virtually every new architecture designed in the last decade follows the RISC principles. Already dominant in high-performance workstations, RISC proponents hope that the new architectures gradually will replace the older-style designs in mainstream personal computers.

IBM had a rocky start in the RISC business. After pioneering RISC work accomplished by the team led by IBM scientist John Cocke in the late seventies and early eighties, IBM lagged upstarts MIPS and SPARC in commercializing the technology. IBM's first commercial RISC-based system, the RT, was a flop—but the company kept pushing forward. In 1990, IBM's RS/6000 family of workstations and servers debuted, introducing a new architecture called POWER. This family has been quite successful in the UNIX market.

Not content to have its RISC architecture serve only this market, IBM entered into a remarkable alliance in the summer of 1991. IBM joined with Apple and Motorola to create the PowerPC architecture, a derivative of POWER that finetunes the architecture with a range of single-chip implementations in mind.

The PowerPC alliance is remarkable in many ways. For IBM, it represents a radical shift away from the "we can do it all ourselves" approach that had dominated the company's thinking for decades. For Apple, it is a partnership with what had been that company's archenemy. And for Motorola, pursuing PowerPC meant de-emphasizing the 88000 architecture in which the company had invested so heavily.

By putting aside their separate agendas and entering into this pivotal alliance, the three companies were able to pool their strengths. The result is an architecture—PowerPC—that many observers believe is the one most likely to wrest control of the personal computer industry away from Intel's aging x86 architecture.

Apple, as the only personal computer other than IBM with control over both its hardware and software, made the brave decision to shift the mainstream of its product line to PowerPC, a transition that is now underway. Apple's use of PowerPC ensures the architecture of a market far larger than that of any RISC design focused on UNIX, as the POWER architecture has been.

At the same time, IBM has started a new division, Power Personal Systems, to build personal computers using PowerPC microprocessors, and IBM Personal Software is developing the Workplace operating system for PowerPC. In yet another sign of its willingness to sacrifice corporate dogma to be a stronger competitor, IBM is working with Motorola to provide a version of Microsoft's Windows NT for PowerPC. Breaking from its proprietary past, IBM is virtually giving away the system designs required for other system makers to build PowerPC computers compatible with IBM's.

The PowerPC architecture won't be limited to desktop and portable computers, either. Motorola and IBM are both developing implementations for embedded control, and Ford Motor Company plans to use PowerPC chips in its next-generation power-train controllers. IBM is developing large multiprocessor systems using the architecture, potentially replacing aging mainframe designs, and there are signs that many of IBM's traditional product lines could be revamped using the POWER and PowerPC architectures. The POWER and PowerPC architectures are therefore of tremendous importance to the future of computing devices, from embedded engine controllers to large-scale computer systems. In addition, the two architectures are particularly interesting to study because they provide an illuminating example of how an instruction-set design can evolve to address different market needs.

This book is unique in both the breadth and depth of its coverage of these architectures. Benefiting from the cooperation of the designers at IBM, the authors have provided not only the details of the architecture, but the even more important "whys"—the reasons behind the design decisions. By covering the implementations (i.e., the actual chip designs) as well as the abstract definitions, the reader is afforded a view of the critical relationships between architecture and implementation. Finally, by comparing the PowerPC 601 to another recent RISC design, Digital's Alpha 21064, the authors provide a perspective on how the PowerPC approach differs from that of one of its key competitors. Any reader seeking a deeper understanding of these hallmark RISC designs and the principles behind them will find this book unusually rewarding.

C O N T E N T S

---

*Reprinted with permission of International Business Machines, Inc. from *RISC System/6000, POWERstation and POWERserver, Hardware Technical Reference, General Information*, Second Edition, 1992.

†Reprinted with permission of International Business Machines, Inc. from *The PowerPC Architecture: A Specification for a New Family of RISC Processors*, Second Edition, Morgan Kaufmann Publishers, 1994.

PREFACE

This book is an in-depth exploration of a very significant family of high-performance computers. This study includes a discussion of the important characteristics of the architectures and their implementations, as well as the important design principles that bind them together. As such, the book forms a detailed case study of the new generation of RISCs (Reduced Instruction Set Computers).

POWER and PowerPC promise to be dominant architectures during the 1990s. Their implementations have already been accepted as the basis for a broad range of commercial computer systems and embedded applications. The POWER architecture was developed by IBM and was introduced in the RS/6000 series of workstations in 1990. More recently, IBM combined with Motorola, Apple, and others in the PowerOpen consortium to develop the PowerPC architecture, with the goal of supporting a range of systems from personal computers to large-scale multiprocessors. The first PowerPC implementation, the PowerPC 601, is poised to challenge Intel for supremacy in low-cost desktop computing.

This book will be of interest to some readers simply because it describes popular computers they may personally use (now or in the future). There is, however, a broader interest. Because POWER and PowerPC were developed expressly for implementation in high-performance processors, and because of the many unique features in these implementations, they give us, collectively, an excellent vehicle for studying modern high-performance computer architecture and the interplay between architecture and implementation.

This book describes the architectures—POWER and PowerPC, processor implementations—POWER1, POWER2, and PowerPC 601, and a variety of system implementations, ranging from PCs to workstations to multiprocessor servers to massively parallel systems. Each is described at a level of detail normally found only in manuals, but from a much broader perspective and with substantially more explanation and discussion. This detail is necessary to clarify the numerous relevant issues. We focus, however, on ideas, techniques, and trade-offs, and often discuss design alternatives not chosen by the implementors.

We have chosen the POWER and PowerPC architectures and implementations as the topic of the book primarily because they are such a good target for study: They incorporate many optimizations at both the architecture and hardware level, and their descriptions naturally lead to discussion of important ideas. Throughout our preparation of the manuscript, we relied on the cooperation of those involved with the development of these architectures and the official IBM technical reference manuals. We also relate these architectures to other commercial designs, such as the DEC Alpha.

By RISC standards, the POWER and PowerPC instruction sets are "rich" in that they often achieve parallelism by expressing multiple operations in the same instruction, and their implementations are targeted at a high degree of parallel operation, rather than a fast clock period. Consequently, the POWER family represents a distinct design style both in architecture and implementation. The family also illustrates an interesting evolution of architecture and implementation. The family now includes two related architectures and the first three of a growing number of distinct implementations, each having its specific goals and constraints.

This book is intended for computer professionals who are interested in acquiring more knowledge of second-generation RISCs, superscalar machines, and the IBM RISC System/6000 or PowerPC in particular. The book can also be used as a case study of a high-performance second-generation RISC in senior undergraduate or first-year graduate courses on computer architecture. This is what the book is truly about: Using a modern second-generation RISC as a vehicle for studying and evaluating computer architecture.

Although the book has a clear hardware orientation, it should also be valuable to software designers interested in performance optimization. To get the most in performance from a modern, high-performance system, it has become necessary to understand the internal working of that system. The differences between optimal and nonoptimal program performance can often hinge on very subtle hardware/software interactions. Indeed, the interplay between hardware and software is at the heart of the RISC revolution.

Organization

The book is organized to offer maximum flexibility to readers who might wish to pursue one topic over another or in an order that better suits their needs. Chapter 1 surveys concepts of modern computer architecture; Chapter 2 describes the POWER architecture; and Chapters 3–5 cover its first implementation, the POWER1, as used in the IBM RS/6000 model 560 workstation. Chapter 6 describes a more recent and higher performance POWER implementation, POWER2. Chapters 7–9 describe the PowerPC architecture and the PowerPC 601 implementation. Chapter 10 covers system components, including main memory and input/output. Chapter 11 compares the PowerPC 601 and the Alpha 21064. Appendix A discusses the IEEE 754 Floating-Point Standard. Appendices B–F list POWER and PowerPC instructions and instruction formats.

Consequently, there are several ways to read the book or parts of it, depending on a reader's interests. One way, obviously, is to follow the outline just described. A reader interested only in POWER and the RS/6000 can read Chapters 2–6 and selected subsections of Chapter 10. On the other hand, a reader interested in PowerPC can read Chapters 7–9 and sections 10.2–10.3 of Chapter 10. Another alternative is topical coverage, as follows:

- Concepts of modern computers: Chapters 1, 4.2, 4.4, and 5.2.

- POWER and PowerPC instruction set architecture: Chapters 2, 6.2, 7, 9.2, 9.3, 9.6, and 11.3.

- Pipelined implementations: Chapters 3, 6.3–6.6, 8.2, 8.5, and 11.2.

- Cache memories: Chapters 5, 6.7, 6.8, 8.4, 9.4–9.6, and a subsection of 11.2.

- Multiprocessing: Chapter 9.

- System organization: Chapter 10.

- Comparative computer architecture: Chapters 7.6, 7.7, 8.5, and 11.

Portions of this material were class-tested in two environments: (1) three-day intensive courses on the architecture and hardware of the RS/6000 taught at the IBM Advanced Workstation Division in Austin, Texas, and at other IBM locations, and (2) a first-year graduate level course on computer architecture at the University of Maryland. Students felt that an in-depth case study provided great help toward understanding concepts, techniques, and design trade-offs in computer architecture.

Acknowledgements

Several years have passed since we last worked together at the University of Wisconsin-Madison, and we both enjoyed the opportunity of collaborating once again. In general, the division of labor can best be described in terms of a sports broadcasting metaphor: S.W. provided the play-by-play while J.S. did the color commentary. The book is a testament to the power of the Internet. During the entire time the book was being written, we spoke only once, over the telephone, for a few minutes. Meanwhile, we had numerous interesting e-mail conversations, and the manuscript has crossed the Atlantic many times in electronic form.

Many people assisted us in bringing the book to its present form and content, and we are very pleased to acknowledge their help. **Mitch Alsup** (Ross Technologies), **Bob Colwell** (Intel), **Greg Grohoski** (IBM - Austin), **Martin Hopkins** (IBM - Yorktown Heights), **Mike Johnson** (AMD), and **Anne Rogers** (Princeton University) reviewed early chapter drafts. **Ed Silha** (IBM - Austin) reviewed the final manuscript. His book review spanned about sixteen typewritten pages of important details that have enhanced the thoroughness of the architectural description. **Guri Sohi** (University of Wisconsin) also provided a careful review of the final manuscript. **Jerry Young** (Motorola) promptly answered questions on the PowerPC 601 pipelines and timing. Special thanks go to **Troy Hicks** (IBM - Austin) for providing important last minute information and quick responses to our many questions on the POWER2 implementation. We would also like to thank IBM for providing us with early releases of their documents for the POWER and PowerPC architectures and implementations.

Finally, **Bruce Spatz**, our editor, made very important contributions. Besides providing valuable advice along the way, he obtained, at an opportune moment, the PowerPC Architecture Specification from IBM. This essential and timely piece of information, published by Morgan Kaufmann as *The PowerPC Architecture: A Specification for a New Family of RISC*

Processors, would serve as a good companion to this book. Others at Morgan Kaufmann to whom we are indebted are **Yonie Overton** for managing the production, **Doug Sery** for helping everything to run smoothly, **Ross Carron** for design, and **Ed Sznyter** for composition.

With new developments and announcements in the POWER/PowerPC world occurring almost daily, one of the most difficult parts of writing the book was saying "STOP! no more new material." We reached that point once…then POWER2 was announced…we re-started. After saying STOP! a second time, we hope you find the finished product both informative and enjoyable.

Shlomo Weiss
James E. Smith

MODERN COMPUTER DESIGN CONCEPTS

1.1 Introduction

As usually defined, computer architecture is the *interface between hardware and software.* Time has shown it to be an unstable interface—like a fault line. Architectures are created for hardware and software technologies as they exist at a specific time. As technologies evolve, stresses build, and hardware and software are no longer matched at the interface; eventually the stress becomes great enough to force architectural changes that accommodate a new alignment of hardware and software.

Often, changes in architecture are relatively small and occur gradually; in other cases they are more dramatic. A major tremor occurred in the early 1980s. At that time, technology, both hardware and software, that was capable of higher performance and lower cost was being held back by architectures and architectural concepts that had been defined years, sometimes decades, earlier.

The dramatic shift in the hardware/software interface that occurred in the early 1980s resulted in processors with simplified architectures known as RISCs, or Reduced Instruction Set Computers. At IBM and leading universities in the United States several new architectures were developed to allow streamlined hardware with a high degree of overlap in instruction processing. A goal of the IBM research project that developed a computer known as the 801 was single-cycle execution of all instructions. For a project at the University of California at Berkeley single-chip implementations were a driving force for architecture simplifications, and at Stanford University overlapped implementations with simple control were the goal. A characteristic of all these research projects was a reliance on studies of instruction usage patterns in real programs to aid in the architecture simplification process. Because high-level languages have to be translated into optimized sequences of relatively primitive RISC instructions, compiler technology was, and continues to be, a key element of the RISC "movement."

RISC-based microprocessors began to appear in commercial products in the mid 1980s at companies such as MIPS (based on the Stanford project) and Sun Microsystems (the SPARC, based on the Berkeley RISC). In 1986, IBM announced the IBM Personal Computer RT (RISC Technology) as its first commercial RISC system. The IBM RT was not particularly successful, and it began to look as though IBM would fail commercially with a technology it had advanced.

Following the initial tremor that led to RISC, however, additional shifting in the hardware/software interface has occurred. Development has continued with a second generation of RISC architectures that take advantage of higher integration levels, more advanced software, and greater demand for processor performance. With the second generation, IBM made a remarkable comeback. The IBM RS/6000 incorporating the POWER architecture was introduced in early 1990 and has become a leading member of the second generation RISCs. The RS/6000 processor achieves high performance by using several innovations such as initiating multiple instructions each clock cycle.

The PowerPC architecture, announced in the fall of 1991, is an evolution of POWER. While the POWER architecture, implemented in the RS/6000, was originally targeted at workstation systems, the PowerPC architecture is suitable for general purpose personal computer applications and multiprocessor servers, as well as workstations. Developed as a joint project of IBM, Motorola, and Apple, the PowerPC, more than anything else, is intended to challenge Intel's supremacy in personal computers. The "battle for the desktop" that is shaping up promises to be one of historical proportions, and the PowerPC will be a major participant.

Because of their many innovations and because they illustrate an evolutionary development based on experience, changing design constraints, and the marketplace, POWER and PowerPC present us with excellent case studies in modern high-performance computer architecture and design. Before beginning our extended study of POWER and PowerPC, we use the remainder of this chapter to provide background on the basic concepts of RISC architectures, implementations, and software.

1.2 RISC Architectures

The acronym RISC was coined by Carlo Sequin of the University of California at Berkeley to describe a microprocessor being developed by a group led by David Patterson and Sequin. The Berkeley project, begun in the early 1980s, was inspired by the IBM 801, but many of the RISC concepts had been articulated for even earlier high-performance systems, beginning at least with the CDC 6600, developed in the early 1960s.

The expression "RISC" seems to suggest that the number of instructions is reduced, but reduction is not a key aspect of what are now classified as RISC architectures. RISC actually reflects a design philosophy in which the implementation is targeted at high performance and is made visible to software (the compiler, to be more precise). This philosophy tends to result in an instruction set with a high degree of regularity and individual instructions performing relatively primitive operations. Features of this type, which are an effect of applying the RISC philosophy, are often confused with the RISC philosophy itself.

To better illustrate the properties of RISCs, let us first consider the alternative: CISCs (Complex Instruction Set Computers). Some CISCs have single machine instructions that can read one or more operands from memory, operate on them, and then store result back to memory. For example, a CISC instruction might perform a memory-to-memory floating-point multiplication:

$$\text{mem}(r1 + r2) = \text{mem}(r1 + r2) * \text{mem}(r3 + disp)$$

The contents of registers r1 and r2 are added to form the memory address for operand 1; r3 and a displacement value are added to form the address for operand 2. Operands 1 and 2 are loaded from memory and multiplied. The result is then stored back to memory at the location formed by adding r1 and r2. Such an instruction might be encoded in several bytes and use several fields to specify the various operands.

A typical RISC would replace the single CISC instruction with the following sequence of simpler instructions:[1]

```
loadf    fp1 = mem(r1 + r2)      # load first floating-point number
loadf    fp2 = mem(r3 + disp)    # load second
multf    fp3 = fp1,fp2           # floating multiply
storef   mem(r1 + r2) = fp3      # store result
```

The first two instructions load memory operands into floating-point registers, the third multiplies them, and the fourth stores the result to memory. This example illustrates some of the properties that RISC architectures often have:

---

[1] We are using an assembly language similar to the one we will use for the POWER architecture; see the end of Section 2.2 for a description.

- The instructions perform primitive operations. An instruction performs only a single load, store, or register operation.

- All instructions loading data from memory place it in an explicit register; all stores take data from a register. Architectures of this type are sometimes referred to as "load-store" or "register-register" architectures.

- There are often separate register files: one for addressing and integer operations, the other for floating-point operations.

Other properties sometimes considered to be "RISCy," although not evident from our example, include the following:

- To simplify decoding, instructions are all the same length with a few interrelated formats.

- There are no implicitly set condition codes; codes are either explicitly set, or branch instructions explicitly test registers.

Some authors have prepared detailed tables and checklists of RISC features to classify architectures by their relative degrees of "RISCiness." We think this checklist mentality gives the wrong idea. The general philosophy is important, not the presence or absence of specific features. In fact, the POWER and PowerPC architectures violate several of the generally accepted RISC "rules."

RISC architectures provide several advantages, including the following:

- The compiler has a direct, often explicit view of performance features. Because the architecture is keyed to implementation, performance features can be directly manipulated by software. This can lead to blurring of "architecture" and "implementation" as traditionally defined, that is, where performance issues are unrelated to the architecture.[2]

- Compilation is simplified. Compilers only have primitives to work with, and there are fewer choices to be made. This simplification was one of the controversial issues surrounding the RISC revolution. Some CISC architectures had been directed toward closing the "semantic gap" with operating systems and high-level languages on one side of the gap, and hardware implementation on the other. In the process of closing the semantic gap, instruction sets became increasingly complicated. RISC architects recognize that the semantic gap, even when wide, can be bridged efficiently with a good compiler—the semantic gap itself is not an obstacle.

---

[2]In fact, the traditional architecture/implementation distinction may have been an obstacle to the widespread discovery of RISCs until the early 1980s. It is interesting to note that computers developed much earlier at the Control Data Corporation, and considered by many to be the original RISCs, do not draw the conventional architecture/implementation distinction. They have architectures defined in terms of a specific hardware implementation.

■ Less integrated circuit area is required. Smaller chips tend to give higher yields during fabrication. A chip with fewer gates will also tend to consume less power. It is interesting to note that a single-chip implementation is not crucial to the success of a RISC, however; the major IBM RS/6000 systems have used multiple-chip processor designs.

■ A simple architecture can lead to shorter design times. Designers have fewer special cases and fewer design bugs to deal with. This means a shorter time-to-market, which can be critical in determining the success or failure of a processor implementation.

With advances in technology, the last advantage seems to be diminishing in importance. Computer-Aided Design (CAD) tools, as well as a base of experience to build upon, are allowing designers to execute increasingly complex implementations while maintaining short design cycles.

RISC architectures also have some disadvantages, such as the following:

■ More instructions are needed than for a CISC to get the same job done. More memory is needed to hold the instructions, and more instructions must be fetched and executed.

■ More registers are needed, as is evident from our brief example, above. The CISC version only requires registers r1, r2, and r3 for computing addresses. The RISC version requires three floating-point registers in addition to r1, r2, and r3.

The first disadvantage can be partially overcome through judicious use of more powerful instructions (seemingly counter to the RISC philosophy); as we shall see, this tactic is an important part of POWER and PowerPC. The second disadvantage is diminishing in importance as integrated circuit technology increases available logic circuits.

Although the RISC philosophy has been defined in rather general terms in this section, we will elaborate on the philosophy and point out specific examples throughout the book.

1.3 An Introduction to Pipelining

Pipelining is a way of achieving high performance by breaking instruction processing into a series of stages that are connected like the stations in an assembly line. This assembly line for instruction processing is referred to as the *pipeline*. As instructions flow down the pipeline, hardware in each stage performs some processing, until instructions leaving the pipeline are completely processed. Pipelining achieves high performance through the parallelism of processing several instructions at once, each in a different pipeline stage.

Pipelining is a fundamental implementation technique that is used for most RISC architectures. Indeed, exposing certain characteristics of the pipeline's structure to software is the basis for many of the commonly enunciated RISC features. As an example of pipelined processing, consider one way instruction processing can be broken into stages:

1. *Instruction fetching:* The program counter is used to fetch the next instruction to be processed. Instructions are usually held in an instruction cache memory that is read during the fetch stage.

2. *Instruction decoding and operand fetching:* The opcode and operands are inspected and control signals are generated. Register specifiers from the instruction are used to read operands from the register file(s).

3. *Instruction execution:* The operation specified by the opcode is performed. For memory access instructions, the operation forms the effective memory address.

4. *Memory access:* Data is loaded from or stored to memory. A data cache memory is typically used.

5. *Result write-back:* The result of the operation is written back into the register file.

Cache memories, used in the instruction fetch and memory access stages, are small high-speed memories that keep recently used blocks of main memory. Statistics, as well as long experience, have shown that such recently used blocks of instructions or data are likely to be used again in the near future. If a memory address matches one of the blocks held in the cache, there is a "hit," and the memory reference is satisfied by the cache. Otherwise, there is a "miss," and the reference is sent to main memory, with the accessed block being transferred into the cache. Cache memories are discussed in detail in Chapter 5. For the reader not familiar with caches, it could be worthwhile to skip ahead and read Section 5.2.

Each pipeline stage consists of combinational logic and/or high-speed memory in the form of a register file or cache memory. The stages are separated by ranks of latches or flip-flops (Figure 1.1). The five pipeline stages in Figure 1.1 are labeled with two-letter abbreviations:

IF:	Instruction Fetch
ID:	Instruction Decode
EX:	EXecution
ME:	MEmory access
WB:	Write-Back results

A common clock signal synchronizes pipeline latches between each stage, so all latches capture data produced by the pipeline stages at the same time. The clock "pumps" instructions down the pipeline. At the beginning of a clock period, or clock cycle, data and control from a partially processed instruction are held in a pipeline latch; this information forms the inputs for the logic making up the next stage. During the clock period, signals propagate through combinational logic, or access high-speed memories, and produce an output in time to be captured in the next pipeline latch at the end of the clock period.

In a well-designed pipeline, all the stages contain logic with roughly the same signal propagation delay. The clock period has to be long enough to accommodate the time required

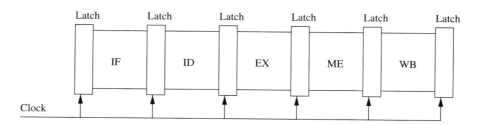

(a) A block diagram showing latches, logic, and the clock signal.

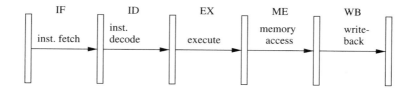

(b) A schematic notation we will be using. The thin vertical rectangles represent the latches, and the lines with arrows indicate the flow of information—data or instructions.

FIGURE 1.1   **A five-stage pipeline.**

by the slowest stage. By making all the stages roughly equal in delay, instruction processing can be done by a minimum number of stages.

The pipeline is designed to start a new instruction (and finish an instruction) each clock period. Therefore, the clock period determines *throughput,* that is, the rate at which instructions can be executed. The time it takes for a single instruction to traverse the entire length of the pipeline is referred to as its *latency.* For example, if the pipeline in Figure 1.1 were clocked at 50 MHz, the maximum throughput is one instruction per 20 ns or 50 million instructions per second (MIPS). The pipeline latency is five clock periods or 100 ns.

Without pipelining, throughput would be the reciprocal of latency. In our example, if there were no pipelining, the maximum throughput would be one instruction per 100 ns or 10 MIPS. In reality, the nonpipelined throughput might be a little better because the pipeline latches add some overhead to the overall latency. Removing them might lead to a slightly smaller latency than 100 ns.

Pipeline Dependences

As we have assumed until now, pipeline throughput is one instruction per clock period if all the instructions are independent entities. In practice, however, they are often *dependent*. An example of dependent instructions occurs when one instruction produces output data used as input by another instruction. Consider again the memory-to-memory floating-point multiplication sequence.

```
loadf    fp1 = mem(r1 + r2)      # load first floating-point number
loadf    fp2 = mem(r3 + disp)    # load second
multf    fp3 = fp1,fp2           # floating multiply
storef   mem(r1 + r2) = fp3      # store result
```

The two load instructions are independent of each other, but the floating-point multiplication uses the data loaded from memory, so it depends on the two loads that precede it. Also, the store instruction depends on the floating-point multiplication, because it stores the product. Because of dependences, an instruction may be held back in a pipeline stage while it waits for data from a previous instruction. When an instruction is held for one or more clock periods, "bubbles" develop in the pipeline.

Another type of dependence involves contention for a hardware resource. For example, a multiplication might use logic in the execution stage for several clock periods. An instruction immediately following the multiplication will be blocked, waiting for the EX stage. This is an example of a *resource dependence*. When two instructions need the same hardware resource at the same time (e.g., logic in the EX stage), one is blocked due to the resource dependence. Other shared resources that might result in resource dependences are data buses or register file read and write ports.

Visualizing Pipeline Flow

Because many instructions can be in a pipeline at once, some blocked due to dependences, it is not always easy to imagine the timing as instructions flow through a pipe. Yet understanding timing is essential to understanding the performance characteristics of pipelines. To help the reader visualize the flow through a pipeline, we introduce a tabular description. Figure 1.2 illustrates the flow for our memory-to-memory multiplication example. There is one row for each instruction, and time (in clock periods) goes across the page, delineating the columns. The table entries name the pipeline stage used by the instruction denoted by the row, at the time denoted by the column. For example, at clock period 3, the instruction i2 is in the execution (EX) stage. Bubbles in the pipeline are denoted as dots. The set of bubbles in the third row illustrates the data dependence involving fp2. The load of fp2 must finish and write fp2 before the multiply can read it. We will use the tabular notation when we want a compact description of pipeline flow.

```
                                    0  1  2  3  4  5  6  7  8  9  10 11 12 13
loadf  fp1 = mem(r1+r2)            IF ID EX ME WB
loadf  fp2 = mem(r3+disp)             IF ID EX ME WB
multf  fp3 = fp1,fp2                     IF  .   .   .  ID EX ME WB
storef mem(r1+r2) = fp3                             IF  .   .   .  ID EX ME WB
```

FIGURE 1.2   **An instruction sequence having pipeline bubbles (shown as dots).**

Figure 1.3 shows three of the key clock periods during the execution of the above sequence. Each latch is labeled with the instruction being held in the latch. The opcode and target register are shown along the top half of the latch, and all source registers are shown along the bottom.

Notice that a pipeline stage is not considered executed until the instruction is clocked into the latches at the beginning of the next stage. In Figure 1.3, the multiply sits in the latches at the beginning of the ID stage. When register fp2 is available it is clocked to the next set of latches; only then is it considered to have executed the ID stage.

Conditional Branches

Unlike our simple examples thus far, real programs contain conditional branch instructions to alter the instruction flow. A conditional branch results in a form of feedback in the pipeline where a test on data is performed by one instruction, typically in the execution stage, and the result is fed back to the I-fetch stage to control fetching of future instructions.

Conditional branches thus lead to another type of dependence, the *control dependence,* where the next instruction to be fetched and started down the pipeline depends on the execution of a preceding branch instruction. Conditional branches may disrupt the flow of instructions through a pipeline because the outcome of a conditional branch is not known until it executes. Consider the instruction sequence shown in Figure 1.4.

In the figure, we use a conditional branch where register r1 is compared with 0 and branches to the instruction labeled NEXT if the condition is true. Assume that the content of r1 is greater than 0. While the conditional branch instruction is fetched, decoded, and executed, the instruction fetch unit must wait until the branch outcome is known before it can proceed. In our pipeline, the comparison is done in the EX stage, and fetching must wait for the next cycle to begin. A "bubble" ensues for two clock periods during which no instructions are fetched and started down the pipe.

Pipeline Bypasses

We now turn to a common pipeline optimization, the *bypass,* the first of many performance optimizations to be discussed throughout this book.

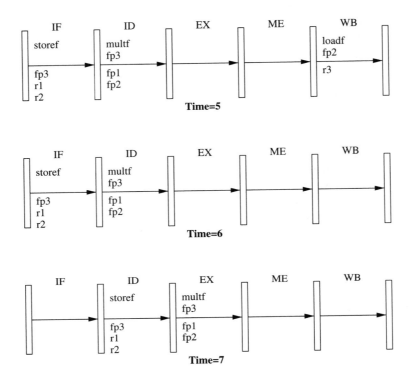

FIGURE 1.3   A detailed drawing of pipeline flow. Three bubbles appear due to a data dependence involving register fp2.

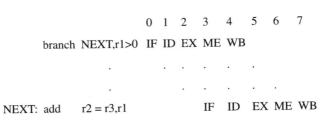

FIGURE 1.4   Pipeline timing for a conditional branch.

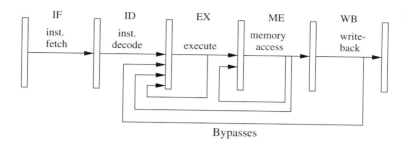

FIGURE 1.5   **A pipeline with bypasses.**

```
                              0  1  2  3  4  5  6  7  8
loadf  fp1 = mem(r1+r2)      IF ID EX ME WB
loadf  fp2 = mem(r3+disp)       IF ID EX ME WB
multf  fp3 = fp1, fp2              IF  .  ID EX ME WB
storef mem(r1+r2) = fp3                  IF ID EX ME WB
```

FIGURE 1.6   **Pipeline flow with bypasses.**

In our example code, we assumed that the result of one instruction can be used by a following instruction no sooner than the clock period after it has been written into the register file. As we have seen, such a register dependence can produce bubbles in the pipeline. Some bubbles can be reduced or eliminated, however, by providing special paths to "bypass" data quickly from one stage to another.

In Figure 1.5, four bypasses have been added. Three go to the Execute stage: from the register write-back stage, the memory access stage, and the execution stage. A fourth bypass connects the memory access stage back to itself. Typically (but not always), such bypasses take signals from the end of a pipeline stage, just before they are latched, and connect them to a multiplexer feeding the latch of the stage to which they are being bypassed. In addition to the data paths, control hardware must be added to detect cases where the bypasses can be used. With these bypasses, the optimized pipeline flow for the earlier code sequence appears in Figure 1.6.

All the bubbles between the multiply and store are now gone, due to the bypass from the ME stage back to itself. The remaining bubble between the second load and the multiply, however, cannot be eliminated; the shortest bypass is from the ME stage back to the EX, and this leaves one bubble.

Figure 1.7 shows clock cycles 2 through 5 in detail. Here, the use of the bypasses is more evident. The bypass paths are shown only when used, labeled with the register values that they contain.

Pipeline Interlocks

As we have seen, a dependence for data, control, or resources might cause one instruction to become blocked (or "stalled") in a pipeline stage waiting for a preceding instruction to produce a result or release a resource. To make sure an instruction is held back when necessary, hardware checks for dependences and blocks instructions from proceeding until any dependences are resolved. The hardware performing these checks is referred to as *interlock* logic.

The following are some of the major interlock checks that may be performed as an instruction passes down a simple pipeline, such as the one we have described. Determining precisely which checks are needed and when they are made is a function of the specific pipeline implementation.

■ *Source registers:* Source operand registers must be available during the decode/operand read stage; there must be no currently executing instruction that will modify them.

■ *Functional units:* In some implementations, a function may take more than one cycle to execute, but it may not be pipelined. This is commonly the case with integer multipliers and dividers. In this case, there may be an interlock at the execution stage to block following instructions that may need the same execution logic.

■ *Comparison results:* In the instruction fetch stage, comparison results for a conditional branch must be complete before instructions following the branch can be fetched. These comparison results are typically produced in the execution stage and must be passed back in the pipeline in the form of condition code bits, register results, or some type of control signals.

■ *Data cache:* If a memory load instruction misses in the data cache, there is a delay while the data are fetched from main memory. In many implementations, this delay means the data cache resource is blocked. An interlock keeps subsequent instructions from proceeding through the memory access stage while the data cache is waiting for memory data. In some more aggressive implementations, memory accesses may continue through the cache until a number of accesses (usually a small number) have missed, then the cache blocks.

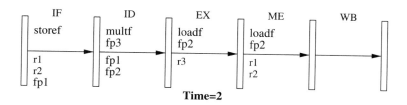

Time=2

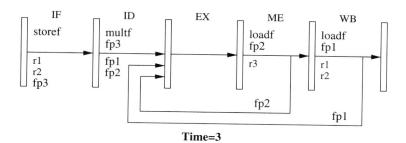

Time=3

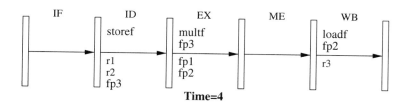

Time=4

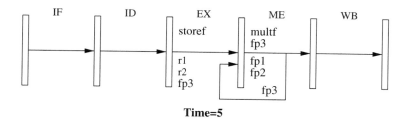

Time=5

FIGURE 1.7   Detail of pipeline flow using bypasses; bypasses are shown only when used.

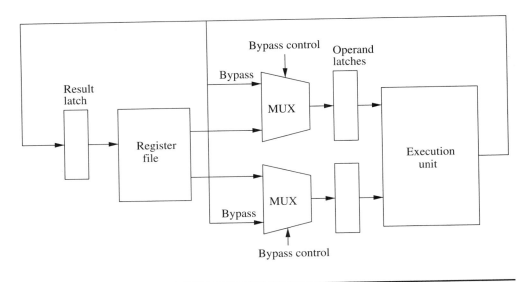

FIGURE 1.8   **Bypass implementation.**

■ *Register write port:* In some pipelined implementations, more than one instruction may finish at the same time. In this case, there must be an interlock in the write-back stage to share a single register file write port. In some implementations with fixed functional unit times, this interlock can be done prior to starting the operation rather than at the end.

For an instruction to move from one pipeline stage to the next, all the interlocks at the stage must "pass." In addition, there must be room for the instruction in the next pipeline stage. That is, if the instruction in the next pipeline stage is blocked, the instruction in the current stage may be forced to hold, even though all its interlocks pass.

Often, the control logic that manages interlocks also manages the bypasses. For example, consider a bypass that moves data from the end of the execution logic into the pipeline latch that receives register file data (Figure 1.8). The interlock logic that is responsible for checking source operands not only checks the status of the registers in the file, but it also compares the source register designator with the result register designator of the instruction currently in the execution stage. If there is a match, the source register interlock is considered to "pass," and the interlock logic provides control to steer the execution data into the decode stage output latch.

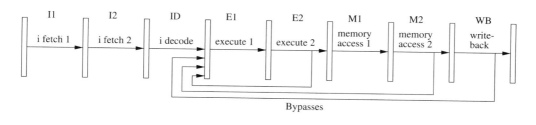

FIGURE 1.9   **A deep pipeline with bypass paths.**

1.4 Beyond Simple Pipelines

We complete our overview of pipelined implementations by considering more complex pipeline structures. These include deep pipelines that allow faster clock rates, parallel pipelines that allow instructions to pass one another, and superscalar implementations that allow multiple instructions to be present in the same pipeline stage simultaneously.

Deep Pipelines

For the pipelines we have discussed thus far, the maximum throughput (i.e., the rate at which instructions can be executed), is one per clock period (this is an upper limit; as we have seen, dependences usually result in fewer than one instruction per clock period).

Given this constraint, a rather obvious method for achieving higher throughput is to make the clock go faster. This can be done, but it means that each pipeline stage must have less signal propagation delay (remember that the delay can be no longer than the clock period). To reduce propagation delay, one could use a more clever design to reduce the number of logic levels required to do the work in each stage, but this reduction cannot always be achieved. Another solution is to use more stages and do less work in each stage. The number of stages in a pipeline is commonly referred to as its *depth,* so by adding stages we are making the pipeline deeper. For example, one might be able to reduce the ID and WB delays through better design, and the IF, EX, and ME stages might be divided into two stages each (Figure 1.9).

As long as instructions are independent, deeper pipelining leads to higher throughput because the clock is faster. More pipeline stages mean more instructions can be processed in parallel.

With dependent instructions, however, performance improvements are limited because some of the additional pipeline stages are filled with bubbles, not instructions. Bubbles occur between instructions because one instruction requires a certain amount of work before it can pass data or control information to a dependent instruction. Dividing this work into more stages simply adds to the number of bubbles separating dependent instructions. As a pipeline

```
                                    0  1  2  3  4  5  6  7  8  9  10 11 12 13 14
loadf  fp1 = mem(r1+r2)            I1 I2 ID E1 E2 M1 M2 WB
loadf  fp2 = mem(r3+disp)             I1 I2 ID E1 E2 M1 M2 WB
multf  fp3 = fp1, fp2                     I1 I2 .  .  .  ID E1 E2 M1 M2 WB
storef mem(r1+r2) = fp3                      I1 .  .  .  I2 .  ID E1 E2 M1 M2 WB
```

FIGURE 1.10   Pipeline flow for deep pipeline.

is made deeper and the number of bubbles increases, a limit can be reached in performance improvements because any additional pipeline stages hold no more instructions, just more bubbles.

For each pipeline stage, some delay typically occurs due to the pipeline register, or latch, that divides the stages. This pipeline overhead means the clock period will not be reduced in direct proportion to the number of added stages. For example, if a four-stage pipe with a 50 ns clock period is evenly divided into eight stages, the clock period will probably be slightly longer than 25 ns due to the fixed overhead; for example, it might be 28 ns. Therefore, performance can actually be reduced for very deep pipelines when instruction dependences limit the number of instructions that can be processed at the same time, and pipeline depth adds to the overall pipeline latency.

Figure 1.10 shows the earlier code sequence being operated on by the deeper pipeline. Because of dependences, there are more bubbles than before, so the performance improvement is not as great as the clock period improvement might suggest. Bypassing is less effective than in the five-stage pipeline, simply because instructions must flow through more stages before reaching the bypass paths. In the eight-stage deep pipeline there is a three-cycle bubble when a load is followed by a dependent arithmetic instruction, and a one-cycle bubble between two dependent arithmetic instructions.

Parallel Pipelines

So far, we have concentrated on "linear" pipelines that have a single path that all instructions follow through the pipe. Parallel pipelines provide different paths depending on the instruction type. Figure 1.11 illustrates a pipeline similar to that used in the CRAY-1, an innovative supercomputer completed in 1976. The POWER processors also use a form of parallel pipeline structure, as do most second-generation RISC implementations.

First, there is a single pipeline for instruction fetching and decoding, then the pipe splits into parallel parts depending on the type of instruction being executed. This type of pipeline

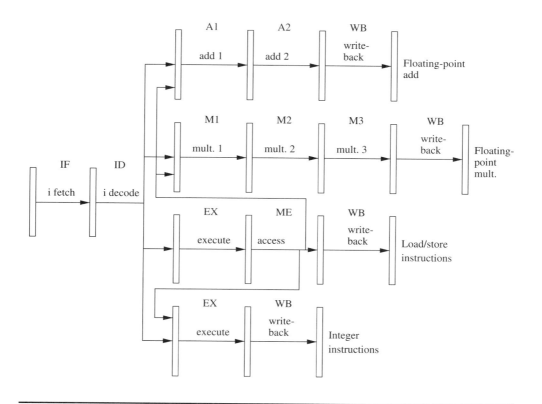

FIGURE 1.11   A parallel pipeline.

allows instructions to proceed with more independence. An instruction is not blocked simply because a preceding instruction may be blocked in the pipeline or using the execution stage for multiple clock periods. The parallel pipelines may be of different lengths, depending on their functions. For example, a floating-point multiply pipeline will likely be longer than a pipeline that performs simple logical operations. Because the pipelines' lengths vary, instructions in them may complete in a different order from which they are initiated.

An important advantage of parallel pipelines occurs when an instruction becomes blocked in the data cache due to a cache miss. If the cache is in a different parallel pipeline from the floating-point operations, a following, independent floating-point instruction can proceed; it is not held up behind the memory instruction that missed in the cache.

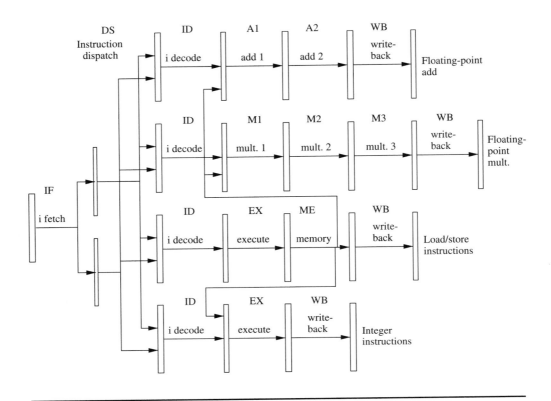

FIGURE 1.12   A superscalar pipeline implementation.

Superscalar Processors

We observed earlier that one way to improve pipeline throughput is to make the pipeline deeper and run the clock faster. Another way is to construct pipelines capable of simultaneously fetching, decoding, and executing more than one instruction at a time. Implementations of this type are referred to as *superscalar,* and they are used in several of the second-generation RISC processors, including those used in the RS/6000 and PowerPC processors.

Superscalar implementations get their name because "scalar" suggests processing one data item at a time (in contrast to the vector processing used in many supercomputers). Superscalar processors go beyond scalar processing by operating on multiple data items at a time, using scalar instructions. Figure 1.12 shows a possible superscalar extension of the parallel pipeline used in Figure 1.11.

In the parallel pipeline, instruction decoding is done in a single ID stage, which limits the maximum decoding rate to one instruction per clock period. In the superscalar implementation, multiple instructions per clock cycle are fetched and dispatched to multiple ID stages. This implementation leads to higher instruction processing rate and better utilization of the parallel pipelines.

Superscalar implementations have significantly increased interlock and resource conflict problems, however, when compared with their simple scalar counterparts. Interlocks must be checked not only with preceding instructions in the pipeline, but with any instructions that are at the same pipeline stage. Also, some pipeline stages, such as a cache lookup, become more complicated if the implementation has to support two accesses at once. For this reason, some superscalar implementations restrict the types of instructions that can be simultaneously executed. For example, in some implementations two memory operations or two floating-point operations cannot be simultaneously processed in the same pipeline stage; however, one memory access instruction and one floating-point operation may be simultaneously processed.

Some Final Comments on Hardware Pipelining

Pipelining has become the accepted implementation method for computers of virtually every class, while the serial one-at-a-time execution model is fading into history—existing only in beginning computer architecture textbooks. Today's computer architect thinks in terms of architectures that map well onto a pipeline, and implementors begin a design by determining the overall pipeline structure. In the next section we see how compiler writers have adapted to pipelined processor designs.

1.5 Instruction Scheduling

For good performance, the hardware implementation of a pipeline is not the only consideration. Software plays an equally important role. We describe here some of the more important aspects of software optimizations for pipelines.

Because every bubble represents a clock period when a pipeline stage is unused, performance can be improved by eliminating bubbles. There is some flexibility in the order in which instructions can be started down the pipeline (e.g., independent instructions can be executed in any order). Carefully adjusting the ordering of instructions can reduce or eliminate bubbles. *Instruction scheduling* is the ordering of instructions either by the compiler or the hardware to try to minimize pipeline bubbles.

Say we want to execute the following two high-level language statements:

$$A \;=\; B + C$$
$$D \;=\; E * F$$

Then a straightforward compilation into assembly code is:

i1:	loadf	fp1 = mem(B)
i2:	loadf	fp2 = mem(C)
i3:	addf	fp3 = fp1, fp2
i4:	storef	mem(A) = fp3
i5:	loadf	fp1 = mem(E)
i6:	loadf	fp2 = mem(F)
i7:	multf	fp3 = fp1, fp2
i8:	storef	mem(D) = fp3

If we use the linear pipeline with bypasses, there will be two sets of bubbles—one for the i1–i4 sequence and the other for the i5–i8 sequence. However, we see that the two statements are actually independent and can be done in parallel. For example, we could start i5 (the load of E) immediately after i3 (the load of C) and fill the pipeline bubble that would ordinarily follow i3. The register assignment used above makes this a little difficult, though, because we can't begin loading fp1 until the floating-point add is started.

This problem can be solved by using a different register assignment. We assume that our architecture has many floating-point registers, as most RISC architectures do, so that we can use the following sequence of machine instructions:

loadf	fp1 = mem(B)
loadf	fp2 = mem(C)
addf	fp3 = fp1, fp2
storef	mem(A) = fp3
loadf	fp4 = mem(E)
loadf	fp5 = mem(F)
multf	fp6 = fp4, fp5
storef	mem(D) = fp6

Now, we can reschedule the instructions to minimize bubbles. Figure 1.13 shows the rescheduled instruction sequence and pipeline flow. The pipeline is assumed to have the bypasses from the EX and ME stages back to the ID stage. The scheduled code can now be executed with no bubbles.

This was a straightforward example, fairly obvious in fact. Instruction scheduling becomes more interesting when loops are involved. Software techniques for optimizing loops are described in the following two subsections.

Loop Unrolling

Consider a simple loop and its compilation into machine code (Figure 1.14(a)). Note that within the loop body not much scheduling can be done. However, the separate loop iterations

		0	1	2	3	4	5	6	7
loadf	fp1 = mem(B)	IF	ID	EX	ME	WB			
loadf	fp2 = mem(C)		IF	ID	EX	ME	WB		
loadf	fp4 = mem(E)			IF	ID	EX	ME	WB	
addf	fp3 = fp1, fp2				IF	ID	EX	ME	WB
loadf	fp5 = mem(F)					IF	ID	EX	ME
storef	mem(A) = fp3						IF	ID	EX
multf	fp6 = fp4, fp5							IF	ID
storef	mem(D) = fp6								IF

FIGURE 1.13   **Pipeline flow for scheduled instructions.**

are independent: iterations could be processed in parallel to increase performance. To achieve this in our pipelined processor, we first *unroll* the loop; after unrolling there are more scheduling opportunities. A loop is unrolled *n* times by making *n* copies of the loop body, with a single branch at the end. Values that are a function of the loop index, such as the address indices, are adjusted to match each of the *n* copies.

Now, registers can be reassigned, and the two copies of the loop body can be rescheduled as a group (see Figure 1.15). When executed on our simple pipeline with bypasses, the scheduled, unrolled loop will execute with bubbles following only the conditional branch at the end of the loop (as in Figure 1.14). Even though there are bubbles after the conditional branch, the overall number of bubbles due to branches has been cut in half because unrolling eliminated half the branches.

In our example, we unrolled the loop twice, but of course a loop could be unrolled more times. Issues such as the number of registers available and the instruction cache size are often used to help determine how many times a loop should be unrolled in practice.

Also, loop unrolling is a little more complicated than the above example suggests, because a loop may not be executed for a number of iterations that is an exact multiple of the unrolling number. In many cases, the number of iterations is not known until runtime. To circumvent this problem, the compiler typically generates "cleanup" code to do any residue loop iterations after unrolling reaches the closest multiple. A test has to be performed at each step to see if the residue is less than the degree of unrolling; if so, the "cleanup" code does the remaining iterations.

```
                Do I=1 to N
                  A(I) = B(I) * C(I)


                load immed    r1 = A
                load immed    r2 = B
                load immed    r3 = C
                load immed    r4 = 0
                load immed    r5 = N
    LOOP:       loadf         fp1 = mem(r1 + r4)
                loadf         fp2 = mem(r2 + r4)
                multf         fp3 = fp1, fp2
                storef        mem(r3+r4) = fp3
                add immed     r4 = r4, 1
                comp lt       c1 = r4, r5
                branchc       LOOP,c1 = true
```

(a) Loop. N ≥ 1.

```
                load immed    r1 = A
                load immed    r2 = B
                load immed    r3 = C
                load immed    r4 = 0
                load immed    r5 = N
    LOOP:       loadf         fp1 = mem(r1 + r4)
                loadf         fp2 = mem(r2 + r4)
                multf         fp3 = fp1, fp2
                storef        mem(r3 + r4) = fp3
                add immed     r4 = r4, 1
                loadf         fp1 = mem(r1+r4)
                loadf         fp2 = mem(r2+r4)
                multf         fp3 = fp1, fp2
                storef        mem(r3+r4) = fp3
                add immed     r4 = r4, 1
                compare lt    c1 = r4, r5
                branchc       LOOP,c1 = true
```

(b) Unrolled loop. N is even and N ≥ 2.

___

FIGURE 1.14   Example of loop unrolling.

	load immed	r1 = A
	load immed	r2 = B
	load immed	r3 = C
	load immed	r4 = 0
	load immed	r5 = N
	load immed	r6 = 1
LOOP:	loadf	fp1 = mem(r1 + r4)
	loadf	fp2 = mem(r2 + r4)
	loadf	fp4 = mem(r1 + r6)
	loadf	fp5 = mem(r2 + r6)
	multf	fp3 = fp1, fp2
	multf	fp6 = fp4, fp5
	storef	mem(r3 + r4) = fp3
	storef	mem(r3 + r6) = fp6
	add immed	r4 = r4, 2
	add immed	r6 = r6, 2
	compare lt	c1 = r4, r5
	branchc	LOOP,c1 = true

FIGURE 1.15   Unrolled loop, rescheduled. N is even and $N \geq 2$.

Software Pipelining

A second technique used to increase loop performance is referred to as *software pipelining*. To understand software pipelining, we look at the processing of a generic loop as being done by a three-stage "pipeline": Load (L), Execute (E), and Store (S). As a loop iteration passes through the pipeline, it performs all its loads in stage L, all the execute instructions in stage E, and all the stores in S. In Figure 1.16(a) loop iterations are on the vertical axis, and time runs across the page. Note that time is in some "time units," not clock cycles. In this conceptual pipeline we assume a loop iteration spends the same time in each of the L, E, and S stages.

Now let's take a "snapshot" of the pipe at time 4, for example. At this time, the pipeline is processing stores of iteration 3 in S, execute instructions of iteration 4 in E, and loads of iteration 5 in L. In general, at time i the software pipeline performs stores of iteration $i - 1$, execute instructions of iteration i, and loads of iteration $i + 1$. In other words, in each iteration the pipeline loads operands for the next iteration and stores results of the previous iteration. The early loads reduce blockage of instructions awaiting operands from memory. The late stores tend to prevent interlocks due to registers awaiting data.

With software pipelining, we will schedule instructions so they naturally fit into the pattern shown in Figure 1.16(a). In particular we will schedule stores for iteration $i - 1$ at the top, executes for iteration i in the middle, and loads for iteration $i + 1$ at the bottom of the loop. In

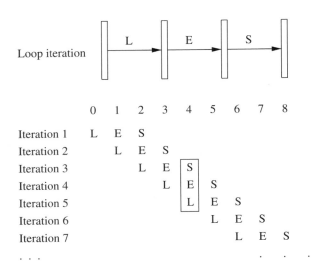

Loop iteration

```
              0   1   2   3   4   5   6   7   8
Iteration 1   L   E   S
Iteration 2       L   E   S
Iteration 3           L   E   S
Iteration 4               L   E   S
Iteration 5                   L   E   S
Iteration 6                       L   E   S
Iteration 7                           L   E   S
. . .                                   .   .   .
```

(a) Conceptual software pipeline.

```
              load immed   r1 = A
              load immed   r2 = B
              load immed   r3 = C
              load immed   r4 = 0
              load immed   r5 = N − 1
              load immed   r6 = −1
              loadf        fp1 = mem(r1 + r4)    # L before the first iteration
              loadf        fp2 = mem(r2 + r4)
              branch       ENTRY                 # nothing to store yet, skip it
LOOP:         storef       mem(r3 + r6) = fp3    # S for iteration i − 1
ENTRY:        add immed    r4 = r4, 1
              add immed    r6 = r6, 1
              multf        fp3 = fp1, fp2        # E for iteration i
              compare lt   c1 = r4, r5
              loadf        fp1 = mem(r1 + r4)    # L for iteration i + 1
              loadf        fp2 = mem(r2 + r4)
              branchc      LOOP,c1 = true
              storef       mem(r3 + r6) = fp3    # cleanup code
              multf        fp3 = fp1, fp2
              add immed    r6 = r6, 1
              storef       mem(r3 + r6) = fp3
```

(b) Software pipeline example. N ≥ 2.

FIGURE 1.16   *Software pipelining.*

each iteration we load operands for the next one, so we have to place the loads for the very first iteration before the loop is entered. If the loop is executed n times, then at the end of iteration n, loads for the nonexisting iteration $n + 1$ will be issued. These data will never be used, and if a memory protection boundary is crossed, a trap can be generated. To be on the safe side, we execute the loop only $n - 1$ times and place the remaining execute and store instructions after the loop exit.

Also, in each iteration we store operands from the previous one. We have to take care not to execute the stores in the first iteration, which would store operands for the previous nonexisting iteration. We simply place an unconditional branch over the store at the top of the loop.

Figure 1.16(b) is the software pipelined version of the loop from Figure 1.14(a). The loop body consists of the same instructions, with the exception of an extra add that bumps register r6, which is used to compute the memory address of the store. Note that loads and stores are independent and their order was reversed. The cleanup code after the branch stores the last result and takes care of the last iteration of the original loop.

1.6 Modern Computer Systems

The microprocessor revolution of the 1980s has led to major changes in virtually every type of computing system. There has been a dramatic shift away from computing based on large centralized systems (mainframes) toward distributed computing based on desktop systems (both personal computers and workstations), department-level multiprocessor servers, and, more recently, clustered multicomputers. Even some large-scale computer systems are being constructed with RISC microprocessors: the "massively parallel" systems. Following is a general characterization of the spectrum of commonly used computer systems, all of which are likely to use POWER- or PowerPC-based processors.

- *Personal computer* systems are driven by cost. They are built of commodity components and have low profit margins. Historically, PCs have been used in isolation, but are now being attached to networks in many applications. PCs typically have a few megabytes of main memory, and tens to hundreds of megabytes of disk storage. For practical purposes, operating systems are limited to proprietary systems developed by IBM, Apple, and Microsoft. Thus far, PCs have been dominated by CISC microprocessors, although several RISC manufacturers are attempting to end this dominance.

- *Workstations* are in many respects similar to PCs. They tend to cost more and provide greater computing power. RISC microprocessors are commonly used, and main memories have tens of megabytes. Because workstations are almost always networked, the bulk of their disk storage is often provided by a file server. Workstation operating systems are usually some variant of UNIX.

■ *Multiprocessor servers* are becoming an increasingly important part of the modern computing environment. They are typically used for file servers or for providing additional computation to clients on a network. They are often bus-based and provide software with a shared main memory containing hundreds of megabytes, sometimes gigabytes. Multiprocessor servers are usually based on RISC processors and run UNIX, just like workstations. File systems often contain tens to hundreds of gigabytes of disk storage.

■ *Multicomputer clusters* are less common than multiprocessors but are becoming increasingly popular. They are usually composed of networked RISC-based computer systems, often of workstation scale. Each processor has its own logical memory image—memory is not logically shared. The interconnection may be a standard local area network, or it may be a special interconnect with higher performance. System software distributes independent processes from a workload to different processors in the cluster. Occasionally, multiple processors can be made to cooperate on a single parallel job.

■ *Massively parallel processors (MPPs)* are still in the process of gaining widespread acceptance. They are typically collections of tens to hundreds to perhaps one or two thousand RISC processors, connected in a regular structure with proprietary, high-performance interconnections. Associated with each processor is a local memory of tens of megabytes. Some MPPs provide applications software with a shared memory image, even though it is physically distributed. Other MPPs maintain a logically distributed view of memory, and tasks running on the processors share data and control information by passing messages. MPPs are constructed to allow very large jobs to run in parallel with supercomputer-class performance. However, they may also be used to act as a throughput server, running many smaller jobs simultaneously.

Of the major categories of modern computer systems listed above, RISCs currently dominate all but the first. POWER- and PowerPC-based systems will eventually span the entire spectrum. POWER-based RS/6000s already form a prominent workstation family. IBM has been a leader in developing and promoting clustered workstations, with RS/6000 clusters being the most popular systems in that class. PowerPC will open up other possibilities, especially as part of an important effort to provide RISC-based personal computers. PowerPC is also well suited for shared memory multiprocessors, and some versions will very likely be a part of future MPP systems.

1.7 POWER and PowerPC: The Big Picture

In the course of the book we will describe POWER and PowerPC-based products at three levels: processor architecture, processor implementation, and system. Because of the way IBM has chosen to name these products, they have a rather confusing array of names, several

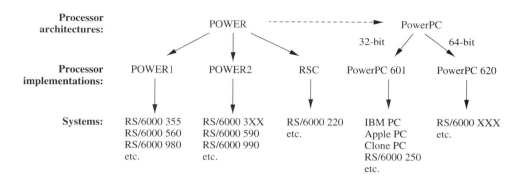

FIGURE 1.17   The relationship of POWER and PowerPC architectures, implementations, and systems.

of which have some variation of "power" in them and some of which have changed since their first introduction. To clarify the nomenclature as well as illustrate the relationships among the various products, we provide the diagram shown in Figure 1.17. At the top of the diagram are the processor architectures. Processor architectures are logical specifications, including such things as instruction sets, registers, and memory translation methods. Architectures are independent of any specific implementation. The POWER architecture was developed first and was announced in 1990. The PowerPC architecture was developed as a joint effort among IBM, Apple, and Motorola, with the actual specification available in 1993. PowerPC is a derivative of POWER, but there are some significant differences which we will explain in this section.

Next in the diagram are the processor implementations. Arrows in the diagram indicate the architecture that each implementation supports. The implementations are specific hardware designs in specific technologies. Performance features are generally an aspect of the implementation. The POWER1 implementation (formerly called RIOS) was done first, and is a multichip implementation of POWER. POWER2 is a very recent implementation of POWER (slightly enhanced), again using multiple chips.[3] RSC (RISC Single Chip) is a single chip implementation of POWER, developed by IBM for low-cost workstations.

PowerPC implementations are just now coming online. The PowerPC 601 (also called the MPC601), was developed jointly by IBM and Motorola and is targeted primarily at low-cost desktop applications. Other implementations of the PowerPC architecture (PowerPC 603,

---

[3]In IBM documentation, this implementation is sometimes referred to as POWER—the same name as the architecture. To avoid such ambiguity, we will always use POWER to denote the architecture and POWER1 or POWER2 to denote the implementation.

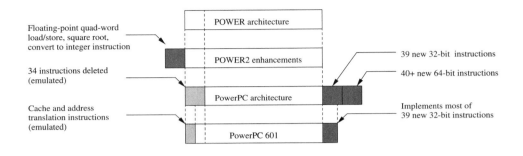

FIGURE 1.18   The relationships among the various POWER and PowerPC instruction sets.

PowerPC 604, and PowerPC 620) have been announced, but no implementation details are available at the time of this writing. All but the PowerPC 620 are 32-bit implementations of PowerPC; the 620 is a 64-bit implementation.

At the bottom of the diagram in Figure 1.17 are the full system implementations that incorporate each of the processors. Arrows indicate which processor implementations are used in the various systems. The RS/6000 systems are implemented with a number of different processors. The lower performance RS/6000s use the RSC processor, and, more recently, the PowerPC 601. Mid-range systems use POWER1 chips in one of two configurations. High-end RS/6000 systems also use POWER1, as do some recently announced versions using POWER2.

Systems implementing PowerPC are just being announced at the time of this writing. Both IBM and Apple will have products based on the PowerPC 601 processor. The chip will also be made available on the open market by Motorla for other system manufacturers to use (most likely to clone the IBM and Apple products). As indicated in the diagram, IBM has plans to use PowerPC implementations in low-end RS/6000 workstations. Because the POWER and PowerPC architectures are not identical, hardware extensions and software will be called upon to implement the POWER architecture in these PowerPC implementations. Besides the uniprocessor systems, there will be other systems using multiprocessors, clustered multicomputers, and MPPs.

The relationships among the various processor architectures are illustrated in Figure 1.18. At the top of the figure is the original POWER architecture, as implemented in POWER1. Shown below POWER is the representation of the architecture used in POWER2. It consists of the POWER instruction set plus floating quadword loads and stores, a floating square root, and a couple of convert to integer instructions. The PowerPC architecture deleted a number of POWER instructions, mostly to simplify implementations, and added 39 new 32-bit instructions and over 40 new 64-bit instructions. Finally, because the first PowerPC implementation, the PowerPC 601, is intended to be a "bridge" between POWER and PowerPC systems, it includes some, but not all, of the instructions deleted from POWER to arrive at PowerPC. And it implements most, but not all, of the 32-bit instructions. Because it is not a 64-bit PowerPC implementation, the PowerPC 601 does not implement any of the new 64-bit PowerPC instructions. The 601 is capable of implementing both POWER and PowerPC by software emulation of instructions not implemented in hardware.

1.8 The Rest of the Book

The first part of the book focuses on the POWER architecture and the POWER1 implementation. Chapter 2 describes the features of the POWER architecture. Chapters 3, 4, and 5 provide details of the POWER1 implementation. These three chapters cover the POWER1 pipelines, branches and interrupts, and cache memories, respectively. Chapter 6 describes the newest member of the POWER family, POWER2. To allow easy comparisons, the POWER2 description follows the same basic flow as for POWER1. The next part of the book shifts attention to PowerPC and the PowerPC 601 implementation. Chapter 7 covers the PowerPC architecture, Chapter 8 covers the PowerPC 601 processor implementation, and Chapter 9 contains a description of multiprocessor features defined in PowerPC and implemented in the PowerPC 601. Chapter 10 discusses a number of system issues and systems. This discussion includes descriptions of memory, input/output systems, and major system buses used in a wide variety of systems incorporating both POWER and PowerPC-based processors. Finally, Chapter 11 provides a different perspective by comparing the PowerPC 601 with a competing RISC architecture and implementation, the DEC Alpha 21064.

1.9 References

To better understand the distinctions between architecture and implementation, the book by Myers [63] begins with a very well articulated discussion on computer architecture. The Myers book also describes the once-dreaded "semantic gap" that was used as the justification for some of the later CISC architectures.

Descriptions of the early RISC processors can be found in [75] (the 801), [72] (the Berkeley RISC), and [35] (the Stanford University MIPS). Also, good summaries of these projects, along with a healthy dose of RISC philosophy, can be found in [34] and [70]. Comparisons of RISC and CISC architectures are in [8, 23].

Pipelining is the subject of the book by Kogge [49]. The following books also cover pipelining at various levels of detail: Hayes [33], Hwang and Briggs [39], Patterson and Hennessy [71], and Stone [88]. Schneck [77] describes several important pipelined machines, including the Stretch which, among other innovations, introduced the first CPU pipeline (see Bloch [9] and Bucholz [10]).

The IBM 360/91 was a classic pipelined computer, developed in the mid 1960s. Fortunately, it was also very well documented in a series of papers in a special issue of the *IBM Journal of Research and Development* [4, 90]. These papers have become required reading for anyone interested in high-performance computer systems.

A study of the trade-off between pipeline depth and performance is in [50]. A discussion of some of the fundamental trade-offs between deeply pipelined and superscalar implementations is in [47]. Superscalar processing is the subject of a book by Johnson [46]. Instruction issuing and other aspects of superscalar processor design are investigated in [1, 24, 69]. Several papers offer different perspectives on the availability of instruction-level parallelism [52, 65, 76, 85, 89, 91].

Discussions of software scheduling techniques are included in Chapter 6 of [71]. The paper [93] contains descriptions and evaluations of loop unrolling and software pipelining methods. Software pipelining is covered in detail by Lam in [51].

POWER ARCHITECTURE

2.1 Introduction

Just as a building's architecture defines its appearance to its inhabitants, a computer's architecture defines its appearance to software. The architecture is the interface between hardware and software, and is the view of a computer system seen by assembly language programmers, operating system developers, and compiler writers. An important part of the architecture is the instruction set, but it contains other elements such as memory addressing methods and interrupt mechanisms.

The POWER (Performance Optimized With Enhanced RISC) architecture is distinguished by two fundamental features. First, the physical partitioning of its implementation in the POWER1 and POWER2 processors is plainly evident in the logical partitioning of the architecture (the "Performance Optimized" part of the architecture). Second, it has a number of instructions that are relatively complex in order to get more "work" done each clock period (the "Enhanced RISC" part). Examples of complex instructions are the combined floating-point multiply-add instruction and instructions that perform both a memory access and an address register update. A set of character string instructions is another complex part of the instruction repertoire.

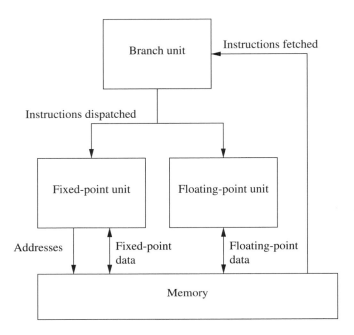

FIGURE 2.1   POWER logical view.

Our description of the architecture is not a detailed specification; for that the reader should refer to [44].[1] Rather, we describe the key elements of the architectures, often via example, so their properties can be clearly understood. We list many instructions but not all—we choose a basic set that will be useful throughout the book. A complete list of instruction forms and a list of the instructions sorted by mnemonic appear in Appendices B and C.

2.2 Instruction Set Basics

In the POWER architecture (Figure 2.1), a processor consists of a Branch Unit (BU), Fixed-Point Unit (FXU), and Floating-Point Unit (FPU). This is a *logical,* not a *physical*, partition.

---

[1]The manual does not describe privileged instructions; the complete POWER architecture specification is not publicly available.

Notation	Meaning
Rn, FRn	Register Rn, FRn, where n is A, B, C, S, T
(Rn), (FRn)	Contents of register Rn, FRn, where n is A, B, C, S, T
R$_i$	Bit i of register R, where R is LR, CTR, CR, XER
R$_{i-j}$	Bits i–j of register R, where R is LR, CTR, CR, XER
//	Unused bits in an instruction.
||	Concatenation
Doubleword	8 bytes
Word	4 bytes
Halfword	2 bytes

FIGURE 2.2   **Notation and terms used to describe instructions. The unused bits are undefined.**

Why partition the architecture into units? The name "units" seems to suggest implementation features, not architectural ones.

The POWER architecture was designed specifically for implementations that exploit instruction-level parallelism. By defining the architecture as a set of three units, each with its own registers, instructions, and interfaces, it is possible to simplify and minimize the resource sharing and synchronization among the units. This, in turn, will enhance parallelism among the units when they process instructions. Partitioning the architecture into units clearly exemplifies the basic RISC philosophy of exposing hardware resources to the compiler.

Instruction Formats

Figure 2.2 contains notation that will be useful in understanding instruction descriptions that follow. Figures 2.3 and 2.4 illustrate the instruction fields and formats used by most instructions. As with typical RISC architectures, the instructions are all 32 bits long and have their fields similarly aligned across all the formats. This simplifies instruction fetching and decoding. The primary opcode fields (OPCD) are all 6 bits. Some of the instructions have extended opcodes (EO, EO′, and XO) because the primary opcode field is not sufficient to encode the entire instruction set. Besides the opcode fields, another important piece of control information contained in many instructions is the Record bit (Rc). This bit causes the Condition Register, held in the branch unit, to be updated depending on the result of the instruction: for example, if the result is positive or negative.

The register fields appear in the same positions in all formats. Source registers are read by instructions and provide operand data or addresses used as input information by instructions. Target registers receive data loaded from memory or results of operate instructions. Also, a number of fields provide immediate data and address information in the instruction itself.

OPCD	Opcode
RT	Target register
FRT	Floating target register
RA, RB, RS	Source registers
FRA, FRB, FRC, FRS	Floating source registers
D	Displacement
SI	Signed immediate
UI	Unsigned immediate
EO, XO, EO$'$	Extended opcode
Rc	Record bit
OE	Overflow enable
MB	Mask begin
ME	Mask end
SH	Shift amount

(a) Instruction fields.

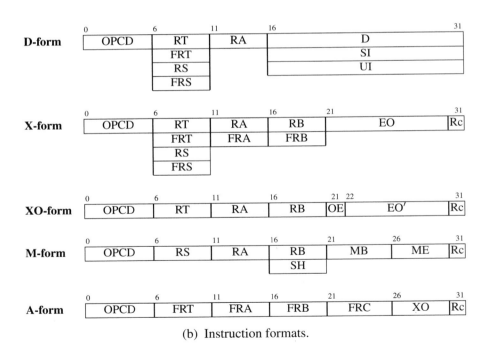

(b) Instruction formats.

FIGURE 2.3   **POWER fixed and floating-point instruction formats.**

OPCD   Opcode
LI   Long immediate
BO   Branch options
BI   Bit in the condition register
BD   Branch displacement
EO   Extended opcode
AA   Absolute address
LK   Link

(a) Instruction fields.

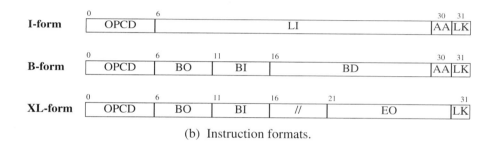

(b) Instruction formats.

FIGURE 2.4   **POWER branch instruction fields and formats.**

Load and store instructions use either the D-form or X-form, which differ in the way the effective address is computed. In D-form instructions the address is computed by adding a displacement to the contents of a register (RA) + D, and in the X-form the address is computed by adding the contents of two registers (RA) + (RB). In traditional IBM terminology, RA is the base register and RB is the index register (the *X* in X-form is for indeX). These two formats are also used in many arithmetic, logical, and shift instructions.

The XO-form is used by some integer arithmetic instructions. XO-form is a variant of the X-form with an overflow enable bit OE (the *O* in XO-form refers to the OE bit) and an extended opcode EO′ made one bit shorter than EO to make space for the OE bit. A typical use of OE is in extended precision arithmetic to disable the setting of overflow indication.

The M-form is used by a set of integer rotate-with-mask instructions. The rotate amount is specified by a register RB or an immediate field SH. The mask is defined by the MB and ME fields (the details will be described later in Section 2.3).

The A-form has four register fields and is used by the four-operand floating multiply-add instruction. For consistency reasons, e.g., to simplify decoding, it is also used by other floating arithmetic instructions that have only three register operands (in which case one of the four register fields is, obviously, unused).

The branch instruction forms include an unconditional branch (I-form) and two similar conditional branch forms (B-form and XL-form). The B-form specifies a branch displacement, and the XL-form gets its branch target from one of the Branch Unit registers.

Assembly Language

An assembly language is a symbolic way of expressing processor instructions. For us the assembly language is only a tool to help illustrate instruction sequences that may be processed by implementations. Consequently, we will describe the language mostly via example. Throughout the book, we will document every assembly language statement so that detailed knowledge of the assembly language is not required.

We do not use the standard IBM assembly language. Rather we use one that is very similar to what the IBM xlc C compiler produces when a flag is set to generate assembly output. We feel this is more readable than the format in the assembly language manual; for example, it contains "=" to indicate assignment and, redundantly, places the name of a variable being loaded or stored as part of the address specification.

An assembly statement usually contains four fields. The first is an optional statement label, used for branches. The second is the opcode mnemonic; third come the operands, typically in a symbolic notation that expresses the access and flow of data. Finally, the fourth field is a comment, beginning with the # symbol. Following are a few examples.

```
        l     r4=s(r1,1)      # load r4 from location r1+1
                              # the variable s is being loaded
        a     r3=r4,r5        # integer add r4 and r5; result to r3
LABEL:  ai    r3=r3,1         # add immediate r3 and 1; result to r3
                              # above instruction is at location "LABEL"
        a     r3=r4,r5        # integer add r4 and r5; result to r3
        bc    LABEL,CTR≠0     # decrement CTR, if CTR≠0
                              # branch to LABEL
        stx   q(r1,r2)=r3     # store r3 at location r1+r2
                              # the variable q is being stored
```

As can be seen from the examples, the arithmetic instructions indicate their data flow in the third field by first giving the target register, followed by "=" followed by the operands separated by commas. Loads indicate the register being loaded, followed by "=", then the variable or array name followed by the expression forming the address in parentheses. A store reverses the flow indicated by a load.

As we define other instruction types in following sections, we will give a few more assembly language examples.

2.3 Fixed-Point Unit

The "core" of the POWER architecture is the Fixed-Point Unit (FXU). The FXU is responsible for the integer operations and all the memory operations (both integer and floating-point). The architectural state belonging to the FXU consists of a set of 32 integer registers and several special purpose registers. The FXU instruction set contains the vast majority of instructions that make up the POWER architecture.

Fixed-Point Unit Registers

The register set used by the FXU is shown in Figure 2.5. The 32 integer registers (r0–r31) are used for both integer and address computations. In most RISCs integer register 0 always has a zero value, which leaves the register file with 31 usable registers. In POWER, however, a value of zero is used only if the RA register designator is zero in a load or store instruction (and a few address computation instructions, such as `cal`; see Figure 2.11). Otherwise, r0 may be used as any other integer register.

Also shown in Figure 2.5 are four special-purpose registers that are part of the architectural state. The Data Address Register (DAR) and Data Storage Interrupt Status Register (DSISR) are used by the operating system to resolve interrupts caused by memory references. For example, in the case of an access attempt that violates memory protection, the DAR will contain the memory address that caused the interrupt. The Multiplier and Quotient (MQ) Register is used by the fixed-point multiply and divide instructions; it holds part of the product for a multiply and the dividend and remainder for a divide.

The Exception Register (XER) holds a number of individually named fields that record exception information and provide additional operand information used by some character string instructions. The fields of the XER are shown in Figure 2.6. The overflow, summary overflow, and carry bits are used by integer arithmetic operations, and two fields (bits 16–23 and 25–31) are used in string instructions. One of these fields contains a string terminator character, and the other, a string length in bytes.

Load and Store Instructions

The FXU executes a set of load and store instructions used to access both memory and input/output devices (Figure 2.7 and Figure 2.8). There are four primary attributes that characterize the different types of load and store instructions (only the first three apply to stores).

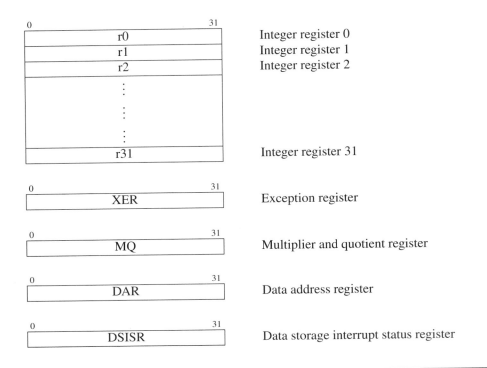

FIGURE 2.5   **Fixed-Point Unit register set.**

1. *Access granularity:* For integer loads and stores, the granularities are byte, two bytes (halfword), and four bytes (word). For floating-point, single-precision numbers (32 bits) or double-precision numbers (64 bits) may be accessed. When a floating-point single is loaded, it is automatically converted to a double when placed in the register. In the other direction, a `store floating single` converts a double-precision operand to single precision.

2. *Addressing mode:* There are two addressing modes. One adds the contents of a register and a displacement value held in the instruction to arrive at the address (D-form). The other adds the contents of two registers (X-form).

3. *Update mode:* The update versions of instructions automatically modify the base register RA by replacing its contents with the newly computed effective address. The update is

Bit	Description
0	**SO** (Summary Overflow)
	Set to 1 to indicate overflow.
	Remains 1 until reset by software.
1	**OV** (Overflow)
	Set to 1 to indicate overflow.
	Reset to 0 by next instruction if there is no overflow.
2	**CA** (Carry)
	Set to 1 to indicate a carry out from the result.
3–15	Reserved
16–23	May contain a string terminator character (byte).
	Used by `lscbx` (load string and compare byte) instruction.
24	Reserved
25–31	May contain a string length (number of bytes).
	Used by several string load and store instructions.

FIGURE 2.6   **Bits in the XER register.**

only done if 1) RA is not also the target of the load and 2) RA specifies a register other than r0.

4. *Sign extension:* "Load algebraic" extends the sign of a data item that is shorter than the register; "load and zero" fills the upper part of the register with zero.

Related to access granularity is *alignment.* An object of size b bytes is *aligned* if its memory address is an integer multiple of b. Otherwise, an object is *misaligned.* Doublewords are aligned at addresses 0, 8, 16, 24,..., words at addresses 0, 4, 8, 12,..., and halfwords at addresses 0, 2, 4, 6,.... Bytes are always aligned.

The Machine State Register (MSR) contains a bit (AL) that determines whether alignment checking is on or off (Figure 2.15). When MSR(AL) = 0, alignment checking is off, and the low-order bits of the address (one bit for halfwords, two bits for words, and three bits for doublewords) are ignored. When MSR(AL) = 1, alignment checking is on, and the architecture specifies that if the hardware cannot handle a misaligned access automatically, an alignment interrupt will be generated. It is then up to the software exception handler whether the program is aborted or the misaligned access is performed in software.

Following are some alignment examples. Assume r1 contains 1024.

```
lhz   r2 = a(r1,6)     # load half from location r1+6
l     r3 = b(r1,8)     # load word from location r1+8
l     r4 = c(r1,34)    # load word from location r1+34
```

D-form

	0	6	11	16	31
	OPCD	RT	RA	D	
		RS			
		FRT			
		FRS			

lbz   load byte, zero rest of RT
lbzu   load byte, zero rest of RT, update RA
lhz   load half, zero rest of RT
lhzu   load half, zero rest of RT, update RA
lha   load half algebraic, sign extend
lhau   load half algebraic, sign extend, update RA
l   load word
lu   load word, update RA
lfs   load floating single
lfsu   load floating single, update RA
lfd   load floating double
lfdu   load floating double, update RA
stb   store lower byte of RS
stbu   store lower byte of RS, update RA
sth   store lower half of RS
sthu   store lower half of RS, update RA
st   store word
stu   store word, update RA
stfs   store floating single
stfsu   store floating single, update RA
stfd   store floating double
stfdu   store floating double, update RA
lm   load multiple
stm   store multiple

$$\text{Effective address} = \begin{cases} (RA) + D & \text{if } RA \neq 0 \\ D & \text{if } RA = 0 \end{cases}$$

FIGURE 2.7   **D-form load and store instructions. RT is the target register for loads, RS is the source register for stores.**

X-form $\begin{array}{c} 0 \\ | \end{array}$ OPCD $\begin{array}{c} 6 \\ | \end{array}$ $\begin{array}{c} \text{RT} \\ \text{RS} \end{array}$ $\begin{array}{c} 11 \\ | \end{array}$ RA $\begin{array}{c} 16 \\ | \end{array}$ RB $\begin{array}{c} 21 \\ | \end{array}$ EO $\begin{array}{c} 31 \\ | \text{Rc}| \end{array}$

lbzx	load byte, zero rest of RT, indexed
lbzux	load byte, zero rest of RT, update RA, indexed
lhzx	load half, zero rest of RT, indexed
lhzux	load half, zero rest of RT, update RA, indexed
lhax	load half algebraic, sign extend, indexed
lhaux	load half algebraic, sign extend, update RA, indexed
lx	load word, indexed
lux	load word, update RA, indexed
lfsx	load floating single, indexed
lfsux	load floating single, update RA, indexed
lfdx	load floating double, indexed
lfdux	load floating double, update RA, indexed
stbx	store lower byte of RS, indexed
stbux	store lower byte of RS, update RA, indexed
sthx	store lower half of RS, indexed
sthux	store lower half of RS, update RA, indexed
stx	store word, indexed
stux	store word, update RA, indexed
stfsx	store floating single, indexed
stfsux	store floating single, update RA, indexed
stfdx	store floating double, indexed
stfdux	store floating double, update RA, indexed

$$\text{Effective address} = \left\{ \begin{array}{ll} (RA) + (RB) & \text{if } RA \neq 0 \\ (RB) & \text{if } RA = 0 \end{array} \right.$$

FIGURE 2.8   **X-form load and store instructions. RT is the target register for loads, RS is the source register for stores.**

The first two loads are aligned: the first is a halfword load from an address that is a multiple of 2 and the second is a word load from a multiple of 4. The final load, however, is unaligned because it is a word loaded from an address that is not an integer multiple of 4. If MSR(AL) = 1, the third instruction will cause an alignment interrupt.

The update mode load and store instructions are useful for sequencing through elements of arrays. For example, the lu instruction can be used to access an integer array, a, of 4-byte words stored in memory beginning at location 512.

```
           cal   r1 = 508              # load immediate, address of a − 4
LOOP:      ...
           lu    r3 = a(r1=r1+4)       # load word with update
                                       # from location r1+4

           ...
           bc    LOOP,CTR≠0            # decrement CTR, if CTR≠0
                                       # branch to LOOP
```

Register r1 is initially set to point 4 bytes before the first element of the array and the displacement D is set to 4. The cal instruction (compute address lower; Figure 2.11) has a rather misleading name. It is often used by the compiler as a load immediate, with RA set to zero and D being the immediate field. Within the LOOP, each execution of the lu instruction updates r1 by adding 4 and uses the updated value to load the next element of the array. This implements a "pre-update"; i.e., the update is done prior to the memory access (the reason r1 is initialized to 4 bytes before the first array element).

In addition to the normal loads and stores, two types of data transfer instructions involve multiple target or source registers: 1) load and store multiple, and 2) string instructions. The load multiple (lm) loads the set of registers beginning with RT and ending with r31. Store multiple (stm) performs a similar data transfer in the other direction. A typical application of these instructions is saving and restoring registers in procedure calls or context switches. As an example, assuming r1 points to an area in memory called "buffer," the following instruction saves registers r25–r31 into that area.

```
stm    buffer(r1) = r25
```

String instructions come in two flavors (Figure 2.9). The first includes four instructions: load string indexed (lsx), load string immediate (lsi), store string indexed (stsx), and store string immediate (stsi). The number of bytes n is specified by a field in the Exception Register XER_{25-31} in instructions lsx and stsx and by an immediate field NB in instructions lsi and stsi. An instruction transfers n bytes beginning with register RT (RS for stores), then using consecutive registers up to r31, and finally wrapping around through r0 if necessary.

There is only one instruction of the second type: load string and compare byte indexed (lscbx). The instruction loads bytes into registers beginning with RT, using consecutive registers and wrapping around, as before. The transfer ends when either the number of bytes specified in XER_{25-31} have been loaded or a match is found with XER_{16-23}.

X-form | OPCD | RT / RS | RA | RB / NB | EO | Rc |

(bit positions: 0, 6, 11, 16, 21, 31)

lsi   load string immediate
lsx   load string, indexed
lscbx load string and compare byte, indexed
stsi   store string immediate
stsx   store string, indexed

$$\text{Effective address (lsi, stsi)} = \begin{cases} (RA) & \text{if } RA \neq 0 \\ 0 & \text{if } RA = 0 \end{cases}$$

$$\text{Effective address (lsx, lscbx, stsx)} = \begin{cases} (RA) + (RB) & \text{if } RA \neq 0 \\ (RB) & \text{if } RA = 0 \end{cases}$$

FIGURE 2.9   **String instructions.**

Figure 2.10 illustrates the use of the `lscbx` instruction in the C `strcpy` function. Loading the number 16 into XER accomplishes two things. It sets the byte count in XER_{25-31} to 16. It also loads zero into XER_{16-23}, which is the correct string delimiter character for C-style strings. In each iteration of the loop, `lscbx` loads 16 bytes, or fewer if a match is found, into integer registers beginning with r6. If a match is found, the instruction modifies the byte count in XER_{25-31} to the number of bytes actually loaded, so that the instruction `stsx` stores the correct number of bytes.

The dot after the instruction's mnemonic (`lscbx.`) indicates that the record bit Rc is set to one. If there is a match, the cr0/eq bit is set. (See Section 2.4 for a description of the Condition Register bits.) This bit is tested by the loop-closing conditional branch.

The `lscbx` instruction has an interesting property: at the time it is initiated, the number of locations that will have to be accessed before there is a match is not known. Because a memory protection boundary may be crossed during the execution of the instruction (e.g., a page boundary may lie between the beginning of a string and its end), there would seem to be a possibility of spurious protection exceptions. These could occur because an implementation is likely to overlap the accessing of data with the byte comparisons by anticipating data to be needed for future comparisons. In the process, some bytes may be accessed (illegally) when they fall beyond a matching one.

```
                                        # a string is copied from t to s
                                        # r4 points to t
                                        # r3 points to s
             cal      r5=16             # load immediate byte count into r5
             mtspr    XER=r5            # move to special register (XER)
             cal      r1=0              # clear index register r1
    LOOP:    lscbx.   r6=t(r4+r1)       # load 16 bytes from t
             stsx     s(r3+r1)=r6       # store to s 16 bytes (fewer if match)
             ai       r1=r1+16          # increment index register
             bc       LOOP, cr0/eq=false  # branch if no match found
```

FIGURE 2.10   Efficient coding of the C strcpy function using the lscbx instruction.

No exception should be signaled in such cases, and an implementation can avoid such spurious exceptions in one of two ways. First, it may perform protection checks prior to crossing protection boundaries, i.e., avoid spurious exceptions in the first place. Second, it may disregard protection boundaries when making the accesses but have hardware mechanisms in place to cancel any exceptions for accesses to data following the match.

Not knowing the full extent of an instruction's effects at the time of its initiation is a type of behavior avoided in other RISCs. The spurious exception problem clearly illustrates the reason. This is an example of the POWER architecture seeming to violate basic RISC philosophy in order to provide more powerful instructions.

A similar, but simpler, issue occurs when a load/store multiple or a string instruction encounters an ordinary page fault part way through its execution. In this case, the faulting access may be perfectly legal and must be handled. In the POWER architecture, the transfer is terminated, the page fault serviced. All transfers up to the termination are complete, but the instruction is restarted from the beginning, a feasible process as long as the registers involved in calculating the effective address (Figure 2.8 and Figure 2.9) are not overwritten. The POWER architecture requires the hardware to perform this check at runtime and inhibit overwriting an address register.

Arithmetic Instructions

The architecture provides the usual set of integer add, subtract, multiply, and divide instructions (Figure 2.11). The XO-form instructions are typical RISC, three-operand instructions. They have an opcode in the OPCD field and an extended opcode in EO$'$. An instruction takes two

XO-form

0	6	11	16	21 22		31
OPCD	RT	RA	RB	OE	EO′	Rc

a   add, place (RA) + (RB) into RT
sf   subtract from, place (RB) − (RA) into RT
ae   add extended, place (RA) + (RB) + CA into RT
sfe   subtract from extended, place (RB) − (RA) + CA into RT
ame   add to minus one extended, place (RA) − 1 + CA into RT
sfme   subtract from minus one extended, place −1 − (RA) + CA into RT
aze   add to zero extended, place (RA) + 0 + CA into RT
sfze   subtract from zero extended, place 0 − (RA) + CA into RT
doz   difference or zero, place (RB) − (RA) into RT, or 0 if (RB) < (RA)
abs   absolute, place the absolute value of (RA) into RT
nabs   negative absolute, place the negative absolute value of (RA) into RT
neg   negate, place −(RA) into RT
mul   multiply, place (RA)×(RB) into RT∥MQ
muls   multiply short, place upper word of (RA)×(RB) into RT, MQ undefined
div   divide, place (RA∥MQ) ÷ (RB) into RT, remainder in MQ
divs   divide short, place (RA) ÷ (RB) into RT, remainder in MQ

D-form

0	6	11	16	31
OPCD	RT	RA	SI	
			D	

cal   compute address lower, place (RA) + D into RT if RA ≠ 0, else place D into RT
ai   add immediate, place (RA) + SI into RT
ai.   add immediate and record, place (RA) + SI into RT
sfi   subtract from immediate, place SI − (RA) into RT
dozi   difference or zero immediate, place SI − (RA) into RT, or 0 if SI < (RA)
muli   multiply immediate, place upper word of (RA)×SI into RT, MQ undefined

FIGURE 2.11   Integer arithmetic instructions.

source registers RA and RB, operates on them, and places the result in a target register RT. The instructions contain the Rc bit which can be used to place an automatic comparison result into the Condition Register held in the Branch Unit. When Rc = 1, as indicated by the dot following the instruction's mnemonic (sf.) in the example below, the result of an instruction is compared to zero and bits in Condition Register field 0 are set accordingly (see Section 2.4 for a description of the Condition Register bits).

```
       . . .
       sf.    r3 = r1–r2          # subtract from, set bit in cr0 accordingly
       bc     EXIT,cr0/eq=true    # branch if result was equal to zero
       . . .
EXIT:  . . .
```

When Rc = 0, the Condition Register is unchanged. This feature allows an operation to be followed immediately by a conditional branch based on the result of the operation; an intervening comparison instruction is not needed. (X-form load and store instructions, however, leave Condition Register field 0 undefined if Rc = 1.)

To support extended-precision integer arithmetic, some add and subtract instructions use the Carry bit from the XER. Also, the OE field is used to enable (or disable) overflow reporting; disabling overflow is useful for implementing extended-precision integer arithmetic where intermediate overflows should be ignored.

All multiply and divide instructions (`muli`, `mul`, `muls`, `div`, `divs`) either use the MQ register or leave it undefined. For holding the 64-bit result of a 32 by 32-bit multiplication, the RT and MQ register are concatenated; the upper 32 bits of the result are in RT, and the lower 32 bits are in MQ. For division, a 64-bit dividend can be supported by using MQ to hold the lower 32 bits with RA holding the upper 32 bits of the dividend. The MQ Register is also used by divisions to hold the remainder; RT holds the quotient.

The D-form instructions use a 16-bit two's complement constant value taken from bits 16 through 31 as one of the operands. The `add immediate with record` (`ai.`) is one of the few D-form instructions that modifies the Condition Register field with a comparison result. There is a separate instruction `add immediate` (`ai`) that has no effect on the Condition Register. Because D-form instructions do not have an Rc bit, the equivalent information must be encoded as part of the opcode.

Rotate and Shift Instructions

POWER provides a large set of rotate and shift instructions, as shown in Figure 2.12. Only rotate left instructions are provided; obviously, rotate right by n positions is identical to rotate left by $32 - n$ positions.

The M-form rotate with mask instructions are unique among RISC instruction sets. These instructions rotate the contents of register RS left by a number of positions specified by register RB, or field SH in immediate instructions. Then a mask of ones that begins from bit position MB and ends at bit position ME is generated. The mask is used in one of two ways: rotate with insert or rotate with AND.

As long as MB ≤ ME, the mask forms as one would expect intuitively. For example, if MB = 26 and ME = 29, the mask is

$$00000000000000000000000000111100$$

M-form

0	6	11	16	21	26	31
OPCD	RS	RA	RB SH	MB	ME	Rc

rlimi rotate left immediate then mask insert
rlmi   rotate left then mask insert
rlinm rotate left immediate then AND with mask
rlnm   rotate left then AND with mask

X-form

0	6	11	16	21	31
OPCD	RS	RA	RB SH	EO	Rc

rrib   rotate right and insert bit
maskg mask generate
maskir mask insert from register
sl   shift left
sr   shift right
slq   shift left with MQ
srq   shift right with MQ
sliq   shift left immediate with MQ
sriq   shift right immediate with MQ
slliq shift left long immediate with MQ
srliq shift right long immediate with MQ
sllq   shift left long with MQ
srlq   shift right long with MQ
sle   shift left extended
sre   shift right extended
sleq   shift left extended with MQ
sreq   shift right extended with MQ
srai   shift right algebraic immediate
sra   shift right algebraic
sraiq shift right algebraic immediate with MQ
sraq   shift right algebraic with MQ
srea   shift right extended algebraic

FIGURE 2.12 **Integer rotate and shift instructions. The rotate/shift amount is specified by the RB register or by the SH field in immediate instructions.**

But, what happens if MB > ME? The sequence of ones still begins at position MB, goes to the end of the word, wraps around and stops at position ME. As a second example, if MB = 29 and ME = 26, the mask is

$$11111111111111111111111111100111$$

Positions 26 and 29 are set to one in both examples.

This general facility defines sequences of ones of length 1 to 32 bits, beginning from any position in a 32-bit word (and wrapping around if necessary). There is no way to specify a mask of all zeros, which would have the effect of simply clearing the target register (this can be done by other instructions).

Instructions `rlimi` and `rlmi` perform rotate with insert. If the mask bit is one, the corresponding bit of the rotated data is inserted into RA; if the mask bit is zero, the corresponding bit in RA remains unchanged. Instructions `rlinm` and `rlnm` perform rotate with AND. The rotated data are ANDed with the mask and placed into register RA. The example below illustrates a use of `rlnm`.

```
                        # source register r1 = 3
                        # rotate positions r2 = 1
   rlnm    r3 = r1,r2,26,29    # MB = 26, ME = 29
                        # now r3 = 4
```

In addition to the usual shift instructions, POWER provides a large set of shifts with MQ and extended shifts that use the MQ Register.

2.4 Branch Unit

The primary function of the Branch Unit (BU) is to direct the correct flow of instructions to the FXU and FPU. The architectural view of the BU consists of a set of special-purpose registers, the branch instructions, and a set of instructions that perform logical operations on bits in one of the special registers, the Condition Register.

Branch Unit Registers

The Branch Unit registers are shown in Figure 2.13. The Condition Register (CR) is a 32-bit register tested by conditional branch instructions. It is divided into eight 4-bit fields (cr0, cr1,..., cr7) that can be accessed separately. In effect, the CR fields may be regarded as a set of independent 4-bit condition registers (Figure 2.14(a)).

The four bits in a field signify the conditions *less than, greater than, equal,* and *summary overflow.* This last bit is a copy of the summary overflow bit from the XER belonging to the FXU, which is set by an overflow and remains set until cleared by software. The condition

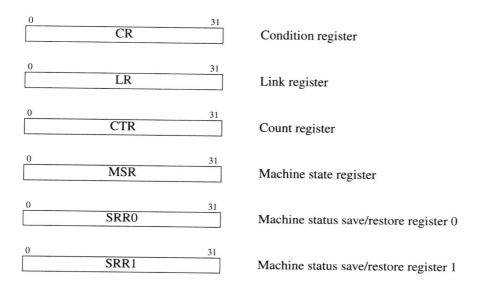

FIGURE 2.13 **Branch Unit registers.**

bits are tested for either a true or false value. Therefore, a "less or equal" condition can be obtained by checking the "greater than" bit for false. Any of these fields can be specified as the target of fixed-point or floating-point compare instruction. In addition, Field 0 and Field 1 have special uses. In fixed-point instructions that have an Rc (Record) bit, if Rc = 1, the result of the instruction is compared to zero and CR Field 0 is set according to this comparison (Figure 2.14(b)). In some instructions, however, setting Rc to 1 makes CR Field 0 undefined (load and store instructions, for example). CR Field 1 has an identical use for floating-point instructions having an Rc bit.

The Link Register (LR) has two uses. The first is to contain the branch target address for one variety of conditional branch instruction (see "Branch Unit Instructions" subsection below). Its second use is to retain the return (i.e., "link") address for subroutines. All branch instructions have a Link (LK) bit. LK is set by the compiler when a branch instruction is used to branch to a subroutine. When a branch instruction with LK = 1 executes, the address of the instruction following the branch is saved in the Link Register and is subsequently used to return from the subroutine.

Like the LR, the Count Register (CTR) also has two uses. The first is to contain the branch target address for one of the conditional branch instructions (see "Branch Unit Instructions" subsection below). Its second use is to hold the iteration count for loops in which the total

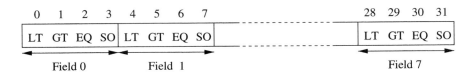

(a) Condition Register fields.

CR bits	Arithmetic instructions	Compare instructions
LT = 1	result < 0	(RA) < (RB), or (RA) < immediate operand
GT = 1	result > 0	(RA) > (RB), or (RA) > immediate operand
EQ = 1	result = 0	(RA) = (RB), or (RA) = immediate operand
SO	Summary overflow—this is a copy of XER(SO), see Section 2.3	

(b) Bits in a CR Field.

FIGURE 2.14   **Condition Register. This definition of bits is for fixed-point operations and fixed-point compare instructions.**

loop count can be computed before the loop is entered. A simple example is a loop of the form "do i=1,n"; in this case n could be loaded into the CTR prior to the loop entry. Conditional branches may test the value of the CTR relative to zero (that is, CTR = 0 or CTR ≠ 0). CTR is automatically decremented by the branch instruction that tests its value, prior to the test.

The Machine State Register (MSR) defines the state of the processor according to the bits defined in Figure 2.15. Some of these bits are the usual controls that disable interrupts or place the processor in a privileged state. A rather uncommon optimization is provided by MSR(FP). When MSR(FP) = 0, the attempt to execute any floating-point instruction causes a "floating-point unavailable" interrupt. If a system call is not normally expected to execute any floating code, instead of saving the floating-point registers prior to the system call, it is sufficient to clear MSR(FP). If, by some chance, a floating-point instruction is encountered, an interrupt will be generated to take care of saving the floating-point registers. MSR(FP) can also be used to support floating point in software, if an implementation does not have hardware

Bit	Name	Value	Description
00–15			Reserved
16	EE	0	External interrupts disabled
		1	External interrupts enabled
17	PR	0	Privileged state
		1	Nonprivileged state
18	FP	0	Floating-point unit unavailable
		1	Floating-point unit available
19	ME	0	Machine check interrupts disabled
		1	Machine check interrupts enabled
20	FE	0	Interrupts disabled for FP exceptions
		1	Interrupts enabled for FP exceptions
21–23			Reserved
24	AL	0	Alignment checking is off
		1	Alignment checking is on
25	IP	0	Interrupts vectored to address x000nnnnn
		1	Interrupts vectored to address xFFFnnnnn
26	IR	0	Instruction address translation is off
		1	Instruction address translation is on
27	DR	0	Data address translation is off
		1	Data address translation is on
28–31			Reserved

FIGURE 2.15   *Machine State Register (MSR) bits.*

floating point, although this situation is becoming increasingly uncommon as chip integration levels rise.

Two additional registers, SRR0 and SRR1, are used to save the machine status on an interrupt and restore the status upon returning from the interrupt. SRR0 contains the address of the instruction that caused the interrupt, or the return address after entering the interrupt service routine. When an interrupt occurs, the upper half (bits 0–15) of SRR1 is loaded with interrupt-specific information, and the lower half (bits 16–31) contains a copy of the lower half of the MSR.

Branch Unit Instructions

The POWER architecture has one unconditional branch and three conditional branch instructions (Figure 2.16). To determine the branch target address in the unconditional branch, a

BO field	Condition to take branch		
0000x	$CTR \neq 0$	AND	$CR_{BI} = 0$
0001x	$CTR = 0$	AND	$CR_{BI} = 0$
001xx			$CR_{BI} = 0$
0100x	$CTR \neq 0$	AND	$CR_{BI} = 1$
0101x	$CTR = 0$	AND	$CR_{BI} = 1$
011xx			$CR_{BI} = 1$
1x00x	$CTR \neq 0$		
1x01x	$CTR = 0$		
1x1xx	Always true		

I-form

0	6		30	31
OPCD	LI		AA	LK

b   Unconditional branch. LI is a word address;
           concatenated with 00 it forms a byte address.

$$\text{Target address} = \begin{cases} LI\|00 + \text{Current instruction address} & \text{if } AA = 0 \\ LI\|00 & \text{if } AA = 1 \end{cases}$$

B-form

0	6	11	16	30	31
OPCD	BO	BI	BD	AA	LK

bc   Conditional branch. BD is a word address;
           concatenated with 00 it forms a byte address.

$$\text{Target address} = \begin{cases} BD\|00 + \text{Current instruction address} & \text{if } AA = 0 \\ BD\|00 & \text{if } AA = 1 \end{cases}$$

XL-form

0	6	11	16	21	31
OPCD	BO	BI	//	EO	LK

bcr   Conditional branch.
           Target address = $LR_{0-29}\|00$
bcc   Conditional branch.
           Target address = $CTR_{0-29}\|00$

FIGURE 2.16   Branch instructions. CR_{BI} is bit BI of the Condition Register. If LK = 1, the Link
                  Register is loaded with the effective address of the instruction following the branch.

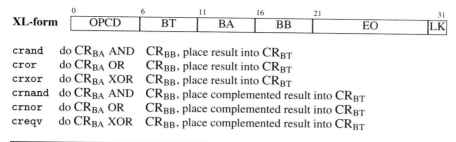

FIGURE 2.17 Condition Register logical instructions.

24-bit immediate field LI is used as either an absolute address or as an address relative to the current instruction, depending on the AA bit. Byte addressing is used for all addresses presented to the hardware, so LI is concatenated with 00 to form a byte address.

In the conditional branch instructions, the condition that determines whether the branch is taken or not is defined by the BO field (Figure 2.16). This condition may be the comparison to zero of the Count Register (CTR), a bit in the Condition Register (CR) defined by field BI of the instruction, or by the logical AND of the two. Conventional conditional branches are implemented by testing a bit in the CR. Loop-closing branches may be implemented by loading the loop count into the CTR and testing its contents in each loop iteration. ANDing the two types of tests is useful for DO loops that contain an exit clause.

The difference between the three conditional branch instructions lies in the way the branch target address is determined. In the bc instruction, a 14-bit immediate field BD (concatenated with 00) is used as either an absolute address or as an address relative to the current instruction, depending on the Absolute Address (AA) bit. The other two conditional branches are similar, the only difference being that the branch target address is the Link Register in the bcr instruction, and the Count Register in the bcc instruction. In either case, the two low-order bits of the special register are replaced by 00.

The Branch Unit also executes a set of instructions that perform logical operations on bits of the CR, as shown in Figure 2.17. Fields BA and BB define the two Condition Register bits to be used in the logical operation, and field BT defines the Condition Register target bit for the result.

Examples

Figure 2.18(a) illustrates the use of the CTR. In the figure, the loop count (512) is loaded into r29 and then transferred into the CTR by the move to special register (mtspr) instruction. This sequence of two instructions is needed because there are no instructions that can load

for (i=0; i<512; i++)

. . .

(a) C statement.

```
        cal     r29=512           # load immediate loop count into r29
        mtspr   CTR=r29           # move to special register (CTR)
LOOP:   . . .

        . . .
        bc      LOOP,CTR≠0    # decrement CTR, branch if CTR≠0
```

(b) Compilation.

FIGURE 2.18   **Example—using the Count Register.**

immediate values into CTR or other special registers. The loop-closing branch decrements the CTR and then tests it at the end of each iteration.

Figure 2.19 shows a code example that demonstrates the use of multiple CR fields and logical CR instructions. On most machines, the two Boolean conditions in the "if" statement are translated to two branch instructions, as shown in Figure 2.19(b). In the assembly code, cri/j indicates bit "j" of condition register field "i"; "j" is given symbolically as the condition it encodes. In POWER, the same "if" statement can be translated to code with a single branch instruction (Figure 2.19(c)). If the two Boolean statements are true, the compare instructions set the "eq" bits in Condition Register fields cr1 and cr2. These two bits are ANDed using a logical CR instruction whose result is sent to cr0 bit 0. Finally, this bit is tested to determine the outcome of the conditional branch.

2.5   Floating-Point Unit

As its name suggests, the primary function of the Floating-Point Unit (FPU) is to handle floating-point arithmetic operations. The architectural view of the FPU consists of 32 64-bit registers for floating-point data, a status register, and a set of instructions.

Floating-Point Unit Registers

The Floating-Point Unit registers are shown in Figure 2.20. The architecture is defined to have 32 64-bit registers to support the IEEE double-precision floating-point format. Exceptions

if ((a == 10) && (b == 20))

. . .

else

. . .

(a) C statement.

```
                          # r1 points to a
                          # r1 + 4 points to b
    l      r7 = a(r1)     # load a
    cmpi   cr1 = r7,10    # compare immediate, set bit in cr1
    bc     ELSE,cr1/eq=false   # branch if 'cr1/eq' bit is false
    l      r7 = b(r1,4)   # load b
    cmpi   cr1 = r7,20    # compare immediate, set bit in cr1
    bc     ELSE,cr1/eq=false   # branch if 'cr1/eq' bit is false
IF:
    . . .
ELSE:
    . . .
```

(b) Assembly language version of C 'if' statement.

```
                          # r1 points to a
                          # r1 + 4 points to b
    l      r7 = a(r1)     # load a
    cmpi   cr1 = r7,10    # compare immediate, set bit in cr1
    l      r8 = b(r1+4)   # load b
    cmpi   cr2 = r8,20    # compare immediate, set bit in cr2
    crand  cr0/eq = cr1/eq,cr2/eq   # AND 'eq' bits, set cr0/eq
    bc     ELSE,cr0/eq=false   # branch if 'cr0/eq' bit is false
IF:
    . . .
ELSE:
    . . .
```

(c) Assembly language version with a single branch instruction.

FIGURE 2.19   **Example—the use of multiple Condition Register fields and logical Condition Register instruction (crand).**

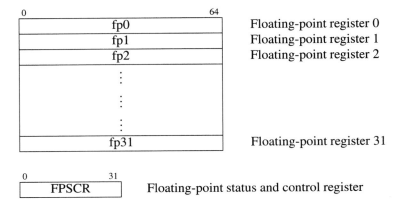

FIGURE 2.20   **Floating-Point Unit registers.**

(e.g., error conditions) are reported via a 32-bit Floating-Point Status and Control Register (FPSCR), shown in detail in Figure 2.21.

Floating-Point Unit Instructions

The centerpiece of the Floating-Point Unit is a set of multiply-add operations. Figure 2.22 provides a list of the FPU instructions. There are four composite instructions in this class: multiply-add and multiply-subtract, $[(FRA) \times (FRC)] \pm (FRB)$, and their negative versions $-[(FRA) \times (FRC)] \pm (FRB)$. These instructions take three input operands from registers FRA, FRB, and FRC, and produce the indicated result. The motivation for these composite instructions is the frequent occurrence of pairs of "multiply" and "add" operations in floating-point code. For example, the inner product that is part of many matrix operations can be implemented using multiply-adds.

An unusual aspect of the POWER multiply-add is that it is a "fused" composite instruction. The architecture explicitly specifies that there is no intermediate rounding operation between the multiply and the add. Because the result of the multiply is not rounded prior to the add, the full precision of the product is kept. Not rounding the product both increases accuracy and saves time. While the results are sometimes more accurate than the IEEE-specified result, at the same time they differ from the IEEE result computed with a separate multiply and add.

Figure 2.23 illustrates the inner loop of a common matrix operation (dot product) using single-precision floating arithmetic. The `lfs` instruction loads a floating-point register from

Bit	Name	Description
0	FX	Exception summary. Set to one if any exception is set to one. Remains one until reset by software.
1	FEX	Enabled exception summary. Set to one if any enabled exception is set to one. Cleared when all enabled exceptions are zero.
2	VX	Invalid operation exception summary. Set to one if an invalid operation exception is set to one. Cleared when all invalid operation exceptions are zero.
3	OX	Overflow exception
4	UX	Underflow exception
5	ZX	Zero divide exception
6	XX	Inexact exception
7	VXSNAN	Invalid operation exception. Result is a signaling NaN.
8	VXISI	Invalid operation exception. Operation is infinity − infinity.
9	VXIDI	Invalid operation exception. Operation is infinity ÷ infinity.
10	VXZDZ	Invalid operation exception. Operation is zero ÷ zero.
11	VZIMZ	Invalid operation exception. Operation is infinity × zero.
12	VXVC	Invalid operation exception. Operation is a comparison involving NaN.
13	FR	Fraction Rounded. Rounding of the result incremented the fraction.
14	FI	Fraction Inexact. Rounding produced an inexact fraction (different than the intermediate result). Or, overflow occurred with disabled overflow exception.
15–19	FPRF	Floating-point result flags
20–23		Reserved
24	VE	Invalid operation exception enable
25	OE	Overflow exception enable
26	UE	Underflow exception enable
27	ZE	Zero divide exception enable
28	XE	Inexact exception enable
29		Reserved
30–31	RN	Rounding control

FIGURE 2.21 **Floating-Point Status and Control Register. Status bits are 0–19. Control bits are 20–31.**

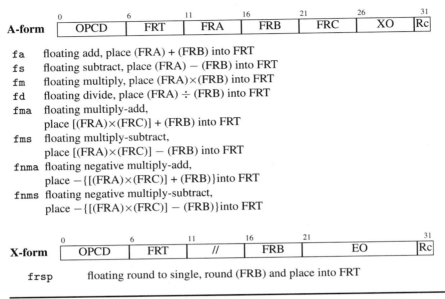

FIGURE 2.22   **Floating-point arithmetic instructions. Field FRC is used in three source operand instructions.**

vector x. The lfsu instruction loads a register from vector y and updates the base register r3 to point (with the same displacements) to the next two vector elements. The POWER compilation inserts a round to single instruction after the multiply add. Note that the frsp could be moved outside of the loop, right after bc, for better performance[2] (see discussion in subsection "Implementation of the IEEE 754 Standard" below for the trade-offs involved).

Implementation of the IEEE 754 Standard

Appendix A describes the IEEE 754 floating-point standard and defines related concepts in floating-point arithmetic. In this section we discuss the POWER implementation of the standard.

In the POWER architecture, all floating-point arithmetic is done in double-precision format. However, the IEEE standard *requires* only single-precision arithmetic; double precision is an *option*. To support single precision, there is a floating round to single (frsp) instruction

---

[2]This option is provided by the FORTRAN compiler, but not by the C compiler (xlc version 2.1).

float q, x[100], y[100];

q = 0;
for (i=0; i<100; i++)
    q = q + x[i]*y[i];

(a) C code.

```
                            # When this loop is entered:
                            # CTR contains the loop count (100),
                            # r1 points to q,
                            # r3 − 396 points to x, and
                            # r3 + 4 points to y.
LOOP:   lfs    fp0=x(r3,−396)   # load floating single
        lfsu   fp1=y(r3=r3+4)   # load floating single with update
        fma    fp0=fp2,fp0,fp1  # floating multiply add
        frsp   fp2=fp0          # round to single precision
        bc     LOOP,CTR≠0       # decrement CTR, branch if CTR≠0
        sts    q(r1) = fp2      # store result
```

(b) POWER compilation (xlc compiler version 2.1) uses the `frsp` instruction to round result to single precision.

FIGURE 2.23   Example—dot product, the inner loop.

---

that converts a double-precision operand to 32-bit single precision. Therefore, programs that use single-precision data are often slower than the double-precision versions because `frsp` instructions are inserted by the compiler to convert results to single precision. This leads to an interesting trade-off between strict standards adherence, performance, and accuracy of results. Both IEEE and FORTRAN 77 standards are at issue.

To mitigate performance loss, the IBM FORTRAN compiler (xlf version 2.2) provides four options listed below in order of decreasing performance, increasing levels of standards conformance, and, generally speaking, decreasing levels of accuracy.

1. *Never round.* This option gives the best performance because no `frsp` instructions are placed in the code, but it is not safe—incorrect results may be produced without warning. A 64-bit result is stored into a 32-bit memory location, usually by truncating the mantissa and the exponent or by converting the result to a denormalized single-precision number if necessary. This is automatically done by `store floating-point single` instructions and is correct as long as the result is within single-precision range. Otherwise, the out-of-range value is incorrectly represented by what appears to be a finite single-precision number. The compiler provides this option for applications (such as graphics) where performance is essential and results are known to be within single-precision range.

2. *Round only before storing a result into a 32-bit memory location.* This option gives the best safe performance but does not conform to FORTRAN 77 and IEEE 754. However, the results are actually more accurate than IEEE or FORTRAN 77 standard single-precision would produce.

3. *Round as required by FORTRAN 77 (this is the compiler's default).* The compiler inserts the `frsp` instructions in certain locations in the program as defined by FORTRAN 77. This option adheres to FORTRAN 77 but not to IEEE 754. Again, any results that deviate from the single-precision standard are more accurate.

4. *Strict FORTRAN 77 and IEEE 754 adherence.* Both standards are met at the cost of a significant reduction in performance due to two factors: rounding instructions are inserted after every floating arithmetic instruction, and the use of the multiply-add instruction is suppressed. Instead, separate multiply and add instructions are used.

Developed more than 10 years ago at a time when microprocessors were heavily micro-programmed with little pipelining, the IEEE standard gives little consideration to problems encountered during overlapped execution of floating-point instructions. The standard requires that a faulting instruction be accurately identified, and this identification is often implemented by providing a precise interrupt for the faulting instruction. Thus, the saved program counter points to the faulting instruction. This feature is desirable if software is to fix up an error and resume execution. But implementing such precise interrupts makes simple, high-performance implementations difficult (more on this in Chapter 4).

Rather than make the implementation overly complex, a decision was made to provide different modes of operation, leading to another trade-off, this time trading off precise floating-point interrupts for performance. To support this trade-off at the architectural level, the POWER architecture provides a bit MSR(FE) in the Machine State Register that can be set if precise interrupts are desired for all floating-point exceptions. This mode is intended for debugging; it considerably limits instruction-level parallelism and slows down the machine by forcing serial execution of floating-point instructions; i.e., one instruction must be known to be exception-free before the next begins. An alternative method is to have software insert test code after each floating-point execution instruction.

There are five types of exceptions defined by the standard: invalid operation, overflow, underflow, division by zero, and inexact exception. For each type of exception, the FPSCR provides a flag (one bit) that is set when the corresponding exception occurs. A flag remains

0	1	2	3	8		31
T	K	S	Not used		Segment ID	

FIGURE 2.24   Segment register format for memory references (T = 0).

set until cleared by the user. The flags may be tested by using a set of move from FPSCR instructions, and cleared using move to FPSCR instructions. Each type of exception has an enable/disable control bit (see Appendix A).

The architecture provides additional information on invalid operation exceptions. Information of this type could be useful for debugging in the absence of precise exceptions. Flags in the FPSCR are set to report that the invalid operation falls in one of the following categories.

- Result is a signaling NaN

- Infinity − Infinity

- Infinity ÷ Infinity

- Zero ÷ Zero

- Infinity × Zero

- A comparison involving NaN

2.6   Virtual Address Generation and Translation

For addressing memory and input/output devices, the architecture defines 16 32-bit segment registers. A segment register is used for memory access when its most significant bit (called T) is zero and for input/output access when T is one. For memory references, the segment register format is shown in Figure 2.24. Bits K and S are used for protection (see Section 2.7).

Address processing begins with the generation of a 32-bit *effective address* whose four most significant bits are used to select one of the segment registers (Figure 2.25). The 24-bit segment ID from the segment register is concatenated with 16 bits from the effective address to obtain a 40-bit virtual page number. This together with a 12-bit page offset forms the 52-bit *virtual address*.

Next, the virtual page number is translated to a real page number. For performance reasons, this address translation is performed most of the time using a Translation Lookaside Buffer (TLB). The TLB contains entries for virtual pages that have been recently accessed. If the requested translation is not found in the TLB (a TLB miss), the page table in memory has to be

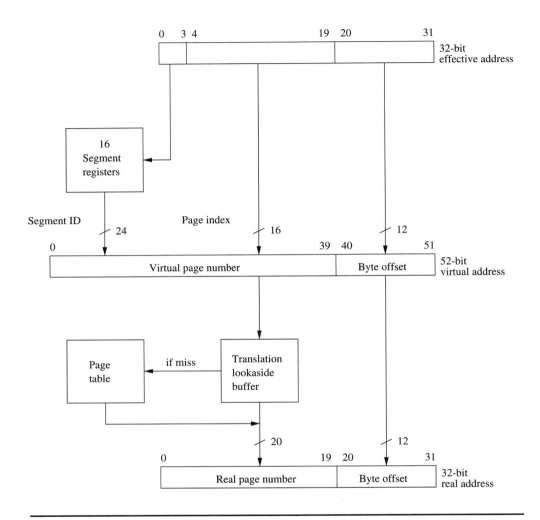

FIGURE 2.25   Virtual address generation and translation.

accessed—a much slower operation that requires several memory references. The real page number is concatenated with the page offset, which remains unchanged during translation, to form the real address.

The 24-bit segment number supports about 16 million segments, system wide. A specific process has access to 16 of these at any given time. A process can access more than 16 segments during its lifetime, but only by calling the operating system to change the segment registers. Because only the operating system can change the segment registers, the users essentially share a single, large virtual address space containing 16 million segments.

Inverted Page Tables

The simplest way to implement a page table is to maintain a table indexed by the virtual page number (VPN) in which each entry contains the mapping of one page, along with other information such as protection. If the page size is 4 Kbytes and a page table entry is 16 bytes, as in the POWER architecture, a 52-bit virtual address space would require 2^{44} bytes just for the page table!

The following observation leads to tremendous savings. At any time, only those virtual pages that have been brought into memory need a page table entry, so it is sufficient to allocate one page table entry per each real page. Using the same page size and page table as in the example above, in a system with 4 Gbytes of physical memory (as much as one can access with a 32-bit real address), the page table needs 16 Mbytes. It takes one byte of "page table overhead" for every 256 bytes of physical memory.

In this *inverted page table* one entry is associated with each real page rather than each virtual page. While the page table size is greatly reduced, the use of an inverted page table introduces a slight complication. Given a virtual page number to be translated, the corresponding page table entry, if there is one, has to be found. This is done using hashing. A hash function is applied to the virtual page number to obtain an index into a hash table. This hash table entry is the head of a linked list of page table entries that is searched serially until either the desired virtual page number is found or the search fails. In the latter case the page is not in memory and a page fault is generated.

Figure 2.26 illustrates the search method. A virtual page number (VPN) is hashed by means of a function and the result is an index into the hash table. The hash table entry points to an entry in the page table, which points to another entry, and so on. The example shows a linked list of length three, which is linearly searched until either a match with one of the VPNs in the three entries is found, or a page fault occurs.

The example demonstrates a problem inherent in the use of hash tables: multiple VPNs may hash to the same entry in the hash table (a situation called *collision*) and a linked list may have to be followed. The longer the linked list, the longer the page table lookup time. The average performance of the search may be controlled by adjusting the size of the hash table. Clearly, making the hash table larger reduces the probability of collisions.

The size of the hash table is chosen as follows. Real memory consists of p pages, 4 Kbytes each. Let $2^n = p$ if p is a power of two, or else n is the smallest integer such that $2^n > p$. The recommended size of the hash table is 2^{n+1} entries. This size is a trade-off between the space allocated to the hash table and the average linked list length. Depending on the size of the memory, n can be between 12 and 20. The lower end corresponds to 16 Mbytes of real

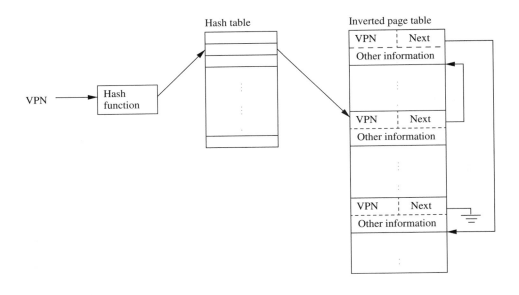

FIGURE 2.26   Searching an inverted page table.

memory (4096 pages), which is assumed by the architecture for the purpose of determining the minimum hash table size. The upper end corresponds to 4 Gbytes of real memory.

The following hash function is used to determine the hash table entry (Figure 2.27). Let the Segment ID be bits 0–23 and Virtual Page Index be bits 24–39 of the virtual page number. Append eight zero bits to the left of the Virtual Page Index to make it into a 24-bit number. Next compute the bitwise exclusive-or of the Segment ID and the Virtual Page Index. The lower $n + 1$ bits of the result are the hash table index. Finally, since each entry is four bytes, append two zero bits to the right of the index. The resulting $n + 3$ bits are the entry's hash table offset from the base of the hash table.

To speed up the access to the hash table, the architecture specifies that software must choose the hash table location in memory such that computation of the real address of the hash table entry can be done without addition. The idea is to drop $n + 3$ bits of the base address and concatenate the remaining bits with the $n + 3$ bits of the hash table offset. Thus, the hash table must be placed on a boundary of 2^{n+3} bytes, in which case the lower $n + 3$ bits of the base address will be zero.

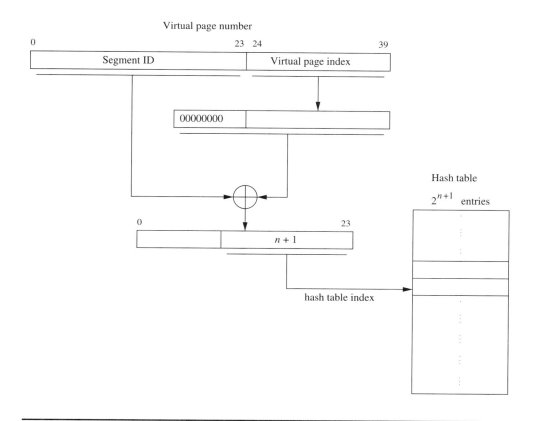

FIGURE 2.27   Hash function. The $\oplus$ sign is exclusive-or. See definition of n in text.

Example

Assume the real memory size is 512 Mbytes. The virtual page number is 19b7a316f9 (hexadecimal). We have to determine the hash table size and select its location in memory. What is the real address of the hash table entry?

Real memory consists of 2^{17} pages ($n = 17$). Therefore, the hash table size is 2^{18} entries, or 2^{20} bytes (1 Mbyte). The hash table must be placed on a 1 Mbyte boundary. We arbitrarily select its base address at memory location 02b00000.

The Segment ID is 19b7a3 and the Virtual Page Index, extended to 24 bits, is 0016f9. The bitwise exclusive-or of these two numbers is 19a15a. The lower 18 bits of this result give the hash table index. The hash table offset 68568 is obtained by appending two zero bits at the right of the index. The five lower hexadecimal digits in the hash table base address, all of which were zero, are replaced by the hash table offset, yielding the real address of the hash table entry: 02b68568.   □

Following is the structure of a hash table entry.

0	1	12	31
i	Unused	Page table index	

If the invalid bit i is one, the search fails. Otherwise, the page table index is used to obtain the real address of the page table entry as follows. Since each entry consists of 16 bytes, append four zero bits to the right of the index. The result is the page table offset of the entry from the base of the page table. The page table offset consists of $n+4$ bits, where n is as defined above.

To compute the real address of the page table entry without addition, the page table must be placed on a boundary of 2^{n+4} bytes, so that the lower $n+4$ bits of the page table base address are all zero. The real address of the page table entry is obtained by replacing the lower $n+4$ bits of the base address with the $n+4$ bits of the page table offset.

Example

Assume the real memory size is 512 Mbytes. The following hash table entry has been accessed after hashing the virtual page number.

0	1	12	31
0	Unused	1c93d	

We have to determine the page table size and select its location in memory. What is the real address of the page table entry?

Real memory consists of 2^{17} pages ($n = 17$). Since there is one entry per page, and each entry consists of 16 bytes, the page table size is 2^{21} bytes (2 Mbytes). The page table must be placed on a 2-Mbyte boundary. We select its base address at memory location 17e00000.

From the hash table we have the page table index, 1c93d. Appending four zero bits we get the page table offset (1c93d0) from the base of the page table. This replaces the lower 21 bits in the base address, all of which were initially zero, giving the real address of the page table entry: 17fc93d0.   □

A page table entry consists of four words in the format shown in Figure 2.28. The first two words contain information used for page table lookup and protection at the page level. The remaining two words contain information used for locking and transaction processing. We discuss protection in the next section.

If the virtual page number valid bit v is one, and the higher 27 bits of the virtual page number match the corresponding field in the page table entry, the search succeeds. The page

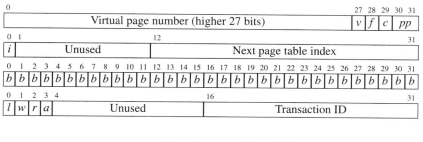

v	Virtual page number valid
f	Reference bit
c	Change bit
pp	Page protection
i	Invalid bit
b	Lock bits
l	Lock type
w	Grant write lock
r	Grant read lock
a	Allow read

FIGURE 2.28   **Format of a page table entry.**

table index is the real page number. Otherwise, if the invalid bit *i* is zero, the search continues by following the next page table index field. If the invalid bit is one, the search fails.

Where is the number 27 coming from? We said earlier in this section that the architecture specifies a minimum real memory size of 16 Mbytes, or 2^{12} pages. The recommended hash table has twice as many entries; hence the smallest hash table has 2^{13} entries. Therefore, at least 13 of the lower-end bits of the virtual page number are used to determine the hash table entry. These bits must be identical in all VPNs that reach any given page table entry in the process of searching the page table, and no more than the upper-end 27 bits (a VPN has 40 bits) are needed for matching.

The reference and change bits in a page table entry are used to keep track of memory references to the corresponding page. This information is used by the software to implement the page replacement policy. When a TLB miss occurs as a result of a memory access to a page whose translation is not in the TLB, the translation is loaded from the page table into the TLB. The architecture specifies that the hardware may choose one of two implementations for handling the reference bit in the page table entry. The bit may be set to one immediately, before checking protection, to indicate that there is an attempt to access the corresponding page. This access attempt may be unsuccessful if the reference is not allowed. With an

pp	K	Access type
00	0	r/w
	1	no access
01	0	r/w
	1	read
10	0,1	r/w
11	0,1	read

FIGURE 2.29   **Page protection. pp are page protect bits in the page table entry. K is the key bit in the segment register.**

alternative implementation, the hardware first determines that the reference is allowed and then sets the reference bit.

2.7 Protection

Protection to limit access to the contents of the main memory is necessary to prevent unauthorized references or to serialize access to shared data in a transaction processing environment. POWER architecture provides protection at two levels: page and record. Most modern architectures support some form of page-level protection, but record-level protection is unusual among RISCs. IBM failed to sell the concept to its partners in the PowerPC venture, with the result that there is no record-level protection in the PowerPC, and even AIX (IBM's implementation of UNIX) is removing all uses. Consequently, we concentrate on page-level protection.

At the hardware level, protection is based on the concept of privileged instructions. A CPU can be in one of two states, privileged or nonprivileged, determined by a bit in the Machine State Register (Figure 2.15). Users run in the nonprivileged state and cannot execute privileged instructions. Therefore, a user cannot modify the contents of the Machine State Register, segment registers, or protection information in page table entries.

The selection between page-level and record-level protection is made by the special bit S in the segment register. Page protection is provided when S is zero. The access type is determined by the two page protect *pp* bits in the page table entry and the key bit K in the segment register, as shown in Figure 2.29.

While the K bit defines two levels of access, there are really three levels. If a user has absolutely no access to a segment, the system simply does not load that segment ID into a segment register. Loading the segment ID and setting K to one provides an access level

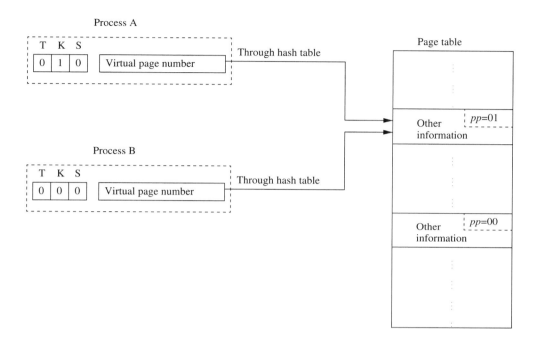

FIGURE 2.30   Example—two processes share a page with different protection key (K).

defined by the page protect bits. Setting K to zero allows read/write access most of the time, unless $pp = 11$.

Consider the example in Figure 2.30. Processes A and B share a page with different access privileges. Process A has read access ($pp = 01$ and $K = 1$) and Process B has read/write access ($pp = 01$ and $K = 0$). Bit $T = 0$ indicates that this is a memory access (not I/O), and bit $S = 0$ selects page-level protection. These three bits are set by the operating system in a segment register (Figure 2.24). While we show sharing of a page, the two processes really share the entire segment. This sharing is accomplished by loading the segment ID into a segment register. Note that the K bit is the same for the entire segment; the pp bits may be set differently for each page.

The second page shown in the figure has $pp = 00$. If it belongs to the same segment, then process B would have read/write access, and A no access. Since process B has $K = 0$, it has at least read access to any page in the segment. If this page exclusively belongs to a third process C, it is protected by not loading its segment ID into the segment register of any other process.

2.8 References

Cocke and V. Markstein [13] relate the evolution of RISC technology at IBM. The POWER instruction set is described in [44] (with the exception of privileged instructions). Hester [36] describes design considerations and architectural decisions. The paper by Oehler and Groves [66] contains additional details on trade-offs in the instruction set and design alternatives that were considered and rejected, as well as code examples.

Stephens et al. [87] describe an instruction level profiling system and profiling experiments on the RS/6000. An interesting study by Hall and O'Brien [31] indicates that update instructions and branches that use the Count Register provide a significant improvement in performance relative to code in which the generation of these instructions was suppressed (by setting certain compiler flags). However, the compiler made little use of multiple condition code fields and their effect was negligible.

3 POWER1 IMPLEMENTATION: PIPELINES

3.1 Introduction

The RISC System/6000 (RS/6000) was introduced in 1990 as the first system using the POWER architecture. The processor used in these systems is a multichip implementation of the POWER architecture called POWER1. Figure 1.17 illustrates the relationships among the various systems, processor implementations, and processor architectures belonging to the POWER family. This chapter and the following two will focus on the POWER1 processor implementation.

Since the time of the original RS/6000 introduction, a rather large number of models have been introduced with different memories, input/output configurations, and performance levels. In Chapter 10, Figure 10.9 lists a few models. Although implementations of the POWER1-based RS/6000 models are similar, they are not identical. For discussing model-dependent features, we have chosen the model 560 as a typical member of the family, and the detailed information we give will be consistent for that specific implementation. Consequently, we often refer to the RS/6000 model 560 simply as the RS/6000.

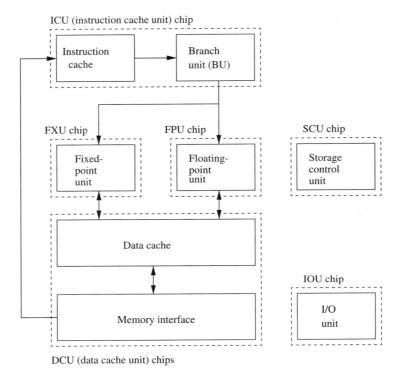

FIGURE 3.1   **POWER1 multichip implementation. Dashed lines indicate chip boundaries.**

The POWER1 processor used in the RS/6000 model 560 is a multichip implementation (Figure 3.1) in which the processor complex consists of nine chips (some lower-cost RS/6000 models have just seven chips). The processor itself is contained in three chips: the FXU (Fixed Point Unit), BU (in the ICU chip), and FPU (Floating Point Unit). The ICU (Instruction Cache Unit) chip contains the instruction cache, and the FXU chip also contains the data cache directory. The storage portion of the data cache is in four DCU chips, which also implement the memory interface and buffering, as well as error checking and correction. Details of the data cache design are discussed in Chapter 5. Finally, two other chips perform system functions. The I/O Unit (IOU) generates the Micro Channel interface and the Storage Control Unit (SCU) provides the RS/6000 memory interface. IOU and SCU functions are described in Chapter 10.

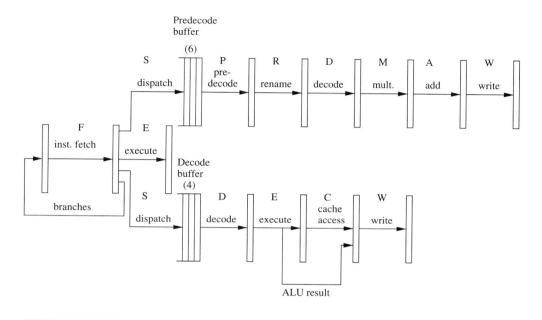

FIGURE 3.2   **POWER1 pipelines.**

3.2 Pipelined Structure of the CPU

Here, we give a brief overview of the POWER1 pipeline structure, which will probably seem complicated at first. Later sections focus on specific parts of the pipelines and should clarify their operation.

The processor is a parallel pipeline organization with each of the three major processor units, the BU, FXU, and FPU, organized as a separate pipeline. Figure 3.2 shows the overall pipeline structure, and Figure 3.3 shows paths taken by different instruction types as they flow through the pipes.

The BU pipeline consists of two stages. In the first, up to four instructions per cycle are fetched from the instruction cache. In the second stage, branches and Condition Register instructions are executed locally (Figure 3.3(a)); all other instructions are dispatched to the FXU and FPU at the rate of up to two instructions per clock cycle. There are buffers at the beginning of both the FXU and FPU pipelines. If a pipeline should become blocked because of a dependence or cache miss, the buffers can absorb a number of instructions until the pipeline blockage goes away. In Figure 3.4, fixed-point instructions (indicated as Xs) and floating-point instructions (Fs) are being distributed into two pipelines, through buffers. The F instructions

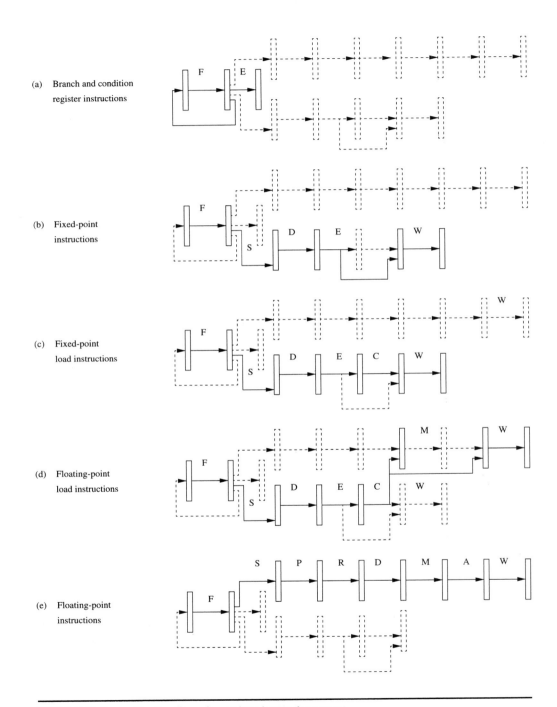

(a)   Branch and condition
      register instructions

(b)   Fixed-point
      instructions

(c)   Fixed-point
      load instructions

(d)   Floating-point
      load instructions

(e)   Floating-point
      instructions

FIGURE 3.3   **Pipeline flows for various instruction types.**

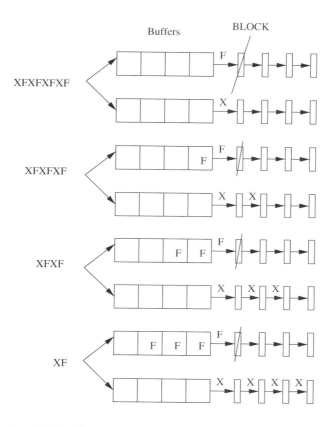

FIGURE 3.4 **A sequence of fixed-point(X) and floating-point(F) instructions being fed into their respective pipelines. The floating-point pipeline becomes blocked, but, because of buffering, fixed-point instructions can proceed.**

become blocked, perhaps because there may be a floating-point divide in the execution units. But because subsequent Fs can be buffered, Xs are allowed to proceed unimpeded.

Fixed-point instructions go through the four stages of the FXU pipeline shown in Figure 3.3(b). Instructions are first decoded; operand registers are read as part of the decode process. Then instructions go to the execute stage of the pipeline. Arithmetic, logical, and shift instructions that do not access memory are then executed and results are written into the fixed-point register file, skipping the cache access stage completely.

For load and store instructions, the address addition and the data cache search are done during the execution stage; if the requested item is found in the data cache, then the cache access occurs in the next stage. (The sequence of events for a cache miss is covered in Chapter 5.) Data loaded from the cache is written into a fixed-point register in the fourth and final FXU pipeline stage. The path taken by load instructions appears in Figure 3.3(c); stores follow a similar path.

The first three stages of the FXU pipeline process instructions at the rate of one instruction per clock cycle. In the fourth stage, results from two different instructions can be written into the register file at once, when the first is data loaded from memory and the second is the result of a fixed-point arithmetic or logic instruction that skips the cache access stage.

Floating-point load and store instructions also pass down the FXU pipeline. As a matter of fact, they pass down both FXU and FPU pipelines. In the FXU, floating-point loads are processed in the same sequence as fixed-point loads, except for the last stage. After accessing the cache, a floating-point operand is sent from the data cache directly to the FPU, where it is written into a floating-point register (Figure 3.3(d)). Floating-point stores pass down the FXU pipeline, generate the address, and are shunted off to the side to wait at the data cache until the store data are delivered from the FPU; the copy of the store instruction that goes down the FPU is responsible for actually delivering the data.

The FPU pipeline consists of six stages (Figure 3.3(e)). In the first, instructions are predecoded in preparation for register renaming. Renaming is essentially a mapping operation: the architectural floating-point registers (named in the instruction) are mapped to physical registers. In most processors this mapping is permanent: If a floating-point instruction names a register fp1, the hardware accesses a register with the name fp1—not so in the POWER1 implementation. The hardware maintains a pool of 38 physical floating-point registers and a mapping table. Logical register fp1 named by the instruction may be mapped by the rename hardware to any of the physical registers. A mapping may only change when a new value is produced by a load instruction and written into a register; until the register is loaded again, its mapping is unchanged. We discuss the motivation and implementation details of register renaming in Section 3.5.

Floating-point multiply, add, and multiply-add instructions go through the full length of the six-stage pipeline. Floating-point loads and stores are predecoded and renamed, after which loads are "sidetracked" to a two-stage pipeline, not shown in Figure 3.3. About the only function of this special load pipeline is to keep track of the load destination register; as we mentioned above, address processing and the memory access are done in the FXU. The FXU delivers the data to the FPU pipeline where the information from the sidetracked load is used to guide the data into the correct floating-point register.

Example

Figure 3.5 shows a code example and its compilation, and Figure 3.6 illustrates the pipelined processing of the loop body. We have the example at this particular point in the chapter to demonstrate the operation of the three pipelines and how they interact; in the rest of the chapter

double x[512], y[512];

for (k = 0; k < 512; k++)
     x[k] = r*x[k] + t*y[k];

(a) C code.

```
                                 # r3 + 8 points to x
                                 # r3 + 4104 points to y
                                 # fp1 contains t,
                                 # fp3 contains r, and
                                 # CTR contains the loop count (512).
LOOP:   lfd    fp0 = y(r3,4104)  # load floating double
        fm     fp0 = fp0,fp1     # floating multiply
        lfd    fp2 = x(r3,8)     # load floating double
        fma    fp0 = fp0,fp2,fp3 # floating multiply-add
        stfdu  x(r3=r3+8) = fp0  # store floating double with update
        bc     LOOP,CTR≠0        # decrement CTR, then branch if CTR ≠ 0
```

(b) Assembly code.

FIGURE 3.5   **Code example and its compilation.**

we look at each pipeline separately. It will be necessary to read the more detailed descriptions of pipelined processing to understand all the details of the example.

We assume in the example that all instructions are in the instruction cache and all data are in the data cache. The first four instructions of the loop are fetched in clock cycle 1 (indicated by the four Fs in the clock period 1 column). Two of these instructions, a load and a floating-point multiply, are dispatched to the FXU and FPU in the next clock cycle. Let's focus on the load. In the next three clock cycles the load goes down the decode, execute, and cache access stages of the FXU pipeline. At the end of the fifth clock period, the cached data are sent to the FPU. The fifth clock period is also the time the floating-point multiply using this operand finishes decoding; the load data arrive just in time for the multiply to begin using the M stage of the pipe. There is no delay between a floating-point load and the use of the data loaded.

Now, focus on the floating-point arithmetic instructions. The first arithmetic instruction (fm) is decoded as soon as it reaches the FPU decode stage. The fma is delayed by one clock cycle waiting for the result of fm. A result of an arithmetic instruction is available as soon as it leaves the add stage of the FPU pipeline due to bypass paths that feed results back to the

```
                                              1 1 1 1 1 1 1 1 1
                          1 2 3 4 5 6 7 8 9 0 1 2 3 4 5 6 7 8

lfd    fp0 = y(r3,4104)   F S P R . W
                              D E C

fm     fp0 = fp0,fp1      F S P R D M A W

lfd    fp2 = x(r3,8)      F . S P R . W
                                D E C

fma    fp0 = fp0,fp2,fp3  F . S P R . D M A W

stfdu  x(r3=r3+8) = fp0     F . S P R . D
                                  D E . . . . . . C

bc     LOOP, CTR ≠ 0        F . S

lfd    fp0 = y(r3,4104)        F S P R . W
                                   D E C

fm     fp0 = fp0,fp1           F S P R . D M A W

lfd    fp2 = x(r3,8)           F . S P R . W
                                     D E C

fma    fp0 = fp0,fp2,fp3       F . S P R . . D M A W

stfdu  x(r3=r3+8) = fp0          F . S P R . . D
                                       D E . . . . . . C

bc     LOOP, CTR ≠ 0             F . S

lfd    fp0 = y(r3,4104)              F S P R . W
                                         D E C

fm     fp0 = fp0,fp1                 F S P R . . D M A W

lfd    fp2 = x(r3,8)                 F . S P R . W
                                           D E C

fma    fp0 = fp0,fp2,fp3             F . S P R . . . D M A W

stfdu  x(r3=r3+8) = fp0                F . S P R . . . D
                                             D E . . . . . .

bc     LOOP, CTR ≠ 0                   F . S
```

FIGURE 3.6   Pipelined processing example. Three iterations of the loop are shown. After dispatching, instructions follow the FPU pipeline (upper path), FXU pipeline (lower path), or both.

beginning of the previous pipeline stage (the multiply stage). Hence `fma` can proceed to the multiply stage on clock cycle 8.

At time 8 the FPU decode stage becomes available and the store decodes, even though the result is not available in register fp0. The result is directed into the Store Data Queue (SDQ) when the `fma` is in the write stage of the pipeline. The actual store into the data cache (FXU cache access stage) may occur as soon as the data are in the SDQ, or it may be delayed if a load instruction, which has higher priority than a store, needs access to the cache in that clock cycle. In the example, the write into the cache is in fact delayed due to the cache access of load instructions in the third loop iteration.

Finally, we see that this example makes good use of update loads and stores and the CTR— the only instructions in the body of the loop are loads, stores and floating-point instructions. By looking at all three loop iterations we see the value of the branching on the CTR to keep the pipes full. Also the high degree of overlap is evident. The third iteration is well underway before the store from the first iteration has been completed.

3.3 Branch Unit

The ICU consists of the instruction cache, instruction fetching and dispatching logic, and hardware that implements the Branch Unit. The architecture of the Branch Unit, its registers and instructions, has been described in Section 2.4. Here we discuss the implementation.

The BU pipeline is a two-stage pipeline (Figure 3.7). Instructions are fetched from the instruction cache into two buffers: the *sequential* buffer and the *target* buffer. The sequential buffer holds up to eight instructions from the sequential instruction stream. The target buffer can hold four instructions from the target address of a branch.

The job of the fetch logic is to try to keep the sequential buffer full. From this buffer, instructions are either dispatched to the FXU and FPU or executed in the BU, depending on their type. In each clock cycle the first five instructions in the sequential buffer are examined simultaneously to see if a branch is coming up. If a branch is found, the branch target address is generated and used to fetch four instructions into the target buffer. If there is more than one branch, the target address of the first is used.

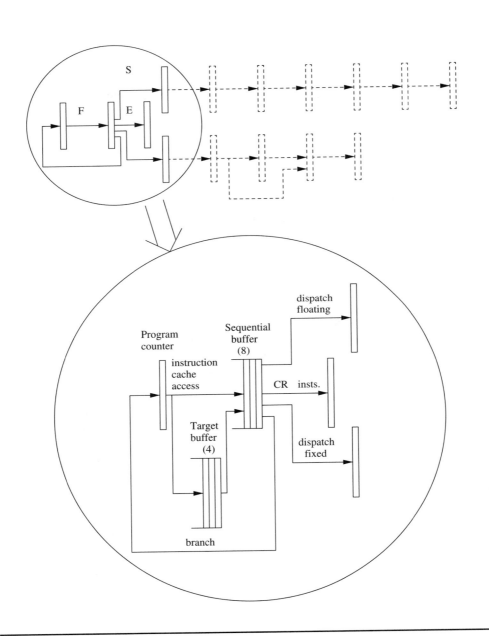

FIGURE 3.7   BU pipeline.

Example

Figure 3.8 illustrates step-by-step instruction fetching and dispatching for an example instruction stream. We assume that all instructions are in the instruction cache. Instructions are partially decoded when fetched from memory into the instruction cache, and information that specifies the instruction type is stored as tag bits in the instruction cache.[1] The tag bits are used later by the fetch and dispatch logic to identify branches and determine whether instructions have to be dispatched to the FXU and FPU or executed locally. The fetch and dispatch logic must be able to inspect and process several instructions every clock cycle. The predecoded tag bits are designed to simplify this process.

In Figure 3.8 the first four instructions are fetched from the instruction cache into the sequential buffer in part (c). Two of these are dispatched the next clock cycle (d), and four more instructions, including a conditional branch, are fetched. The branch is identified and the target address generated in the following clock cycle (e). Next, four instructions are fetched from the target address into the target buffer as shown in (f).

Whether the conditional branch is taken may not be known at this time. The purpose of prefetching into the target buffer is to have instructions ready in case the branch is taken. Prefetching is done only if instructions are already available in the instruction cache. Otherwise, memory would have to be accessed—an expensive operation done only when it is known that the branch is taken.

Even though the conditional branch is removed from the sequential buffer and is considered "executed" by the BU (Figure 3.8(f)), it will remain pending for a number of additional clock cycles until the Condition Register is updated by an arithmetic or compare instruction. Meanwhile, instructions may be conditionally dispatched from the sequential buffer. That is, the branch is predicted not taken. If this prediction turns out to be correct, the conditionally dispatched instructions are allowed to complete and the target buffer is purged. Otherwise, instructions from the sequential instruction stream are canceled, and the target buffer is copied into the sequential buffer.

3.4 Fixed-Point Unit

The FXU functions as both the integer unit and the load/store unit. It is a four-stage pipeline as shown in Figure 3.9. Instructions arrive at the rate of up to two instructions per clock cycle from the BU and are held in a buffer. Whenever the buffer is empty, the first instruction is sent directly to decoding. In the second pipeline stage instructions are executed. The execution of most arithmetic, logical, shift, and compare instructions takes one clock cycle, with the

---

[1]These tag bits should not be confused with the instruction cache tag bits used to find instructions in the cache.

$I_1 \; I_2 \; I_3 \; I_4 \; I_5 \; I_6 \; BR \; I_7 \; I_8 \; I_9 \; I_{10} \; I_{11} \; I_{12} \ldots\ldots T_1 \; T_2 \; T_3 \; T_4 \; T_5$

(a) Example instruction stream. $I_1 - I_{12}$ are fixed-point or floating-point instructions. *BR* is a conditional branch. T_1 is the instruction at the branch target address.

Sequential buffer   Target buffer

(b) Instruction buffers. The buffer tails are to the left, their heads to the right. Following is a clock-by-clock description of buffer contents.

$I_1 \quad I_2 \quad I_3 \quad I_4$
Sequential buffer   Target buffer

(c) First four instructions fetched into the sequential buffer.

$I_3 \quad I_4 \quad I_5 \quad I_6 \quad BR \quad I_7$
Sequential buffer   Target buffer

(d) First two instructions dispatched to FXU and FPU. Four more instructions fetched from the instruction cache. The branch at a distance of five instructions from the head of the buffer is detected in the next clock cycle.

$I_5 \quad I_6 \quad BR \quad I_7 \quad I_8 \quad I_9 \quad I_{10} \quad I_{11}$
Sequential buffer   Target buffer

(e) Branch target address is generated. Two more instructions are dispatched. Four more instructions fetched into the sequential buffer.

$I_7 \quad I_8 \quad I_9 \quad I_{10} \quad I_{11}$ $T_1 \quad T_2 \quad T_3 \quad T_4$
Sequential buffer   Target buffer

(f) Four instructions are fetched into the target buffer from the branch target address. Two more instructions are dispatched and the branch is executed.

FIGURE 3.8   **Instruction fetch buffers.**

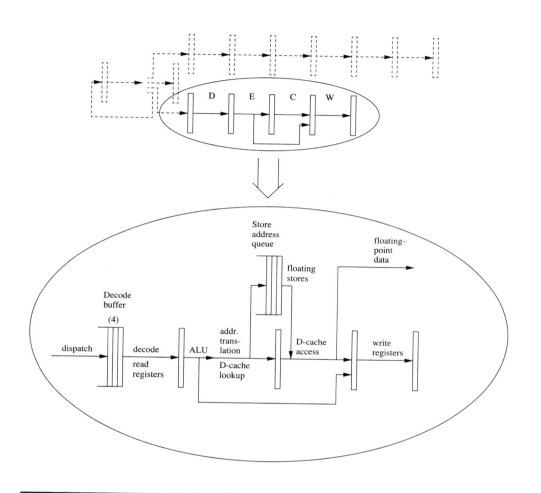

FIGURE 3.9   FXU pipeline.

exception of integer multiply (three to five clock cycles) and divide (19 clock cycles). During the execution of a multiply or divide instruction, the execution stage is reserved, and the next instruction is held in the decode stage. After execution, the result is written to one of the 32 integer registers.

Following decoding, load and store instructions are "executed," meaning that the effective address is generated in one of two ways that depends on the instruction format: (a) in X-form instructions the contents of two integer registers are added, or (b) in D-form instructions the contents of an integer register is added to a 16-bit displacement. The generation of the effective address takes one half of the execution stage. In the second half, the virtual address is generated, then translated, and the data cache directory lookup is performed (a more detailed description is in Chapter 5).

At the end of the execute stage it is known whether the referenced data are in the cache or not. Cache access is performed for all load instructions and fixed-point stores in the next clock cycle. Floating-point stores may have to be delayed because the floating-point data normally are not yet available from the longer FPU pipeline. Hence, the addresses of floating-point stores are held in a Store Address Queue (SAQ) and the FXU pipeline can continue to process instructions. A subsequent load can bypass pending floating-point stores if its address does not match any of the addresses in the SAQ; otherwise, it has to wait until the match goes away. The SAQ has room for four floating-point stores. Figure 3.6 illustrates this situation in several cases: for example, following the first `stfdu`, all the remaining loads in the next two iterations complete before the store does. An identically sized Store Data Queue (SDQ) in the FPU (see Section 3.5) holds the data. When both queues are nonempty, the store at the head of the queues is ready for execution and is performed in the first available cache cycle.

3.5   Floating-Point Unit

The FPU architecture contains 32 double-precision (64-bit) floating-point registers and the FPSCR (Floating-Point Status and Control Register) as defined by the POWER architecture. It implements a single arithmetic pipeline that performs the fused multiply-add ($A \times C + B$) operation. Addition is considered a special case of the multiply-add instruction in which one of the multiplication operands is set to 1.0: $A \times 1.0 + B$. Similarly, multiplication is performed by setting the addend to 0: $A \times C + 0.0$.

Floating-point division is implemented by a state machine. While the floating-point execution units are reserved, a sequence of multiply-add instructions performs division via Newton-Raphson approximation. The high-precision intermediate multiply-add unit permits this method to give IEEE standard–compliant results. Using a dedicated state machine for division is another example in which the POWER1 deviates from a "pure" RISC for the sake of performance.

FPU Pipeline

Floating-point instructions dispatched from the BU go to a buffer or, if the buffer is empty, directly to the predecode stage of FPU pipeline, as shown in Figure 3.10. Instructions are then renamed, and, with the exception of loads, sent to decoding. The first two stages of the pipeline process instructions at the rate of two per clock cycle; from the decode stage on, the rate is reduced to one instruction per clock cycle.

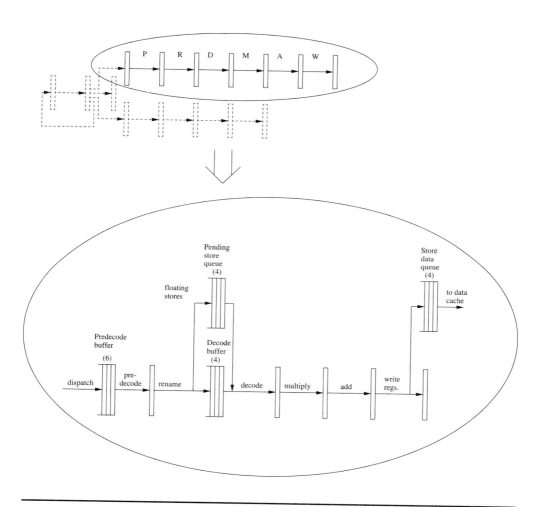

FIGURE 3.10   Floating-point pipeline.

Even though there are separate queues for stores (Pending Store Queue) and for arithmetic instructions (Decode Buffer), the instructions are issued from those queues in program order. If a store immediately follows an arithmetic instruction (multiply-add, multiply, or add) that produces the result to be stored, the store decodes right away even though the result is not available yet. Then, when the arithmetic instruction is in the write stage of the pipeline, its result is directed to the Store Data Queue (SDQ). This important optimization prevents the pipeline from becoming blocked by store instructions.

Data in the SDQ is matched with the memory address of the store instruction from the Store Address Queue (SAQ) in the FXU and sent to the data cache. Stores have lower priority than load instructions and the data remain in the SDQ until the FPU data cache bus, which may be busy transferring load operands, becomes available.

The processing of load instructions is shown in Figure 3.11. The same load instruction is dispatched simultaneously to both the FXU and FPU. Assuming there are no previous instructions held in the buffers, the load passes at the same time through the FXU decode stage and FPU predecode stage. In the next clock cycle, the load is renamed in the FPU and executed in the FXU, where the effective address is generated, the virtual address is translated, and D-cache directory lookup is performed. In the third clock cycle, while the D-cache is accessed, the FPU pipeline keeps track of the load instruction's destination register designator so that the operand arriving from the D-cache is written into the correct register in the following clock cycle.

In the above discussion we have assumed no delays, i.e., that the same load instruction is in the rename stage of the FPU and the execute stage of the FXU. Delays in the pipelines may lead to situations in which instruction processing in one unit "slips" ahead or behind the other. As long as the FXU does not slip behind the FPU, there is no delay between a floating-point load and the use of the operand loaded.

Multiply-Add Instruction

Figure 3.12 illustrates two implementations of floating-point arithmetic pipelines. The conventional implementation has two separate pipelines, one for multiplication and one for addition, and it requires a total of six ports (inputs and outputs) for source and destination operands. The POWER1 implementation consists of a single multiply-add pipeline, which requires only four ports. Since each port is 64 bits wide for double-precision floating-point operands, saving two ports and their associated logic leads to significant reduction in hardware. The implementation saves additional hardware in the multiply-add pipeline by doing normalization and rounding only at the pipeline output and not between the multiply and add stages.

The multiply-add instruction has significant performance consequences. With a decoding rate of one instruction per clock cycle, the peak throughput is two floating-point operations per cycle for the fused multiply-add instruction. For individual multiply and add instructions, it is one floating-point operation per clock cycle.

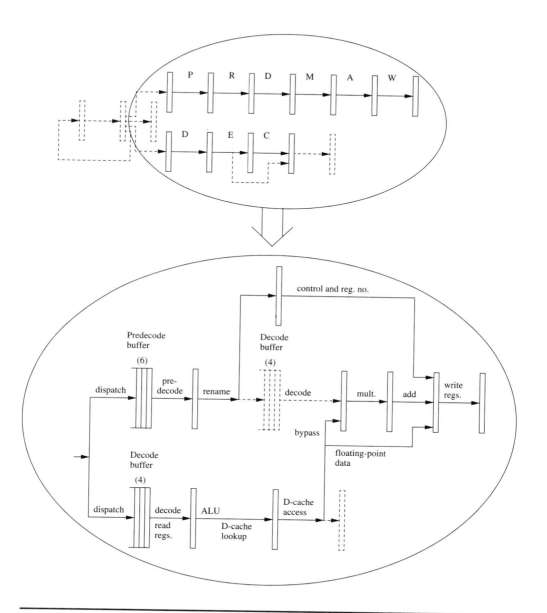

FIGURE 3.11   Processing of floating-point loads in the FXU and FPU.

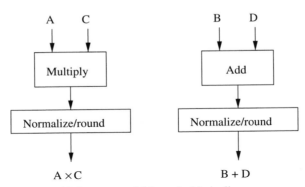

(a) Separate multiply and add pipelines.

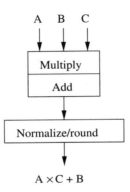

(b) Single multiply-add pipeline.

FIGURE 3.12   **Floating-point arithmetic pipelines.**

Multiply-Add Implementation

The pipeline shown in Figure 3.13 implements the multiply-add operation (see Section 2.5) on double-precision floating-point operands. For clarity, the figure shows only the hardware involved in processing the significands (see Appendix A for floating-point number formats), which is the major part of the pipeline.

In ordinary floating-point addition, it is necessary to *align* the significands before they can be added (i.e., make adjustments so they effectively have the same exponent). The alignment operation consists of two steps: (1) subtracting the exponents, and (2) shifting the significand

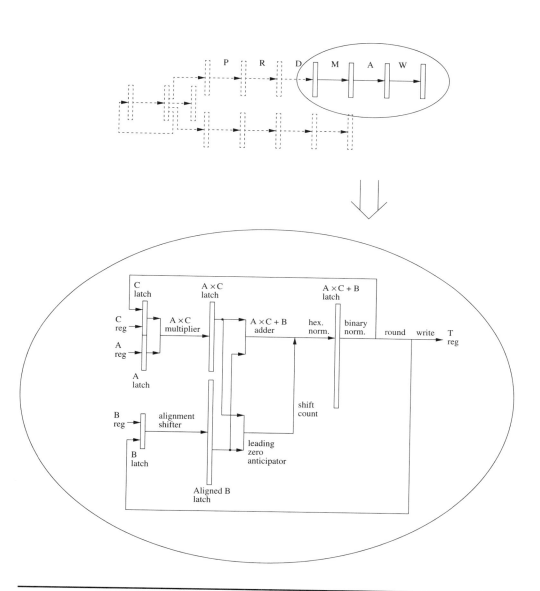

FIGURE 3.13 **Multiply-add pipeline implementation. The widths of the latches are proportional to the number of bits of data: 53 bits (source operands), 106 bits (A×C product), and 159 bits (aligned B and A×C + B).**

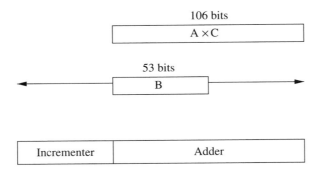

FIGURE 3.14 **Alignment prior to addition.**

of the addend with the smaller exponent to the right by a number of positions equal to the difference in exponents.

If this approach were to be followed in the multiply-add pipeline, alignment would be done after multiplication. Either B or A×C would have to be aligned, depending on which one has the smaller exponent. Note that no operation would be performed on B during multiplication. To save time and increase performance, a different approach was adopted in the POWER1 multiply-add implementation. While A and C are multiplied, the alignment of B takes place. This approach implies that B may have to be shifted to either left or right depending on the size of its exponent. Alignment and multiplication are overlapped and addition can be done right after multiplication.

This capability requires some additional hardware. The multiplication of two 53-bit significands A and C generates a 106-bit product A×C. Prior to alignment, A×C and B are flushed left, as shown in Figure 3.14. To perform the alignment, as long as B is shifted to the right, the addition can be performed using a 106-bit adder. When B is shifted to the left, the part of B that exceeds the range of A×C may have to be incremented if a carry is generated by the addition. Hence an incrementer is the extra hardware needed when B is left-shifted.

Addition is performed in the second stage of the pipeline. In parallel, a Leading Zero Anticipator predicts the number of hexadecimal zero digits at the left of the most significant nonzero hexadecimal digit. The count of leading zeros is the number of positions that the result A×C + B has to be left-shifted for normalization. Using this count, hexadecimal normalization is performed immediately after addition, and in the same clock cycle.

Normalization is done in two phases: first, there is a hexadecimal (4-bit) normalization that gets the result to within 4 bits of being correct. Then, a final binary normalization finishes the job. Binary normalization is performed in the third and final stage of the multiply-add pipeline, followed by rounding. The result is written into the destination register in the same clock cycle.

The length of an arithmetic pipeline has a significant effect on the throughput when there are dependences between instructions. An instruction waiting for an operand will be delayed until the instruction producing that operand reaches the end of the pipeline. In a three-stage pipeline the second of a sequence of two dependent instructions would have to be delayed for two clock cycles until the result becomes available.

The POWER1 multiply-add pipeline is essentially a three-stage pipeline, but it appears to function like a two-stage pipeline due to two bypass paths that route the result back to inputs B and C. The path to B takes the result after rounding, which means that the result will not be available for alignment at the beginning of the multiply cycle, because binary normalization and rounding have to be performed first. This is not a problem, however, because exponent subtraction (not shown in Figure 3.13), which determines the number of positions B has to be shifted, has to be done prior to alignment anyway. Hence, binary normalization and rounding are overlapped with exponent subtraction.

The bypass path to C takes the result before rounding because there is not enough time in one clock cycle to perform rounding and multiplication serially. Rounding is done in the multiplier itself as follows. If the result, which we shall simply call C because it is routed to input C, is rounded down, then C is truncated to 53 bits. If the result is rounded up, then B is incremented by 1. Hence the multiplier performs the operation $A \times (C + \epsilon)$, where ϵ is either 0 or 1, depending on the direction of rounding.

To summarize, this remarkable design performs double-precision floating-point multiplication and addition in a pipeline in which the second of two consecutive dependent instructions is delayed for only one clock cycle. This performance has been achieved by the following techniques: (1) alignment of B done in parallel to multiplication of A and C, (2) leading zero count done in parallel to addition, and (3) bypass paths to inputs B and C allow the use of a result prior to writing it into the destination register.

Register Renaming

Register renaming is the process of associating logical register names with members of a pool of physical registers. This unusual feature of the POWER1 implementation is important because of the previously noted "slip" that can occur between the FXU and the FPU. It is very common for the FXU to slip ahead of the FPU, allowing the FXU to get a head start on loading data from the data cache or memory. A rather extreme example of "slip" is illustrated in Figure 3.4.

The FXU slipping ahead occasionally leads to a situation in which the FXU would like to load a floating-point register that is the source of a previous (in program order) floating-point instruction in the FPU that has not been decoded yet. (Registers are read in the decode stage of the pipe, an instruction that has not been decoded still needs its source registers.)

The following sequence shows an example in which register fp1 is used by the first instruction and loaded by the second one.

```
fm    fp0 = fp2,fp1    # floating multiply executed by the FPU
lfd   fp1 = a          # load floating double executed by the FXU
```

In this simple example, the problem can be easily fixed by having the compiler make a different register assignment, say, letting the load use fp3 instead of fp1. However, when a conditional branch separates the two dependent instructions, reassignment may not be so easy. An important case occurs in small loops where a register is loaded at the top of the loop and used by a floating-point operation, then has to be reloaded at the top of the loop. The following example shows the elements of an array z being multiplied by a constant held in fp2, then stored into array x.

```
LOOP:   lfd     fp1 = z(r3,8200)    # load floating double
        fm      fp3 = fp2,fp1       # floating multiply
        stfdu   x(r3=r3+8) = fp3    # store floating double with update
        bc      LOOP,CTR≠0          # decrement CTR, then branch if CTR ≠ 0
```

This example contains a register dependence of the type we have just described between the load of fp1 for loop iteration i and the multiply for iteration $i - 1$.

Register renaming eliminates this type of register dependence by assigning a different register, obtained from a register pool, as the destination of the load instruction. Instructions that follow the load and refer to fp1 are also renamed so that the reference is to the correct register.

Figure 3.15 shows the renaming stage of the FPU pipeline. The main components of the register renaming scheme are the following:

- *Map Table.* The POWER architecture has 32 architectural floating-point registers. The POWER1 FPU implementation consists of a pool of 38 physical registers. The map table maintains the mapping of each architectural register to a physical register, taking care of 32 of the physical registers. The remaining 6 are in either the Free List or Pending Target Return Queue.

- *Pending Target Return Queue (PTRQ).* The PTRQ holds those registers that are no longer in the map table but still in use. It is managed as a circular list with head and tail pointers.

- *Free List (FL).* This is a list of free registers, also managed as a circular queue.

Consider again the short loop in the above code example. Figure 3.16 illustrates two iterations of the loop passing through the renaming stage of the pipeline. To limit the size of the figure, we assume the map table has only eight entries (corresponding to eight architectural registers), and the PTRQ and FL each have four entries. Hence, the pool of physical registers

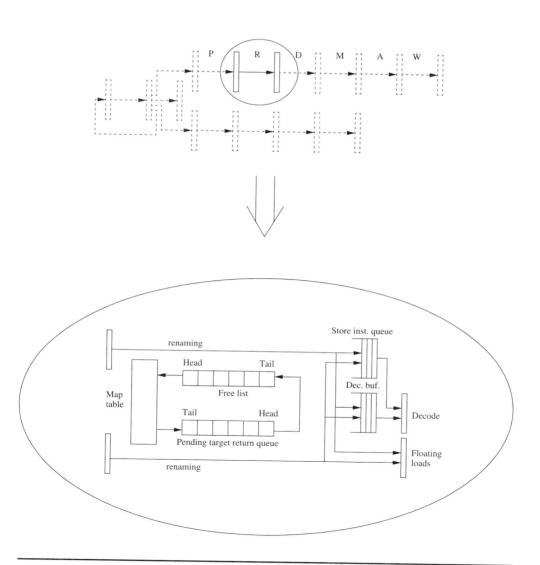

FIGURE 3.15   Register renaming. Two instructions may be renamed per clock cycle.

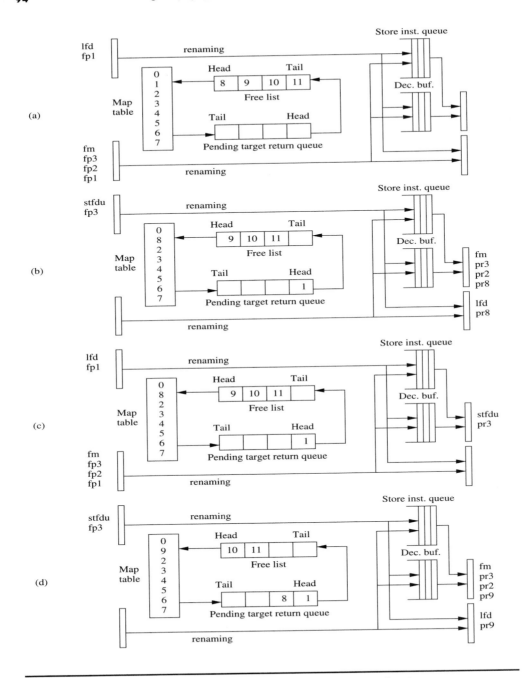

FIGURE 3.16   Register renaming example. Note that "pr" is physical register.

has twelve registers. The map table is indexed by architectural registers, and each entry designates the corresponding physical register. We assume that initially the table contains the identity mapping.

In (a) the load and the floating multiply arrive at the register renaming stage of the pipeline. Note that the order is significant; the upper latch holds the first of the two instructions in program order. In (b) both instructions are renamed, but the load goes first. A fresh register (8) from FL is assigned as the load target, and the map table is changed accordingly. Physical register 1 is removed from the map table and placed in the PTRQ. The floating multiply is renamed in the same clock cycle, using the modified map table. The physical register pr8, which was just pulled out from the Free List, maintains the data dependence between the load and floating multiply instructions.

In the next clock cycle (c), these two instructions go down the FPU pipeline (not shown in the figure). The store is renamed and sent to decoding. Two instructions from the second loop iteration arrive. Finally, in (d), the load is again renamed and assigned a new register from the FL.

How does the hardware determine that a physical register's value is no longer needed, so the physical register can be transferred from the PTRQ to the FL? The instruction that precedes a load in the program order is marked. When the marked instruction decodes, all previous instructions must have decoded and read their registers, so the register moved into the PTRQ is no longer needed and may be returned to the Free List. Hence, a register is released from the PTRQ when a marked instruction decodes. Because registers are released in the same order that they are inserted in the PTRQ, a marked instruction always releases the next register.

3.6 References

The original 801 RISC project was followed by a research project at IBM Yorktown Heights. The America project, as it was called, used multiple execution units and was investigated for a CMOS implementation. Grohoski [27] describes the organization of America including a description of a rather complex register renaming method that allocated fresh registers not only for loads but for arithmetic instructions. A simpler version was implemented in POWER1.

Bakoglu and Whiteside [7] is an overview of the RS/6000 implementation. Additional details on the BU and FXU are in Grohoski et al. [28]. Olsson et al. [67] describe the FPU. Montoye, Hokenek, and Runyon [60] contains additional material on the design of the FPU and the multiply-add pipeline. Hokenek and Montoye [38] describe the Leading Zero Anticipator. Markstein describes the sequences used to implement IEEE divide and square root in [56].

Decoupled architectures [83] and [94] have many characteristics in common with the POWER1. These systems use architectural queues for holding load data instead of register renaming.

POWER1 IMPLEMENTATION: BRANCHES AND INTERRUPTS

4.1 Introduction

The rate of instruction execution can be no better than the rate at which instructions are fetched and injected into the pipelines. As long as the instruction stream comes from sequential memory locations, maintaining a high rate of instruction flow is relatively easy. Branch instructions, however, break the smooth flow and cause instruction fetching to be disrupted.

When a branch instruction is encountered, a new program counter value must be determined before sequential fetching can resume. This requirement can temporarily suspend pipeline filling, with bubbles rather than instructions being injected into the pipeline. Conditional branches are especially difficult because final determination of the next program counter value depends on the result of a previous instruction, and that result is often not known until the previous instruction is far along in the pipeline.

Generally speaking, we see two problems associated with branches. The first is the *instruction flow* problem. That is, the instruction flow is changed from one sequence of consecutive addresses to another, and the instruction fetch unit must adjust for this change in flow. The second is the *decision* problem associated with conditional branches. The place to begin fetching the next sequence of instructions must sometimes wait for a decision based on just-computed data values.

Interrupts are caused by instruction faults or external requests for service, e.g., for Input/Output. Interrupts cause pipeline disruptions by changing the instruction flow, just as branches do, but they occur much less often than branches and are easier to handle from the instruction fetch perspective. Interrupts cause other difficulties, however. In highly pipelined processors like the POWER1, the order in which instructions are completed may be different from their sequential program order. At the time of an interrupt, however, it must be possible to capture cleanly the machine state so that system software can respond to the interrupt condition and then restore the machine state and resume execution.

Because of its aggressive design, the branch and interrupt mechanisms in the POWER1 are based on highly evolved strategies. To provide some background, we first discuss commonly used methods for handling the flow and branch decision problems in RISC processors. We then focus on the POWER1 implementation of branch instructions.

The discussion on interrupts is likewise divided into two parts. We first provide some background by looking at the problem of interrupts in pipelined machines in general and then describe the implementation of interrupts in POWER1.

4.2   Solving the Branch Problems

A variety of ways to solve the branch problems have been developed over the years. In this section we consider two of them: delayed branches and branch prediction. Delayed branches are a solution to the flow problem and are used in several RISC architectures. Branch prediction is a solution to the decision problem and is used in RISCs as well as conventional CISCs.

Maintaining Instruction Flow: Delayed Branches

To understand how the flow problem appears in a typical RISC pipeline, we consider the pipeline discussed in Chapter 1. The program counter, held in the IF stage, addresses the instruction cache and increments every clock period while it is fetching sequential instructions. When a conditional branch instruction is fetched, it is not actually determined to be a branch until it is decoded in the ID stage. By that time, the next consecutive instruction is already in the process of being fetched. If the branch turns out to be taken, the next consecutive instruction is discarded and the instruction at the branch target is fetched.

In the example in Figure 4.1(a), the pipeline flow for the case just described is shown. We see that instruction i4 is fetched and then discarded, resulting in a bubble that passes down the pipeline.

To eliminate the bubble in the pipeline, the semantics of branch instructions can be modified to specify that the effect of the branch is *delayed* by one instruction. This implies that the instruction immediately following the branch is always executed regardless of the branch

```
i1        C1    =    A1 > 0      IF   ID   EX   ME   WB
i2        A3    =    A5 − A6          IF   ID   EX   ME   WB
i3    BC i6,C1  =    true                  IF   ID   EX   ME   WB
i4               .                              IF   .    .    .    .
i5               .
i6        A2    =    A3 + A1                              IF   ID   EX   ME   WB
```

(a) Pipeline timing for a conditional branch.

```
i1        C1    =    A1 > 0      IF   ID   EX   ME   WB
i2    BC i6,C1  =    true             IF   ID   EX   ME   WB
i3        A3    =    A5 − A6               IF   ID   EX   ME   WB
i4               .
i5               .
i6        A2    =    A3 + A1                         IF   ID   EX   ME   WB
```

(b) Timing with delayed branch.

FIGURE 4.1   Delayed branch.

outcome. In our example, the branch and subtract instructions are independent and their order can be changed as shown in Figure 4.1(b). This optimization can be performed by the compiler. With delayed branching the subtract is fetched and executed immediately after the branch, keeping the pipeline full.

If the branch depends on the immediately preceding instruction, the order cannot be changed and another instruction has to be found to execute after the branch. If no instruction can be found, a no-op must be inserted. In this case, the effect is the same as when a bubble is introduced.

The IBM 801, RISC II, MIPS, and a number of other RISC machines with short pipelines have used the delayed branch. This technique can be generalized for longer pipelines by delaying the effect of the branch by n instructions. As n is increased beyond one, however, it becomes increasingly difficult to find n instructions to be moved after the branch. McFarling and Hennessy [58] investigated a typical pipeline with delayed branches and found that the second slot could not be used over 75% of the time.

Making Decisions Early: Branch Prediction

If the outcome of a conditional branch (taken or not taken) is not known at the time the branch is decoded, then, logically, the next instruction to be fetched and sent down the pipeline is unknown. Only when the branch outcome is known can the program counter be given the correct value and the instruction fetching resume. The worst case occurs when the instruction that determines the branch outcome (e.g., a compare instruction) immediately precedes the branch instruction.

During the delay between the occurrence of a conditional branch in the instruction stream and the determination of its outcome, the pipeline would normally be unused. However, the fetch logic can "guess" or, to put a more positive spin on it, "predict" the outcome of the branch and begin fetching instructions based on the predicted outcome. If the prediction turns out to be correct, then the pipeline has been doing useful work when it otherwise would not have. If the prediction is incorrect, any predicted instructions in the pipeline must be flushed, and any changes to the process state, such as registers and memory, must be reversed. The hardware that handles pipeline flushing can be considerably simplified if instructions are allowed to proceed down the pipeline but are stopped before they change any process state.

The simplest branch prediction strategy is to assume that branches are either always taken or always not taken. A more refined method also takes into account the branch's direction (forward or backward in the instruction stream). For example, loop-closing branches are normally backward branches and are taken most of the time. These are examples of *static* prediction methods because they never change during the time a program is executing.

A *dynamic* branch prediction strategy is typically based on the past history of a specific branch instruction, and the prediction may vary during the execution of a program. The recent execution history of branch instructions may be retained in a table and used to make more accurate branch predictions. The branch history table is accessed using the program counter address of the branch instruction. Information is stored in each entry of the table as one or more bits, encoding the outcome(s) of previous branch executions. If a single bit is maintained, a good strategy is to use it to encode the outcome the last time the branch was executed and predict that its next outcome will be the same. Several history bits can be used to implement more complex prediction strategies.

Instead of or in addition to a history bit, each prediction table entry may hold either the address of the instruction executed after the branch or the instruction itself. This last approach also helps with the flow problem by saving the instruction fetch cycle, because the instruction from the predicted program path is obtained directly from the history table and does not have to be fetched.

4.3   Branches in the POWER1

The POWER architecture defines branch instructions that test bits in the Condition Register (CR). These bits may be set by compare or arithmetic instructions that have the Record bit set. A synchronization problem occurs because the CR is written and read by different pipeline stages at different times. CR–updating instructions are executed by the FXU or FPU, and CR–testing instructions (branches) are executed by the BU.

Consider the following instruction sequence.

```
cmpi    cr0=r8,0            # compare immediate
l       r10=d(r1,12)        # load d
l       r11=e(r1,16)        # load e
bc      ELSE,cr0/gt=false   # branch if bit false
```

The conditional branch cannot be executed until cr0 has been assigned its value by the compare. But the BU has no direct way of knowing how far the compare has progressed down the pipeline. It could be finished, it could be blocked waiting for the value of r8 to be computed, or it could be blocked behind some other instruction. How does the BU know when the CR has been assigned its correct value so that the branch can be completed?

The answer is that interlock bits are associated with Condition Register fields. As shown in Figure 4.2, this interlock bit is set when the compare instruction is decoded and dispatched to the FXU. As long as the interlock bit remains set, it blocks subsequent instructions that attempt to either use (or modify[1]) any bit in the locked Condition Register field. Eventually, when the CR–modifying instruction executes, it updates the CR field, and the interlock bit is cleared. Then the conditional branch outcome can be evaluated by the BU.

Because of implementation constraints specific to POWER1, there are only four interlock bits available for the CR. Therefore, one bit guards the access to two CR fields, as shown in Figure 4.2. To avoid false blockages, the compiler attempts to assign CR fields that have different interlock bits to consecutive CR–modifying instructions.

Branch instructions in the POWER architecture fall into three categories: (1) unconditional branches, (2) loop-closing branches using the Count Register (CTR), and (3) conditional branches. To simplify presentation, we assume in all the examples below that references to the instruction and data caches are hits; the cache miss cases are discussed in Chapter 5.

Figure 4.3 shows an example of a short loop ending with a branch that uses the CTR. In cycle 1, all four instructions of the loop body are fetched into the sequential buffer. In the next cycle, the sequential buffer is scanned, a branch is discovered at a distance of less than five instructions from the top of the buffer, and the branch target address is generated. In cycle 3, four instructions are fetched from the branch target address (beginning of the loop) into the target buffer.

The first two instructions are dispatched to the FXU in cycle 2. Following decoding and execution of the load instruction, the cache is accessed and the operand is written into register r0 in cycle 6. The register file has a read-through capability that allows the operand to be read in the cycle it is written. Cycle 6 is the earliest time the add immediate instruction, which needs the operand loaded into r0, can execute. So the decoding of the add is delayed until cycle 5. In general, there is a delay of one cycle between the load and use of an operand in the FXU.

---

[1]This could happen when the same CR field is the destination of another CR–modifying instruction.

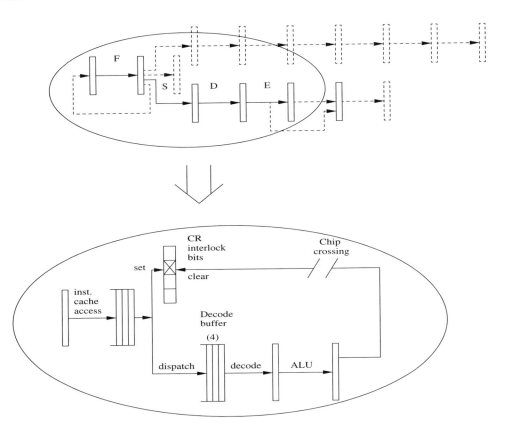

(a) Setting and clearing an interlock bit.

Condition register field	Interlock bit
0 4	0
1 5	1
2 6	2
3 7	3

(b) One interlock bit is associated with every two CR fields.

FIGURE 4.2   **Condition Register interlock.**

for (i=0; i<100; i++)
        a[i] = a[i] + 1;

(a) C code.

```
                                    # When the loop is entered:
                                    # r3 points to a, and
                                    # CTR contains the loop count.
LOOP:    l    r0 = a(r3)            # load a
         ai   r0 = r0,1             # add immediate
         stu  a(r3=r3+4) = r0       # store with update
         bc   LOOP,CTR ≠ 0          # decrement CTR, branch if CTR ≠ 0
```

(b) Assembly code.

		1	2	3	4	5	6	7	8	9	1 0	1 1	1 2
l	r0 = a(r3)	F	S	D	E	C	W						
ai	r0 = r0,1	F	S	.	.	D	E	W					
stu	a(r3 = r3+4) = r0	F	.	S	.	.	D	E	C				
bc	LOOP, CTR > 0	F	.	S									
l	r0 = a(r3)		F	S	.	.	D	E	C	W			
ai	r0 = r0,1		F	S	.	.	.	D	E	W			
stu	a(r3 = r3+4) = r0		F	.	S	.	.	.	D	E	C		
bc	LOOP, CTR ≠ 0		F	.	S								

(c) POWER1 processing, two iterations of the loop.

FIGURE 4.3   **Code example with loop-closing branch using the Count Register.**

   This example illustrates the way POWER1 solves the flow problem. Instructions can be fetched and buffered at a rate that is faster than they can be dispatched to the FXU and FPU. Therefore, the fetch unit can often build a "stockpile" of instructions in the target and sequential buffers. Furthermore, the fetch unit is able to look ahead in the sequential buffer to detect branch instructions early. When a branch is encountered, the buffers can be used to continue feeding the pipeline while the branch target is fetched. In many cases this leads to a *zero-cycle* branch, because the instruction flow into the pipelines is uninterrupted.

   The instruction flow for unconditional branches is similar to that just described for the

CTR branches. In both cases, determining the branch outcome is not an issue; at the time the branch is encountered the outcome is always known.

Conditional Branches

For conditional branches, POWER1 must deal with the decision problem. POWER1 predicts all conditional branches not taken, but then uses the target buffer as a "hedge" against a wrong prediction. Consider the code example in Figure 4.4. Part (a) of Figure 4.5 shows the pipelined processing of the code when the prediction is correct. The cmpi instruction is executed in clock cycle 9 and the result of the comparison is forwarded to the Branch Unit in the next cycle. Meanwhile, based on the not-taken prediction, instructions from the sequential stream are dispatched, decoded, and executed conditionally (indicate by a prime). When the branch is resolved, conditional instructions are allowed to write results to their destination registers, and instruction processing continues normally. There are no delays, and the pipeline is kept full despite the branch.

As a hedge, as soon as the branch is discovered as one of the five instructions at the top of the sequential buffer (from which instructions are dispatched), four instructions from the branch target address are fetched and and held in a second buffer, the target buffer. The target buffer is purged when the branch is resolved as not taken.

Part (b) of the figure shows the timing when the branch is taken and the prediction is incorrect. This time the conditionally dispatched instructions must be flushed from the pipeline. Instruction dispatching begins from the target instructions in clock cycle 11. The result is that no instructions are executed in clock cycles 10, 11, and 12 (with the exception of one conditionally dispatched instruction that is canceled). The mispredicted branch causes a three-cycle bubble in the pipeline.

One of these three-delay cycles is a direct consequence of the multichip implementation. Even though the outcome of cmpi is known at the end of cycle 9, it takes one clock cycle to transmit this result to the Branch Unit, which is in a different chip.

The compiler can entirely eliminate this delay by scheduling the code as shown in Figure 4.6. The compare instruction is shifted up in the instruction stream, an optimization that can be performed here because the compare is independent of the previous three load instructions. Now the compare is executed earlier, target instructions are dispatched earlier, and the execute stage of the pipeline is kept full. Another way to look at it is that three load instructions execute "for free" in what otherwise would be a bubble of three cycles between the compare and branch instructions. The optimized code executes at the maximum rate without any delays.

if (a > 0)

    a = a + b + c + d + e;

else

    a = a − b − c − d − e;

(a) C code.

```
                          # When this code is entered:
                          # r1 points to a,
                          # r1+4 points to b,
                          # r1+8 points to c,
                          # r1+12 points to d,
                          # r1+16 points to e.
        l     r8=a(r1)          # load a
        l     r12=b(r1,4)       # load b
        l     r9=c(r1,8)        # load c
        l     r10=d(r1,12)      # load d
        l     r11=e(r1,16)      # load e
        cmpi  cr0=r8,0          # compare immediate
        bc    ELSE,cr0/gt=false # branch if bit false
IF:
        a     r12=r8,r12        # add
        a     r12=r12,r9        # add
        a     r12=r12,r10       # add
        a     r4=r12,r11        # add
        st    a(r1)=r4          # store
ELSE:
        sf    r12=r8,r12        # subtract
        sf    r12=r12,r9        # subtract
        sf    r12=r12,r10       # subtract
        sf    r4=r12,r11        # subtract
        st    a(r1)=r4          # store
```

(b) Assembly code.

FIGURE 4.4   **Code example with conditional branch.**

```
                                  1 1 1 1 1 1
                1 2 3 4 5 6 7 8 9 0 1 2 3 4 5
    l    r8 = a(r1)       F S D E C W
    l    r12 = b(r1,4)    F S . D E C W
    l    r9 = c(r1,8)     F . S . D E C W
    l    r10 = d(r1,12)   F . S . . D E C W
    l    r11 = e(r1,16)     F . S . . D E C W
    cmpi cr0 = r8,0         F . S . . . D E
    bc   ELSE,cr0/gt=false  F . S
IF: a    r12 = r8,r12       F . . S´ . . . D´ E´ W
    a    r12 = r12,r9         F . S´ . . . D´ E W
    a    r12 = r12,r10        F . . S´ . . . . D E W
    a    r4 = r12,r11         F . . S´ . . . . . D E W
    st   a(r1) = r4           F . . . S´ . . . . . D E C
    b    OUT
ELSE: sf r12 = r8,r12           F . . . . .
    sf   r12 = r12,r9           F . . . . .
    sf   r12 = r12,r10          F . . . . .
    sf   r4 = r12,r11           F . . . . .
    st   a(r1) = r4
OUT:
```

(a) Not-taken (correctly predicted) branch.

```
                                  1 1 1 1 1 1 1 1 1
                1 2 3 4 5 6 7 8 9 0 1 2 3 4 5 6 7 8
    l    r8 = a(r1)       F S D E C W
    l    r12 = b(r1,4)    F S . D E C W
    l    r9 = c(r1,8)     F . S . D E C W
    l    r10 = d(r1,12)   F . S . . D E C W
    l    r11 = e(r1,16)     F . S . . D E C W
    cmpi cr0 = r8,0         F . S . . . D E
    bc   ELSE,cr0/gt=false  F . S
IF: a    r12 = r8,r12       F . . S´ . . . D´ E´
    a    r12 = r12,r9         F . S´ . . . . D´
    a    r12 = r12,r10        F . . S´ . . . .
    a    r4 = r12,r11         F . . S´ . . . .
    st   a(r1) = r4           F . . . S´ . . .
    b    OUT
ELSE: sf r12 = r8,r12           F . . . . . . S D E W
    sf   r12 = r12,r9           F . . . . . . S . D E W
    sf   r12 = r12,r10          F . . . . . . . S . D E W
    sf   r4 = r12,r11           F . . . . . . . S . . D E W
    st   a(r1) = r4                        F . S . . D E C
OUT:
```

(b) Taken (incorrectly predicted) branch.

FIGURE 4.5   POWER1 execution of the code example from Figure 4.4. A prime indicates conditional dispatching.

```
                                                          1 1 1 1 1 1
                                      1 2 3 4 5 6 7 8 9 0 1 2 3 4 5
        l     r8 = a(r1)             F S D E C W
        l     r12 = b(r1,4)          F S . D E C W
        cmpi  cr0 = r8,0             F . S . D E
        l     r9 = c(r1,8)           F . S . . D E C W
        l     r10 = d(r1,12)           F . S . . D E C W
        l     r11 = e(r1,16)           F . S . . . D E C W
        bc    ELSE,cr0/gt=false        F . S
IF:     a     r12 = r8,r12             F . . S´ . .
        a     r12 = r12,r9              F . S´ . .
        a     r12 = r12,r10             F . . S´ .
        a     r4 = r12,r11              F . . S´ .
        st    a(r1) = r4                F . . . S´
        b     OUT
ELSE:   sf    r12 = r8,r12                  F . . . S D E W
        sf    r12 = r12,r9                  F . . . S . D E W
        sf    r12 = r12,r10                 F . . . . S . D E W
        sf    r4 = r12,r11                  F . . . . S . . D E W
        st    a(r1) = r4                      F . . . . S . . D E C
OUT:
```

FIGURE 4.6   POWER1 taken (mispredicted) conditional branch, scheduled code. A prime indicates conditional dispatching.

4.4 Precise Interrupts

When an interrupt occurs, processing is halted, the process state is saved, and an interrupt handling routine is invoked. Upon completion of the interrupt service, the process state must be restored to resume the execution of the interrupted program.

In a sequential (nonpipelined) processor model, an instruction is fetched and executed only when the previous one is finished. When an interrupt occurs the address of the next instruction to be fetched is saved—this is the address to which the interrupt service routine returns. Figure 4.7(a) illustrates the case in which instruction *i2* encounters a fault, such as an overflow or a virtual memory page fault. If the process state is saved for the instruction sequence in Figure 4.7(a), the interrupt is said to be *precise,* because all instructions prior to the faulting instruction are executed, and all instructions following it are not started. The

Instruction	Status		Instruction	Status
i0	Executed		i0	Executed
i1	Executed		i1	Executed
i2	Executed		i2	Partially executed
i3	Not started		i3	Partially executed
i4	Not started		i4	Executed
i5	Not started		i5	Partially executed
i6	Not started		i6	Not started
i7	Not started		i7	Not started

(a) Sequential processing.   (b) Pipelined processing.

FIGURE 4.7   **Execution of an instruction sequence.**

faulting instruction is either unexecuted (as with a virtual memory page fault) or completed (as with an overflow).

In a pipelined machine, a number of instructions may be in various stages of the pipelines at any given time, and instructions may modify the process state out of order, i.e., in an order other than the logical program order defined by the program counter. At the time a fault requiring an interrupt is detected, the instructions might be as illustrated in Figure 4.7(b), where i4 has been dispatched to a short pipeline and already executed, while two previous instructions, i2 and i3, are still in progress in a longer pipeline.

When an interrupt occurs under these circumstances, there are a number of ways of dealing with it. Two possibilities follow:

1. *Freeze the pipelines and save their contents along with the normal process state.* The pipeline contents include intermediate data and control information of partially executed instructions. Much of this information is implementation-dependent. In this case the interrupt is said to be *imprecise*.

2. *Stop dispatching new instructions to the pipeline, but let instructions in the pipeline complete as much as possible.* Then modify the process state so that it is the same as would have occurred under the sequential execution model (Figure 4.7(a)). That is, implement a precise interrupt model, even though the execution is pipelined.

In the first case, the interrupt may be *recoverable* even though it is imprecise. That is, execution can resume where it left off by restoring the process state and the machine-dependent pipeline state and then resuming execution. In some processor implementations, the pipeline state is not saved, so the imprecise interrupt is not recoverable. In general, imprecise interrupts make program debugging more difficult, because the saved process state may not correspond to a sequential execution model at the time a fault occurs.

For external interrupts (such as I/O interrupts), the implementation of precise interrupts is straightforward. Dispatching of new instructions is stopped and those instructions already in the pipelines are allowed to finish execution. The interrupt is serviced after the pipelines are drained.

For internal interrupts, the implementation of precise interrupts is more complex, because an internal interrupt is caused by an instruction in the currently executing process. Consider again the example in Figure 4.7(b). If instruction $i2$ is a load that causes a page fault, it cannot finish execution. With $i2$ "stuck" in a pipeline waiting for a page to be brought in from disk, it is not reasonable to simply wait for the pipelines to drain. Furthermore, instructions following $i2$ may be processed by a different pipeline and may run to completion and modify the process state.

4.5 Interrupts in POWER1

POWER Interrupt Architecture

Interrupts are caused by faults due to instruction execution or external causes such as Input/Output. Error conditions that occur when an arithmetic instruction is executed are referred to as *exceptions*. Sometimes the interrupt that is caused by an exception is referred to as a *trap*.

There are nine different interrupt types in the POWER architecture.

1. *The system reset interrupt* is an external, nonmaskable interrupt that causes the processor to reset, reinitialize the system software, and begin processing.

2. *The machine check interrupt* is a maskable interrupt that is caused by a hardware error detected in the system. The machine check interrupt provides system software with an opportunity to try to recover from the hardware error. The mask bit held in the MSR allows this interrupt to be disabled, in which case a hardware error causes the processor to stop, but the interrupt handler is not invoked.

3. *The instruction storage interrupt* is a precise internal interrupt caused by instruction references that cause page faults or protection violations.

4. *The data storage interrupt* is a precise internal interrupt caused by data references that cause page faults or protection violations.

5. *The alignment interrupt* is a precise internal interrupt that occurs when MSR(AL) = 1 and the hardware cannot handle a reference to misaligned data. This interrupt allows software to support misaligned data accesses (see Section 2.3).

6. *The program interrupt* is a precise internal interrupt that occurs when there is (1) an invalid operation, (2) a privileged operation in nonprivileged mode (MSR(PR) = 1), (3) an enabled floating-point exception occurring when MSR(FE) = 1, or (4) a software interrupt.

7. *The floating-point unavailable interrupt* occurs if MSR(FP) = 0 and there is an attempt to execute a floating-point instruction. This interrupt can be used to avoid saving and restoring floating-point registers during context switches to software not expected to use floating point (see Section 2.4). It could also be used to allow software emulation of floatingpoint in an implementation without floating-point hardware.

8. *The external interrupt* is a maskable interrupt generated by an external source such as the Input/Output system.

9. *The supervisor call (SVC) interrupt* is generated when an SVC instruction is executed in the Branch Unit. The SVC is used when a program requires some operating system service to be provided.

Besides the interrupt conditions listed above, there are a number of arithmetic exceptions. The floating-point exceptions are reported via the FPSCR (see Section 2.3), which also holds trap-enable bits for each of the floating-point exceptions. Because of the difficulties of implementing precise interrupts (see subsection "POWER1 Interrupt Implementation" below), floating-point exceptions cannot produce precise interrupts when the processor is operating in full-speed pipelined mode. Consequently, when interrupts are enabled for floating-point exceptions (MSR(FE) = 1), the processor is put into a serial mode in which all FPU and FXU instructions must be known error-free before the next instruction is begun. In this manner, the interrupts can be made precise.

A higher-speed alternative is to use software polling to explicitly check for floating-point exceptions. Software may be used to support debugging by inserting exception test code in certain places in the program. The compiler may provide several options at different levels: subroutine, loop exit, statement assignment, or after each floating-point instruction.

When an interrupt occurs, the POWER architecture modifies state registers held in the Branch Unit (Figure 2.13).

1. Depending on the type of the interrupt, the address of the instruction following the interrupted one, the address of the interrupted instruction, or the address of the last instructions completed before taking the interrupt is placed into the Status Save/Restore Register 0 (SRR0).

2. The current value of the Machine State Register (MSR) and some information related to the specific interrupt condition are placed in the Status Save/Restore Register 1 (SRR1).

3. After they have been saved in SRR1, most of the MSR bits are cleared.

4. The program counter is set to a value that is determined by the interrupt type, and interrupt processing begins at that point. In effect, there is a branch to the interrupt handling software.

POWER1 Interrupt Implementation

As we have seen, the POWER1 processor consists of three units, the BU, FXU, and FPU, implemented as three pipelines. Because some instructions are executed in the BU, never reaching the FXU or FPU, and because the FXU and FPU execute somewhat independently, instructions often finish execution in an order different from that defined by a sequential program execution model. This ability to execute instructions in a decoupled manner is responsible for many of the POWER1's performance advantages, but it also complicates the implementation of precise interrupts.

The problem of implementing precise interrupts is simplified by forcing each of the pipelines to complete its instructions in order. That is, all the instructions that execute in the BU modify the process state in order with respect to one another, all the instructions in the FXU modify the process state in order, and all the FPU instructions modify the process state in order. Within a pipeline, then, all instructions following a faulting one can simply be canceled because they modify the state in order. The problem then becomes one of ordering among the three major pipelines.

We say that pipeline *A* is *behind* pipeline *B* (or *B* is *ahead* of *A*) if, at any given time, an instruction still in pipeline *A* logically precedes an already completed instruction in pipeline *B*. Consider the following sequence of two unrelated instructions.

    fm   fp0 = fp2,fp1   # floating multiply. Goes to FPU pipe.
    a   r4=r12,r11   # integer add. Goes to FXU pipe.

Assuming both instructions are dispatched in the same clock cycle, and assuming both flow down their respective pipelines without any delays, then the floating multiply will finish second even though it precedes the add in the program order (refer back to Figure 3.2). The logical order of the program is that the floating multiply should modify the state of the FPU (register fp0), and then the add should modify the state of the FXU (register r4). But due to the difference in the lengths of the pipelines, the write to register fp0 will occur *after* the write to register r4. We say the FPU pipe is *behind* the FXU pipe.

If pipeline *A* is behind pipeline *B* and an instruction from *A* generates an interrupt, any instructions in *B* that logically follow the faulting instruction must not be allowed to modify the process state, or if they already have, the state change must be "undone." If instructions in *B* cannot be canceled, an alternative is to never let *A* fall behind *B*.

Because we have reduced the precise interrupt problem to one of maintaining the ordering among the major three pipelines, we describe the precise interrupt method implemented in POWER1 by describing what is done for all six ordered pairs of pipelines. In each case, pipeline *A* is behind *B*, and a fault is detected in an instruction being executed in *A*.

1. *BU behind FXU.* A branch executes right away, even if its outcome cannot be immediately resolved. As long as the branch is pending, FXU instructions can be dispatched conditionally, but cannot complete. This means that the BU cannot get behind the FXU. In any case, BU instructions (branches and logical Condition Register instructions) do not cause interrupts.

2. *FXU behind BU.* Certain FXU instructions may cause an interrupt. Examples include load and store instructions, which may lead to page faults or protection violations, software interrupts, and privileged instructions executed in user mode. If an interruptible instruction causes an interrupt, BU instructions that have been executed ahead of the FXU need to be undone. BU instructions may change three registers: (a) Link Register (LR), modified by a branch to subroutine; (b) Count Register (CTR), decremented in each loop iteration when used by a loop-closing branch; and (c) Condition Register (CR), whose contents are modified by logical Condition Register instructions. A history buffer method is used to restore the state. There is a separate history buffer associated with each of the three registers in the BU. After dispatching to the FXU an interruptible instruction, any subsequent instruction that modifies the CR, CTR, or LR causes the old value of that register to be saved in the history buffer. If an interrupt occurs in the FXU, the old value of the register is restored, leading to a precise interrupt. Otherwise, if there is no fault, the old value of the register is no longer needed and it is purged from the buffer.

3. *FPU behind FXU.* Instructions processed in the FPU may cause any of a number of floating-point exceptions. As we have seen, however, in POWER1, floating-point traps are enabled only when the processor executes instructions serially. In this mode, an instruction must finish execution before the next one is dispatched. This means the FPU never falls behind the FXU, and floating-point interrupts are precise.

In the normal mode of operation, floating-point traps are disabled, the FPU can be behind the FXU, and floating-point exceptions are detected by software polling.

4. *FXU behind FPU.* As described in (2) above, a variety of instructions executed in the FXU may cause interrupts. A different solution from that in (2) has been adopted, however, primarily because the state of the FPU, to be restored in case of an interrupt, is much larger than the state of the BU. The BU has only three registers, CR, CTR, and LR, that can be modified by relatively infrequent BU instructions. The FPU has 40 floating-point registers implemented by the hardware (the architecture specifies 32 registers) as well as other state information.

Precise interrupts are implemented by using an *interruptible instruction counter* in the FPU. This counter prevents the FPU from going ahead of the FXU when an interruptible instruction comes up, until it is known that the instruction does not lead to an interrupt. The counter does allow the FXU to be ahead of the FPU.

5. *BU behind FPU.* Same as (1) above.

6. *FPU behind BU.* Same as (3) above. The only situation when the FPU can be behind BU is when floating-point traps are disabled.

We have now considered all the pairings of pipelines. To summarize the major points of the precise interrupt method:

1. All instructions within a pipeline finish in order.

2. The history buffer method is used within the BU.

3. The FXU is synchronized with respect to the FPU so that the distance it can fall behind is restricted. The distance is chosen so that the FPU cannot modify its state too far ahead of the FXU.

Having described synchronization among the three pipelines for the purpose of handling interrupts, we find this a good place to describe another synchronization mechanism that also limits the distance between the FXU and FPU in both directions, but for different reasons. There is a synchronization counter that allows the FXU to be two instructions ahead and six instructions behind the FPU. This restriction exists in addition to the one described in item (4) above.

1. The FXU may be at most two instructions ahead of the FPU. The reason for this limitation has to with synchronization of floating loads. When the FXU executes floating loads ahead of the FPU, data sent from the cache to the FPU must be buffered. It cannot be written into the destination register because the floating load has not yet reached the write stage of the FPU pipeline (Figure 3.11). Limited data-buffering space does not allow the FXU to be more than two instructions ahead.

2. FXU is at most six instructions behind the FPU. This restriction is the result of limited instruction-buffering space in the FXU. There are four instruction buffers and two decode slots that can hold a total of six instructions.

4.6 References

The general problem of dealing with branches is described in Lilja [54], McFarling and Hennessy [58], and in a recent monograph by Cragon [17]. The basic static and dynamic branch prediction methods were studied in J. E. Smith [82]. A later, and much more detailed study was reported in Lee and A. J. Smith [53].

A comprehensive discussion of the precise interrupt problem is in J. E. Smith and Pleszkun [84]. Other relevant work is Hwu and Patt [40] and Sohi [86]. To see how another recent RISC implementation with out-of-order completion does precise interrupts, refer to Diefendorff and Allen [18].

POWER1 IMPLEMENTATION: CACHE MEMORIES

5.1 Introduction

As in most modern computers, the RS/6000 memory hierarchy consists of a set of registers, cache memory, main memory, and secondary storage (usually implemented as hard disk drives). In a typical memory hierarchy, data and instructions are moved up and down the hierarchy depending on their usage. At the top of the hierarchy, data of immediate use are generally loaded into the register file or they reside in the cache memory. At the bottom, blocks of data that have not been used for a long period of time are eventually placed in secondary storage by the virtual memory system or explicitly placed there as files. In between, main memory holds instructions and data for an actively executing program.

The lower in the hierarchy, the cheaper and slower the memory tends to be. Register files that usually contain a few hundred bytes are at the top of the hierarchy. They can support multiple reads and writes in a fraction of one pipeline stage. A data cache is typically tens to a few hundreds of kilobytes, and each access takes one or two pipeline stages. A main memory usually contains a few to a few hundred megabytes, and can typically be accessed in seven to ten clock cycles. Finally, secondary storage implemented as a hard disk may contain hundreds of megabytes to a few gigabytes or more and take milliseconds to access. The goal of a memory hierarchy is to provide an apparent memory the size of the lower levels of the hierarchy, but with access times of the higher levels.

The POWER1 registers are part of the processor architecture and are described in Chapter 2. In this chapter we look at the next level of the hierarchy, the cache memory. The final two levels of the hierarchy, main memory and secondary storage, are discussed in Chapter 10.

In general, caches can be *unified* into a single cache for both instructions and data or *split* into separate instruction and data caches. Most RS/6000 processors have split caches that come in different sizes depending on the model, but the very low end models use a single-chip processor (the RSC) and have a unified cache.

5.2 Cache Memory Overview

A cache reference consists of two steps: *lookup* and *access*. A cache lookup is performed when an instruction or data item has to be fetched from memory. If the requested item is in the cache, the reference is a *hit*, and the lookup is followed by the second step, the cache access. Otherwise, a *miss* occurs—the requested item is not in the cache and must be fetched from main memory. The *hit ratio* is the ratio of references that hit to the total number of references. The *miss ratio* is simply 1 − *hit ratio*. In references that hit, the access time is the cache access time, usually just one or two clock cycles. Hit ratios vary greatly from one program to another, but hit ratios of over 90% are not uncommon.

Computer designers usually prefer to use the miss ratio rather than the hit ratio because comparisons of miss ratios tend to better reflect the actual performance effects. For example, the difference between a 90% and a 95% hit ratio seems to be relatively small. However, these are equivalent to miss ratios of 10% and 5%—a factor of two. The larger apparent difference in miss ratios suggests a relatively large overall performance difference, which is probably closer to reality (although the actual relationship between cache miss rates and processor performance is quite complex).

Accessing main memory is more time consuming than accessing a cache, but it must be done in the case of a cache miss. A miss presents an opportunity to do some prefetching: main memory has to be accessed anyway, so data or instructions at adjacent addresses may be brought in along with the requested item. These additional data or instructions often prove useful since most programs exhibit *spatial locality*. That is, items at addresses close to the referenced address are likely to be accessed in the near future. This tendency is most obvious with instructions, which are executed sequentially until a taken branch alters the program flow, but it also occurs with data, for example when the elements of an array are accessed in sequential order.

Therefore, an entire block or *line* of consecutive memory locations is brought in whenever a miss occurs. The line is the basic unit of transfer between memory and the cache, so the cache storage space is partitioned naturally into lines. When a line is brought into the cache, usually another line has to be removed to make room for it. Most caches remove lines that have not been used recently or that have been in the cache for the longest time. The cache generally holds recently used data or instructions that are likely to be used again. The principle that a recently accessed location will likely be accessed again soon is called *temporal locality*. It is locality, both spatial and temporal, that leads to low miss ratios, even though the cache memory may be orders of magnitude smaller than main memory.

Because the cache memory is much smaller than main memory but can potentially hold the contents of any memory location, it can't be accessed in the same way as main memory. Cache lookup is done by *association*—by comparing the address being accessed with addresses of locations being held in the cache. Each cache line has a portion of the main memory address, or a *tag*, stored along with it; the tag is compared with the memory address to determine if there is a hit. The next section describes the cache lookup process in more detail.

Cache Lookup

There are three types of cache organizations in common use: *fully associative, set associative,* and *direct-mapped*. The set associative organization includes the other two as special cases, so we will consider it first. To reduce the number of address comparisons that must be done when the cache is accessed, the lines are grouped into *sets* containing one or more lines (usually a power of 2). An "*n*-way set associative cache" is a cache in which each set has n lines. For a given memory address, only the lines belonging to one set have to be searched to see if there is a hit.

For a cache lookup, the memory address is interpreted as having three fields: *tag, set number,* and *line offset* (Figure 5.1). The length of these fields is determined in a right-to-left order as follows. If the line size is 2^b bytes, the line offset field is b bits. The line offset locates the correct data once the line is found. If the cache has 2^s sets, the set number field is s bits. The remaining address bits are the tag.

Figure 5.1 is a 2-way set associative cache with 128-byte lines and 64 sets, each containing two lines. Hence, the line offset and set number fields have 7 and 6 bits, respectively. The remaining 19 bits of the 32-bit address are the tag.

These three fields are used in the cache lookup as follows. First, the set number directly accesses the members of the set in which the requested item may be found. This is set 03 in Figure 5.1. There are two lines in this set, each with its own tag. Next, the two tags are simultaneously compared with the tag field part of the address. If there is a match, a hit occurs and the matching line is selected (line A in the figure). Finally, the line offset determines the location within the line of the requested data item.

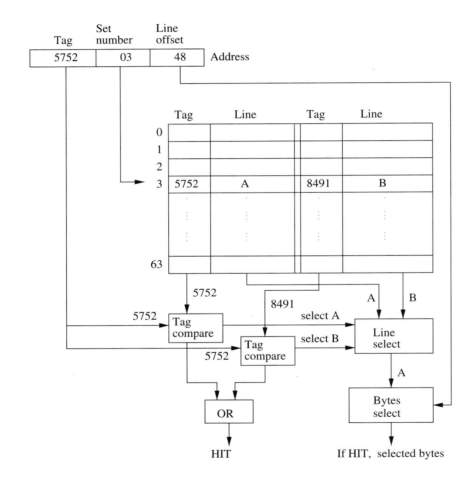

(a) Fields in the 32-bit address.

(b) Block diagram.

FIGURE 5.1   **Cache memory organization. Cache shown is a 2-way set associative cache with 64 lines and 128 bytes per line.**

Handling Writes

So far we have been assuming the cache access is a read. In case of a write, the cache lookup proceeds as described above. Then, there are two ways write accesses are usually handled: *write-through* and *write-back*.

■ In a *write-through* cache, if there is a hit, the write operation updates both the cache and the main memory. If there is a miss, most systems update only main memory. That is, a cache line is not allocated on a write miss.

■ In a *write-back* cache, if there is a hit, only cache is updated. If there is a miss, most systems bring the line into the cache, then update it. This is referred to as a *write allocate* policy. With a write-back cache, multiple updates may be performed to a line without writing to the main memory. Eventually, when the cache line must be replaced, its contents are first written back to main memory.

The main argument in favor of a write-through policy is that the cache and main memory always have the same data. This simplifies certain operations, such as flushing the cache (or part of it). With a write-through cache, flushing can be done by simply marking lines as invalid. With a write-back cache, there is often a burst of memory activity as flushed lines are written back (actually, only the modified lines have to be written back, but all lines must be checked to see if they have been modified).

In contrast, a write-through cache generates higher bus traffic, the same item may be updated multiple times, and each update must make it to memory. Also, frequent writes of short items interfere with line transfers and often lead to underutilized bus bandwidth. In a write-back cache, the cache–main memory interface may be optimized to transfer fixed-size lines at a high rate.

Cache Organizations

Important design parameters that determine the cache cost and performance are the cache size, line size, and associativity (number of lines in a set).

A 1-way set associative cache (usually called a *direct-mapped* cache) has a single line per set. Direct-mapped caches are simple: for a given address, there is only one place the data can possibly be (if it is in the cache at all). But, if there is a miss, there is also only choice for the line to be replaced, regardless of whether the replaced line has been recently used and may be accessed again in the near future. Despite relatively worse miss ratios, direct-mapped caches are used because their simplicity often translates into shorter access times.

Somewhat more flexibility exists in a 2-way set associative cache because it can retain two lines that map to the same set. When a new line is brought in, it can replace the older, or the one used less recently. Increasing the associativity from a 1-way to a 2-way cache, while keeping the cache size and line size constant, improves the miss ratio. Some improvement, although

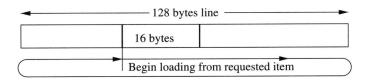

FIGURE 5.2   Wraparound load.

considerably smaller, can be observed when the organization is changed from a 2-way to a 4-way cache.

If a cache has only one set, it is *fully associative*. Fully associative caches tend to give the best miss ratios, but they are expensive because they require tag comparisons with all the lines, and they may be slow for that reason. When fully associative caches are used, they tend to be small.

The line size is another important design consideration. There is one tag per line in the cache, and the storage space taken up by tags is often considered "overhead," because it is not used for storing data or instructions. In a fixed-size cache, increasing the line size reduces this overhead. Also, increasing the line size beyond very short lines will initially reduce the miss ratio because more useful information is brought in when a miss occurs (spatial locality). Some of this information may not be used before the line is discarded from the cache, however, and the proportion of unused data increases as the line size becomes larger, eventually leading to a higher miss ratio (again, assuming a fixed-size cache).

The line length and the cache memory bandwidth determine the time it takes to load a line from memory into the cache. In the RS/6000–560 it takes 8 cycles to load a 128-byte line into the data cache, at the rate of 16 bytes per cycle (following a delay of a few cycles to initiate the transfer). To reduce the delay caused by a miss, a combination of two techniques is commonly used: (a) fetch bypass, and (b) wraparound load. Using fetch bypass, the requested item, which caused the miss, is sent to the processor as soon as it arrives from memory, bypassing the cache. Since the requested item may be somewhere in the middle of a line, a wraparound load (Figure 5.2) is used to begin loading the line from the requested item, continue until the end, and finally wrap around and load the remainder of the line from the beginning.

5.3 POWER1 Instruction Cache

The RS/6000–560 has an 8 Kbyte instruction cache (I-cache) whose organization is shown in Figure 5.3. There are two lines per set (a 2-way set associative cache). A line holds 16 fixed-length, 32-bit instructions, numbered in the figure from 0 to 15.

The performance demands on the instruction cache are quite high. The pipelines can

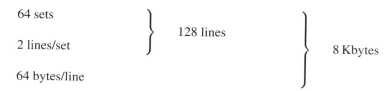

64 sets
2 lines/set
64 bytes/line
} 128 lines } 8 Kbytes

(a) Instruction cache structure.

Set number	Tag	Array 0	Array 1	Array 2	Array 3	Tag	Array 0	Array 1	Array 2	Array 3
0		0	1	2	3		0	1	2	3
		4	5	6	7		4	5	6	7
		8	9	10	11		8	9	10	11
		12	13	14	15		12	13	14	15
1		0	1	2	3		0	1	2	3
		4	5	6	7		4	5	6	7
		8	9	10	11		8	9	10	11
		12	13	14	15		12	13	14	15
⋮	⋮	⋮	⋮	⋮	⋮	⋮	⋮	⋮	⋮	⋮
63		0	1	2	3		0	1	2	3
		4	5	6	7		4	5	6	7
		8	9	10	11		8	9	10	11
		12	13	14	15		12	13	14	15

(b) Cache arrays. The thick lines show one line. The numbers 0–15 represent the sixteen instructions in the line.

FIGURE 5.3   RS/6000–560 instruction cache.

consume instructions at the maximum rate of four per clock cycle. While these instructions are often from consecutive addresses, which simplifies the task, branch instructions can go to the middle of a line and complicate matters. The POWER1 instruction cache is specially built so that it can sustain four consecutive instruction references per clock cycle, regardless of where in a cache line the string of four instructions starts. To accomplish this, the physical structure of a line is similar to a matrix with four columns, called *arrays,* and four *rows.* Each of the four cache arrays is a single-port memory that can supply one instruction per cycle adding up to a maximum fetch rate of four instructions per cycle over all four arrays.

Instruction Cache Operation

Figure 5.4(a) shows how a 32-bit address is interpreted by the instruction cache. The rightmost 2 bits (marked XX in the figure) have no use in instruction addressing and are simply ignored, as all instructions are 4 bytes long. The next 2 bits determine the cache array (array address). Finally, the following 2 bits are the row address. The array and row fields are based on the physical structure of the cache. Logically, they are part of the line offset field.

As a simple example, consider fetching four instructions as shown in Figure 5.4(b). These are the first four instructions in the line, they have the same set number and row address, and they are fetched by presenting row address 00 to the four cache arrays.

Now consider fetching the four instructions in Figure 5.4(c). The first three of these are in arrays 01, 10, and 11; they are fetched using the same row address 00. The fourth instruction is in array 00 at row address 01. Hence, the row address of array 00 must be incremented, a function performed by row increment logic as shown in Figure 5.5. Depending on the location (that is, which cache array) of the first of the four instructions, row addresses for the other cache arrays may also have to be incremented, with the exception of array 11.

A final example is shown in Figure 5.4(d). These four instructions span two lines, in two different sets. The first three instructions are in set 000000, while the fourth instruction is in set 000001. To fetch these four instructions in a single cycle, two cache sets must be searched simultaneously. The normal operation of a generic cache is to perform associative lookup of the lines in a single set. The POWER1 solution to this problem is based on the observation that when the four instructions span two sets, these sets are always consecutive. Hence, the instruction cache directory (the part of the cache that contains the tags and comparators and is used for lookup) is split into two directories, one containing odd-numbered sets, and the other containing even-numbered sets. The two directories can be searched in parallel and support simultaneous access to two consecutively numbered sets.

Instruction Cache Miss Processing

An instruction cache miss loads a line of 16 instructions (64 bytes) into the instruction cache. As shown in Figure 5.6, this transfer involves the use of error detection and correction logic and a buffer (Instruction Reload Buffer or IRB) located on the DCU (Data Cache Unit) chips.

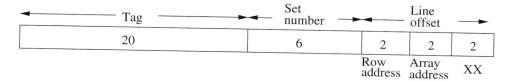

(a) Fields in the 32-bit instruction address.

Instruction address	Set number	Row address	Array address
000...00000000	000000	00	00
000...00000100	000000	00	01
000...00001000	000000	00	10
000...00001100	000000	00	11

(b) Four instructions beginning at address 000...00000000.

Instruction address	Set number	Row address	Array address
000...00000100	000000	00	01
000...00001000	000000	00	10
000...00001100	000000	00	11
000...00010000	000000	01	00

(c) Four instructions beginning at address 000...00000100.

Instruction address	Set number	Row address	Array address
000...00110100	000000	11	01
000...00111000	000000	11	10
000...00111100	000000	11	11
000...01000000	000001	00	00

(d) Four instructions beginning at address 000...00110100.

FIGURE 5.4   **Fetching four instructions from the instruction cache. All numbers are in binary.**

Array number	Logic function
00	Increment row address if array address field > 00
01	Increment row address if array address field > 01
10	Increment row address if array address field > 10
11	Increment row address if array address field > 11

FIGURE 5.5   Logic to increment row address. Note that the situation in the last entry of the table never occurs, since array addresses have only two bits and are never larger than 11. Hence, there is never a need to increment the row address of array 11.

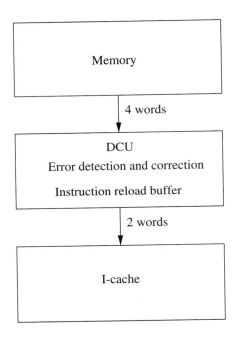

FIGURE 5.6   Instruction cache miss processing.

FIGURE 5.7   RS/6000–560 data cache structure.

After a delay of several cycles needed for the memory system to begin the transfer, 4 words (16 bytes) are sent in each cycle from memory to the IRB. From the IRB to the ICU, the transfer occurs at the slower rate of 2 words per cycle because of the narrower bus between the DCU and the I-cache. At this rate, it takes 8 cycles to load an I-cache line after the transfer has begun.

I-cache misses are not processed until the outcome of pending branch is known. That is, misses are not initiated based on a prediction alone. Thus, the memory bus, which is used to load both the instruction and data caches, is not tied up servicing the miss of an instruction that ends up not being executed. Instructions loaded into the I-cache are partially decoded and a tag (not to be confused with the cache tag) indicating the instruction type is stored in the cache with each instruction. This decode tag is used by the dispatch logic to simplify the recognizing of branches within the sequential buffer and the dispatching of multiple instructions per cycle to the FXU and FPU.

5.4 POWER1 Data Cache

The RS/6000–560 has a 64 Kbyte, 4-way set associative data cache (D-cache) with 128 byte lines. Figure 5.7 illustrates the data cache organization. The following sections cover the D-cache and the memory interface in more detail.

Virtual Addresses and Aliasing

A program refers to virtual addresses, but main memory is accessed with physical addresses (we use the terms *physical* address and *real* address interchangeably). Address translation (see Section 2.6), is used to convert the virtual address to a physical address. Which type of address should be used to access the data cache? If the virtual address is used, then there is a possibility of an *alias* problem in the data cache. Aliases occur when two virtual addresses map to the same physical address. This is no problem for main memory, because it is accessed with physical addresses. For a virtually addressed data cache, however, a physical memory location may appear at two different places in the cache. Then, if a store is made to one of the aliased virtual address locations, followed by a load from the other, the load result will be incorrect.

A second kind of alias problem occurs when identical virtual addresses of two different processes map to different physical memory locations (which is often the case). To avoid this interprocess alias problem, the processor can be made to flush the cache whenever the process changes. Another solution is to append a process number to the cache tag and compare it with the process number of the currently running process.

An obvious solution to the alias problem is to do address translation before the cache is accessed; that is, use physical addresses. Logically, this process would mean accessing the page tables before the cache, which could be a very slow process indeed. To speed up the process, recently accessed page table entries are cached in a Translation Lookaside Buffer (TLB), which is a table maintained in hardware (Figure 5.8(a)). Internally, a TLB is organized like a set associative cache. Even with the TLB, however, the address translation and cache access still seem to be a serial sequence that we would like to speed up.

We base one way of doing this on the observation that the page offset part of the virtual address is not translated. If the information contained in the page offset field of the address is sufficient to access the cache set, then the TLB and cache access may be overlapped. The set number field (Figure 5.1) must fit into the page offset field, which is 12 bits in a 4 Kbyte page. However these 12 bits are split between the set number and line offset fields, the size of a direct-mapping cache cannot exceed 4 Kbytes. The cache can be made larger by increasing the associativity, which has no effect on the length of the set number and line offset fields.[1]

A second solution is to use the virtual address to access the cache set, even though some of these bits will be translated, then use the translated physical address to do the tag compare. This "virtual index–physical tag" solution is used in POWER1 and is becoming increasingly common in other RISC implementations. With this method, there can still be some aliases in general. In the RS/6000, however, aliasing is prevented as follows.

■ Virtual addresses are unique, preventing the type of aliasing in which identical virtual addresses used by two processes map to different physical addresses. In the POWER architecture the 52-bit virtual address space is sufficiently large to support many concurrent processes without having to "reuse" virtual addresses. The controlled sharing of the single large virtual space among different processes is accomplished by having the operating system manage the segment registers.

■ At any given time only one virtual address can be mapped to a particular physical address. This property prevents the type of aliasing in which two different virtual addresses map to the same physical address.

---

[1] As a rather extreme example, the IBM 3033 had a 64 Kbyte cache, organized with 16-way set associativity so that this overlap technique could be used.

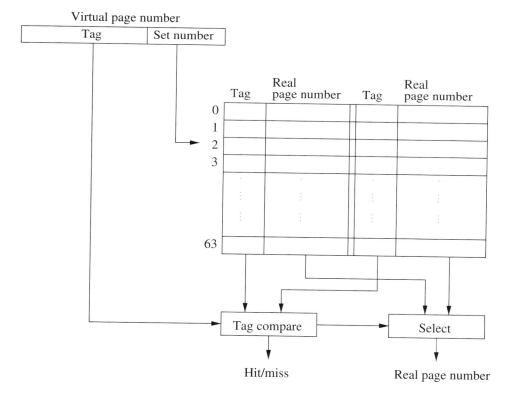

(a) Conceptual TLB.

(b) POWER1 Data TLB organization.

FIGURE 5.8   **Translation Lookaside Buffer (TLB).**

The property holds because of the inverted page table used by the POWER architecture (see Chapter 2). In the inverted page table, two different virtual addresses V1 and V2 cannot simultaneously map to the same physical address P1 because each page table entry, corresponding to a unique page frame, points back to a single virtual page.

However, care must be taken whenever the page table mapping changes. In this case we have two virtual pages, a new one that was just brought in, and an old one that was discarded to make place for the new page. Both the new and old virtual pages map to the same physical page. Because the cache is indexed with the virtual address, we can still encounter the problem that *a physical memory location appears at two different places in the cache.* The obvious solution is to have the operating system flush the entries corresponding to a physical page whenever the virtual page that maps to it is changed.

Aliases may occur in the RS/6000 when the same data are accessed with translation both on and off. Translation *on* refers to the normal translation of the effective address to virtual address to real address. Translation *off* means that the effective address is directly used as the real address. A typical example is page tables. Hardware accesses page tables with translation off. Hence, the cache is indexed with the real address. Now, if system software attempts to access the page tables with translation on, it will index the cache with the virtual address. Software may prevent aliasing by ensuring that the cache set index bits are identical in the virtual and physical addresses.

Data Cache Directory Lookup

To access the cache in POWER1, the set number field is taken directly from the effective address. These bits are identical in the effective and virtual addresses, since the virtual address is obtained by concatenating the 28 rightmost bits of the effective address with the 24-bit segment ID.

POWER1 implements two TLBs, one for instructions (I-TLB) located on the ICU, and one for data (D-TLB) located on the FXU. The D-TLB is a 2-way set associative cache with 64 sets for a total of 128 entries (Figure 5.8(b)). Since each entry translates the virtual page number of one page, and the machine has 4 Kbyte pages, the D-TLB contains translation information for 512 Kbytes of physical memory.

For the purpose of accessing the D-TLB, the 40-bit virtual page number is interpreted as shown in Figure 5.9. The 6-bit set number is used to select one of 64 sets. The tags in the two entries of the selected set are compared with the tag field from the virtual page number. If there is a match, the corresponding real page number is returned, otherwise a D-TLB miss is signaled.

In POWER1, virtual address generation, translation, and D-cache directory lookup (Figure 5.10) are performed in one half of a clock cycle. This remarkably short time is obtained by overlapping the following three operations.

1. To generate the virtual address, a segment register is selected using bits 0–3 from the

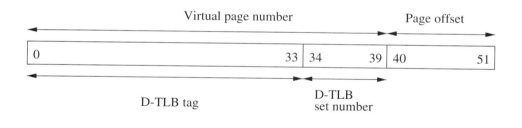

FIGURE 5.9   **D-TLB tag and set number fields from the virtual page number.**

effective address. The least significant 24 bits from the segment register are concatenated with bits 4–13 of the effective address to form the D-TLB tag (see also Figure 5.9).

2. The D-TLB is accessed using bits 14–19 of the effective address to select the D-TLB set.

3. The D-cache directory is accessed using bits 18–24 of the effective address to select the D-cache set.

Next two comparisons are performed.

1. The D-TLB is a 2-way set associative cache and the selected set has two entries, each with its own tag. These two tags have to be compared with the D-TLB tag from the virtual address to determine whether the D-TLB access is a miss or a hit. If it is a hit, the real page number (RPN) corresponding to the matching tag is obtained from the D-TLB.

2. The D-cache is a 4-way set associative cache and the selected set has four lines, each with its own tag. The four tags have to be compared with the D-cache tag from the RPN to determine whether the D-cache access is a miss or a hit.

It seems that these two operations have to be serialized, since the D-TLB tag comparison is needed to obtain the RPN, which is then used to perform the D-cache tag comparison. The two operations can be overlapped, however, as shown in Figure 5.10, by comparing the tags of both RPNs with the D-cache tags. Two matches may result and the correct one is selected after the D-TLB tag comparison is finished. Finally, a D-TLB miss always leads to a D-cache miss because no RPN is available to perform the D-cache lookup.

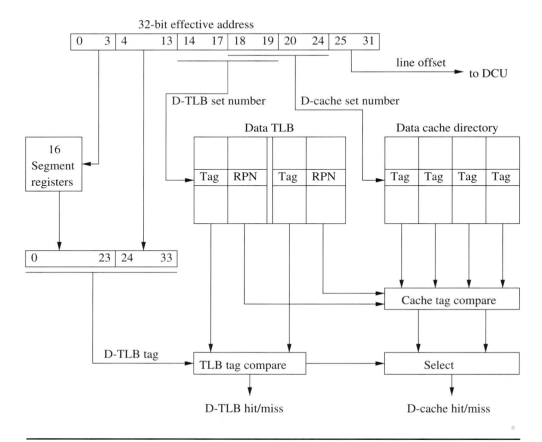

FIGURE 5.10   Virtual address generation, translation, and D-cache directory lookup.

Data Cache Miss Processing

When a D-cache miss occurs, two operations may have to be performed: (a) a line must be loaded from memory, and (b) another line must be stored into memory, if the line discarded from the cache is dirty (modified). These two operations (Figure 5.11) are overlapped to some extent due to two buffers located on the DCU: Cache Reload Buffer (CRB) and Store Back Buffer (SBB). Each buffer can hold a full line.

Data coming from memory following a miss is buffered in the CRB until a full line is loaded. The transfer rate is 16 bytes (one quadword) per cycle, and the requested item is sent to the processor as soon as the first quadword arrives, since the load begins with the quadword

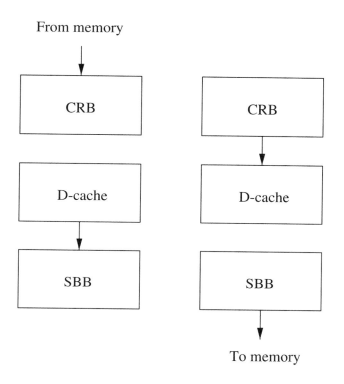

(a) Load CRB from memory and transfer dirty line into SBB.

(b) Transfer line from CRB into D-cache and store SBB into memory.

FIGURE 5.11   **D-cache miss processing.**

containing the requested item (see wraparound load, Figure 5.2). As the CRB is being loaded, data are made available to the processor even before the line is transferred into the D-cache. During the same time, the dirty line to be discarded from the cache is moved into the SBB, a transfer that takes two cycles.

Once the entire line is in the CRB, the second phase of the miss processing may begin. The CRB is loaded into the cache and concurrently the dirty line is stored from the SBB into memory. If a second miss occurs while the processing of the first one is in progress, the store of the SBB is delayed to give priority to the load of the missing data.

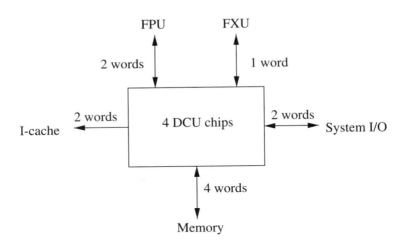

FIGURE 5.12   DCU data paths. A word is four bytes.

Data Cache Physical Implementation

The storage part of the data cache is physically located on the four DCU chips. Its directory, which consists of tags and other management information (LRU bits, dirty bits, valid bits), is on the FXU. The D-TLB, as well as the segment registers, are also located on the FXU.

The four DCU chips located on the processor board provide paths of different widths to the FPU, FXU, memory, I-cache, and System I/O (SIO) (Figure 5.12). Since there are two separate caches, one for instructions and another for data, it may seem unusual that the I-cache path passes through the DCU instead of being connected directly to the memory bus. There are two reasons for this. The first is that pin limitations of the ICU chip restrict the I-cache load bus to two words. Using the wider four-word memory–DCU bus, an I-cache line is loaded at the rate of four words per cycle into a buffer on the DCU (Figure 5.6), and from the buffer the I-cache line is transferred to the I-cache at a slower rate of two words per cycle. The memory bus is busy only for the duration of the high-speed transfer from memory to DCU.

The second reason follows from the error checking and correction (ECC) method. If the I-cache load bus were connected directly to the memory bus, the ICU would have ECC logic to detect and correct errors in loading instructions from memory, duplicating ECC logic already present in the DCU chips. The ECC hardware located in the DCU is shared for transfers between memory and I-cache, memory and D-cache, and memory and I/O devices using the SIO bus.

5.5 References

Several books, including Patterson and Hennessy [71] and Stone [88], discuss caches at various levels of detail. A. J. Smith [80] is a comprehensive survey. Kessler et al. [48] discuss implementations of set associative caches. Hill [37] examines design trade-offs in cache memory with specific focus on direct-mapped caches. This paper also contains interesting discussions on implementation alternatives and timing paths.

A. J. Smith [81], Przybylski, Horowitz, and Hennessy [74], and Przybylski [73] study trade-offs involving the line size. One of the conclusions in [74] is that if certain assumptions hold (separate instruction and data caches, a line as the unit of transfer between memory and cache, see [74]), a good selection of the line size is $4b$ or $8b$, where b is the number of bytes transferred per cycle between memory and the data cache. This is supported in the RS/6000–560, where $b = 16$ bytes and the line size is $8b = 128$ bytes. The relation is the same in lower-end models with split caches in which both the memory bus width and line size are halved.

Grohoski et al. [28] describe the POWER1 instruction cache and the data cache directory lookup. A performance evaluation of the RS/6000 by Simmons and Wasserman [78] includes a discussion on data cache misses.

POWER2: THE NEXT GENERATION

6.1 Introduction

In the competitive high-end workstation market, manufacturers are constantly leapfrogging one another, producing ever higher performance systems. IBM, in 1990, made a significant leap into the lead with the superscalar POWER1 chip set and the initial RS/6000 workstations. By 1993, however, a number of other companies had introduced products that surpassed even the top-end RS/6000s in performance. In late 1993 it was IBM's turn to leap ahead once again. This it did with the POWER2 chip set and an accompanying set of new RS/6000 workstation products.

Compared with its single-chip RISC competitors, the eight-chip, 23 million–transistor POWER2 is a beast. Virtually every pipeline used in POWER1 has been doubled in POWER2. In a single clock cycle, a POWER2 implementation can issue up to six instructions and perform two data cache accesses, in the process transferring up to 32 bytes between the data cache and the registers. The main memory to cache path can transfer up to 32 bytes per cycle. Large low-latency instruction and data caches also contribute to the performance bottom line. In POWER2's full configuration, eight chips are mounted on a state-of-the-art multichip module that allows very high signal counts and low chip crossing times.

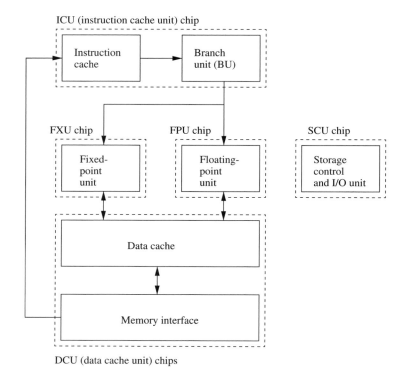

FIGURE 6.1   **POWER2 multichip implementation. Dashed lines indicate chip boundaries.**

The POWER2 chip set (Figure 6.1) essentially retains the same functional partitioning as that used in POWER1: the processor consists of three chips, the ICU, FXU, and FPU, and the data cache is a set of four DCU chips. Smaller processors can be configured with two DCU chips. However, the new POWER2 SCU chip combines the I/O and memory control functions that previously were implemented in two separate chips in POWER1 (SCU and IOU), reducing the maximum chip count from nine in POWER1 to eight in POWER2.

At the time of this writing, three POWER2-based RS/6000 models have been introduced. POWER1- and POWER2-based RS/6000 systems have similar memory and Input/Output structures (Chapter 10). The primary difference is the much higher POWER2 main memory bandwidth.

In this chapter we describe POWER2 configured as it is used in the RS/6000 model 590, a high-end deskside system using the full eight-chip implementation.[1] Just as the POWER1 family of RS/6000 systems provided a range of performance by using different combinations of POWER1 chips (Figure 10.10), the POWER2 chips are likely to be used in different configurations as new members of the RS/6000 family are introduced.

6.2 POWER Architecture Extensions

The POWER architecture as implemented in POWER2 largely resembles that introduced in POWER1. The most significant change comes in the form of new quadword floating load and store instructions (Figure 6.2) that provide architectural support for higher memory bandwidth implementations. The data transfer occurs between the data cache and a pair of adjacent floating-point registers. The register designated in the instruction (FRT in loads and FRS in stores) is the first of these two registers. The dual-ported cache is built to supply (or accept) two 128-bit operands per clock cycle, allowing two quadword memory instructions to execute simultaneously.

Computational bandwidth is easier to increase than memory bandwidth, and a characteristic of many of the superscalar RISCs is relatively low memory bandwidth as compared with floating-point bandwidth. To some extent, POWER1 suffers from this problem—it is capable of two floating-point operations but only one load or store per cycle. POWER2, in contrast, addresses the problem head-on. Consider the example in Figure 6.3, which illustrates the application of the quadword loads and stores.

Figure 6.3(a) is a simple code sequence that multiplies two arrays, adds the product to a third array, and stores the result. This loop requires a total of four loads and stores per loop iteration. When executed on POWER1, each loop iteration requires a minimum of four cycles because the data cache is capable of handling only one load or store per clock cycle.

Figure 6.3(b) is an example compilation for POWER2, using the quadword floating loads and stores. Here, the compiler takes advantage of consecutive array element accesses by using the quad load/stores to access two elements at a time. The loop is essentially unrolled twice, with a single quad load or store performing operations for two iterations' worth of accesses. In addition, because the data cache can handle two such quadword accesses per cycle, all four of the load/stores can be handled in two clock cycles. The POWER2 implementation averages one clock cycle per original loop iteration, one fourth the number of cycles required by POWER1.

The POWER2 instruction set includes three other new instructions (Figure 6.2(c)). These are a square root instruction—a function that required software emulation in POWER1—and two new instructions to convert floating-point numbers to integers. The last two instructions

---

[1] All of the first three POWER2-based RS/6000s use the full eight-chip processor implementation; what distinguishes each processor from the others is the clock frequency, ranging from 55 to 71.5 MHz.

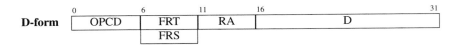

0	6	11	16	31

D-form | OPCD | FRT / FRS | RA | D |

```
lfq       load floating quad
lfqu      load floating quad, update RA
stfq      store floating quad
stfqu     store floating quad, update RA
```

$$\text{Effective address} = \begin{cases} (RA) + D & \text{if } RA \neq 0 \\ D & \text{if } RA = 0 \end{cases}$$

(a) D-form floating load and store instructions. FRT is the target register for loads, FRS is the source register for stores.

0	6	11	16	21	31

X-form | OPCD | FRT / FRS | RA | RB | EO | Rc |

```
lfqx      load floating quad
lfqux     load floating quad, update RA
stfqx     store floating quad
stfqux    store floating quad, update RA
```

$$\text{Effective address} = \begin{cases} (RA) + (RB) & \text{if } RA \neq 0 \\ (RB) & \text{if } RA = 0 \end{cases}$$

(b) X-form floating load and store instructions. FRT is the target register for loads, FRS is the source register for stores.

FIGURE 6.2   **New POWER2 floating-point instructions. Part (c) continued on page 139.**

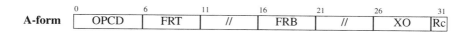

A-form

0	6	11	16	21	26	31
OPCD	FRT	//	FRB	//	XO	Rc

fsqrt   floating square root, place sqrt (FRB) into FRT

X-form

0	6	11	16	21	31
OPCD	FRT	//	FRB	EO	Rc

fcir   floating convert to integer, round (FRB), place into FRT
         rounding done according to the rounding mode set in the FPSCR
fcirz   floating convert to int with round to zero, round (FRB), place into FRT

(c) Double-precision, square root, and convert to integer instructions.

FIGURE 6.2 (continued)   **New POWER2 floating-point instructions.**

differ in the way rounding is done (again, see Figure 6.2(c)). All three instructions are available in double precision only.

Page Table Structure

POWER2 retains the POWER virtual address scheme (see Figure 2.25), but the page table structure is different. Instead of an inverted page table and a separate hash table, POWER2 uses a page table that is itself hashed. As shown in Figure 6.4, the hashed virtual page number (VPN) is used as an index into a page table in which each row consists of eight PTEs (page table entries). The eight entries are searched linearly until a matching VPN is found or the search fails. In the latter case, a second search is attempted using a secondary hash function.

This page table structure and lookup is identical to that of PowerPC, as described in Section 7.5. The page table access takes one memory reference less than in POWER because the page table is accessed directly. Furthermore, the page table entries are cacheable. Eight PTEs fit in a cache line, so they can all be searched with only one cache miss penalty.

double a[512], b[512], c[512], d[512];

for (k = 0; k < 512; k++)
    a[k] = b[k]*c[k] + d[k];

(a) C code.

```
                                      # r3 + 16 points to a.
                                      # r3 + 4112 points to b.
                                      # r3 + 8208 points to c.
                                      # r3 + 12304 points to d.
                                      # CTR holds half loop count (256).
LOOP:   lfq     fp0 = b(r3,4112)      # load b floating quad.
        lfq     fp2 = c(r3,8208)      # load c floating quad.
        lfq     fp4 = d(r3,12304)     # load d floating quad.
        fma     fp6 = fp4,fp0,fp2     # floating multiply-add.
        fma     fp7 = fp5,fp1,fp3     # floating multiply-add.
        stfqu   a(r3=r3+16) = fp6     # store floating quad with update.
        bc      LOOP,CTR≠0            # decrement CTR; branch if CTR ≠ 0.
```

(b) Assembly code.

FIGURE 6.3   **Code example and its compilation.**

6.3 Pipeline Overview

In this section we give a brief overview of the POWER2 pipelines. Later sections will fill in detail for specific areas. The POWER2 processor has the same three basic units as POWER1: the BU, FXU, and FPU, each with its own set of pipelines. Figure 6.5 shows the basic pipeline flow. For clarity, not all paths, buffers, and latches are shown in Figure 6.5; many of them appear in detailed drawings in later sections.

Each of the major units implements two pipelines: two integer arithmetic pipelines in the FXU, two floating-point arithmetic pipelines in the FPU, and two execution units in the BU. The individual pipelines are similar to those in POWER1 implementations.

The BU pipeline begins by fetching up to eight instructions per cycle. In the next stage, up to two branches and Condition Register instructions are executed in the BU. Up to four other instructions are partially decoded and dispatched to the FPU and FXU pipelines. The eight buffers at the beginning of these pipelines are each capable of absorbing as many as four instructions per cycle.

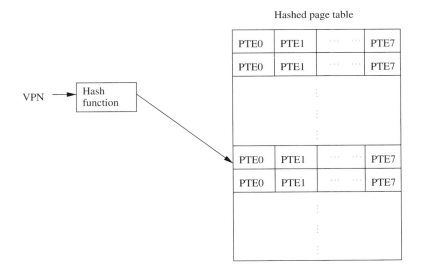

FIGURE 6.4   **POWER2 page table structure and lookup.**

These buffers (named decode buffers in the FXU and predecode buffers in the FPU) allow the FXU and FPU pipelines to run somewhat independently and permit instruction fetching and processing in one of the pipelines when the other pipeline is blocked (this principle is illustrated for POWER1 in Figure 3.4).

Instructions are read from the FXU decode buffers at the rate of up to two instructions per cycle and are passed down the two FXU pipelines. Each of these pipelines has its own ALU, and they share a data cache that can service both pipelines during the same clock cycle. In general, instructions must be independent to be issued down both pipelines at the same time, but an important exception is described below. In every case, FXU instructions are removed from the instruction queue and sent down the pipelines in strict program order. This order facilitates the implementation of precise (and restartable) interrupts for FXU exceptions, most importantly addressing exceptions and page faults.

Each of the two FPU pipelines supports its own fused multiply-add unit. Instructions in the FPU are read from the predecode buffers at the rate of up to four per cycle. Then they are predecoded, renamed, and placed in one of three queues: for floating-point arithmetic, for loads, and for stores. Instructions may be removed from these three queues somewhat independently, providing opportunities for out-of-order execution (only the arithmetic paths are shown in Figure 6.5). Additional buffering in each of the two independent floating-point units permits floating-point instructions to pass one another within the FPU pipelines.

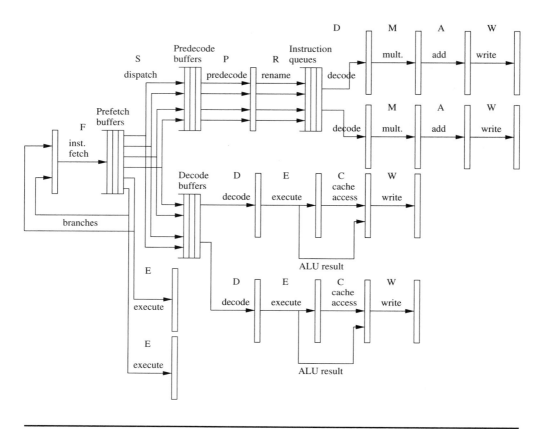

FIGURE 6.5   **POWER2 pipeline overview.**

Considerable flexibility in allowing FPU instructions to be processed out of order exists because floating-point exceptions are not required to generate precise interrupts, as is the case with FXU instructions.

Floating-point load and store instructions pass down both the FXU and FPU pipelines. On a load, the FXU pipeline accesses the data cache and the data are sent to the FPU. The copy of the load in the FPU provides control information to "catch" the data when it arrives and send it to the correct floating-point register and/or the floating-point unit that is waiting for it.

For stores the address is processed in the FXU and queued, waiting for data to be produced by the FPU. The FPU copy of the store instruction waits for the arithmetic units to produce the result and provides the control information required to send the data to the FXU. Floating-point data are stored when both the address and data are available to the data cache.

	POWER1	POWER2
Instruction cache bandwidth	4 instructions/cycle	8 instructions/cycle
Instruction dispatch bandwidth	4 instructions/cycle	6 instructions/cycle
Sequential buffer	8 instructions	16 instructions
Target buffer	4 instructions	8 instructions
Decoders in the target buffer	no	yes
Maximum branch taken delay	3 cycles	1 cycle

FIGURE 6.6   **POWER1 versus POWER2 implementation of the Branch Unit.**

6.4 Branch Unit

The POWER2 ICU chip contains the instruction cache, instruction fetching, decoding, and dispatching logic, plus the hardware that implements the Branch Unit (BU). The POWER BU registers and instructions are described in Section 2.4. Here we focus on the implementation (see Figure 6.6 for a comparison of POWER1 and POWER2 BU capabilities).

When instructions are fetched into the instruction cache, they are predecoded and predecode bits are stored in the cache along with the instructions. These bits help the dispatch logic determine the instruction type quickly. From the instruction cache, instructions are fetched into two buffers: the *sequential* buffer and the *target* buffer (Figure 6.7). The sequential buffer holds up to 16 instructions from the sequential instruction stream. The target buffer can hold eight instructions from the target address of a branch.

The fetch logic attempts to keep the sequential buffer full. This task is assisted by a high-bandwidth instruction cache that can supply eight instructions per clock cycle, even when the instructions span two cache lines. From the sequential buffer, instructions are dispatched to the FXU and FPU or executed in the BU, according to their type. In each clock cycle the first six instructions in the sequential buffer are decoded in preparation for dispatching. Two more instructions (the seventh and eighth slots in the sequential buffer) are partially decoded for the purpose of detecting branches. From the first six instructions any mixture of up to four fixed-point or floating-point instructions can be dispatched simultaneously to the FXU and FPU. And, in the same clock cycle, up to two instructions (branches or Condition Register instructions) can be executed by the BU.

Besides determining whether an instruction is to be dispatched to FXU and FPU or executed locally in the BU, decoding is done because some fixed-point and floating-point instructions modify the state of the BU. For example, the contents of the Condition Register (in the BU) may change as a result of FXU or FPU execution of compare instructions (or X-form instructions that have the Rc bit set). These instructions must set interlock bits in the BU to make sure that

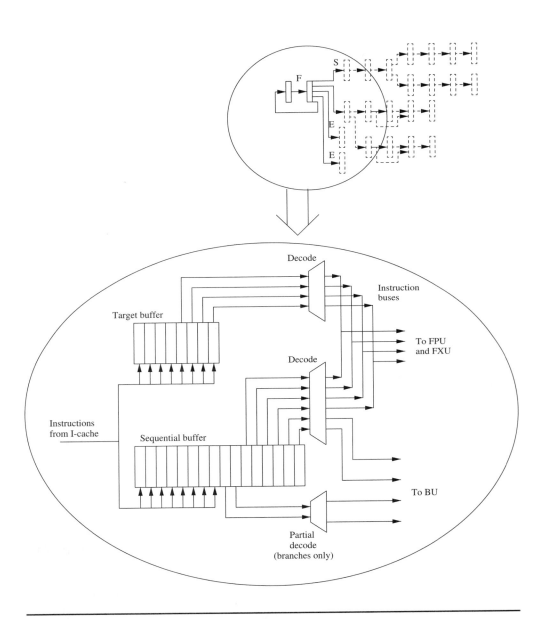

FIGURE 6.7   POWER2 buffer and decode logic.

the Condition Register is not tested before it is updated. The Condition Register interlocks are implemented as in POWER1 (Figure 4.2), except that each field has its own interlock bit.

In addition to decoding the first six instructions in the sequential buffer, the BU also decodes four instructions from the target buffer, allowing instructions that follow a conditional branch to be conditionally dispatched from both the sequential and target buffers. Figure 6.8 illustrates the example of this procedure described below.

Consider the "worst case," in which a conditional branch is immediately preceded by a compare operation that updates the CR field which the branch must use. At the end of cycle 0 the branch and compare have been dispatched. As the branch is dispatched, the fetch unit is directed to fetch from the branch target address. At this point the sequential buffer holds a block of instructions (s1, s2, s3, and s4) that logically follows the branch. These four instructions will be dispatched to the decode buffers on following clock period(s). All four will be dispatched, unless dispatch becomes blocked for some reason other than a full decode buffer.

At the end of cycle 1 a block of target instructions, t1 through t4, has been fetched into the target buffers. Assuming no blockages, the four sequential instructions (s1 through s4) have been dispatched to the decode buffers in the FXU. Meanwhile the compare instruction has finished decoding and is ready for execution.

During cycle 2 a block of target instructions is dispatched to the FXU. (The instructions are not actually latched into the decode buffers but are held on the instruction bus.) The previously dispatched sequential instructions are being decoded, and the compare instruction is now executing. At the end of cycle 2, as shown in the figure, one of two things happens, depending on the result of the compare. If the branch is not taken, the dispatched target instructions are canceled and the sequential instructions are permitted to complete; the result is that the pipeline is kept full and there is no delay. If the branch is taken, the executing sequential instructions are canceled, and the target instructions proceed into the decode buffers. In this case there is a one-cycle delay in instruction processing.

This one-cycle penalty of taken conditional branches is significantly lower than the maximum three-cycle delay in POWER1. The savings come from the following:

■ One cycle, the dispatch cycle, is saved because target instructions are conditionally dispatched.

■ Another cycle is saved by resolving the pending branch earlier, in the same cycle the compare executes.

Example

Figure 6.9 shows an example with a conditional branch instruction. Figure 6.10(a) illustrates the pipelined processing of the code when the branch is not taken. Eight instructions are fetched into the sequential buffer at time 1. Five of these, four integer instructions and the conditional branch, are dispatched in the next clock cycle. The first two instructions can be

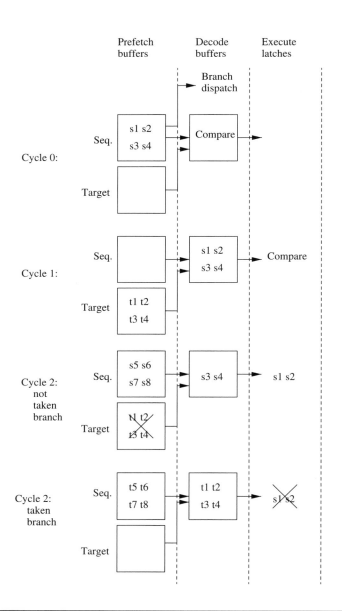

FIGURE 6.8   Overview of conditional dispatching, fixed-point instructions.

if (a > 0)

$$a = a + b + c;$$

else

$$a = a - b - c;$$

(a) C code.

```
                                          # r1 points to a
                                          # r1+4 points to b
                                          # r1+8 points to c
        l      r8=a(r1)                   # load a
        l      r12=b(r1,4)                # load b
        l      r9=c(r1,8)                 # load c
        cmpi   cr0=r8,0                   # compare immediate
        bc     ELSE,cr0/gt=false          # branch if bit false
IF:
        a      r12=r8,r12                 # add
        a      r12=r12,r9                 # add
        st     a(r1)=r12                  # store
        b      OUT                        # done
ELSE:
        sf     r12=r8,r12                 # subtract
        sf     r12=r12,r9                 # subtract
        st     a(r1)=r12                  # store
OUT:
```

(b) Assembly code.

FIGURE 6.9   **Code example with conditional branch.**

---

decoded simultaneously because they are independent. The next two instructions, however, are decoded serially because the `cmpi` depends on the first load and cannot decode until cycle 5. It is then executed, and the conditional branch is resolved. Meanwhile, three instructions are conditionally dispatched from sequential buffers; up to four could be dispatched, but in the example the unconditional branch blocks the sequential instruction stream. The unconditional branch cannot execute before the resolution of the previous (conditional) branch. Instructions are fetched from the target address at cycle 3 and conditionally dispatched in the next clock cycle; they are held on the instruction busses. Finally, at time 6 the `cmpi` executes, the `bc` is resolved, and the conditional instructions are allowed to finish execution and write results. There were no delays in the instruction flow as a result of the branch.

```
                                       1  2  3  4  5  6  7  8  9
        l      r8 = a(r1)              F  S  D  E  C  W
        l      r12 = b(r1,4)           F  S  D  E  C  W
        l      r9 = c(r1,8)            F  S  .  D  E  C  W
        cmpi   cr0 = r8,0              F  S  .  .  D  E
        bc     ELSE,cr0/gt=false       F  S
IF:     a      r12 = r8,r12            F  .  S´ .  D´ E´ W
        a      r12 = r12,r9            F  .  S´ .  .  D´ E  W
        st     a(r1) = r12             F  .  S´ .  .  .  D  E  C
        b      OUT                        F  .  .  .  .  S
ELSE:   sf     r12 = r8,r12                  F  S´ .  .
        sf     r12 = r12,r9                  F  S´ .  .
        st     a(r1) = r12                   F  S´ .  .
OUT:
```

(a) Not taken (correctly predicted) branch.

```
                                                            1
                                       1  2  3  4  5  6  7  8  9  0
        l      r8 = a(r1)              F  S  D  E  C  W
        l      r12 = b(r1,4)           F  S  D  E  C  W
        l      r9 = c(r1,8)            F  S  .  D  E  C  W
        cmpi   cr0 = r8,0              F  S  .  .  D  E
        bc     ELSE,cr0/gt=false       F  S
IF:     a      r12 = r8,r12            F  .  S´ .  D´ E´
        a      r12 = r12,r9            F  .  S´ .  .  D´
        st     a(r1) = r12             F  .  S´ .  .  .
        b      OUT                        F  .  .  .  .
ELSE:   sf     r12 = r8,r12                  F  S´ .  .  D  E  W
        sf     r12 = r12,r9                  F  S´ .  .  D  E  W
        st     a(r1) = r12                   F  S´ .  .  .  D  E  C
OUT:
```

(b) Taken (incorrectly predicted) branch.

FIGURE 6.10   POWER2 execution of the code example from Figure 6.9. A prime indicates conditional dispatching.

Part (b) of Figure 6.10 shows the same example when the branch is taken. As soon as the cmpi is executed and the outcome of the branch is known, the conditionally dispatched instructions from the sequential instruction stream are canceled. Instructions from the target stream have also been dispatched and are ready for decoding. Both subtract instructions can execute in the same cycle, even though they are dependent, due to the three input adder (see the section on the FXU below). There is one clock cycle (cycle 7) during which the E stage of the pipe is idle, and the code example takes one cycle longer to execute than when the branch is not taken.   □

We have assumed so far in this discussion that the conditional branch depends on a fixed-point instruction (the most common case) and that there is a single branch. A floating-point CR–updating instruction leads to a longer delay because the floating-point pipeline is longer. In the FPU conditionally dispatched instructions from the sequential stream are held in the rename stage (see Section 6.6 below) until the branch is resolved. Target instructions are dispatched but are not actually latched into the predecode buffers until branch resolution. Then, if the branch is taken, the target instructions are copied into the instruction predecode buffers.

Finally, instruction dispatching blocks when the dispatcher encounters a second branch while the first one is not yet resolved. Two branches can be handled simultaneously only if the first one is a conditional branch known not to be taken. If the first branch is a known-taken conditional branch or an unconditional branch, it changes the instruction flow, and a second branch cannot be executed in the same clock cycle.

6.5   Fixed-Point Unit

As in POWER1, the POWER2 FXU functions as both the integer unit and the load/store unit. Instructions are dispatched from the BU to the FXU at the rate of up to four instructions per clock cycle and held in eight decode buffers at the beginning of the FXU (Figure 6.11).

In the FXU decode stage up to two instructions at a time are removed from the head of the decode queue and issued to the FXU pipelines in program order. If the two instructions are independent, they both issue, read their operand registers, and go to separate execution stages. Dependent instructions, with one important exception, issue sequentially. The exception occurs when there is a sequence of two add instructions, and the first instruction feeds its result to the second:

$$a \quad r1=r3,r4$$
$$a \quad r2=r1,r5$$

The FXU issue logic detects this situation and sends both instructions to execution. The first instruction is executed by a normal two-input adder. The second instruction is executed by a three-input adder that performs the operation $r2 = r3 + r4 + r5$ (Figure 6.12). The two ALUs

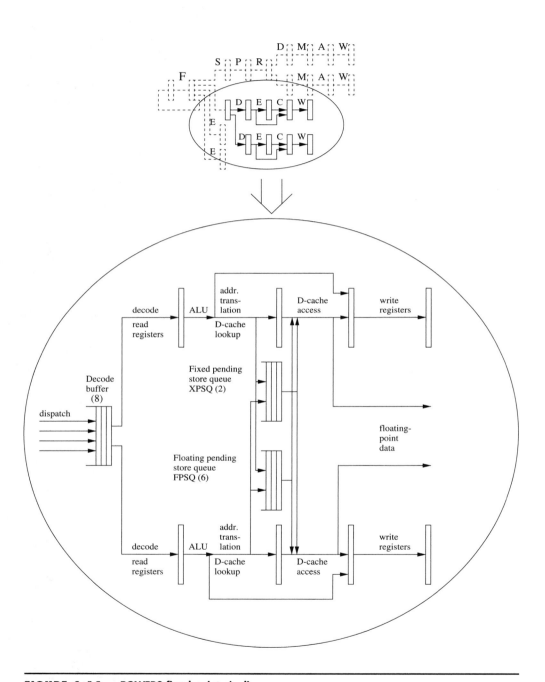

FIGURE 6.11   POWER2 fixed-point pipelines.

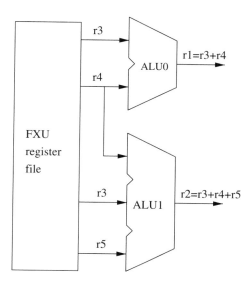

FIGURE 6.12   POWER2 dual ALUs execute dependent instructions.

are also used to compute two effective addresses in parallel, allowing simultaneous execution of two load instructions, both of which can be load-with-update.

The three-input ALU also contains a multiply/divide unit. A 36-by-36 combinational multiplier array executes multiply instructions in two cycles, a significant improvement over the POWER1 three to five–cycle multiplication. In most cases the time for division has also been reduced to 13–14 cycles, down from 19–20 cycles in POWER1.

Up to two load and store instructions pass through the decode and execute stages. During the last portion of the execute stage, the two effective addresses are translated first to virtual and then to real addresses, which requires dual-ported segment registers and a dual-ported data TLB. The cache tag directory is also searched at this time. Finally, during the next cycle, the cache data memories are accessed. In the case of hits, both addresses can be processed in the same cycle. The ability to process more than one memory access per clock period is a key part of the POWER2 implementation that is covered in more detail in Section 6.8.

After passing through one of the execute stages (Figure 6.11), store instructions wait for results in the Floating Pending Store Queue (FPSQ) or in the fiXed Pending Store Queue (XPSQ). Addresses of incoming loads are compared with addresses of stores in the queues; a match indicates that the load must be held until the matching store completes. From the queues, stores can access the cache through either of the two ports. The FPSQ has lower

FPU	Max instructions per cycle	
stage	POWER1	POWER2
Predecode	2	4
Rename	1L or 2A/S	2L (including quad) or 4A/S
Decode	1L and 1A/S	2L and 2A and 2S
Multiply	1	2
Add	1	2
Write	1L and 1A	2L (including quad) and 2A

FIGURE 6.13   **POWER1 and POWER2 maximum instruction processing rate. L is loads, A is arith- metic instructions, and S is stores. Combinations of A, L, and S instructions, not shown in the table, may also be processed in parallel.**

priority than the XPSQ. Stores wait in the FPSQ until data are ready in the SDQ and then transfer the data into the DCU when a bus cycle becomes available.

6.6 Floating-Point Unit

The POWER2 FPU consists of the same six pipeline stages as in POWER1: predecode, rename, decode, multiply, add, and write. However, POWER2 stages have two times the bandwidth (or sometimes even higher). Figure 6.13 gives the maximum numbers; the text below offers more detailed explanations.

Instructions dispatched from the BU, at the rate of up to four instructions per clock cycle, go to eight Instruction Predecode Buffers (IPB) (Figure 6.14). Here the four instructions are predecoded; this information is used for renaming and for synchronization with the FXU, as discussed below. Fixed-point instructions go no farther.

Next, instructions are renamed. The renaming process resembles the one used in POWER1 (see Section 3.5). It maps the 32 logical registers to physical registers to avoid some depen- dences involving instructions that write to the same logical register. The POWER2 renaming implements more physical registers than does that in POWER1 (54 compared with 38) and can process instructions at a higher rate. Up to four arithmetic instructions, four stores, or any combination of these can move through the renaming stage. Loads, however, are limited to two, but both can be quadword loads. Four load target registers (two per quadword load instruction) can exist, four times more than in the POWER1 single-load renaming bandwidth.

After passing through renaming, instructions split up according to their type. Loads go into the Load Instruction Queue (LIQ), arithmetic instructions into the Arithmetic Instruction Queue (AIQ), and stores into the Store Instruction Queue (SIQ). Each queue supplies instruc- tions to two units, adding up to a total of six: two load units, two arithmetic units, and two

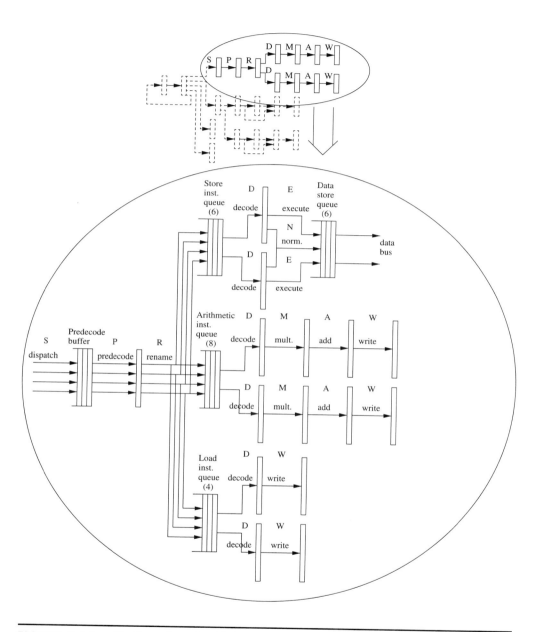

FIGURE 6.14   Floating-point unit with three instruction queues.

store units. These units are free to execute instructions out of program order so register and data dependences among the out-of-order streams must be properly handled.

Dealing with Dependences

To understand the way the various types of dependence conditions are handled, we consider every pair of instruction types that may be reordered as they pass through the FPU: load/store, load/arithmetic, and store/arithmetic.

Although loads and stores may pass one another in the FPU, the same instructions must pass through the FXU in order. Consequently, data dependences involving memory, i.e., loads and stores to the same address, are taken care of in the FXU by matching addresses there. (See the description of the POWER1 Store Address Queue in Section 3.4.) The FXU serializes cache references of loads and stores that have the same address, so there is no need for anything additional in the FPU.

As for loads and arithmetic instructions, the situation is considerably simplified by register renaming. There are three types of dependences that are of concern, often referred to as "output dependences," "anti-dependences," and "true data dependences." In an *output dependence* an instruction writes a register written to by a previous instruction. These register writes must be done in order. For example, register fp1 exhibits an output dependence in the following:

```
fm    fp1 = fp2,fp1
lfd   fp1 = a
```

In an *anti-dependence* a register is written after a previous instruction reads it. The register must be read before it is written. Register fp1 exhibits an output dependence in the following:

```
fm    fp0 = fp2,fp1
lfd   fp1 = a
```

A *true data dependence* involves reading a register written by a previous instruction. Clearly the read must follow the write for correct operation. For example, fp1 is the object of a true data dependence in the following:

```
lfd   fp1 = a
fm    fp0 = fp2,fp1
```

The case of a read followed by a read poses no problem, because the reads may be done in any order.

Because loads and arithmetic instructions execute from different queues and can pass one another, all three of the above dependences must be handled correctly. Output and anti-dependences are eliminated by register renaming. Recall that register renaming is done while the instructions are still in program order, and in the renaming stage each load instruction is assigned a fresh register from the register pool. With register renaming, instructions that originally have output and anti-dependences become free to pass one another.

True data dependences reflect situations in which instructions simply cannot be allowed to pass one another because one produces data used by the other. Interlock logic that blocks the dependent instruction in the Arithmetic Instruction Queue until the preceding register load is finished takes care of this problem.

Because stores do not write registers, there are only two dependence conditions that can affect arithmetic and store instructions: true data dependences and anti-dependences. In the case of a true data dependence, the floating-point instruction must produce a result before the store unit attempts to store it. In the case of an anti-dependence, the floating-point unit must not overwrite a result register that is waiting to be stored. The remainder of this subsection describes a mechanism that takes care of these situations.

Eight store counters (SC) are associated with the eight entries of the AIQ (Figure 6.15). Specifically, counter SCi contains the count of pending stores that are ahead (in the program order) of the arithmetic instruction in AIQ entry AQi. Here we discuss how these counters are maintained.

When an arithmetic instruction is entered into the AIQ (say AQi), its corresponding store count is computed in the following way. The current number of pending stores (i.e., stores in the SIQ) is added to the number of stores ahead of the arithmetic instruction in the rename stage. From this, the number of stores that execute in this cycle (i.e., leave the SIQ) is subtracted. The result is entered into SCi. When a store instruction is removed from the SIQ (to execution), all nonzero counters are decremented.

The store counters are used by the issue logic to determine when it is safe to issue store and arithmetic instructions. There are no stores ahead of an arithmetic instruction in AQ0 if SC0 = 0, and the instruction is free to issue. If SC0 = i, and $i > 0$, then the instruction's target register designator must be compared with the source registers of the stores in the first i entries of the SIQ. If there is a match, the instruction cannot issue because it would overwrite the source register of a previous store (i.e., there is an anti-dependence). Similar logic handles the arithmetic instruction in AQ1.

If all the store counters are nonzero, a store instruction to be issued in entry SQ0 of the SIQ precedes all arithmetic instructions in the AIQ and can be allowed to execute. Otherwise, its source register designator must be compared with the target registers of all the arithmetic instructions whose store counters are zero. If there is a match, the store cannot issue, because the instruction that produces the result to be stored has not executed yet (i.e., there is a true data dependence).

The same store counters, but different issue logic, are used for the store in SQ1. This store can issue if all store counters are larger than or equal to two, which indicates that at least two store instructions are ahead of all arithmetic instructions in the AIQ. Otherwise, its source register designator is compared with the target registers of all the arithmetic instructions in the AIQ whose store counters are either zero or one. Zero indicates that the arithmetic instruction is ahead of both stores in SQ0 and SQ1. A count of one means that the arithmetic instruction is behind the store in SQ0 but ahead of the store in SQ1. Again, if there is a match, the store cannot issue.

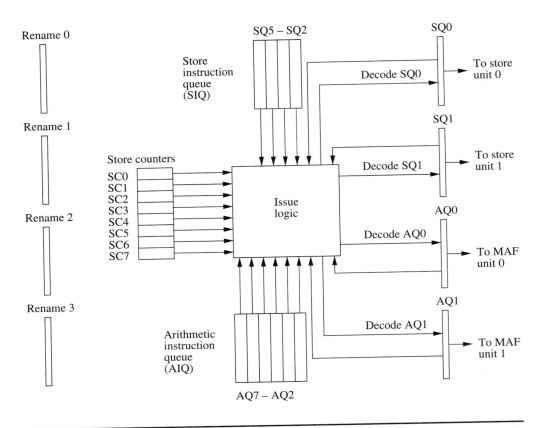

FIGURE 6.15   Using store counters to issue arithmetic and store instructions. Only control paths are shown (no data paths). The AIQ's first two entries, AQ0 and AQ1, function as the decode latches of the arithmetic pipelines, and the SIQ's first two entries, SQ0 and SQ1, are the decode latches of the store units.

Example

To illustrate the use of the store counters to resolve dependences involving AQ and SQ instructions, consider a compilation of the loop in Figure 6.3(a). To make the example more interesting, we used doubleword loads and stores and have unrolled the loop twice. An excerpt of the compiled loop appears in Figure 6.16(a). Figure 6.16(b) shows the contents of the AQ, SQ, and SCi during two consecutive clock periods while the loop executes (these are labeled time = 0 and time = 1). Dashed arrows show the association of the fma instructions and stfdu

LOOP: lfd   fp0 = b(r3,4104)   # load b floating double
　．　　　　．
　．　　　　．
　．　　　　．
　　　　　　fma   fp6 = fp4,fp0,fp2   # floating multiply-add
　　　　　　fma   fp7 = fp5,fp1,fp3   # floating multiply-add
　　　　　　stfdu   x(r3=r3+8) = fp6   # store floating double with update
　　　　　　stfdu   x(r3=r3+8) = fp7   # store floating double with update
　　　　　　bc   LOOP,CTR≠0   # decrement CTR; branch if CTR ≠ 0

(a) Code excerpt of compilation for loop in Figure 6.3(a).

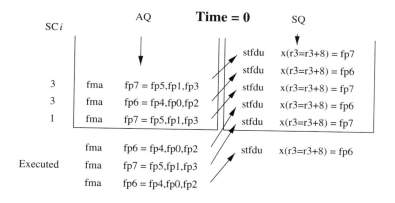

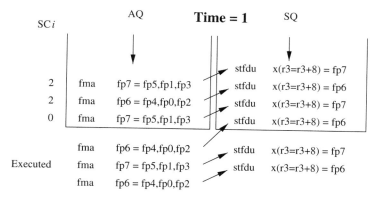

(b) AQ and SQ contents during execution of the loop.

FIGURE 6.16   **Example of store counters resolving dependences among AQ and SQ instructions.**

instructions. That is, the fma produces the result stored by the stfdu to which the arrow points.

To keep things simple, let's first assume that there is a single store unit and a single MAF unit. First consider the fma at the head of the AQ (i.e., in position AQ0). At time = 0, SC0 = 1, so the fma can issue only if its target register does not match the source register of the store in the first (because SC0 = 1) position of the SQ. It does match, so the fma cannot issue. Thus, the fma cannot overwrite the value in fp7 before it is stored. Because all the store counters are nonzero, the stfdu at the head of the SQ can issue safely; it must logically precede all the instructions in the AQ.

At time = 1, the store has issued, and the SCi have all decremented. Now, the fma in AQ0 is safe to issue because SC0 = 0. Turning to the SQ, because SC0 is zero the stfdu at the head of the SQ can issue only if its source register does not match the target register of any AQ instruction whose store counter is zero. The only AQ instruction whose SC value is zero is in AQ0. The registers do not match, so the stfdu in SQ0 is also able to safely issue.

Now, when there are two store units and two MAF units, as in POWER2, the first store will issue during time = 0, as explained above. Moreover, the second store can also issue at this time because the source register of the store in SQ1 does not match the only fma instruction (in AQ0) whose SC value is zero or one. Then, at time = 1, the first two fma instructions can issue: the first because SC0 = 0 and the second because its target register does not match the source register of the first store in the SQ.

Dual MAF Units

From the decode latches AQ0 and AQ1 instructions issue to the multiply-add (fused) units MAF0 and MAF1, respectively (Figure 6.17). The effectiveness of the dual arithmetic pipelines would be somewhat limited if dependences held up both pipes. Of particular concern are multicycle instructions, such as divide or square root. Consider the following example.

```
fsqrt    fp0 = fp1
fm       fp0 = fp0,fp3
fa       fp4 = fp4,fp2
```

Unless special steps are taken, both MAF units could be simultaneously blocked for many clock cycles: one with the fsqrt and the other with the dependent fm. To solve this problem, each MAF unit has a backup register (BRi) that is used to hold multiple cycle instructions while they execute. With the backup registers, the fsqrt in the above example executes from BR0. The fm is held in AQ0, where it remains for the duration of the execution of the fsqrt. The fa, which is independent of the previous two instructions, can issue from AQ1 to MAF1 and execute out of program order. Other instructions following the fa are also free to execute in MAF1, providing no other dependence conditions inhibit them.

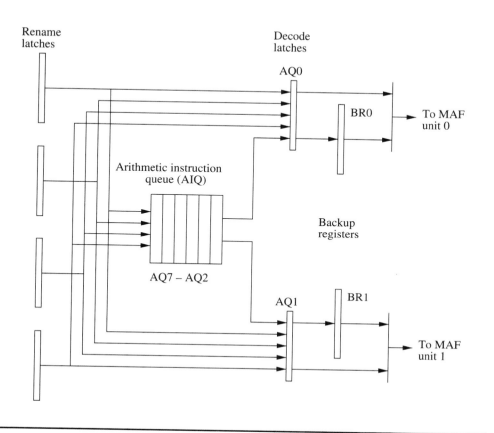

FIGURE 6.17   Arithmetic Instruction Queue with backup registers.

Bypasses

As shown in Figure 6.18, bypass paths connect the outputs of MAF0 and MAF1 to the B and C inputs of both pipelines. The bypass path to B feeds the result after rounding. The path to C is taken from the pipeline output before rounding; to save time, rounding is done in the multiplier itself (discussed in Section 3.5).

As long as data dependences are handled through the B and C inputs, the pipes appear to have a two-cycle latency only; there is a single-cycle delay between dependent instructions (with the exception of divide and square root, of course, which take multiple cycles). The pipeline interlock logic compares the source register designators of instructions that are about to issue from the instruction queue with the target registers of instructions whose execution is

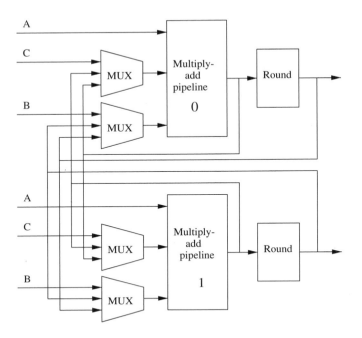

FIGURE 6.18   Bypasses in the MAF units.

in progress. If there is a match, the control inputs of the multiplexers are set to receive data from the bypass paths. The data must be a normalized number. Infinity, NaN (Not a Number, see Appendix A), denormalized numbers, and zero are handled as special values and cannot use the bypass paths.

In addition to the MAF bypasses, the register file is write-through, and a result is available for reading in the same cycle as it is written. The register file has ten 64-bit read ports and six 64-bit write ports (Figure 6.19). The ten read ports allow two multiply-add instructions (each of which requires three input operands) and two quadword stores to decode and read registers simultaneously. The six write ports allow two quadword loads and two arithmetic instructions to write results in the same clock cycle. The actual implementation consists of two five-read, six-write register files, both written at the same time and always containing the same data.

	MAF unit 0	MAF unit 1	Load unit 0	Load unit 1	Store unit 0	Store unit 1	Total
Read ports	3	3			2	2	10
Write ports	1	1	2	2			6

FIGURE 6.19   **Floating-point register file ports.**

Load Instruction Processing

Figure 6.20 shows the processing of a load instruction in the FXU and FPU, assuming the two units proceed without blocking. At time 1, the FXU decodes the instruction, and the FPU predecodes it. At time 2, the FXU computes the effective, virtual, and real addresses (see Section 6.8), and it searches the data cache directory; the FPU renames the instruction. Next, at time 3, the cache is accessed. At time 4, the data arrive from the cache and are loaded into a temporary register (the load register) in the FPU. At the same time the data are bypassed to the inputs of the multiply-add pipelines and are available for arithmetic instructions. In the next clock cycle, the operand is moved into the load destination register.

Only one pipeline is shown in the figure, but POWER2 can perform this entire process for two floating-point loads simultaneously. The two cache ports are associated with the two FXU execution pipelines. If a cache port becomes blocked due to a miss, it blocks the corresponding FXU pipe for memory instructions; arithmetic instructions can continue as long as they do not depend on the blocked instruction. Meanwhile, the second cache port and the second FXU pipe can keep instructions flowing. Consequently, the cache does not become fully blocked until there are two outstanding misses.

Store Instruction Processing

In the first two clock cycles, the processing of store instructions is identical to that of load instructions (Figure 6.20). After that, in the FXU the store is shunted off to a Floating Pending Store Queue (FPSQ) to wait for data from the FPU. In the FPU the store goes into the SIQ. The store reads its data, when it becomes available, from its source floating register. This read can occur in the write cycle of the arithmetic instruction that produced the data because the register file is write through.

Then stores may pass through a normalize/denormalize unit. This pass is necessary if a store double is performed on single-precision data, or a store single on a double-precision number. The first case can occur if a floating round to single (frsp) instruction, which rounds and normalizes the data in a register to single-precision format, was performed prior to storing the data with a double precision store. The sequence does not make much practical sense, but must be handled nevertheless. The second case can occur if a store single

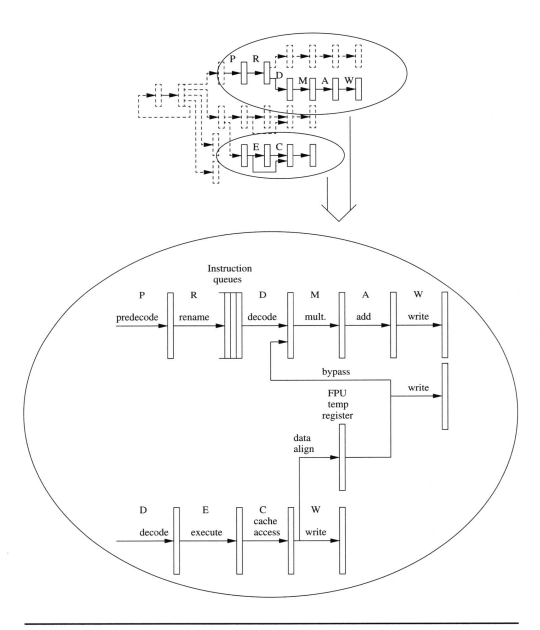

FIGURE 6.20   Processing a floating-point load instruction.

is performed (on double-precision data) without first executing a `frsp` instruction. Because both cases are considered unusual, the two store units share a single normalize/denormalize unit.

If there is no need to perform normalization/denormalization, the store's source operand is transferred into the Data Store Queue. Control information is passed to the FXU indicating that the data are available. The final phase of the store, the access of the data cache, is again controlled by the FXU and takes place when there is an available cache cycle.

FPU and FXU Synchronization

POWER2 and POWER1 handle interrupts in similar ways (see Section 4.5 for a description of the POWER interrupt structure and interrupts in POWER1). As in POWER1, floating exceptions in POWER2 do not trap in the normal mode of operation. A bit MSR(FE) in the Machine State Register intended for debugging can be turned on to provide precise floating interrupts by running the FPU in a much slower serial mode. Support also exists at the compiler level in the form of a compiler option that inserts test code and software interrupts after floating arithmetic instructions. And POWER2 introduces floating imprecise interrupts that are supported in hardware while the machine runs programs in the normal high-performance mode of operation.

Two types of instructions can lead to interrupts in the FXU: memory instructions and software interrupts. FXU interrupts are always precise. The implementation is based on a concept similar to that in POWER1: the FPU is not allowed to execute past an interruptible FXU instruction. However, the FXU in POWER2 has more freedom to run ahead of the FPU than it does in POWER1. The synchronization hardware lets the FPU run at full speed as long as the FXU is ahead (which is often the case because of the shorter FXU pipe and because floating-point instructions often depend on loads executed in the FXU). If the FXU gets behind, synchronization will occur when the FPU encounters an interruptible FXU instruction, and the FPU is forced to wait for the FXU instruction to be known error-free.

6.7   Instruction Cache

Figure 6.21 shows the organization of an instruction cache in POWER2. There are two lines per set (a 2-way set associative cache). A line holds 32 fixed-length 32-bit instructions, numbered in the figure from 0 to 31.

The bandwidth demands on the POWER2 instruction cache are very high. Up to eight instructions can be fetched per clock cycle. The fetch rate is actually higher than the rate at which instructions are processed in the pipelines because some instructions are conditionally dispatched and later canceled. Branches are frequent, and instructions have to be dispatched from the branch target address, which can be anywhere in the middle of a cache line. The POWER2 instruction cache is designed to sustain a fetch rate of eight instructions per clock

(a) Instruction cache structure.

Set number	Tag	Array number								Tag	Array number							
		0	1	2	3	4	5	6	7		0	1	2	3	4	5	6	7
0		0	1	2	3	4	5	6	7		0	1	2	3	4	5	6	7
		8	9	10	11	12	13	14	15		8	9	10	11	12	13	14	15
		16	17	18	19	20	21	22	23		16	17	18	19	20	21	22	23
		24	25	26	27	28	29	30	31		24	25	26	27	28	29	30	31
1		0	1	2	3	4	5	6	7		0	1	2	3	4	5	6	7
		8	9	10	11	12	13	14	15		8	9	10	11	12	13	14	15
		16	17	18	19	20	21	22	23		16	17	18	19	20	21	22	23
		24	25	26	27	28	29	30	31		24	25	26	27	28	29	30	31
⋮	⋮																	
127		0	1	2	3	4	5	6	7		0	1	2	3	4	5	6	7
		8	9	10	11	12	13	14	15		8	9	10	11	12	13	14	15
		16	17	18	19	20	21	22	23		16	17	18	19	20	21	22	23
		24	25	26	27	28	29	30	31		24	25	26	27	28	29	30	31

(b) Cache arrays. The numbers 0–31 represent the instructions in one cache line.

FIGURE 6.21   POWER2 instruction cache.

FIGURE 6.22   RS/6000–590 data cache structure.

cycle, regardless of where in a cache line the string of eight instructions begins. If there are fewer than eight instructions until the end of the line, the next line is also accessed in the same clock cycle (as long as the next line is not in a different page).

The physical structure of a line resembles a matrix with eight columns, called *arrays*, and four *rows*. Each of the four cache arrays is a single-port memory that can supply one instruction per cycle, adding up to a maximum fetch rate of eight instructions per cycle over all eight arrays.

The detailed operation of the POWER1 instruction cache is described in Section 5.3. The POWER2 instruction cache works in a similar way, with the exception that eight (instead of four) instructions are fetched from eight cache arrays.

6.8 Data Cache

POWER2, as used in the RS/6000–590, has a 256 Kbyte, 4-way set associative data cache (D-cache) with 256 byte lines. Figure 6.22 illustrates the data cache organization. The storage part of the data cache is physically located on the four DCU chips. Its directory, however, which consists of tags and other management information (LRU bits, dirty bits, valid bits), is on the FXU. The D-TLB, as well as the segment registers, is also located on the FXU.

In addition to the cache arrays, the error checking and correction (ECC) hardware is also located on the DCU chips (see Chapter 10 for details on the ECC). This ECC logic is shared for transfers between memory and I-cache, memory and D-cache, and memory and I/O devices using the System I/O (SIO) bus. Figure 6.23 shows the paths that connect the DCU to the FPU, FXU, memory, I-cache, and System I/O.

Data Cache Lookup and Access

To access the cache, the set number field is taken directly from the effective address. These bits are identical in the effective and virtual addresses, since the virtual address is obtained by concatenating the 28 rightmost bits of the effective address with the 24-bit segment ID.

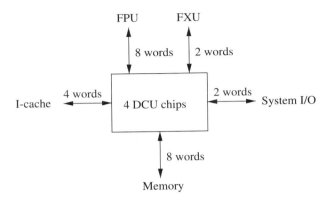

FIGURE 6.23　　**DCU data paths. A word is four bytes.**

	POWER1				POWER2			
	Associativity	Sets	Bytes/line	Size	Associativity	Sets	Bytes/line	Size
I–cache	2-way	64	64	8 KB	2-way	128	128	32 KB
D–cache	4-way	128	128	64 KB	4-way	256	256	256 KB

(a) Caches.

	POWER1			POWER2		
	Associativity	Entries	Ports	Associativity	Entries	Ports
I-TLB	2-way	32	1	2-way	128	1
D-TLB	2-way	128	1	2-way	512	2

(b) TLBs.

FIGURE 6.24　　**POWER1 (RS/6000-560) and POWER2 (RS/6000-590) caches and TLBs.**

POWER2 implements two TLBs (Figure 6.24), one for instructions (I-TLB) located on the ICU, and one for data (D-TLB) located on the FXU. The I-TLB is a 2-way set associative cache with 64 sets for a total of 128 entries. The D-TLB is also 2-way associative but larger, 256 sets and 512 entries. Since each entry translates the virtual page number of one page, and the machine has 4 Kbyte pages, the D-TLB contains translation information for 2 Mbytes of physical memory.

For the purpose of accessing the D-TLB, the 40-bit virtual page number is interpreted as

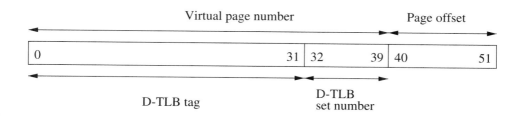

FIGURE 6.25 D-TLB tag and set number fields from the virtual page number.

shown in Figure 6.25. (See also Figure 2.25 for the POWER virtual address scheme.) The 8-bit set number is used to select one of 256 sets. The tags in the two entries of the selected set are compared with the tag field from the virtual page number. If there is a match, the corresponding real page number is returned, otherwise a D-TLB miss is signaled.

The virtual address generation, translation, and D-cache directory lookup are shown in Figure 6.26). The following three operations overlap.

1. To generate the virtual address, a segment register is selected using bits 0–3 from the effective address. The least significant 24 bits from the segment register are concatenated with bits 4–11 of the effective address to form the D-TLB tag.

2. The D-TLB is accessed using bits 12–19 of the effective address to select the D-TLB set.

3. The D-cache directory is accessed using bits 16–23 of the effective address to select the D-cache set.

Next, two comparisons are performed.

1. The D-TLB is a 2-way set associative cache and the selected set has two entries, each with its own tag. These two tags have to be compared with the D-TLB tag from the virtual address to determine whether the D-TLB access is a miss or a hit. If it is a hit, the Real Page Number (RPN) corresponding to the matching tag is obtained from the D-TLB.

2. The D-cache is a 4-way set associative cache and the selected set has four lines, each with its own tag. The four tags have to be compared with the D-cache tag from the RPN to determine whether the D-cache access is a miss or a hit.

These two operations can be overlapped, however, as shown in Figure 6.26, by comparing the tags of both RPNs with the D-cache tags. Two matches may result and the correct one is

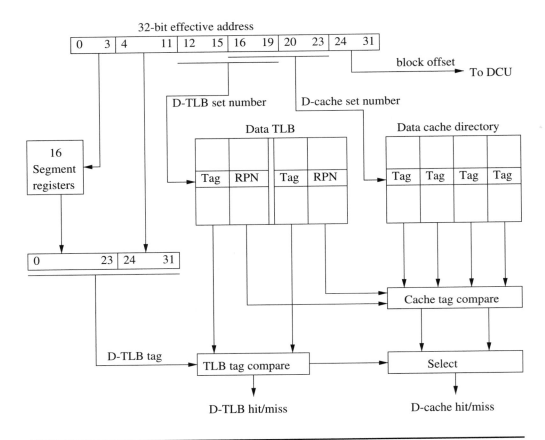

FIGURE 6.26   Virtual address generation, translation, and D-cache directory lookup for a single effective address. In POWER2 this operation is performed on two effective addresses in parallel.

selected after the D-TLB tag comparison is finished. Finally, a D-TLB miss always leads to a D-cache miss since no RPN is available to perform the D-cache lookup.

Dual-Ported Caches

We have described above the D-cache lookup of a single address. However, POWER2 is designed to execute two memory instructions in tandem, requiring dual-ported D-TLBs, dual-ported D-cache directory, and comparators to match the tags of two lookups in parallel.

   The cache arrays on the DCU chips are actually single ported (a wide 128-bit port, see Figure 6.23). They are implemented using SRAMs that are fast enough to be accessed two times in a clock cycle for loads and stores. Furthermore, toward the end of the clock cycle, a third access can be made for filling the cache from main memory. This technique emulates a dual-ported cache that supports two load/stores per clock cycle. Any combination of memory instructions (two loads, two stores, or one load and one store) is allowed.

   To understand the significance of this type of cache design, compare it with some alternatives (Figure 6.27). One alternative is to use dual-ported RAM cells (Figure 6.27(a)). With this alternative, the RAM cells are more complex and larger, consuming more chip real estate. Also, some provisions must be made for a store followed by a load to the same location. Such an event must be handled in the cache access logic because conflict is typically not known until after the effective addresses have been formed. Although solvable, this problem does add to the complexity of the cache design.

   Another alternative is to use an interleaved cache (Figure 6.27(b)), in which one bank handles even addresses and the other handles odds. This alternative adds no chip real estate and can handle loads and stores to the same address, but in the process it adds some significant complications to the cache access logic. Addresses must be sorted according to a low-order address bit and must be steered to the correct bank. If two addresses want to simultaneously access the same bank, one must be held up and buffered for a cycle. Memory ordering problems may also occur if the addressing stream for one bank is allowed to get ahead of the other bank.

   The alternative used in POWER2 (Figure 6.27(c)). solves most of the above problems. The box marked with the delta symbolizes a delay, necessary to operate the cache in phases (this can be accomplished by switching the mux partway through the clock cycle). Real estate for the RAM is not increased because the RAM cells remain single ported. Because the cache is really accessed sequentially, any pair of loads and stores can be accommodated. In theory, if a load follows a store, the store is completed first, then the load accesses the stored data. In the POWER2 implementation, however, tight timing paths require a modification that partially offsets this advantage. Because a store requires more time in the RAM than does a load, doing the store first does not leave quite enough time for the following load data to pass from the DCU chip to the FXU or FPU chip. So when a store is followed by a load, the cache controller swaps them so that the load gets done first. Bypass logic must exist for the case in which the load and store are to the same address.

   Implementing a multiple-ported cache by using multiple cycles is a reasonable solution if the cache is fast enough to allow it. Many other RISCs with higher clock rates simply cannot access their caches more than once in the same clock period. When considering it from this perspective, we see that a disadvantage of the POWER2 method is that any particular load operation has extra latency added because it takes a full clock period to do a fraction of a clock period's worth of work.

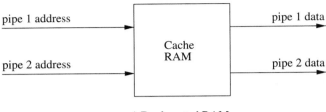

a) Dual-ported RAM.

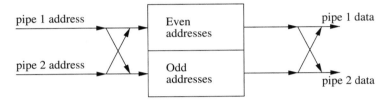

b) Interleaved cache.

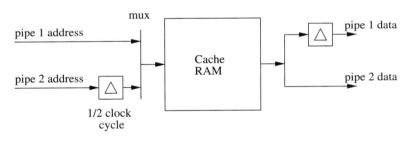

c) Time-shared, sequential access cache.

FIGURE 6.27   **Methods for implementing dual-ported caches.**

6.9 Summary

POWER2 is a worthy successor to the successful POWER1, providing significant performance improvements while employing many of the same principles. High performance is a major goal, but not through clock period alone. In fact, there is not much difference in clock period between the first POWER2 (71.5 MHz) and the last POWER1 (62.5 MHz). Essentially, all the instruction pipelines are doubled. A total of up to six instructions per clock period can be dispatched—a new high for RISC processors.

To support balanced instruction processing at these rates, several innovations were required. The instruction fetch unit with its ability to fetch eight instructions and decode ten every cycle is much more powerful than any contemporary RISC. The coupled integer ALUs allow the processing of dependent integer adds in about the same time as a single add would take. The dual-ported cache allows any combination of two loads and stores to be executed every cycle. Besides the dual-ported cache, another feature for enhancing memory bandwidth, quad floating loads and stores, allows another doubling of effective memory bandwidth for many floating-point applications. Finally, there is enhanced flexibility in instruction issuing in the floating-point unit, leading to more opportunities for out-of-order instruction execution and fewer pipeline blockages due to dependences.

6.10   References

Because it is so new, POWER2 has relatively few references. A good summary can be found in [29]. As it usually does with major new products, IBM is planning to publish an issue of its *Journal of Research and Development* dedicated to POWER2 and the new RS/6000 products. As of this writing, it is not yet available.

A discussion of dual ALUs similar to those used in POWER2 can be found in [55]. Processors using other approaches for dual-ported caches are the Intel Pentium [3] and SGI TFP [30], both of which chose to implement an interleaved structure. Like POWER2, TFP implements dual multiply-add pipelines.

POWERPC ARCHITECTURE

7.1 Introduction

The development of the PowerPC architecture followed that of the POWER architecture by a few years. PowerPC was developed for a broader range of implementations and had the benefit of the experience gained implementing the RS/6000 series of workstations. Consequently, relative to POWER, the PowerPC architecture was developed with three goals in mind.

1. *Simplification* reduces hardware requirements and implementation complexity. A smaller processor implementation leads to a smaller chip, important in very low cost systems, or leaves additional chip area that can be used for larger cache memories and system hardware (such as bus interface logic). Another consideration in simplifying the architecture is performance. For example, a few seldom-used POWER instructions required extra hardware in the integer data path that lengthened the clock cycle. As another example, integer multiply and divide instructions in POWER shared the same resource, the MQ Register, leading to a potential bottleneck in high-performance implementations.

2. *Extension* allows a broader range of products to be supported. Extensions include optional 64-bit addressing, single-precision floating instructions, and multiprocessor support. In some cases new instructions had to be provided to replace POWER instructions removed to simplify the hardware.

3. *Compatibility* with the POWER architecture allows previously developed POWER software to run on either type of processor. The opcodes of removed instructions were defined as *reserved* rather than being reused for new instructions, so that implementations of the combined POWER and PowerPC instruction sets are feasible. PowerPC implementations can remain compatible with the POWER architecture by trapping on the unimplemented opcodes and emulating the missing POWER instructions in software.

The 64-bit extensions and 32-bit compatibility are both accommodated through the definition of 32- and 64-bit versions of PowerPC. Implementations are allowed to have 32-bit addressing only, but 64-bit machines must also have a 32-bit mode, allowing 64-bit machines to run 32-bit code. The mode is selected via a bit in the Machine State Register. The relationship between the POWER and PowerPC instruction sets is illustrated in Figure 1.18.

Although POWER and PowerPC have a lot in common, we have decided to describe them separately; attempting to describe both at once is unnecessarily confusing. So, we have two architecture chapters, one on POWER and one on PowerPC. Naturally, there is some overlap between the two chapters, some portions are identical, in fact. With this organization, a reader interested in the PowerPC only will find a description of the key components of the instruction set architecture and the memory model in the first few sections of this chapter. This part of the chapter is self-contained and requires no knowledge of POWER. Sections 7.6 and 7.7 go beyond "just the facts" into some of the considerations and trade-offs that shaped the PowerPC instruction set architecture.

A PowerPC microprocessor (Figure 7.1) consists of three entities, the Fixed-Point Unit, Branch Unit, and Floating-Point Unit (abbreviated FXU, BU, and FPU). This functional partitioning applies to architectural registers and to instructions, and its goal is to increase overlap by reducing interlocks and resource sharing among the units. It suggests a "natural" way to split the instruction stream into three threads according to instruction types.

Figure 7.2 contains notation that will be useful in understanding instruction descriptions that follow.

Instruction Formats

Figure 7.3 and Figure 7.4 illustrate the instruction fields and formats used by most instructions. As with typical RISC architectures, the instructions are all 32 bits long and have their fields similarly aligned across all the formats. This simplifies instruction fetching and decoding. The primary opcode fields (OPCD) are all 6 bits. Some of the instructions have extended opcodes (EO, EO′, and XO) because the primary opcode field is not sufficient to encode the entire instruction set. Besides the opcode fields, another important piece of control information

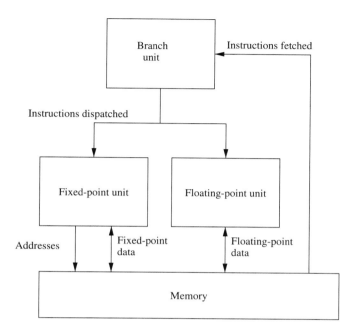

FIGURE 7.1   **PowerPC logical view.**

Notation	Meaning
Rn, FRn	Register Rn, FRn, where n is A, B, C, S, T
(Rn), (FRn)	Contents of register Rn, FRn, where n is A, B, C, S, T
R_i	Bit i of register R, where R is LR, CTR, CR, XER
R_{i-j}	Bits i–j of register R, where R is LR, CTR, CR, XER
//	Unused bits in an instruction.
||	Concatenation
Doubleword	8 bytes
Word	4 bytes
Halfword	2 bytes

FIGURE 7.2   **Notation and terms used to describe instructions. The unused bits must be zero.**

RT	Target register	FRT	Floating target register
RA, RB, RS	Source registers	FRA, FRB, FRC, FRS	Floating source registers
D, DS	Displacement	SI,UI	Signed/Unsigned immediate
EO, XO, EO′	Extended opcode	OE	Overflow enable
MB, mb	Mask begin	ME, me	Mask end
SH, sh	Shift amount	Rc	Record bit

(a) Instruction fields.

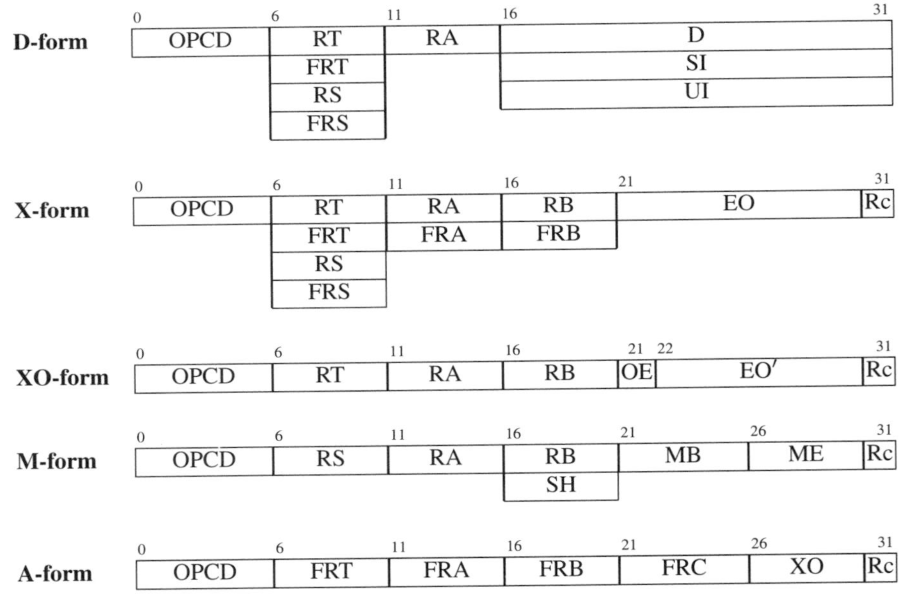

(b) Instruction formats.

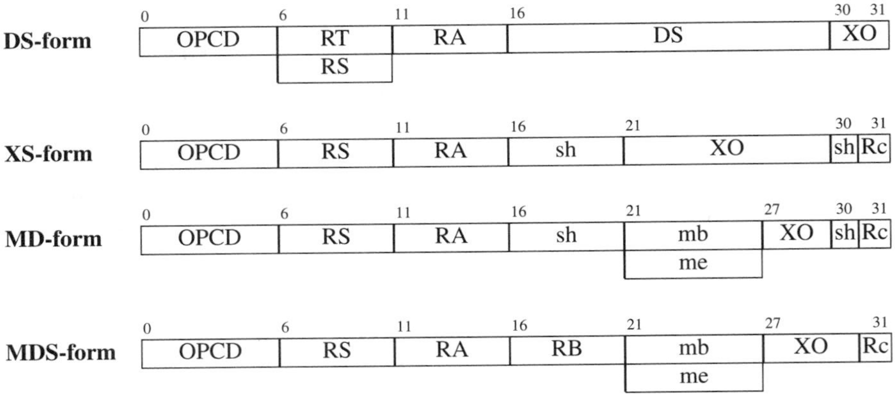

(c) 64-bit-only instruction formats.

FIGURE 7.3   Most PowerPC instructions use one of these instruction formats.

OPCD   Opcode
LI   Long immediate
BO   Branch options
BI   Bit in the CR
BD   Branch displacement
EO   Extended opcode
AA   Absolute address
LK   Link

(a) Instruction fields.

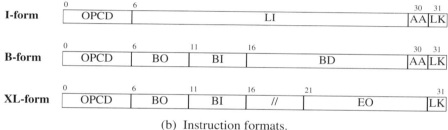

(b) Instruction formats.

FIGURE 7.4   **PowerPC branch instruction fields and formats.**

contained in many instructions is the Record bit (Rc). This bit causes the Condition Register, held in the Branch Unit, to be updated depending on the result of the instruction, for example if the result is positive or negative.

The register fields are typically aligned across all formats. Source registers are read by the instructions and provide operand data or addresses used as input information by instructions. Target registers receive the results of instructions or data loaded from memory. There are also a number of instruction fields that provide immediate data and address offset values.

Load and store instructions use either the D-form or X-form, which differ in the way the effective address is formed. In D-form instructions the address is computed by adding a displacement to the contents of a register (RA) + D, and in the X-form the address is computed by adding the contents of two registers (RA) + (RB). In traditional IBM terminology, RA is the base register and RB is the index register (the X in X-form stands for indeX). These two formats are also used in many arithmetic, logical, and shift instructions.

The XO-form used by some integer arithmetic instructions is a variant of the X-form with an overflow enable bit OE (the *O* in XO-form refers to the OE bit) and an extended opcode EO′ made one bit shorter than EO to make space for the OE bit. A typical use of OE is in extended-precision arithmetic to disable the setting of the overflow bits in a special purpose exception register held in the Fixed-Point Unit.

The M-form is used by a set of integer rotate-with-mask instructions. The rotate amount is specified by a register RB or an immediate field SH. The mask is defined by the MB and ME fields (the details will be described later in Section 7.2).

The A-form has four register fields and is used by the four-operand floating multiply-add instruction. To simplify instruction decoding, it is also used by other floating arithmetic instructions that have only three register operands (in which case one of the four register fields is, obviously, unused).

The Branch instruction forms include an unconditional branch (I-form) and two similar conditional branch forms (B-form and XL-form). The B-form specifies a branch displacement, and the XL-form gets its branch target from one of the Branch Unit registers.

64-bit Instruction Formats

Figure 7.3(c) shows that 64-bit PowerPCs have a few more instruction formats. Three of these (XS, MD, and MDS) were necessary because a 6-bit instead of 5-bit field is needed to specify the shift amount or the beginning and end of a mask in a 64-bit register. The 5-bit fields are labeled SH, MB, and ME, the 6-bit fields are labeled sh, mb, and me. In MD-form the sh field is split.

Since the 6-bit mb and me fields do not fit in the fixed-length 32-bit instruction, MD- and MDS-form instructions contain either an mb or me field, but not both. In instructions that have an mb field, the mask is a sequence of ones beginning at position mb and ending at position 63. In instructions that have an me field, the mask is a sequence of ones beginning at position 0 and ending at position me.

7.2   Fixed-Point Unit

The Fixed-Point Unit (FXU) is responsible for the integer operations and all the memory operations (both integer and floating point). The architectural state belonging to the FXU consists of a set of 32 integer registers and several special-purpose registers. The FXU instruction set contains the vast majority of the instructions that make up the PowerPC architecture.

Fixed-Point Unit Registers

The register set used by the FXU is shown in Figure 7.5. The 32 integer registers (r0–r31) are used for both integer computations and address computations. In most RISCs integer register 0 always has a zero value, which leaves the register file with 31 usable registers. In

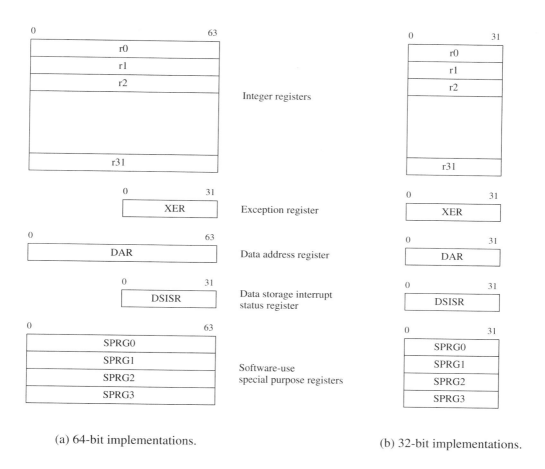

(a) 64-bit implementations.   (b) 32-bit implementations.

FIGURE 7.5   Fixed-Point Unit register set.

PowerPC, however, a value of zero is used if the RA register designator is zero in a load or store instruction. Otherwise, r0 may be used as any other integer register.

The Data Address Register (DAR) and Data Storage Interrupt Status Register (DSISR) are used by the operating system to resolve interrupts caused by memory references. For example, in case of an access attempt that violates memory protection, the DAR will contain the memory address that caused the interrupt.

The Exception Register (XER) holds a number of individually named fields that record exception information and provide additional operand information used by some of the character

Bit	Description
0	**SO** (Summary Overflow) Set to 1 to indicate overflow. Remains 1 until reset by software.
1	**OV** (Overflow) Set to 1 to indicate overflow. Reset to 0 by next instruction if there is no overflow.
2	**CA** (Carry) Set to 1 to indicate a carry out from the result.
3–24	Reserved
25–31	Specify the string length (number of bytes) Used by `load string word indexed` (`lswx`) and `store string word indexed` (`stswx`) instructions.

FIGURE 7.6   **Bits in the XER register.**

string instructions. The fields of the XER are shown in Figure 7.6. The overflow, summary overflow, and carry bits are used by integer arithmetic operations, and an 8-bit field is used in two of the string instructions to specify the string length in bytes.

Load and Store Instructions

The FXU contains a set of load and store instructions used to access both memory and input/output devices (see Figure 7.7 and Figure 7.8). Four primary attributes characterize the different types of load instructions (only the first three apply to stores).

1. *Access granularity:* For integer loads and stores, the granularities are byte, 2 bytes (halfword), 4 bytes (word), and, in 64-bit PowerPC, 8 bytes (doubleword). For floating point, single-precision numbers (32 bits) or double-precision numbers (64 bits) may be accessed.

2. *Addressing mode:* There are two addressing modes. One adds the contents of a register and a displacement value held in the instruction to arrive at the address (D-form). The other adds the contents of two registers (X-form).

3. *Update mode:* The update versions of instructions automatically modify the index register RA by replacing its contents with the newly computed effective address. If RA is also the target of the load, or RA = 0, the instruction is invalid. Implementations are not required to check at runtime that the instruction is valid, the compiler must produce correct code.

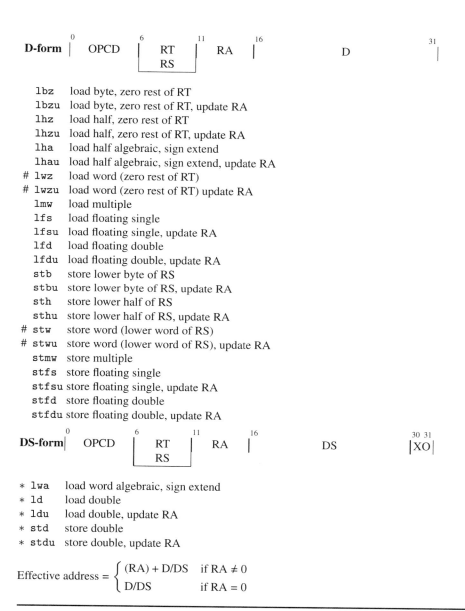

D-form

lbz	load byte, zero rest of RT
lbzu	load byte, zero rest of RT, update RA
lhz	load half, zero rest of RT
lhzu	load half, zero rest of RT, update RA
lha	load half algebraic, sign extend
lhau	load half algebraic, sign extend, update RA
# lwz	load word (zero rest of RT)
# lwzu	load word (zero rest of RT) update RA
lmw	load multiple
lfs	load floating single
lfsu	load floating single, update RA
lfd	load floating double
lfdu	load floating double, update RA
stb	store lower byte of RS
stbu	store lower byte of RS, update RA
sth	store lower half of RS
sthu	store lower half of RS, update RA
# stw	store word (lower word of RS)
# stwu	store word (lower word of RS), update RA
stmw	store multiple
stfs	store floating single
stfsu	store floating single, update RA
stfd	store floating double
stfdu	store floating double, update RA

DS-form

* lwa	load word algebraic, sign extend
* ld	load double
* ldu	load double, update RA
* std	store double
* stdu	store double, update RA

$$\text{Effective address} = \begin{cases} (\text{RA}) + \text{D/DS} & \text{if RA} \neq 0 \\ \text{D/DS} & \text{if RA} = 0 \end{cases}$$

FIGURE 7.7 **D-form and DS-form load and store instructions. RT is the target register for loads, RS is the source register for stores. 64-bit PowerPC extensions are marked with *. Instructions marked with # have different semantics in 64-bit PowerPC, as shown in parentheses.**

	0	6	11	16	21	31
X-form	OPCD	RT	RA	RB	EO	Rc
		RS				

	lbzx	load byte, zero rest of RT, indexed
	lbzux	load byte, zero rest of RT, update RA, indexed
	lhzx	load half, zero rest of RT, indexed
	lhzux	load half, zero rest of RT, update RA, indexed
	lhax	load half algebraic, sign extend, indexed
	lhaux	load half algebraic, sign extend, update RA, indexed
#	lwzx	load word (zero rest of RT), indexed
#	lwzux	load word (zero rest of RT) update RA, indexed
*	lwax	load word algebraic, sign extend, indexed
*	lwaux	load word algebraic, sign extend, update RA, indexed
*	ldx	load double, indexed
*	ldux	load double, update RA, indexed
	lfsx	load floating single, indexed
	lfsux	load floating single, update RA, indexed
	lfdx	load floating double, indexed
	lfdux	load floating double, update RA, indexed
	stbx	store lower byte of RS, indexed
	stbux	store lower byte of RS, update RA, indexed
	sthx	store lower half of RS, indexed
	sthux	store lower half of RS, update RA, indexed
#	stwx	store word (lower word of RS), indexed
#	stwux	store word (lower word of RS) update RA, indexed
*	stdx	store double, indexed
*	stdux	store double, update RA, indexed
	stfsx	store floating single, indexed
	stfsux	store floating single, update RA, indexed
	stfdx	store floating double, indexed
	stfdux	store floating double, update RA, indexed

$$\text{Effective address} = \begin{cases} (RA) + (RB) & \text{if } RA \neq 0 \\ (RB) & \text{if } RA = 0 \end{cases}$$

FIGURE 7.8   **X-form load and store instructions. RT is the target register for loads, RS is the source register for stores. 64-bit PowerPC extensions are marked with ∗. Instructions marked with # have different semantics in 64-bit PowerPC, as shown in parentheses.**

4. *Sign extension:* "Load algebraic" extends the sign of an object that is shorter than the register; "load and zero" fills the upper part of the register with zero.

Related to access granularity is *alignment.* An object of size *b* bytes is *aligned* if its memory address is a multiple of *b.* Otherwise an object is *misaligned.* Doublewords are aligned at addresses 0, 8, 16, 24,..., words at addresses 0, 4, 8, 12,..., and halfwords at addresses 0, 2, 4, 6,.... Bytes are always aligned.

The architecture specifies that if the hardware cannot handle a misaligned access, an alignment interrupt will be generated. It is up to the software exception handler whether the program is aborted or the misaligned access is performed in software.

Following are some alignment examples. (Section 2.2 describes the assembly language we use throughout the book.) Assume r1 contains 1024.

```
lhz    r2 = a(r1,6)     # load half from location r1+6
lwz    r3 = b(r1,8)     # load word from location r1+8
lwz    r4 = c(r1,34)    # load word from location r1+34
```

The first two loads are aligned—the first is a halfword load from an address that is a multiple of 2 and the second is a word load from a multiple of 4. The final load, however, is unaligned because it is a word loaded from an address that is not an integer multiple of 4. The third instruction will cause an alignment interrupt if the hardware cannot handle it.

The update mode load and store instructions are useful for sequencing through elements of arrays. For example, the lwzu instruction can be used to access an integer array, a, of 4-byte words stored in memory beginning at location 512.

```
        addi    r1 = 508          # add immediate (to 0), load address of a - 4
LOOP:   ...
        lwzu    r3 = a(r1=r1+4)   # load word with update
                                  # from location r1+4

        ...
        bc      LOOP,CTR≠0        # decrement CTR, if CTR≠0
                                  # branch to LOOP
```

Register r1 is initially set to point 4 bytes before the first element of the array and D is set to 4. Within the LOOP, each execution of the lwzu instruction will update r1 by adding 4 and use the updated value to load the next element of the array, implementing a "pre-update." That is, the update is done prior to the memory access (the reason r1 is initialized to 4 bytes before the first array element).

In addition to the normal loads and stores, two types of data transfer instructions involve multiple destination or source registers: 1) load and store multiple and 2) string instructions. The load multiple word (lmw) loads the low-order word of registers beginning with RT and ending with r31. In 64-bit PowerPC the high-order 32 bits of these registers are set to zero. While this leads to a somewhat inefficient use of the 64-bit registers, it maintains a

	0	6	11	16	21	31

X-form

OPCD	RT	RA	RB	EO	Rc
	RS		NB		

`lswi`   load string word immediate
`lswx`   load word string
`stswi` store string word immediate
`stswx` store string word

$$\text{Effective address (lswi, stswi)} = \begin{cases} (RA) & \text{if } RA \neq 0 \\ 0 & \text{if } RA = 0 \end{cases}$$

$$\text{Effective address (lswx, stswx)} = \begin{cases} (RA) + (RB) & \text{if } RA \neq 0 \\ (RB) & \text{if } RA = 0 \end{cases}$$

FIGURE 7.9   **String instructions.**

consistent definition of the instruction across all PowerPC versions. `Store multiple word` (`stmw`) performs a similar data transfer in the other direction. A typical application of these instructions is saving and restoring registers in procedure calls or context switches. As an example, assuming r1 points to an area in memory named "buffer," the following instruction saves registers r25–r31 into that area.

        stmw   buffer(r1) = r25

There are four string instructions (Figure 7.9). The number of bytes n is specified by a field in the exception register XER_{25-31} in instructions `lswx` and `stswx` and by an immediate field NB in instructions `lswi` and `stswi`. An instruction transfers n bytes, beginning with register RT (RS for stores), then using consecutive registers up to r31, and finally wrapping around through r0 if necessary.

    If a load/store multiple or a string instruction encounters a page fault part way through its execution, the transfer is terminated, the page fault serviced, and then the instruction is restarted. This is feasible as long as the registers involved in calculating the effective address (Figure 7.8 and Figure 7.9) are not overwritten. If these registers are in the range to be loaded, the instruction is invalid. Implementations are not required to check at runtime that the instruction is valid, the compiler must generate correct code.

Arithmetic Instructions

The architecture provides the usual set of integer add, subtract, multiply, and divide instructions (Figure 7.10). The XO-form instructions are typical RISC, three-operand instructions. They

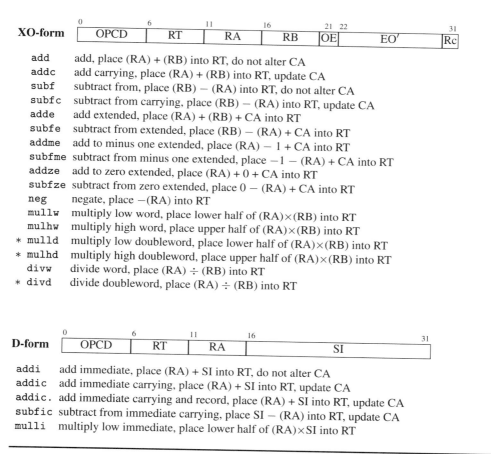

(see Section 7.3 for a description of the Condition Register bits)

FIGURE 7.10   Integer arithmetic instructions. 64-bit PowerPC extensions are marked with ∗.

have an opcode in the OPCD field and an extended opcode in EO′. An instruction takes two source registers RA and RB, operates on them, and places the result into a target register RT. The instructions contain the Rc bit, which can be used to place an automatic comparison result into the Condition Register held in the Branch Unit. When Rc = 0, the Condition Register is unchanged. When Rc = 1, as indicated by the dot following the instruction's mnemonic (subf. in the example below), the result of an instruction is compared to zero and bits in Condition Register field 0 are set accordingly (see Section 7.3 for a description of the Condition Register bits).

```
        ...
   subf.   r3 = r1–r2              #subtract from, set bit in cr0 accordingly
   bc      EXIT,cr0/eq=true        # branch if result was equal to zero
        ...
EXIT:   ...
```

This feature allows a condition for a branch to be set without requiring a separate compare instruction.

Some of the add and subtract instructions come in two versions: with carry update or without it. The architecture specifies that addi, add, and subf are the preferred instructions because they alter fewer special registers; updates of special registers may become a bottleneck in aggressive implementations. However, to support extended-precision integer arithmetic, some of the add and subtract instructions use the Carry (CA) bit from the XER. Examples are addic, addc, and subfc. Also, the OE field is used to enable (or disable) overflow reporting; disabling overflow is useful for implementing extended-precision integer arithmetic where intermediate overflows should be ignored.

The D-form instructions use a 16-bit two's complement constant value taken from bits 16 through 31 as one of the operands. The add immediate with record (addi.) is one of the few D-form instructions that modifies the Condition Register field with a comparison result. There is a separate instruction add immediate (addi) that has no effect on the Condition Register. Because D-form instructions do not have an Rc bit, the equivalent information must be encoded as part of the opcode.

Rotate and Shift Instructions

The rotate and shift instructions appear in Figure 7.11. Only rotate left instructions are provided, obviously, rotate right by n positions is identical to rotate left by $32 - n$ positions (or $64 - n$ positions in the 64-bit version of PowerPC).

The 32-bit M-form rotate with mask instructions rotate the contents of register RS left by a number of positions specified by register RB, or field SH in immediate instructions. A mask of ones that begins from bit position MB and ends at bit position ME is then generated. The mask is used in one of two ways: rotate with insert or rotate with AND.

As long as MB $\leq$ ME the mask formation is as one would expect intuitively. For example, if MB = 2 and ME = 5, the mask is

$$00111100000000000000000000000000$$

But, what happens if MB > ME? The sequence of ones still begins at position MB, goes to the end of the word, wraps around, and stops at position ME. As a second example, if MB = 5 and ME = 2, the mask is

$$11100111111111111111111111111111$$

M-form

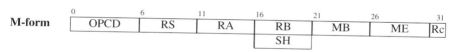

rlwimi rotate left word immediate then mask insert
rlwinm rotate left word immediate then AND with mask
rlwnm rotate left word then AND with mask

MD-form

0	6	11	16	21	27	30 31
OPCD	RS	RA	sh	mb	XO	sh Rc
				me		

*   rldic rotate left doubleword immediate then clear
*   rldicl rotate left doubleword immediate then clear left
*   rldicr rotate left doubleword immediate then clear right
*   rldimi rotate left doubleword immediate then mask insert

MDS-form

0	6	11	16	21	27	31
OPCD	RS	RA	RB	mb	XO	Rc
				me		

*   rldcl rotate left doubleword then clear left
*   rldcr rotate left doubleword then clear right

X-form

0	6	11	16	21	31
OPCD	RS	RA	RB	EO	Rc
			SH		

slw	shift left word
srw	shift right word
sraw	shift right algebraic word
srawi	shift right algebraic word immediate
* sld	shift left doubleword
* srd	shift right doubleword
* srad	shift right algebraic doubleword

XS-form

0	6	11	16	21	30 31
OPCD	RS	RA	sh	XO	sh Rc

*   sradi shift right algebraic doubleword immediate

FIGURE 7.11 Integer rotate and shift instructions. 64-bit PowerPC extensions are marked with ∗.

Positions 2 and 5 are set to one in both examples.

This general facility defines sequences of ones of length 1 to 32 bits, beginning from any position in a 32-bit word (and wrapping around if necessary). There is no way to specify a mask of all zeros, which would simply clear the destination register; this can be done by other instructions.

Instruction `rlwimi` performs rotate with insert. If a mask bit is one, the corresponding bit of the rotated data is inserted into RA; if a mask bit is zero, the corresponding bit in RA remains unchanged. Instructions `rlwinm` and `rlwnm` perform rotate with AND. The rotated data are ANDed with the mask and placed into register RA. The example below illustrates a use of `rlwnm`.

```
                          # source register r1 = 3.
                          # rotate positions r2 = 25.
        rlwnm   r3 = r1,r2,2,5   # MB = 2, ME = 5.
                          # now r3 = 2^26.
```

In 64-bit rotate with mask instructions, two 6-bit fields (mb and me) are needed to specify the beginning and the end of the mask. But because both fields do not fit in the instruction, it takes two instructions to perform a rotate with AND: `rldcl` and `rldcr`. The former contains a mask begin (mb) field, and a mask of ones is generated from bit mb through bit 63. The latter contains a mask end (me) field, and a mask of ones is generated from bit 0 through bit me.

Using the same example as above, with mb = 2 for `rldcl` and me = 5 for `rldcr`, the two 64-bit masks are:

```
        rldcl:  0011111111111111...111
        rldcr:  1111110000000000...000
```

As a result of executing both instructions, the rotated data are ANDed with both masks, leaving bits 2 to 5 unchanged and clearing the remainder of the doubleword.

The instructions `rldicl` and `rldicr` are similar, but the amount the data are rotated is determined by a 6-bit immediate field sh. This field is split, so that the beginning of the mb, me, and sh fields can be aligned with the MB, ME, and SH fields.

In the remaining two rotate with mask instructions, `rldic` and `rldimi`, the immediate field sh specifies the number of bits the register is rotated and also determines the end of the mask: the mask is a sequence of ones from mb through 63–sh.

Finally, the usual set of shift instructions is provided in both 32-bit and 64-bit versions.

7.3 Branch Unit

The primary function of the Branch Unit (BU) is to direct the correct flow of instructions to the FXU and the FPU. The architectural view of the BU consists of a set of special-purpose

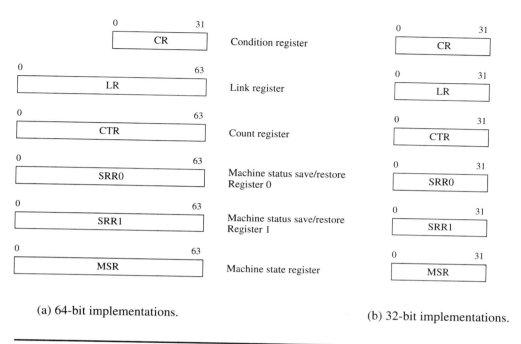

(a) 64-bit implementations.

(b) 32-bit implementations.

FIGURE 7.12   Branch Unit registers.

registers, the branch instructions, and a set of instructions that perform logical operations on bits in one of the special registers, the Condition Register.

Branch Unit Registers

The Branch Unit registers are shown in Figure 7.12.

The Condition Register (CR) is a 32-bit register tested by conditional branch instructions. It is divided into eight 4-bit fields (cr0, cr1, ... cr7) that can be accessed separately. In effect, the CR fields may be regarded as a set of independent 4-bit condition registers (Figure 7.13(a)).

The four bits in a field signify the conditions *less than, greater than, equal,* and *summary overflow*. This last bit is a copy of the summary overflow bit from the XER belonging to the FXU that is set by an overflow and remains set until cleared by software. The condition bits are tested for either a true or false value. Consequently, a "less or equal" condition can be obtained by checking the "greater than" bit for false. Any of these fields can be specified as the destination of fixed-point or floating-point compare instruction. In addition, Field 0 and Field 1 have special uses. In fixed-point instructions that have an Rc (Record) bit, if Rc = 1, the

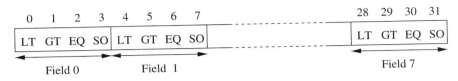

(a) Condition Register fields.

CR bits	Arithmetic instructions	Compare instructions
LT = 1	result < 0	(RA) < (RB), or (RA) < immediate operand
GT = 1	result > 0	(RA) > (RB), or (RA) > immediate operand
EQ = 1	result = 0	(RA) = (RB), or (RA) = immediate operand
SO	Summary overflow—this is a copy of XER(SO) (see Section 7.2)	

(b) Bits in a CR field.

FIGURE 7.13   Condition Register. This definition of bits is for fixed-point operations and fixed-point compare instructions.

result of the instruction is compared to zero and CR Field 0 is set according to this comparison (Figure 7.13(b)). CR Field 1 has an identical use for floating-point instructions having an Rc bit.

The Link Register (LR) has two uses. First, it contains the branch target address for one variety of conditional branch instruction (see subsection "Branch Unit Instructions" below). Second, it retains the return (i.e., "link") address for subroutines. All branch instructions have a Link (LK) bit. LK is set by the compiler when a branch instruction is used to branch to a subroutine. When a branch instruction with LK = 1 executes, the address of the instruction following the branch is saved in the Link Register and subsequently used to return from the subroutine.

Like the LR, the Count Register (CTR) also has two uses. First, it contains the branch target address for one of the conditional branch instructions (see subsection "Branch Unit Instructions" below). Second, it holds the iteration count for loops in which the total loop count can be computed before the loop is entered. A simple example is a loop of the form do i=1,n; in this case n could be loaded into the CTR prior to the loop entry. Conditional branches may test the value of the CTR relative to zero (that is, CTR = 0 or CTR ≠ 0). CTR is autodecremented by the branch instruction that tests its value, prior to the test.

The Machine State Register (MSR) defines the state of the processor according to the bits defined in Figure 7.14. Some of these bits are the usual controls that disable interrupts or place the processor in a privileged state. A mode bit (SF) controls 32-bit or 64-bit operation in 64-bit implementations. This bit determines whether the results of integer operations are regarded as 32-bit or 64-bit quantities for the purpose of modifying condition code bits.

The FPU Unavailable bit (FP) provides an interesting optimization. When MSR(FP) = 0, the attempt to execute any floating-point instruction causes a "floating-point unavailable" interrupt. If a system call is not expected to execute any floating code, it is sufficient to clear MSR(FP) instead of saving the floating-point registers prior to the system call. If, by some chance, a floating-point instruction is encountered, an interrupt will be generated to take care of saving the floating-point registers.

Two bits (SE and BE) are provided to enable tracing. When SE is enabled the CPU executes an interrupt after the completion of each instruction (assuming the instruction did not cause an interrupt for a different reason). This bit is useful for tracing instructions or memory references. A second bit (BE) is provided for specifically tracing branches, whether taken or not.

The LE bit controls the way the order of bytes is interpreted by memory access instructions. There are two ways to order bytes in an object, beginning from the least significant byte (Little-Endian) or from the most significant byte (Big-Endian), as shown in Figure 7.15. The LE bit provides a way to select the desired mode. That this control bit is called Little-Endian mode and not Big-Endian mode is not a coincidence. POWER is a Big-Endian machine and PowerPC provides the additional Little-Endian capability and a bit to turn it on. There is also an Interrupt Little-Endian (ILE) bit, which is copied into the LE bit when an interrupt occurs, allowing the interrupt context to execute in a different mode.

The PowerPC 601 implements a 32-bit PowerPC architecture and a 32-bit MSR. The definition of some aspects of the architecture, such as the MSR(LE) and MSR(ILE) bits, was completed after the 601 was designed. Consequently, these bits are not implemented in the 601. The function of MSR(LE) is provided by a bit in a Hardware Implementation–Dependent (HID) register. (In our later discussion of the PowerPC 601 we will ignore this minor difference.)

Two additional registers, SRR0 and SRR1, are used to save the machine status on an interrupt and restore the status upon returning from the interrupt. Depending on the type of the interrupt, the address of the instruction following the interrupted one, the address of the interrupted instruction, or the address of the last instruction completed before taking the interrupt is placed into SRR0. When an interrupt occurs, SRR1 is loaded with interrupt-specific information and with a copy of certain MSR bits.

Bit position		Name	Value	Description
64-bit version	32-bit version			
0		SF	0	CPU is in 32-bit mode
			1	CPU is in 64-bit mode
1–31				Reserved
32–44	0–12			Reserved
45	13	POW	0	Power management disabled (normal)
			1	Power management enabled (reduced power)
46	14			Implementation-dependent function
47	15	ILE		Interrupt Little-Endian mode
48	16	EE	0	External interrupts disabled
			1	External interrupts enabled
49	17	PR	0	Privileged state
			1	Nonprivileged state
50	18	FP	0	Floating-point unit unavailable
			1	Floating-point unit available
51	19	ME	0	Machine check interrupts disabled
			1	Machine check interrupts enabled
52	20	FE0	0	FP exception mode 0
53	21	SE	0	Single-step trace disabled (normal)
			1	Single-step trace enabled
54	22	BE	0	Branch trace disabled (normal)
			1	Branch trace enabled
55	23	FE1		FP exception mode 1
56	24			Reserved
57	25	IP	0	Interrupts vectored to address x000nnnnn
			1	Interrupts vectored to address xFFFnnnnn
58	26	IR	0	Instruction address translation is off
			1	Instruction address translation is on
59	27	DR	0	Data address translation is off
			1	Data address translation is on
60–61	28–29			Reserved
62	30	RI	0	Interrupt is not recoverable
			1	Interrupt is recoverable
63	31	LE	0	CPU is in Big-Endian mode
			1	CPU is in Little-Endian mode

FIGURE 7.14   Machine State Register (MSR) bits. The FE0 and FE1 bits are described in Section 7.4.

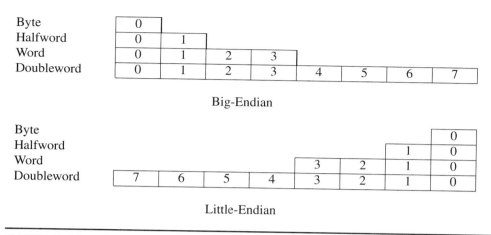

FIGURE 7.15   The order of bytes in an object.

Branch Unit Instructions

The PowerPC architecture has one unconditional branch and three conditional branch instructions (Figure 7.16). To determine the branch target address in the unconditional branch, a 24-bit immediate field LI is used as either an absolute address or as an address relative to the current instruction, depending on the Absolute Address (AA) bit. Byte addressing is used for all addresses presented to the hardware, so LI is concatenated with 00 to form a byte address.

In the conditional branch instructions, the condition that determines whether the branch is taken or not is defined by the BO field (Figure 7.17). This condition may be the comparison to zero of the Count Register (CTR), a bit in the Condition Register defined by field BI of the instruction, or by the logical AND of the two. Conventional conditional branches are implemented by testing a bit in the Condition Register. Loop-closing branches may be implemented by loading the loop count, if known, into the Count Register and testing its contents in each loop iteration. ANDing the two types of tests is useful for DO loops that contain an exit clause.

Branch prediction in the PowerPC depends on the branch instruction itself and on the direction of the branch, as shown in the following:

- ■ Branch conditional (bc) with a negative displacement is predicted taken. Normally this is a loop-closing branch.

- ■ Branch conditional (bc) with a positive displacement is predicted not taken.

- ■ Branch conditional to link register (bclr) and branch conditional to count register (bcctr) are predicted not taken.

I-form

0	6		30	31
OPCD		LI	AA	LK

b   Branch unconditional. LI is a word address;
         concatenated with 00 it forms a byte address.
         The byte address is signed extended

$$\text{Target address} = \begin{cases} \text{LI}||00 + \text{current instruction address} & \text{if AA} = 0 \\ \text{LI}||00 & \text{if AA} = 1 \end{cases}$$

B-form

0	6	11	16	30	31
OPCD	BO	BI	BD	AA	LK

bc   Branch conditional. BD is a word address;
         concatenated with 00 it forms a byte address.
         The byte address is signed extended

$$\text{Target address} = \begin{cases} \text{BD}||00 + \text{current instruction address} & \text{if AA} = 0 \\ \text{BD}||00 & \text{if AA} = 1 \end{cases}$$

XL-form

0	6	11	16	21	31
OPCD	BO	BI	//	EO	LK

bclr   Branch conditional to link register.

$$\text{Target address} = \begin{cases} \text{LR}_{0-29}||00 & \text{if version} = \text{32-bit} \\ \text{LR}_{0-61}||00 & \text{if version} = \text{64-bit and mode} = \text{64-bit} \\ \text{LR}_{32-61}||00 & \text{if version} = \text{64-bit and mode} = \text{32-bit} \end{cases}$$

bcctr   Branch conditional to count register.

$$\text{Target address} = \begin{cases} \text{CTR}_{0-29}||00 & \text{if version} = \text{32-bit} \\ \text{CTR}_{0-61}||00 & \text{if version} = \text{64-bit and mode} = \text{64-bit} \\ \text{CTR}_{32-61}||00 & \text{if version} = \text{64-bit and mode} = \text{32-bit} \end{cases}$$

FIGURE 7.16   Branch instructions. CR_{BI} is bit BI of the Condition Register. If LK = 1, the Link Register is loaded with the effective address of the instruction following the branch. The BO field is defined in Figure 7.17.

BO field	Test to take branch
0000y	Count $\neq 0$ AND $CR_{BI} = 0$
0001y	Count $= 0$ AND $CR_{BI} = 0$
001zy	$CR_{BI} = 0$
0100y	Count $\neq 0$ AND $CR_{BI} = 1$
0101y	Count $= 0$ AND $CR_{BI} = 1$
011zy	$CR_{BI} = 1$
1z00y	Count $\neq 0$
1z01y	Count $= 0$
1z1zz	Always true

$$\text{Count} = \begin{cases} CTR_{0-31} & \text{if version = 32-bit} \\ CTR_{0-63} & \text{if version = 64-bit and mode = 64-bit} \\ CTR_{32-63} & \text{if version = 64-bit and mode = 32-bit} \end{cases}$$

FIGURE 7.17   Encoding of the BO field in conditional branches. The z bit must be always zero. The y bit is the branch prediction reversal bit.

When y = 1 in the BO field (Figure 7.17), the branch prediction is reversed. This bit may be set by the compiler if it can predict the most likely branch behavior, based on the kind of control construct it is compiling.

The difference between the three conditional branch instructions lies in the way the branch target address is determined. In the bc instruction, a 14-bit immediate field BD (concatenated with 00) is used as either an absolute address or as an address relative to the current instruction, depending on the Absolute Address (AA) bit. In the `bclr` instruction, the branch target address is determined by the Link Register. It is determined by the Count Register in the `bcctr` instruction. In either case, the two low-order bits of the special register are replaced by 00.

The Branch Unit also executes a set of instructions that perform logical operations on bits of the Condition Register, as shown in Figure 7.18. Fields BA and BB define the two Condition Register bits to be used in the logical operation and field BT defines the Condition Register destination bit for the result.

Examples

Figure 7.19(a) illustrates the use of the Count Register. The loop count (512) is loaded into r29 (`addi`), and then transferred into the CTR by the move to special register (`mtspr`)

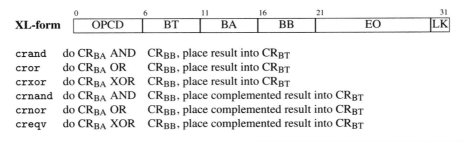

XL-form

crand do CR_{BA} AND CR_{BB}, place result into CR_{BT}
cror   do CR_{BA} OR CR_{BB}, place result into CR_{BT}
crxor do CR_{BA} XOR CR_{BB}, place result into CR_{BT}
crnand do CR_{BA} AND CR_{BB}, place complemented result into CR_{BT}
crnor do CR_{BA} OR CR_{BB}, place complemented result into CR_{BT}
creqv do CR_{BA} XOR CR_{BB}, place complemented result into CR_{BT}

FIGURE 7.18   Condition Register logical instructions.

for (i=0; i<512; i++)

. . .

(a) C statement.

```
        addi    r29=512        # load immediate loop count into r29
        mtspr   CTR=r29        # move to special register (CTR)
LOOP:   . . .
        . . .
        bc      LOOP,CTR≠0     # decrement CTR, branch if CTR≠0
```

(b) Compilation.

FIGURE 7.19   Example—using the Count Register.

instruction. This sequence of two instructions is needed because there are no instructions that can load immediate values into CTR or other special registers. The loop-closing branch decrements the CTR and then tests at the end of each iteration.

Figure 7.20 shows a code example that demonstrates the use of multiple CR fields and logical CR instructions. On most machines, the two Boolean conditions in the "if" statement are translated to two branch instructions as shown in Figure 7.20(b). In the assembly code, cri/j indicates bit j of Condition Register field i; i is given explicitly as its number or symbolically as the condition it encodes. In PowerPC, the same "if" statement can be translated to code with a single branch instruction (Figure 7.20(c)). If the two Boolean statements are true, the compare instructions set the "eq" bits in Condition Register fields cr1 and cr2. These two bits

if ((a == 10) && (b == 20))

. . .

else

. . .

(a) C statement.

```
                                    # When this code is entered:
                                    # r1 points to a, and
                                    # r1 + 4 points to b.
        lwz     r7 = a(r1)          # load a
        cmpi    cr1 = r7,10         # compare immediate, set bit in cr1
        bc      ELSE,cr1/eq=false   # branch if 'cr1/eq' bit is false
        lwz     r7 = b(r1,4)        # load b
        cmpi    cr1 = r7,20         # compare immediate, set bit in cr1
        bc      ELSE,cr1/eq=false   # branch if 'cr1/eq' bit is false
IF:

        . . .

ELSE:

        . . .
```

(b) Assembly language version of C 'if' statement.

```
                                    # When this code is entered:
                                    # r1 points to a, and
                                    # r1 + 4 points to b.
        lwz     r7 = a(r1)          # load a
        cmpi    cr1 = r7,10         # compare immediate, set bit in cr1
        lwz     r8 = b(r1+4)        # load b
        cmpi    cr2 = r8,20         # compare immediate, set bit in cr2
        crand   cr0/0 = cr1/eq,cr2/eq  # AND 'eq' bits, set cr0/0
        bc      ELSE,cr0/0=false    # branch if 'cr0/0' bit is false
IF:

        . . .

ELSE:

        . . .
```

(c) Assembly language version with a single branch instruction.

FIGURE 7.20   **Example—the use of multiple Condition Register fields and logical Condition Register instruction (crand).**

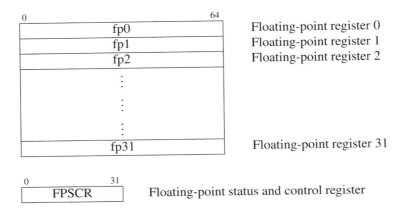

are ANDed using a logical CR instruction whose result is sent to cr0 bit 0. Finally, this bit is tested to determine the outcome of the conditional branch.

7.4   Floating-Point Unit

As its name suggests, the primary function of the Floating-Point Unit (FPU) is to handle floating-point arithmetic operations. The architectural view of the FPU consists of 32 64-bit registers for floating-point data, a status register, and a set of instructions.

Floating-Point Unit Registers

The Floating-Point Unit registers are shown in Figure 7.21. The architecture is defined to have 32 64-bit registers to support the IEEE double-precision floating-point format. Exceptions are reported via a 32-bit Floating-Point Status and Control Register (FPSCR), which is described in detail in Figure 7.22.

Floating-Point Unit Instructions

The Floating-Point Unit is built around a set of multiply-add operations. Figure 7.23 provides a list of the FPU instructions. There are four composite instructions in this class:

Bit	Name	Description
0	FX	Exception summary. Set to one if any exception is set to one. Remains one until reset by software.
1	FEX	Enabled exception summary. Set to one if any enabled exception is set to one. Cleared when all enabled exceptions are zero.
2	VX	Invalid operation exception summary. Set to one if an invalid operation exception is set to one. Cleared when all invalid operation exceptions are zero.
3	OX	Overflow exception
4	UX	Underflow exception
5	ZX	Zero divide exception
6	XX	Inexact exception
7	VXSNAN	Invalid operation exception. Result is a Signaling NaN.
8	VXISI	Invalid operation exception. Operation is Infinity − Infinity.
9	VXIDI	Invalid operation exception. Operation is Infinity ÷ Infinity.
10	VXZDZ	Invalid operation exception. Operation is Zero ÷ Zero.
11	VZIMZ	Invalid operation exception. Operation is Infinity×Zero.
12	VXVC	Invalid operation exception. Operation is a comparison involving NaN.
13	FR	Fraction rounded. Rounding of the result incremented the fraction.
14	FI	Fraction inexact. Rounding produced an inexact fraction (different from the intermediate result). Or, overflow occurred with disabled Overflow exception.
15–19	FPRF	Floating-point result flags
20		Reserved
21	VXSOFT	Invalid operation exception. Software request.
22	VXSQRT	Invalid operation exception. Square root of a negative number.
23	VXCVI	Invalid operation exception. Integer convert of a NaN, a large number, or infinity.
24	VE	Invalid operation exception enable
25	OE	Overflow exception enable
26	UE	Underflow exception enable
27	ZE	Zero divide exception enable
28	XE	Inexact exception enable
29	NI	Non–IEEE mode. If NI=1, the FPSCR bits may have other meanings than defined in this table, and the results may not conform to IEEE.
30–31	RN	Rounding control

FIGURE 7.22   **Floating-Point Status and Control Register. Status bits are 0–23. Control bits are 24–31.**

0	6	11	16	21	26	31

A-form

OPCD	FRT	FRA	FRB	FRC	XO	Rc

fadd	floating add, place (FRA) + (FRB) into FRT
fadds	floating add single, place (FRA) + (FRB) into FRT
fsub	floating subtract, place (FRA) − (FRB) into FRT
fsubs	floating subtract single, place (FRA) − (FRB) into FRT
fmul	floating multiply, place (FRA)×(FRB) into FRT
fmuls	floating multiply single, place (FRA)×(FRB) into FRT
fdiv	floating divide, place (FRA) ÷ (FRB) into FRT
fdivs	floating divide single, place (FRA) ÷ (FRB) into FRT
fmadd	floating multiply-add,
	place [(FRA)×(FRC)] + (FRB) into FRT
fmadds	floating multiply-add single,
	place [(FRA)×(FRC)] + (FRB) into FRT
fmsub	floating multiply-subtract,
	place [(FRA)×(FRC)] − (FRB) into FRT
fmsubs	floating multiply-subtract single,
	place [(FRA)×(FRC)] − (FRB) into FRT
fnmadd	floating negative multiply-add,
	place −{[(FRA)×(FRC)] + (FRB)}into FRT
fnmadds	floating negative multiply-add single,
	place −{[(FRA)×(FRC)] + (FRB)}into FRT
fnmsub	floating negative multiply-subtract,
	place −{[(FRA)×(FRC)] − (FRB)}into FRT
fnmsubs	floating negative multiply-subtract single,
	place −{[(FRA)×(FRC)] − (FRB)}into FRT

0	6	11	16	21	31

X-form

OPCD	FRT	//	FRB	EO	Rc

frsp	floating round to single, round (FRB) and place into FRT
fctiw	floating convert to integer word
fctiwz	floating convert to integer word with round toward zero
* fctid	floating convert to integer doubleword
* fctidz	floating convert to integer doubleword with round toward zero
* fcfid	floating convert from integer doubleword

FIGURE 7.23 **Floating-point arithmetic instructions. Field FRC is used in three source operand instructions. 64-bit PowerPC extensions are marked with ∗.**

multiply-add and multiply-subtract, $[(FRA) \times (FRC)] \pm (FRB)$, and their negative versions $-[(FRA) \times (FRC)] \pm (FRB)$. These instructions take three input operands from registers FRA, FRB, and FRC, and produce the result; e.g., $[(FRA) \times (FRC)] + (FRB)$. The motivation for these composite instructions is the frequent occurrence of pairs of "multiply" and "add" operations in floating-point code. For example, the inner product that is part of many matrix operations can be implemented using multiply-adds.

An unusual aspect of the PowerPC multiply-add is that it is a "fused" composite instruction— the architecture explicitly specifies that there is no intermediate rounding operation between the multiply and the add. The result of the multiply is not rounded prior to the add; the full precision of the product is kept. Not rounding the product both increases accuracy and saves time. While the results are sometimes more accurate than the IEEE-specified result, at the same time they differ from the IEEE result computed with a separate multiply and add. However, if full IEEE conformance is desired, a compiler option may be provided to suppress multiply-add instructions.

Implementation of the IEEE 754 Standard

Appendix A describes the IEEE 754 floating-point standard and defines related concepts in floating-point arithmetic. In this section we discuss the PowerPC implementation of the standard.

Developed more than 10 years ago at a time when microprocessors were heavily microprogrammed with little pipelining, the standard gives little consideration to problems encountered during overlapped execution of floating-point instructions. The standard requires that a faulting instruction be accurately identified, and this is often implemented by providing a precise interrupt for the faulting instruction. The saved program counter, therefore, points to the faulting instruction. Although this feature is desirable if software is to fix up an error and resume execution, implementing such precise interrupts makes simple, high-performance implementations difficult (see also Chapter 4).

Rather than make the implementation overly complex, a decision was made to provide different modes of operation, leading to another trade-off, this time balancing precise floating-point interrupts with performance. To support this trade-off at the architectural level, the PowerPC architecture provides two bits, FE0 and FE1, in the Machine State Register, that can be used to set the exception mode to one of the following.

MSR(FE0)	MSR(FE1)	Mode
0	0	Interrupts disabled
0	1	Imprecise nonrecoverable
1	0	Imprecise recoverable
1	1	Precise

In the interrupts disabled mode floating-point exceptions are ignored, and the exception handler is not invoked. The other modes provide various degrees of support for debugging, at the expense of reduced performance.

An alternative method is to have software insert test code in certain places in the program. For example, test code may be placed after every floating instruction that may cause an exception, or it may be placed only at subroutine exits, depending on the performance and exception resolution desired.

Five types of exceptions are defined by the standard: invalid operation, overflow, underflow, division by zero, and inexact exception. For each type of exception, the FPSCR provides a flag (one bit) that is set when the corresponding exception occurs. A flag remains set until cleared by the user. The flags may be tested by using a set of move from FPSCR instructions, and cleared using move to FPSCR instructions.

The architecture provides additional information on invalid operation exceptions. Flags in the FPSCR are set to report that the invalid operation falls in one of the following categories:

- Result is a signaling NaN

- Infinity $-$ Infinity

- Infinity $\div$ Infinity

- Zero $\div$ Zero

- Infinity $\times$ Zero

- A comparison involving NaN

- Square root of a negative number

- Floating convert to integer of a NaN, a number too large to fit in the integer format, or an infinity

7.5   Virtual Address Generation and Translation

Address processing in the PowerPC begins with an *effective address,* obtained by adding a base register to either a displacement or an index register. Next, the effective address is simultaneously processed by two address translation schemes: segmented translation and block translation. Segmented translation provides access to fixed-size 4 Kbyte pages. Block translation provides access to blocks ranging from 128 Kbytes to 256 Mbytes. A typical use of block translation is a memory-mapped display buffer. Once loaded, this buffer is not subject to normal virtual memory paging.

Both segmented and block translation are simultaneously performed to save time. Typically, only one translation will be successful, or none if the information is not in memory. If both are successful, block translation has priority.

32-bit PowerPC Segmented Address Translation

The architecture defines 16 32-bit segment registers that may be modified only by privileged instructions. A Segment Register is used for memory access when its most significant bit (called T) is zero and for I/O access when T is one. For memory references, the Segment Register format is:

0	1	2	3	8	31
T	Ks	Ku	Not used	Segment ID	

Ks and Ku are supervisor and user memory key, respectively (see subsection on protection at the end of this section).

The four most significant bits of the effective address are used to select one of the segment registers (Figure 7.24). The 24-bit Segment ID from the Segment Register is concatenated with 16 bits from the effective address to obtain a 40-bit virtual page number, which together with a 12-bit byte offset forms the 52-bit *virtual address*.

Next, the virtual page number is translated to a real page number. For performance reasons, this translation is performed most of the time using a Translation Lookaside Buffer (TLB). The TLB contains entries for virtual pages that have been recently accessed. If the requested translation is not found in the TLB (TLB miss), the page table must be accessed, a much slower operation that requires several memory references. Once found, the real page number is concatenated with the byte offset, which remains unchanged during translation, to form the real address.

32-bit Page Table

The architecture defines a variable-sized hashed page table. Each page table entry (PTE) translates a virtual page number to a real page number. The number of entries in the page table reflect a trade-off between the page table size and performance. If the page table is too small, it may not be able to contain translations for all memory-resident pages, and many hash collisions will occur.

Eight PTEs form a PTE Group (PTEG). The hash function identifies a PTEG (Figure 7.25), and the entries in the PTEG are then searched until a matching virtual page number is found.

Two hash functions are used. First, the primary hash function is used, and, if the desired PTE is not found, another attempt is performed with the secondary hash function. Accordingly, a PTE can be placed in a primary or secondary PTEG, distinguished by the H bit in the PTE (Figure 7.27). A page table lookup is a hit if the Segment ID and Abbreviated Page Index match, and if H = 0 for a primary hashing, or H = 1 for a secondary hashing.

The following primary hash function is used (Figure 7.26). Append three zero bits to the left of the Virtual Page Index to make it into a 19-bit number. Next, compute the bitwise exclusive-OR of the 19 lower bits of the Segment ID and the Virtual Page Index. The lower n bits of the result are the hash table index, where 2^n is the number of PTEGs in the page

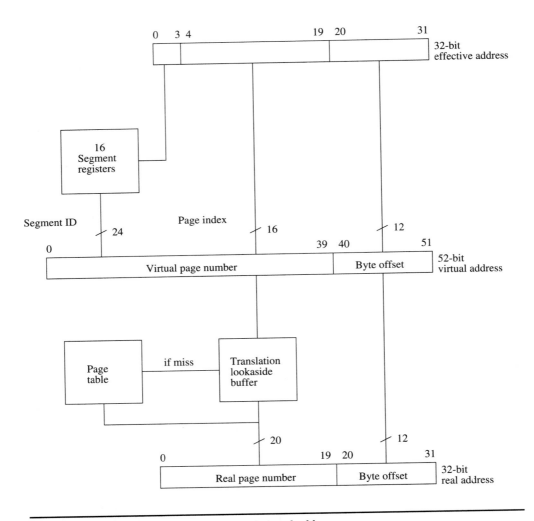

FIGURE 7.24   32-bit PowerPC segmented virtual address.

table. Finally, since each PTEG is 64 bytes, append six zero bits to the right of the index. The resulting $n + 6$ bits are the PTEG's offset from the base of the page table.

To speed up the access to the page table, the architecture specifies that software must choose the page table location in memory such that computation of the PTEG's real address can be done without addition. This can be done by dropping $n + 6$ bits of the base address

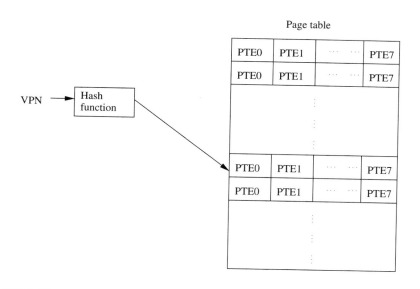

FIGURE 7.25   *Searching the page table.*

and concatenating the remaining bits with the $n + 6$ bits of the PTEGs offset. The page table must be placed on a boundary of 2^{n+6} bytes. The architecture specification recommends that the number of PTEGs be at least one-half the number of real pages (which means the number of PTEs is four times the number of real pages).

Example

Assume the real memory size is 256 Mbytes. The virtual page number is 27a9b1f6a3 (hexadecimal). We have to determine the page table size and select its location in memory. What is the real address of the PTEG?

Real memory consists of 2^{16} pages. The recommended number of PTEGs is (at least) one-half of that, which is 2^{15}. Using our previous definition of n, we have $n = 15$. The page table must be placed on a boundary of 2^{n+6}, which is 2^{21} (2 Mbytes). We arbitrarily select its base address at memory location 14e00000.

The 19 lower bits of the Segment ID are 7a9b1, and the Virtual Page Index, extended to 19 bits, is 0f6a3. The bitwise exclusive-OR of these two numbers is 75f12. The lower 15 bits of this result give the PTEG index in the page table. The page table offset 17c480 is obtained by appending six zero bits at the right of the index. The 21 lower bits in the page table offset,

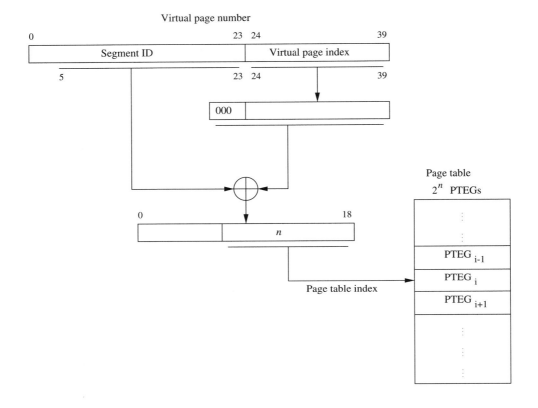

FIGURE 7.26   **32-bit PowerPC. The computation shown is the primary hash function. $\oplus$ is exclusive-OR. The secondary hash function is identical, other than the 19-bit result produced by the exclusive-OR being bitwise complemented. The page table has 2^n PTEGs, which is 2^{n+3} entries. $10 \leq n \leq 19$.**

all of which were zero, are replaced by the page table offset, yielding the real address of the PTEG: 14f7c480.   □

Figure 7.27 shows the structure of a page table entry (PTE). Note that a VPN consists of a Segment ID and a 16-bit Page Index (Figure 7.24). However, the PTE contains only a 6-bit Abbreviated Page Index, which is sufficient because at least 10 bits of the Page Index are hashed (the 10 bits correspond to a minimum size page table with 2^{10} PTEGs). All VPNs that hash to a particular PTEG must have identical bits in the 10 low-order bit positions, so it is

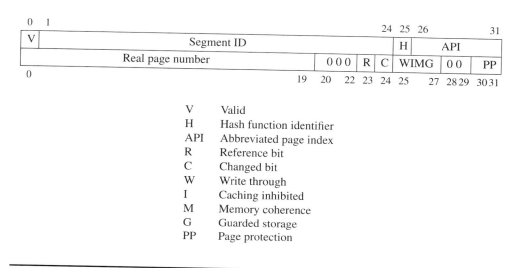

FIGURE 7.27   **32-bit PowerPC page table entry.**

sufficient to compare the remaining VPN bits and the hash function identifier (H) to determine a match.

The PTE contains the usual Reference and Changed bits, indicating whether a page has been accessed or modified since it was brought in. The software uses this information to implement the page replacement policy. The Page Protection (PP) bits are described in the subsection on protection at the end of this section.

There are four memory and cache control bits (WMIG). W determines whether the cache is write-through ($W = 1$) or write-back ($W = 0$). If caching is inhibited ($I = 1$), a memory access instruction references the main memory directly, bypassing the cache. The M bit is applicable to shared-memory multiprocessors; when $M = 1$, the hardware must enforce cache coherence (we discuss this topic in detail in Chapter 9). Finally, the G bit identifies memory areas in which prefetching must be avoided (such as an address that represents an I/O device).

64-bit PowerPC Segmented Address Translation

Figure 7.28 illustrates the mechanism for generating and translating the virtual address in 64-bit versions of PowerPC. Compare with Figure 7.24. Obviously, the lengths of the effective, virtual, and real addresses are different. The second main difference is that the segment registers are replaced with a segment table.

Each 16-byte segment table entry (STE) maps an Effective Segment ID to a Virtual Segment

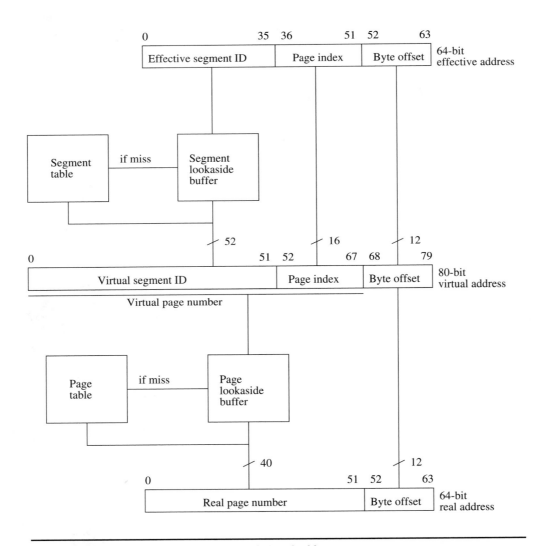

FIGURE 7.28   64-bit PowerPC segmented virtual address.

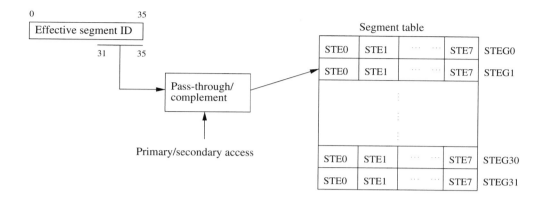

FIGURE 7.29   **Indexing into the segment table (64-bit implementations).**

ID. Eight STEs form an STE Group (STEG) The entire segment table consists of 32 STEGs, fully contained in a 4 Kbyte page. The table must be placed on a page boundary.

To access the segment table, the lower 6 bits of the Effective Segment ID are used as an index (Figure 7.29), creating an essentially degenerate hash function referred to as the *primary* index. It identifies a PTEG whose eight entries are then searched linearly. If no match is found, the lower 6 bits of the Effective Segment ID are complemented, producing a *secondary* index. This in turn identifies a second PTEG, which is also scanned. If there is again no match, the search fails and the result is a page fault.

A segment table entry is used for memory access when its T bit is zero and for I/O access when T is one. For memory references, the segment table entry format is shown below.

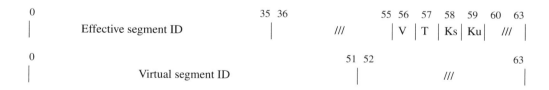

Ks and Ku are supervisor and user memory key, respectively (see the subsection on protection at the end of this section), and V is the valid bit. For performance reasons, segment table entries are cached in a Segment Lookaside Buffer (SLB).

64-bit Page Table

The page table structure and searching method are identical in 32-bit and 64-bit implementations (Figure 7.25): the virtual page number is hashed to obtain an index into the page table, in which each entry is a PTEG. A PTEG consists of eight PTEs, as in 32-bit implementations, but there is one difference: PTEs are twice as wide (16 bytes), since more bits are needed to identify virtual and real pages.

The hash function is similar but more bits are used, as one would expect, given the 80-bit virtual address (versus 52-bit virtual address in 32-bit implementations). Figure 7.30 shows the details of the hash function. Append 23 zero bits to the left of the Virtual Page Index to make it into a 39-bit number. Next, compute the bitwise exclusive-OR of the 39 lower bits of the Virtual Segment ID and the Virtual Page Index. The lower n bits of the result are the hash table index, where 2^n is the number of PTEGs in the page table. Finally, since each PTEG is 128 bytes, append seven zero bits to the right of the index. The resulting $n + 7$ bits are the PTEG's offset from the base of the page table.

To speed up the access to the page table, the architecture specifies that software must choose the page table location in memory such that computation of the PTEG's real address can be done without addition. The same method used in 32-bit implementations is used to compute the PTEG's real address without addition: $n + 7$ bits of base address are dropped and remaining bits are concatenated with the $n + 7$ bits of the PTEG's offset. The page table must be placed on a boundary of 2^{n+7} bytes. It is recommended that the number of PTEGs be at least one-half the number of real pages.

Figure 7.31 shows the structure of a page table entry (PTE). Note that a VPN consists of a Virtual Segment ID and a 16-bit Page Index (Figure 7.28). However, the PTE contains only a 5-bit Abbreviated Page Index, which is sufficient because at least 11 bits of the Page Index are hashed (the 11 bits correspond to a minimum-size page table with 2^{11} PTEGs). All VPNs that hash to a particular PTEG must have identical bits in the 11 low-order bit positions, so it is sufficient to compare the remaining VPN bits and the hash function identifier (H) to determine a match. The remaining bits in the page table entry are identical to those in 32-bit implementations.

Block Address Translation

The block address translation (BAT) scheme maps a large block of data into a contiguous real memory area. These data are not swapped in and out as virtual memory pages. The architecture provides a set of eight distinct special-purpose registers; each pair of registers (called Upper and Lower BAT registers) maps the effective address of a block to its real memory address. The BAT registers may be accessed using the normal move to special register and move from special register instructions.

Figure 7.32 illustrates the format of the BAT registers. The Block Effective Page Index (BEPI) is compared with the high-order bits of the effective address; a match indicates a hit.

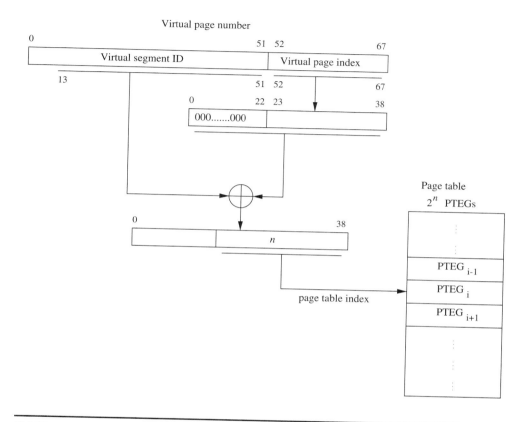

FIGURE 7.30   **64-bit PowerPC. The computation shown is the primary hash function. $\oplus$ is exclusive-OR. The secondary hash function is identical, other than the 39-bit result produced by the exclusive-OR being bitwise complemented. The page table has 2^n PTEGs, which is 2^{n+3} entries.** $11 \leq n \leq 39$.

In 32-bit PowerPC, the number of bits compared is $32 - n$, where 2^n is the block length in bytes. The block length is between 128 Kbytes and 256 Mbytes, which corresponds to $17 \leq n \leq 28$. Consequently, 15 bits are sufficient for the BEPI field. BRPN is the real address of the block in memory, and again 15 bits are sufficient because the smallest block is 128 Kbytes.

The length of the BAT register fields in 64-bit PowerPC can be easily determined following the same reasoning. The two valid bits are in conjunction with the Privileged State (PR) bit from the Machine State Register as follows:

Valid = (Vu AND MSR(PR)) OR (Vs AND /MSR(PR))

	51 52	56 57	61 62 63

Virtual segment ID	API	//	H	V
Real page number	//	R	C	WIMG	//	PP

0   51 52 54 55   56 57   60 61 62 63

V	Valid
H	Hash function identifier
API	Abbreviated page index
R	Reference bit
C	Changed bit
W	Write-through
I	Caching inhibited
M	Memory coherence
G	Guarded storage
PP	Page protection

FIGURE 7.31   *64-bit PowerPC page table entry.*

where '/' is logical NOT. The rest of the bits have been defined earlier, with the exception of PP, Ks, and Ku, which are described in the section on protection below.

Protection

The architecture provides protection at the page and block levels. At the page level, the access type is determined by the following.

■ The two page protect *PP* bits in the page table entry.

■ The Ku (user mode) and Ks (supervisor mode) bits in the segment register (32-bit PowerPC) or segment table entry (64-bit PowerPC).

■ The Privileged State (PR) bit in the Machine State Register.

A Boolean value (Key) is obtained according to the following equation.

Key = (Ku AND MSR(PR)) OR (Ks AND /MSR(PR))

where '/' indicates logical NOT. Then the access type is determined according to Figure 7.33.

For block level protection, Key is assumed to be one, and the PP bits are obtained from the lower BAT register. The access privileges are again as shown in Figure 7.33.

Vs   Supervisor state valid bit
Vu   User state valid bit
W   Write-through
I   Caching inhibited
M   Memory coherence
G   Guarded storage
PP   Page protection

Block length	Block length mask (BLM)
128 KB	000 0000 0000
256 KB	000 0000 0001
512 KB	000 0000 0011
1 MB	000 0000 0111
2 MB	000 0000 1111
4 MB	000 0001 1111
8 MB	000 0011 1111
16 MB	000 0111 1111
32 MB	000 1111 1111
64 MB	001 1111 1111
128 MB	011 1111 1111
256 MB	111 1111 1111

(a) BAT Register fields.

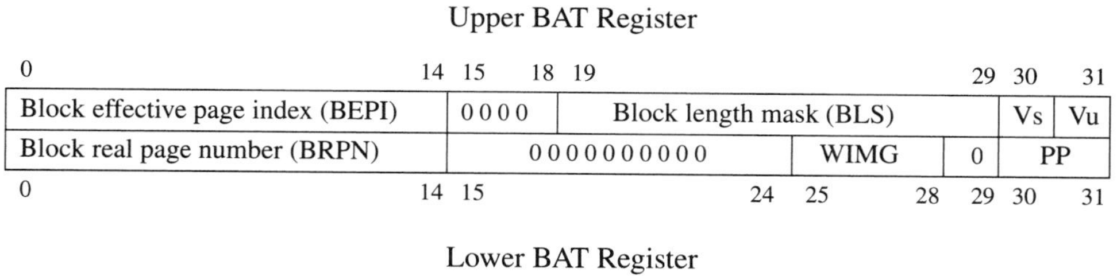

Upper BAT Register

0	14 15	18 19	29 30	31
Block effective page index (BEPI)	0 0 0 0	Block length mask (BLS)	Vs	Vu
Block real page number (BRPN)	0 0 0 0 0 0 0 0 0 0	WIMG	0	PP
0	14 15	24 25 28	29 30	31

Lower BAT Register

(b) 32-bit PowerPC.

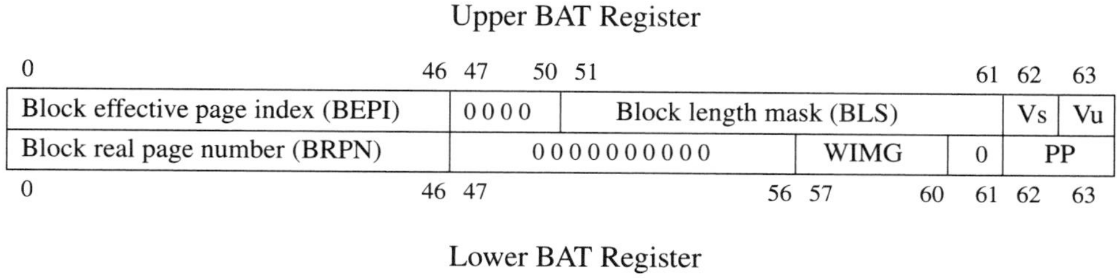

Upper BAT Register

0	46 47	50 51	61 62	63
Block effective page index (BEPI)	0 0 0 0	Block length mask (BLS)	Vs	Vu
Block real page number (BRPN)	0 0 0 0 0 0 0 0 0 0	WIMG	0	PP
0	46 47	56 57 60	61 62	63

Lower BAT Register

(c) 64-bit PowerPC.

FIGURE 7.32   **Block Address Translation (BAT) registers.**

PP	Key	Access type
00	0	r/w
	1	no access
01	0	r/w
	1	read
10	0,1	r/w
11	0,1	read

FIGURE 7.33   **Access type.**

7.6 PowerPC versus POWER: Simplification

In this section we discuss the simplification aspects of the PowerPC architecture, including POWER instructions that were removed and instructions that were retained, but with simplified architectural specifications. PowerPC extensions are described in the next section.

Load with Update Instructions

Load instructions with update place the effective address into RA and load an operand into RT, the target register. What happens if RA = RT? There is an apparent conflict because the same register should receive both the update value and the operand from memory. The POWER architecture resolves this dilemma by specifying that the value placed in the register is the data from memory, not the updated effective address. The hardware must check whether RA and RT are the same and, if so, handle the situation as a special case.

In PowerPC this hardware requirement has been removed so that such a conflict will lead to an undefined value in the register. The compiler is then used to prevent the RA = RT case from occurring by simply not using an update form when the base address and target registers are the same. This method clearly does not restrict in any way the usefulness of update instructions; a POWER load with update in which RA = RT does not perform an update, so a simple load instruction can be always used instead.

String Instructions

String instructions move data between memory and one or more integer registers. High-performance implementations of these multiple clock cycle instructions require the sequencing to be done by either sequential hardwired control or microcode—this is an implicit requirement of the POWER architecture. The PowerPC architecture specifies that string instructions may be implemented in software. Interestingly enough, the first PowerPC implementation (the 601) retained the hardware string unit.

Another difference concerns restartability. A string instruction that encounters a page fault in the POWER architecture is terminated and restarted after the page is brought in. To restart the instruction successfully, the registers involved in calculating the effective address must not be overwritten. POWER specifies that implementations must check and prevent this override at runtime. But the POWER compilers also prevent the situation by not generating this kind of code. Consequently, in POWER this problem is addressed by a redundant effort in both software and hardware. In PowerPC this problem is handled by software only: the implementation requirement to perform runtime checks is removed.

Integer Register File Bandwidth

A high-performance implementation of the POWER architecture may incorporate an integer register file with three read ports and two write ports.

The three read ports are needed by several POWER instructions that have three source registers. Prominent examples are the X-form fixed-point store instructions that read RS and store the contents into the memory location whose effective address is obtained by adding RA and RB. More obscure examples are several instructions that insert data into a register (`rlmi`, `rrib`, `maskir`).

A high-performance implementation is likely to have one write port for memory load data and the other for fixed-point arithmetic results. The load with update instructions require two register file writes: one for the update and one for the load data.

An attempt was made in PowerPC to reduce the integer register file bandwidth requirements. Three POWER instructions that have to read three source registers (`rlmi`, `rrib`, `maskir`) have been removed. Because of their fundamental nature, X-form store instructions are retained. However, in some implementations these instructions may take multiple clock cycles, for example, if the register file has only two read ports.

PowerPC implementors may also choose to provide a single write port, in which case the load with update instructions will take multiple clock cycles to write results. The architecture specification warns programmers that in some implementations `load with update` instructions may take longer to execute than a functionally equivalent sequence of `load` and `add` instructions.

The MQ Register

The POWER architecture's MQ (Multiplier and Quotient) Register is a special-purpose 32-bit register in the FXU used in integer divide instructions and in one of the integer multiply instructions. In the `divide` (`div`) instruction, the MQ Register holds the lower half of the 64-bit dividend. In both `divide` (`div`) and `divide short` (`divs`) instructions, the remainder is placed into the MQ. In the `multiply` (`mul`) instruction the lower half of the 64-bit product is placed into the MQ.

When there is a sequence of fixed-point multiplies and divides, the MQ Register becomes a shared resource among the instructions. This could restrict the overlapped execution of such multiply/divide sequences and force them to execute serially (without significant hardware complexity). So the POWER instructions that use the MQ Register (`div`, `divs`, `mul`) are not in the PowerPC instruction set. New 32-bit integer multiply and divide instructions have been added, instead. This change simplifies the issue logic for multiple integer instructions: in the PowerPC there is no need to check MQ Register conflicts, and integer arithmetic instructions can be handled in a uniform way.

In addition to the changes to the multiply and divide, a number of shifts that operate on the MQ Register have been removed. If necessary, these shifts can be emulated by one or more PowerPC instructions.

Instructions Requiring a Select Operation

The execution of several POWER instructions requires a "select" operation between two possible results. The `absolute` (`abs`) instruction produces (RA), the contents of the source register RA if RA's sign is positive, or −(RA) otherwise. The hardware must then select between two possible results, (RA) or −(RA). As shown in Figure 7.34, the implementation of this instruction requires a multiplexer to select between the two alternatives. This extra hardware lengthens the execution time of all integer instructions that use the ALU; other instructions that do not need the multiplexer still have to pass through it. The same multiplexer with complemented select logic is needed for the POWER `negative absolute` (`nabs`) instruction, which produces the negative absolute value of the source register.

The POWER instruction set also contains two instructions whose primary application is the efficient computation of the minimum or maximum of signed integers. The instructions lead to a shorter code sequence without branches. The `doz` instruction and its immediate companion `dozi` involve a select operation between two possible results, the difference of the source operands or zero. Again, the hardware implementation requires a multiplexer to select between two alternatives.

Consequently, the four instructions `abs`, `nabs`, `doz`, and `dozi` were not included in the PowerPC instruction set. This change simplifies the execution hardware of integer instructions. If the time it takes to execute integer instructions determines the clock cycle, the streamlined hardware will permit a shorter clock cycle.

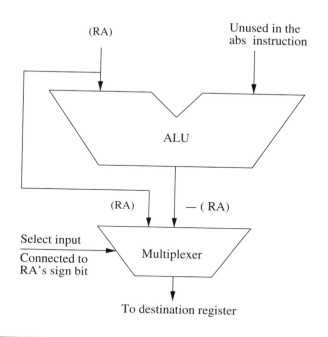

FIGURE 7.34   **An extra multiplexer is needed on the data path to implement the POWER** absolute (abs) **instruction.**

7.7 PowerPC versus POWER: Extensions

64-bit Addressing and Integer Arithmetic

The PowerPC architecture has been extended to include doubleword (64 bit) integer load and store instructions. The instruction set has also been supplemented with a set of double-word multiply, divide, shift, and rotate instructions (Figure 7.10 and Figure 7.11). PowerPC processors may implement a 32-bit subset architecture or the full 64-bit architecture. 64-bit implementations must also have a 32-bit mode, which allows 64-bit machines to run 32-bit code without changes.

The mode is controlled by a new bit in the Machine State Register, the Sixty-Four (SF) mode bit.   This bit redefines the integer registers and many special-purpose registers in the FXU and BU. Most instructions do not depend on the addressing size; some instructions have different architectural definitions for each addressing mode and produce different results depending on the mode.

The 64-bit integer versions of PowerPC include multiply instructions that produce either the lower doubleword or the upper doubleword of two doubleword operands, as well as a set of doubleword divide instructions. As for addition and subtraction, the same instructions are used regardless of the mode bit; a 32-bit result is simply the lower half of a 64-bit result. However, the mode bit determines whether the carry and overflow bits are set by the 32-bit result or by the 64-bit result (overflow for multiply and divide instructions is independent of the mode).

Since the integer registers have 64 bits, the shift field must have 6 bits to specify the amount of rotate or shift in immediate instructions. The mask begin and mask end fields in rotate instructions must also have 6 bits to specify the beginning and the end of a mask of ones. These 6-bit fields simply do not fit in the space available in the instruction, so a new set of six doubleword rotate instructions were defined. Four other instructions were added to perform shifts on 64-bit data.

Extended Loads

When we move from the 32-bit integers of POWER to 64-bit versions of PowerPC, some loose ends appear when words are loaded from memory. First, in 64-bit versions of PowerPC, the semantics of load word instructions were defined to be consistent with the byte and halfword loads; that is, the upper half of the 64-bit register is zeroed out. Second, it was necessary to add load word algebraic instructions (Figure 7.7 and Figure 7.8).

Interestingly enough, only three of the four versions of load word algebraic instructions are provided. These are DS-form load word algebraic (lwa), X-form load word algebraic indexed (lwax), and X-form load word algebraic with update indexed (lwaux). The fourth version, DS-form load word algebraic with update, was not included in the instruction set, apparently because of *ad hoc* implementation considerations and in order to save limited opcode space for future extensions. However, an extend sign word (extsw) instruction is provided, which extends the word sign bit out to doubleword length, so the missing instruction can be emulated by a simple load followed by extsw. Similarly, there was no load byte algebraic in the original POWER architecture. To help make up for this in PowerPC, there is an extend sign byte (extsb) instruction, so that a load byte algebraic can be emulated by a simple load followed by extsb.

Alignment

POWER has an Alignment Check (AL) bit in the Machine State Register. If MSR(AL) = 0, alignment checking is off. In this case, the low-order bits (three bits for doublewords, two bits for words, and one bit for halfwords) are ignored. If MSR(AL) = 1, alignment checking is on, and either the misaligned access can be done by the hardware, or an alignment interrupt is generated.

In PowerPC the MSR(AL) bit has been removed, which is equivalent to having alignment checking always on. Therefore, all misaligned accesses that cannot be done properly by hardware will cause an alignment interrupt. Also, certain (implementation-dependent) misaligned accesses may be handled in software and may perform much more slowly than accesses done entirely by hardware. The following references are expected to be done in hardware and should have good performance in all implementations:

1. Word and halfword integer loads and stores, regardless of alignment

2. Word-aligned doubleword integer loads and stores

3. Word-aligned floating-point loads and stores

References with other alignments may have worse performance, depending on the implementation.

Byte Order

POWER is a Big-Endian architecture, which means that bytes in a word are ordered from left to right (Figure 7.15). Load and store instructions that reverse the byte order are provided, and these are especially useful in efficiently interfacing with Little-Endian I/O systems. PowerPC provides selectable Big- or Little-Endian access by a mode bit (LE) in the Machine State Register.

There is some asymmetry between Little-Endian and Big-Endian modes in the PowerPC, however, to simplify the implementation. A simple hardware trick can be used to efficiently implement both endians. In particular, as part of the addressing hardware, low-order address bits are selectively complemented by exclusive-ORing them with a mask. If a word is being accessed, the low-order address bits are exclusive-ORed with '100', a halfword (2 byte) address with '110', and a byte address with '111'. This trick causes the physical address used by hardware to swap the data entity end to end. Consequently, the PowerPC architecture defines Little-Endian mode in terms of this kind of simple modification to the low-order 3 bits of an effective address.

As an example, consider two consecutive words stored in Big-Endian order at memory location 110000 (we assume a 6-bit address).

Address	Data
110000	word0
110100	word1

If the processor is to view these data in Little-Endian order, word1 should be loaded before word0. This is easily accomplished by exclusive-ORing the addresses with 000100, which has the effect of complementing the third lower bit of the address (the bit that determines the word location in a doubleword).

Address	Addr XOR 000100	Data loaded
110000	110100	word1
110100	110000	word0

This exclusive-OR method is inexpensive to implement and adds little delay to the address computation. Unfortunately, it cannot handle misaligned data. In the above example, the first word was aligned on a doubleword boundary. Now consider the same example when the first word is not on a doubleword boundary.

Address	Addr XOR 000100
110100	110000
111000	111100

Clearly, the exclusive-OR did not accomplish the desired result. Instead of reversing the order in which the two words are loaded, we got two different addresses! Therefore, all unaligned accesses must be trapped to software when in Little-Endian mode, as must all string and load/store multiple instructions. It is up to the interrupt handler to complete the misaligned access in software or to report an error.

Note that the above two words are *aligned* on a word boundary. Misalignment refers to the *doubleword in which the two words are contained.* We have defined the endian concept relative to a doubleword: Big-Endian means objects in a doubleword begin from the upper end, Little-Endian means objects in a doubleword begin from the lower end.

Floating Point

The PowerPC architecture specifies a set of single-precision floating arithmetic instructions (Figure 7.23), which allows single-precision programs to run faster because there is no need to insert rounding instructions. The definition of the multiply-add instruction was not changed: rounding is done after the addition but not the multiplication. Again, results are slightly more accurate than the standard, but if strict conformance to IEEE 754 is desired, PowerPC compilers may provide a flag to suppress this instruction.

As an option, implementors of PowerPC may choose to save integrated circuit die area by using single-precision hardware to provide somewhat slower double-precision arithmetic.

Unused Bits

Unused bits in some POWER instructions and special registers do not have a defined value. Undefined bits in registers are occasionally put to "good use" by resourceful programmers. A well-known example is the IBM 360/370 architecture, which originally had a set of 32-bit integer registers but 24-bit addresses. The extra upper byte in the register found its use in programs, and when the 370 address space was extended, many old programs could not run with the new, longer addresses.

In the PowerPC unused bits in instructions are defined to be zero, otherwise the instruction is invalid.[1] Also, unused bits in special registers are defined to be zero, and instructions that modify special registers must read the unused bits (along with the rest of the register) and write them back unchanged. If these bits are not set to zero, the result of the instruction is undefined, and the instruction may produce incorrect results on some implementations.

Page Table Structure

There are some rather interesting differences in the 32-bit POWER and PowerPC page table structures. (POWER has no 64-bit table.)

POWER maintains a fixed-size inverted page table. Its size is simply determined by the size of the physical memory: there is one page table entry for each page of physical memory. Page table entries are linked in lists; the head of each list is an entry in a hash table.

So there are two tables: a hash table and a page table. Why is there a need to keep a separate hash table? First, the page table is fixed size; the size of the hash table may be adjusted to control collisions. Second, page table entries are items in dynamically allocated linked lists, and each list is headed in a hash table entry through which the list is entered for lookup, insertion, or deletion.

PowerPC also uses hashing to access its page table. However, there are significant differences from POWER:

1. There is no separate hash table; the page table is accessed directly.

2. The size of the page table is variable.

3. Page table entries form a statically allocated, fixed-length list.

PowerPC saves some memory by not using a hash table. However, it uses additional memory by using a larger page table (in which some entries may be empty) to reduce collisions. To compare the space needed for the POWER and PowerPC tables, assume a physical memory with 2^n pages and an 8-byte page table entry. This assumption is certainly valid for PowerPC (Figure 7.27). As for POWER, assume the last two words of the page table entry in Figure 2.28 are not in use, as we discussed in Section 2.7. In the table below we use the recommended size of the hash table in the POWER architecture specification, and the recommended size of the page table in the PowerPC architecture specification.

---

[1] But the hardware is not required to check that the instruction is invalid.

	POWER	PowerPC
Page table entry (bytes)	8	8
Number of page table entries	2^n	2^{n+2}
Page table (bytes)	2^{n+3}	2^{n+5}
Hash table (bytes)	2^{n+3}	0
Total (bytes)	2^{n+4}	2^{n+5}

It appears that the space needed by the PowerPC page table is twice as large as the combined space of the POWER page and hash tables. But PowerPC saves the extra memory reference needed in POWER to access the hash table.

7.8   Summary and Conclusions

PowerPC is the result of both streamlining the POWER architecture and extending it in several ways. Several integer instructions that required three register ports were removed to simplify hardware requirements. Instructions using the MQ Register were removed so that the MQ will not become a bottleneck in aggressive implementations. The new instructions that were added include a set of 64-bit doubleword integer instructions. These changes accomplished the PowerPC architecture goals but at the expense of some asymmetries in the instruction set.

The design decisions that shaped the PowerPC instruction set architecture reflect a fundamental trade-off between the desire to provide a rich instruction set and the need to limit the complexity of the implementation. There is evidence that state-of-the-art compilers can exploit a rich instruction set and also that a direct relationship between complexity and the clock period exists. Despite the occasional irregularity, the PowerPC may prove to be a well-balanced design.

7.9   References

Two articles by Case contain relevant material, a description of POWER [11] and a discussion of the differences between POWER and PowerPC [12]. Paap and Silha [68] is an overview of the PowerPC instruction set, including discussions on the considerations that motivated changes relative to the POWER architecture.

Additional details are in the PowerPC architecture specification [42] and in the Motorola 601 manual [62]. For an interesting discussion of Big and Little-Endian addressing, refer to Cohen's paper [15].

8
POWERPC 601 IMPLEMENTATION

8.1 Introduction

The PowerPC 601 (Motorola's part MPC601) is the first implementation of the PowerPC architecture, so it serves as a "transition" between POWER and PowerPC. Even though the PowerPC architecture is designed to simplify the POWER instruction set and relax the implementation requirements, the 601 implementation took little advantage of the simplifications. In fact, its instruction set includes elements from both the PowerPC and POWER instruction sets. PowerPC 601–based systems can execute either instruction set, although software emulation is needed in a few cases.

The 601 implements POWER instructions in addition to the full 32-bit PowerPC instruction set for two main reasons. First, all existing POWER applications will run on a 601-based system, and the operating system does not have to provide emulation for POWER instructions. Second, the performance of POWER applications running on a 601 will be good, even if they make frequent use of POWER instructions that were not included in the PowerPC instruction set.

Just as in the POWER1, the implementation of the 601 centers around two main techniques: pipelining and dispatching multiple instructions per cycle. In the PowerPC 601, up to three

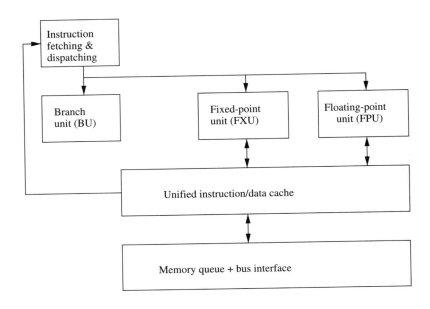

FIGURE 8.1   **601 block diagram.**

instructions can be dispatched per clock cycle, one to each of the three processing units shown in Figure 8.1: Fixed-Point Unit (FXU), Branch Unit (BU), and Floating-Point Unit (FPU). The 601 supports a restricted form of out-of-order dispatching. The goal is to resolve, or at least predict, branches early so that the instruction flow to pipelines may continue with minimal disruption.

Obviously, the 601 inherited much of the original POWER1 pipelined structure, but, as we will see, significant differences exist. These differences can be traced to the following:

1. The 601 is a single-chip implementation versus the multichip POWER1. There are fewer total gates to work with (even though the 601 is implemented with a denser chip technology), and the physical interfaces between major units are quite different. For example, some interfaces may have been pin-limited in the POWER1, but this limitation disappears in the 601.

2. The 601 is directed toward PC applications, therefore, the floating point, especially 64-bit, is de-emphasized.

3. Experience gained from the first POWER1 implementations has no doubt found its way into the PowerPC 601.

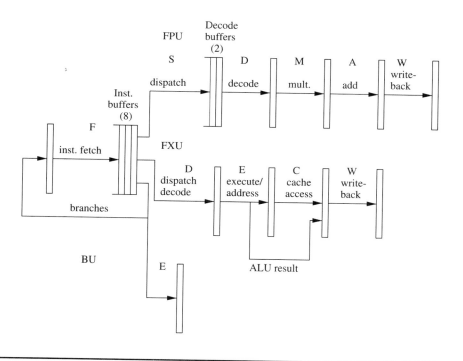

FIGURE 8.2   PowerPC 601 pipeline structures.

Throughout most of this chapter we describe the 601 without relying on any knowledge of the POWER1. Toward the end of the chapter, in Section 8.5 there is a side-by-side comparison of the 601 and a multichip POWER1. Multiprocessing capabilities, new in the PowerPC architecture, are described in Chapter 9.

8.2 Pipelines

Figure 8.2 illustrates the 601 pipelines. All instructions are processed in the fetch and dispatch stages. Branch and Condition Register instructions go no farther. Fixed-point and load/store instructions are also decoded in the dispatch stage of the pipe and are then passed to the FXU to be processed. Most fixed-point arithmetic and logical instructions take just two clock cycles in the FXU: one to execute, the second to be written into the register file. All load/store instructions take three cycles in the FXU: address generation, cache access, and register write. This assumes a cache hit, of course; cache miss handling is described later.

The 601 design places emphasis on getting the FXU instructions processed in as few pipeline stages as possible. This low-latency design is evident in the combining of the dispatch and decode phases of instruction processing. The effect of an instruction pipeline's length on performance is most evident after a branch, when the pipeline may be empty or partially empty. (See, for example, Figure 8.11(b), where the pipeline is empty after an incorrectly predicted branch.) The shorter the pipeline, the more quickly instruction execution can get started again. Most of the time, the first instructions following a branch are FXU instructions (even in floating-point–intensive code), because a program sequence following a branch typically begins by loading data from memory (or by preparing addresses with fixed point instructions). Clearly, this makes a short FXU pipeline desirable.

In contrast, the processing of floating-point instructions proceeds a little more slowly. FPU decoding is not done in the same clock cycle as dispatching. The first floating-point instruction following a branch is likely to be dependent on a preceding load, so the extra delay in the floating-point pipeline will not affect overall performance in a significant way. This extra delay reduces the interlock between a floating load and a subsequent dependent floating-point instruction to just one clock cycle.

The buffer at the beginning of the FPU can hold up to two instructions; the second buffer slot is actually the decode latch, where instructions are decoded. In the FXU pipeline, there is a one-instruction decode buffer (not shown in Figure 8.2) that can be bypassed. The decode buffers provide a place for instructions to be held if one of the pipelines blocks due to some interlock condition or an instruction that consumes the execute stages for multiple cycles. By getting instructions into the decode buffers when a pipeline is blocked, the instruction buffers are allowed to continue dispatching instructions (especially branches) to nonblocked units.

Instruction Fetching and Dispatching

Instructions are fetched from the cache at a rate of up to eight instructions per clock cycle and held in an eight-slot instruction buffer (Figure 8.3). The fetch logic attempts to keep the buffer full. If there is a cache miss and the buffer still contains four or more instructions, the fetch request will be canceled; cache misses for instructions are serviced only when more than half of the buffer is empty. The more instructions in the buffer, the more likely one of them is a branch; a branch in the buffer could make the prefetched instructions unneeded.

Unlike many RISC implementations, the PowerPC 601 uses a single, unified cache for both instructions and data. Instruction fetching and data accesses must contend for the cache resource. The unified cache has its lines divided into two 32-byte *sectors*. The sectors share the same address tag, but only one sector at a time is brought into the cache on a miss; occasionally a line will have an invalid sector that holds no useful instructions or data.

Instruction fetching does not cross cache sector boundaries. A cache sector contains 32 bytes (see Section 8.4), or exactly eight instructions. Hence, instructions may be fetched at the peak rate if the instruction buffer is empty and the requested instruction is the first one in a cache sector.

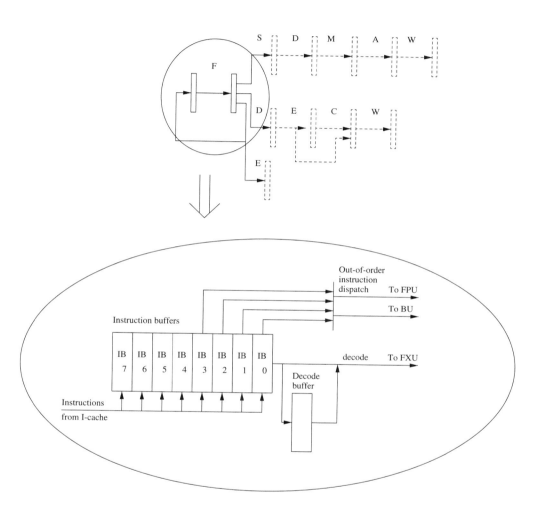

FIGURE 8.3   **PowerPC 601 instruction dispatching.**

Because the cache is unified, there is cache contention and arbitration between instruction and data accesses. A request to fetch instructions may be delayed for any one of the following reasons:

■ There is an ongoing transfer between the cache and main memory.

■ The cache status is updated as a result of multiprocessing activity (see Chapter 9).

■ The FXU requests access to the cache to perform a load or store operation. FXU data access is given priority over instruction fetching.

Contention for the cache, with instructions having a lower priority than data, provides the reason for fetching up to eight instructions at a time, even though the absolute maximum processing rate is three per clock cycle. When the instruction fetch unit has a chance to fetch, it *FETCHES!*—it may not have another chance for a while.

Once fetched into the buffer, multiple instructions can be dispatched, and, under certain conditions, they may dispatch out of logical program order. A single FXU instruction can be dispatched from the head of the buffer (IB0) only, because FXU decoding is done in the same pipeline stage as dispatching. Forcing the FXU instruction to dispatch from the IB0 eliminates the need for buffer selection logic prior to the FXU dispatch logic; in fact, the FXU dispatch/decode logic can be merged with the logic forming the head instruction buffer. If the FXU pipeline should be blocked, there is a decode buffer following IB0 that the IB0 instruction moves into, freeing up the IB0 slot for another instruction. The instruction in the decode buffer moves into the FXU when it becomes free.

One BU instruction and one FPU instruction may be dispatched from any of the four head slots, IB0–IB3. The instruction flow to each unit, BU, FXU, and FPU, must be in program order, but instructions to different units may be dispatched out of order (Figure 8.4). The dispatching rules are summarized as follows.

■ A single FXU instruction may be dispatched from IB0 only.

■ A single BU instruction may be dispatched from IB0–IB3, even if FXU and FPU instructions closer to the buffer head remain in the buffer.

■ A single FPU instruction may be dispatched from IB0–IB3, even if FXU and BU instructions closer to the buffer head remain in the buffer.

As instructions are dispatched and removed from the buffers, other valid buffer entries slide forward toward the head. This "compacts" the instructions and makes room for new instructions in the tail buffers.

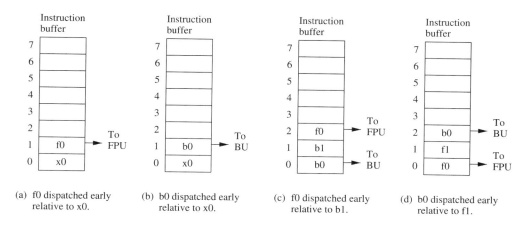

FIGURE 8.4   Out-of-order dispatching examples. x*i* is FXU instruction, b*i* is BU instruction, and f*i* is FPU instruction.

Fixed-Point Pipeline

The FXU is a four-stage pipeline shown in Figure 8.5. Most integer instructions take one cycle to execute. Exceptions are the multiply, divide, and multiple word memory operations, which spend several cycles in the execute pipeline stage. As long as the execute stage of the pipeline is available, instructions are dispatched and decoded in the instruction buffer IB0 in the same clock cycle, bypassing the FXU decode buffer. This in effect shortens the pipeline latency by one cycle. However, if the execute stage is occupied by a multicycle instruction, or the operands are not available, the instruction goes to the decode buffer. In this case, dispatching and decoding occur in different clock cycles.

Bypass paths are provided from the execute and cache access pipeline stages back to the beginning of the execute stage. Dependent, single-cycle execution instructions may be fully pipelined, and there is a one-cycle interlock delay only between a load (that hits in the cache) and a subsequent dependent instruction.

Load and store instructions share the decode and execute stages of the pipeline with the other FXU instructions. The same adder in the execute stage is used for arithmetic addition/subtraction and effective address generation.

As defined in the architecture, the effective address is obtained in one of two ways depending on the instruction format: (a) in X-form instructions the contents of two integer registers are added, and (b) in D-form instructions the contents of an integer register are added to a 16-bit displacement. The effective address is produced in the first part of the execute cycle, and the rest of the address processing (virtual address generation, translation, and cache

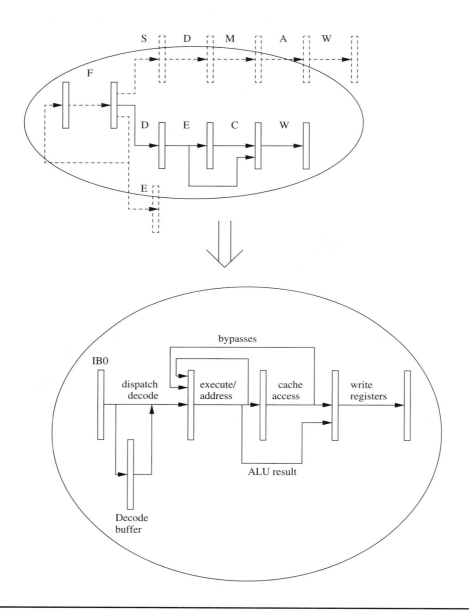

FIGURE 8.5   PowerPC 601 FXU pipeline.

directory lookup) is performed in the remainder of that cycle. If there is a hit, cache access is performed in the next clock cycle.

A queue prior to the cache holds store instructions forwarded by the FXU until the data to be stored becomes available. Note that this situation never comes up for fixed-point stores. When a fixed-point store executes, all previous FXU instructions must have executed, which implies that the store source register must contain the result. Hence, the store can complete right away. The FPU pipeline, however, is longer and normally lags the FXU. Therefore, floating stores are buffered in the cache until the result becomes available, clearing the FXU execute stage for other instructions.

Floating-Point Unit

The FPU implements a single arithmetic pipeline that performs the fused multiply-add (A × C + B) operation. Addition is considered a special case of the multiply-add instruction in which one of the multiplication operands is set to 1.0: A × 1.0 + B. Similarly, multiplication is performed by setting the addend to 0: A × C + 0.0.

Single-precision multiply, add, or multiply-add operations, as well as double-precision add instructions may flow through the pipe at the rate of up to one instruction per clock cycle. Figure 8.6 illustrates the PowerPC FPU pipelines. Double-precision multiplication takes two passes through the multiply stage, which saves hardware at the cost of an extra cycle of latency. The peak throughput of double-precision instructions that use the multiply stage is one instruction every two clock cycles.

There are no bypass paths from the multiplier back to the input of the adder. Nor does the register file write through. Therefore, a dependent instruction must wait for the register write cycle to be finished before it can decode and read the data. This applies only to data coming from the FPU pipeline. Data coming from the cache as a result of executing a floating load is available in the same clock cycle that it is written into the destination register.

Floating stores go down both the FXU and FPU pipelines. Address processing is done in the FXU, and the address is forwarded to the cache even though the data are not ready yet.

Example

Figure 8.7 shows a code example and its compilation and Figure 8.8 illustrates the pipelined processing of the loop body. To simplify the presentation, we assume in all the examples below that instruction and data references hit in the cache, and that the code is aligned with the cache sector (the first instruction in the loop is the first one in the cache sector).

All six instructions of the loop are fetched in clock cycle 1 (actually, eight are fetched but the remaining two are irrelevant and not shown). The first two, a load and a floating multiply, are dispatched to the FXU and FPU in the next clock cycle. The load is decoded in the same cycle and then goes down the execute and cache access stages of the FXU pipeline.

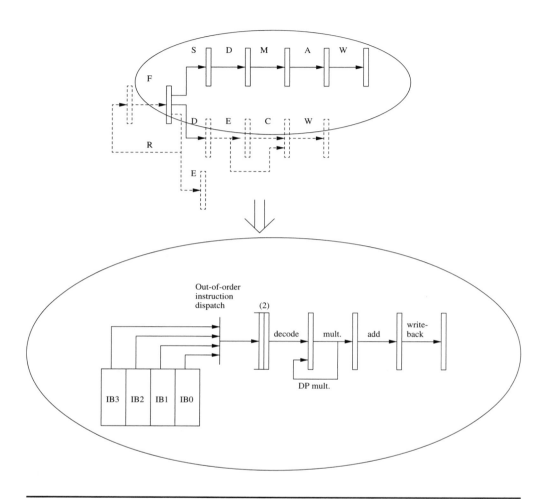

FIGURE 8.6   Floating-point pipeline. B is Buffer, IB is Instruction Buffer.

The `fmuls` is delayed for two cycles in the decode stage pending arrival of the operand from the cache; it decodes in the same cycle in which the operand is written into the register file.

The `fmadds` is delayed waiting for the result of `fmuls`. There are no bypass paths, so it must wait until the result is written into the register file at time 8; the `fmadds` decodes in the next clock cycle. A dependent instruction is delayed in the decode stage for three cycles if

float x[512], y[512];

for (k = 0; k < 512; k++)
    x[k] = r*x[k] + t*y[k];

(a) C code.

```
                            # r3 + 4 points to x
                            # r3 + 2052 points to y
                            # fp1 contains t,
                            # fp3 contains r, and
                            # CTR contains the loop count (512).
LOOP:   lfs     fp0 = y(r3,2052)    # load floating single
        fmuls   fp0 = fp0,fp1        # floating multiply
        lfs     fp2 = x(r3,4)        # load floating single
        fmadds  fp0 = fp0,fp2,fp3    # floating multiply-add single
        stfsu   x(r3=r3+4) = fp0     # store floating single with update
        bc      LOOP,CTR≠0           # decrement CTR, then branch if CTR ≠ 0
```

(b) Assembly code.

FIGURE 8.7   Code example and its compilation.

---

it depends on an arithmetic instruction that spends no more than one cycle in every pipeline stage. Otherwise the delay is longer.

Finally, the store is dispatched to both pipes in clock cycle 5, when the FPU buffer becomes available. It remains buffered in the FPU, while the FXU executes it and forwards the address to the cache. It decodes right after the fmadds, even though the data to be stored are not available yet. The branch is dispatched out of order, while the store is still in the instruction buffer.

Whereas instructions could be fetched from the branch target as early as clock cycle 4, at that time the cache is being accessed for data and not available for instructions. The first opportunity comes up at time 6, and instructions of the second loop iteration are fetched. The load decodes right after that. The fmuls, however, cannot be dispatched; one previous instruction (fmadds) is stuck in the FPU decode stage, and another (stfsu) in the single-slot FPU buffer. The first of these decodes at time 9, the second one goes from the buffer to the decode stage, and the fmuls is dispatched.

		1	2	3	4	5	6	7	8	9	10	11	12	13	14	15	16	17	18	19
lfs	fp0 = y(r3,2052)	F	D	E	C	W														
fmuls	fp4 = fp0,fp1	F	S	·	·	D	M	A	W											
lfs	fp2 = x(r3,4)	F	·	D	E	C	W													
fmadds	fp5 = fp4,fp2,fp3	F	·	S	·	·	·	·	·	D	M	A	W							
stfsu	x(r3=r3+4) = fp5	F	·	·	·	S D	E	·	·	·	· D	·	·	C						
bc	LOOP, CTR ≠ 0	F	·	S																
lfs	fp0 = y(r3,2052)					F	D	E	C	W										
fmuls	fp4 = fp0,fp1					F	·	·	S	·	D	M	A	W						
lfs	fp2 = x(r3,4)					F	·	·	·	D	E	C	W							
fmadds	fp5 = fp4,fp2,fp3					F	·	·	·	S	·	·	·	·	D	M	A	W		
stfsu	x(r3=r3+4) = fp5					F	·	·	·	·	S D	E	·	·	·	· D	·	·	·	C
bc	LOOP, CTR ≠ 0					F	·	·	·	S										

FIGURE 8.8   PowerPC 601 pipelined processing example. Two iterations of the loop are shown. After dispatching, instructions follow the FPU pipeline (upper path), FXU pipeline (lower path), or both. Loads execute in the FXU pipe, but the write is in the FPU. Stores are both dispatched (to the FXU and FPU) and decoded (as part of the FXU processing) in the same cycle.

8.3 Branch Processing

The Branch Unit executes all three types of PowerPC branch instructions: unconditional branches; loop-closing conditional branches using only the Count Register (CTR); and conditional branches using the Condition Register (CR), including those that use both the CR and the CTR. Unconditional branches and conditional branches that test only the CTR (not the CR) are executed in a similar way. Consider the example in Figure 8.9.

for (i=0; i<100; i++)
    a[i] = a[i] + 1;

(a) C code.

```
                                    # r3 points to a, and
                                    # CTR contains the loop count.
LOOP:   lwz     r0 = a(r3)          # load a
        addi    r0 = r0,1           # add immediate
        stwu    a(r3=r3+4) = r0     # store with update
        bc      LOOP,CTR≠0          # decrement CTR, branch if CTR ≠ 0
```

(b) Assembly code.

```
                                    1 1
                        1 2 3 4 5 6 7 8 9 0 1
lwz    r0 = a(r3)       F D E C W
addi   r0 = r0,1        F . S D E W
stwu   a(r3 = r3+4) = r0  F . . S D E C
bc     LOOP            F S
lwz    r0 = a(r3)           F . S D E C W
addi   r0 = r0,1            F . . S . D E W
stwu   a(r3 = r3+4) = r0    F . . . S . D E C
bc     LOOP, CTR ≠ 0        F . S
```

(c) Pipelined processing.

FIGURE 8.9   Code example with loop-closing branch using the Count Register.

The four instructions forming the loop are fetched in cycle 1 (others fetched past the branch are not shown). The lwz is dispatched right away. The addi is dispatched the next cycle, but waits a cycle to decode because it depends on the load of r0. The operand loaded is forwarded past the register file to the execute stage of the pipeline, and the addi executes in cycle 5.

Note that for the rest of the example, instruction dispatching and decoding occur on different clock cycles because there is always an instruction in the decode buffer. Hence, the following instruction in IB0 can be dispatched but not decoded; the instruction in the decode buffer must be decoded first.

The branch is dispatched during cycle 2, out of order (logically preceding integer instructions that are still in the instruction buffer). The branch can be resolved immediately by inspecting the contents of the CTR. In the next clock cycle instructions are fetched from the branch target address (the top of the loop).

The example in Figure 8.9 illustrates the *zero-cycle* branch: no pipeline cycles are wasted because of the branch. Instructions are dispatched and executed as fast as the FXU pipeline is able to handle them; the only delay is due to the one cycle interlock between the `load` and the `add immediate`.

Unconditional branches can also be resolved immediately, so their timing is the same as that shown in the figure.

Conditional Branches

The PowerPC uses static branch prediction with assistance from the compiler. A bit in the branch instruction allows the compiler to make a prediction of "taken" or "not taken" (see Section 7), which is useful when the compiler generates a code structure with a predictable flow. For example, if the compiler inserts test code that checks for floating exceptions or other errors, branches to the error-reporting subroutine are not taken as long as the program executes correctly; the compiler can predict "not taken" with high accuracy.

Whatever the prediction is, if it turns out to be correct, then the instruction flow through the pipeline has been maintained. If the prediction is incorrect, any predicted instructions in the pipeline must be flushed; we refer to this as *conditional execution*. The hardware that handles pipeline flushing can be considerably simplified if conditionally executed instructions are stopped before they change the memory or any registers.

Consider the example in Figure 8.10. Let's first assume that the branch is predicted not taken (Figure 8.11). Part (a) of the figure shows the pipelined processing of the code when the prediction is correct. The branch cannot be dispatched until it is one of the first four instructions in the buffer. This happens at clock cycle 5. The branch is dispatched at that time but can't be resolved—it is awaiting the result of the `cmpi`. Since the prediction is "not taken," instructions are conditionally dispatched and executed from the sequential instruction stream. (Actually, in the example, a single instruction is conditionally dispatched and decoded.) The `cmpi` instruction is executed in clock cycle 8 and the prediction turns out to be correct. The conditional instruction is allowed to execute and write its result to the destination register. There are no delays and the pipeline is kept full despite the branch.

Note that the instruction fetch logic attempts to keep the instruction buffer full, but no instructions can be fetched during cycles 4–8 while the cache is busy with data accesses (the load instructions are in the cache access stage of the pipeline). As it turns out, the fetch rate is sufficient to keep the pipeline full despite the cache contention. Because the prediction is "not taken," no instructions are fetched from the branch target address.

Part (b) of the figure shows the timing when the branch is taken and the prediction is incorrect. One instruction is conditionally dispatched and executed as before, but it must be canceled when the branch is resolved and the prediction is known to be incorrect at the end of

if (a > 0)

    a = a + b + c + d + e;

else

    a = a − b − c − d − e;

(a) C code.

```
                                      # r1 points to a,
                                      # r1+4 points to b,
                                      # r1+8 points to c,
                                      # r1+12 points to d,
                                      # r1+16 points to e.
      lwz    r8=a(r1)                 # load a
      lwz    r12=b(r1,4)              # load b
      lwz    r9=c(r1,8)               # load c
      lwz    r10=d(r1,12)             # load d
      lwz    r11=e(r1,16)             # load e
      cmpi   cr0=r8,0                 # compare immediate
      bc     ELSE,cr0/gt=false        # branch if bit false
IF:
      add    r12=r8,r12               # add
      add    r12=r12,r9               # add
      add    r12=r12,r10              # add
      add    r4=r12,r11               # add
      stw    a(r1)=r4                 # store
      b      OUT                      # unconditional branch
ELSE:
      subf   r12=r8,r12               # subtract
      subf   r12=r12,r9               # subtract
      subf   r12=r12,r10              # subtract
      subf   r4=r12,r11               # subtract
      stw    a(r1)=r4                 # store
OUT:
```

(b) Assembly code.

FIGURE 8.10   Code example with conditional branch.

(a) Correct prediction. Branch was not taken.

		1	2	3	4	5	6	7	8	9	10	11	12	13	14
	lwz r8 = a(r1)	F	D	E	C	W									
	lwz r12 = b(r1,4)	F	.	D	E	C	W								
	lwz r9 = c(r1,8)	F	.	.	D	E	C	W							
	lwz r10 = d(r1,12)	F	.	.	.	D	E	C	W						
	lwz r11 = e(r1,16)	F	.	.	.	.	D	E	C	W					
	cmpi cr0 = r8,0	F	.	.	.	.	.	D	E						
	bc ELSE,cr0/gt=false	F	.	.	.	S									
IF:	add r12 = r8,r12	F	.	.	.	.	.	.	.	.	D´	E	W		
	add r12 = r12,r9			F	.	.	.	.	.	.		D	E	W	
	add r12 = r12,10			F	.	.	.	.	.	.			D	E	W
	add r4 = r12,r11									F	.	.	D	E	W
	stw a(r1) = r4									F	.	.	D	E	C
	b OUT														
ELSE:	subf r12 = r8,r12														
	subf r12 = r12,r9														
	subf r12 = r12,r10														
	subf r4 = r12,r11														
	stw a(r1) = r4														
OUT:															

(a) Correct prediction. Branch was not taken.

(b) Incorrect prediction. Branch was taken.

		1	2	3	4	5	6	7	8	9	10	11	12	13	14	15	16
	lwz r8 = a(r1)	F	D	E	C	W											
	lwz r12 = b(r1,4)	F	.	D	E	C	W										
	lwz r9 = c(r1,8)	F	.	.	D	E	C	W									
	lwz r10 = d(r1,12)	F	.	.	.	D	E	C	W								
	lwz r11 = e(r1,16)	F	.	.	.	.	D	E	C	W							
	cmpi cr0 = r8,0	F	.	.	.	.	.	D	E								
	bc ELSE,cr0/gt=false	F	.	.	.	S											
IF:	add r12 = r8,r12	F	.	.	.	.	.	.	.	.	D´						
	add r12 = r12,r9			F	.	.	.	.	.								
	add r12 = r12,10			F	.	.	.	.	.								
	add r4 = r12,r11																
	stw a(r1) = r4																
	b OUT																
ELSE:	subf r12 = r8,r12										F	D	E	W			
	subf r12 = r12,r9										F	.	D	E	W		
	subf r12 = r12,r10										F	.	.	D	E	W	
	subf r4 = r12,r11										F	.	.	.	D	E	W
	stw a(r1) = r4										F	.	.	.	D	E	C
OUT:																	

(b) Incorrect prediction. Branch was taken.

FIGURE 8.11   Branch prediction: not taken. Conditionally dispatched and executed instructions marked with a prime.

clock cycle 8. Instructions are fetched from the branch target address in the next clock cycle and dispatching resumes at the rate of one instruction per cycle. The result is that the execute stage of the pipeline did not do any work in clock cycles 9 and 10, and the mispredicted branch caused a two-cycle bubble in the pipeline.

Now let's consider the case that the branch is predicted taken (Figure 8.12). The branch is dispatched and predicted in clock cycle 5, and the fetch logic places a request to access the cache to fetch instructions from the branch target address. This request, however, can't be granted right away. During cycles 4–8 the unified cache is busy with data access operations of the load instructions. Data requests as a result of instructions already executing in the pipeline are always given priority over instruction fetching.

The earliest available cache cycle is clock period 9. Instruction dispatching does not resume until clock cycle 10. The two-cycle bubble in the pipeline is a result of cache contention rather than branch misprediction.

In Figure 8.12(b), the branch is predicted taken, but the prediction is incorrect. A request to fetch instructions from the cache is placed as early as cycle 5, but it is delayed because the cache is unavailable. Instructions are never fetched from the branch target address because the branch is resolved in cycle 8 before the cache becomes available, and the prediction is found to be incorrect. Hence, the previous instructions are still in the instruction buffer, ready for dispatching. This saves the fetch cycle, and instruction processing can resume one cycle earlier. Interestingly enough, the code with the correct prediction takes one cycle longer than the code with the incorrect prediction, because the delay in gaining access to the cache is longer than the misprediction recovery.

To summarize this example, if the prediction is correct, the instruction dispatch logic may be capable of keeping the pipeline full, depending on the availability of instructions. When a not-taken branch is correctly predicted, instructions are likely to be available in the instruction buffer. When a taken branch is correctly predicted, instructions must be quickly fetched, but cache contention may be a source of lost cycles.

The compiler may be able to reduce or entirely eliminate the misprediction penalty by scheduling the code. The compare instruction is shifted up in the instruction stream, an optimization that can be performed in our example because the compare is independent of the previous load instructions (with the exception of the first one).

```
cmpi    cr0=r8,0
lwz     r10=d(r1,12)
lwz     r11=e(r1,16)
bc      ELSE,cr0/gt=false
```

Now that the compare executes earlier, the branch may be resolved early enough to keep instructions flowing. One instruction between the cmpi and bc is sufficient if the branch is predicted taken, because in the case of misprediction, instructions are likely to be in the buffer. Two instructions between the cmpi and bc are needed if the branch is predicted not taken to allow for a fetch cycle if the prediction is incorrect.

Instruction	1	2	3	4	5	6	7	8	9	10	11	12	13	14	15	16
lwz r8 = a(r1)	F	D	E	C	W											
lwz r12 = b(r1,4)	F	.	D	E	C	W										
lwz r9 = c(r1,8)	F	.	.	D	E	C	W									
lwz r10 = d(r1,12)	F	.	.	.	D	E	C	W								
lwz r11 = e(r1,16)	F	.	.	.	.	D	E	C	W							
cmpi cr0 = r8,0	F	.	.	.	.	.	D	E								
bc ELSE,cr0/gt=false	F	.	.	.	S											
IF: add r12 = r8,r12	F	.	.	.	.	.	.	.								
add r12 = r12,r9			F	.	.	.	.	.								
add r12 = r12,10			F	.	.	.	.	.								
add r4 = r12,r11																
stw a(r1) = r4																
b OUT																
ELSE: subf r12 = r8,r12									F	D	E	W				
subf r12 = r12,r9									F	.	D	E	W			
subf r12 = r12,r10									F	.	.	D	E	W		
subf r4 = r12,r11									F	.	.	.	D	E	W	
stw a(r1) = r4									F	.	.	.	.	D	E	C
OUT:																

(a) Correct prediction. Branch was taken.

Instruction	1	2	3	4	5	6	7	8	9	10	11	12	13	14	15
lwz r8 = a(r1)	F	D	E	C	W										
lwz r12 = b(r1,4)	F	.	D	E	C	W									
lwz r9 = c(r1,8)	F	.	.	D	E	C	W								
lwz r10 = d(r1,12)	F	.	.	.	D	E	C	W							
lwz r11 = e(r1,16)	F	.	.	.	.	D	E	C	W						
cmpi cr0 = r8,0	F	.	.	.	.	.	D	E							
bc ELSE,cr0/gt=false	F	.	.	.	S										
IF: add r12 = r8,r12	F	.	.	.	.	.	.	.	.	D	E	W			
add r12 = r12,r9			F	.	.	.	.	.	.	.	D	E	W		
add r12 = r12,10			F	.	.	.	.	.	.	.	.	D	E	W	
add r4 = r12,r11										F	.	.	D	E	W
stw a(r1) = r4										F	.	.	.	D	E	C
b OUT															
ELSE: subf r12 = r8,r12															
subf r12 = r12,r9															
subf r12 = r12,r10															
subf r4 = r12,r11															
stw a(r1) = r4															
OUT:															

(b) Incorrect prediction. Branch was not taken.

FIGURE 8.12 Branch prediction: taken.

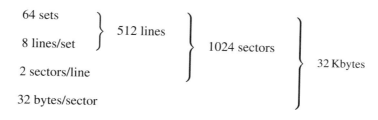

(a) Cache structure.

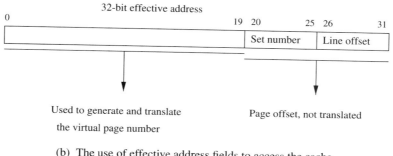

(b) The use of effective address fields to access the cache.

FIGURE 8.13   PowerPC 601 unified cache.

8.4 Cache Memory

Figure 8.13(a) illustrates the PowerPC 601 cache organization. In such a large cache, increasing associativity beyond 2 or 4 brings very little improvement in the miss ratio, so improving the miss ratio is not the reason for using 8-way associativity. If the cache is not larger than the product of the page size (4 Kbytes) and the associativity (8-way), the set number field is contained entirely in the page offset field (Figure 8.13(b)). Since the page offset field is not changed by address translation, the cache directory lookup may be overlapped with virtual address translation.

The unit of transfer between the cache and main memory is a 32-byte *sector*. A line with a single tag is split into two sectors. The line/sector structure reduces the storage space needed for tags by associating tags with lines and reduces the memory bus traffic by transferring smaller units to/from main memory.

A sector is brought in when there is a cache miss. The miss can be a line hit, but a sector miss, in which case the new sector takes its place in the already-present line. If there is a line

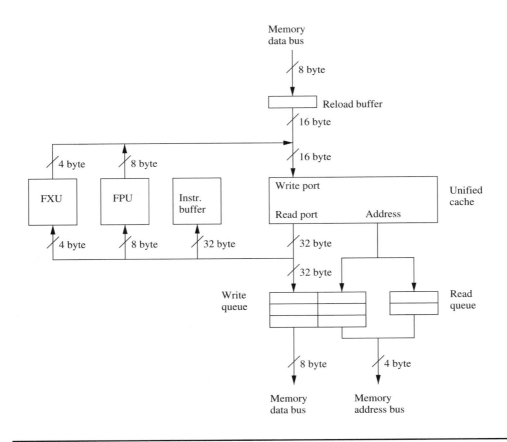

FIGURE 8.14   PowerPC 601 cache interfaces.

miss, an entire line must be replaced; one sector is valid, and the other is invalid. Both sectors of a replaced line must be written back to memory if they are valid and modified. Finally, one sector may be invalidated independently of the other by a cache instruction or multiprocessing activity.

Cache Interfaces

The cache has a 32-byte read port, unusually large, but apparently affordable because the cache is on-chip and reads are internal to the chip (Figure 8.14). This interface matches the size of the 32-byte sector and the size of the instruction buffer. One important use is instruction fetching—a full 32-byte instruction buffer may be fetched in a single cycle if instructions do not cross sector boundaries. The 32-byte read is also used to read a sector that must be written back to memory. While the write operation itself will take multiple cycles on the 8-byte memory bus, reading the sector from the cache takes just one clock cycle, immediately freeing the cache for other requests.

The 32-byte read port also allows unaligned data to be handled in a single cycle; most other RISCs do not allow unaligned references. For example, if a 32-bit word begins in the last byte of a word, as long as the addressed word plus the next word are in the same sector, they are both read from the cache at the same time. Select/alignment logic can be used to read and align the bytes from the two words. If an unaligned access happens to cross a sector boundary, then the cache must be held for two clock periods while two sectors are accessed.

Store operations into the cache usually take a single cycle, even though performing a store requires reading a sector, modifying it, and writing it back into the cache. As with loads, if the store data are unaligned, but both parts are in the same sector, the store can be done in a single cache cycle. Otherwise, when the data span two sectors, two access cycles are needed.

The 16-byte write port allows a sector to be transferred into the cache in two clock cycles. The cache does not block after a miss but remains available to service subsequent accesses while a miss is being serviced. Once the memory responds, it takes four clock cycles to transfer a cache sector onto the chip via the 8-byte memory data interface. The incoming data are buffered as they arrive. When the entire sector is available, it is loaded into the cache in two single-cycle transfers of four words each. It is only during this two-cycle time period that the cache is required for the miss service.

The memory queue buffers memory requests as they go on or off the chip. It provides "speed matching" between the 601 external bus and the higher bandwidth internal cache interface. It also allows memory accesses to be performed in an order that may be different from the order in which they arrive. This flexibility can improve performance, for example, by letting loads pass stores. The memory queue is really implemented as two queues, a two-entry read queue and a three-entry write queue. The read queue holds addresses waiting to leave the chip. Each entry in the write queue holds a full sector of instructions or data and its address.

The memory queue control logic supports a form of hardware prefetching by automatically loading the second sector of a cache line after fetching the first one, provided the bus is idle. The control logic that performs prefetching was needed to implement the PowerPC data cache block touch instruction, which is essentially a load without a destination register (see Section 9.6). Hardware prefetching was provided at little extra cost, and it can be turned on and off via a mode bit in a hardware implementation–dependent register.

Cache Lookup

Figure 8.15 illustrates the cache lookup logic. Following are the main components involved in this process:

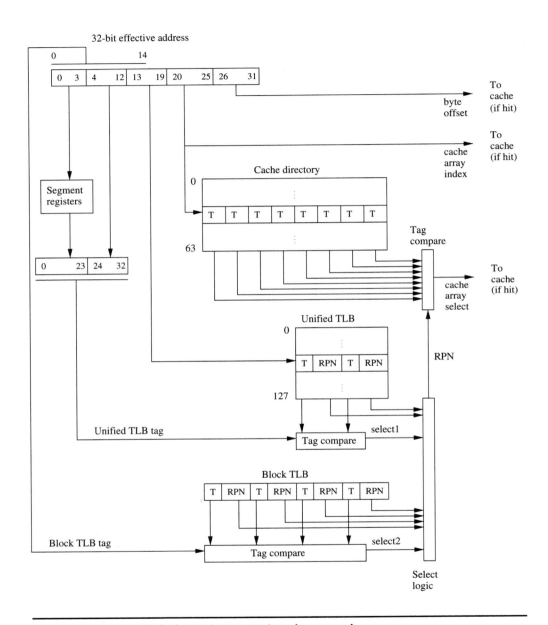

FIGURE 8.15 Cache lookup. T is tag. RPN is real page number.

■ An 8-way associative cache directory that consists of 64 sets (numbered 0 to 63) with eight tags per set.

■ A 2-way associative Unified TLB (U-TLB) with 128 sets (numbered 0 to 127). If there is a hit, the U-TLB produces the real page number (RPN) associated with the matching tag.

■ A fully associative Block TLB (B-TLB) with four entries. In case of a hit, the B-TLB produces the RPN associated with the matching tag.

■ A set of 16 segment registers.

■ Tag comparators and select logic.

The architecture provides for a block address translation (BAT) mechanism that maps large blocks of data into physical memory. Up to four blocks may be defined; the remaining memory is paged. Translation of block addresses is performed by four pairs of registers, called Upper and Lower BAT registers (see Section 7.5). For fast translation, the 601 implements associative lookup of the BAT registers. The B-TLB consists of the BAT registers and the tags and comparators that implement the associative lookup. (We use the term B-TLB here because it is used for address translation, and it is searched associatively, like a TLB. There is an important distinction, however. The B-TLB does not cache information from a memory-resident table. Rather, the B-TLB itself is the block translation table.)

Bits 26–31 of the effective address are used as the byte offset into the 64-byte cache line. Bits 20–25 select one of the 64 cache sets. These two fields of the effective address form the page offset, which is not translated. Hence, the cache directory can be immediately accessed, and the eight tags are brought to the input of the tag comparator without waiting for the virtual address translation.

At the same time, bits 13–19 (which are the lower bits of the virtual page number) of the address are used to select one of the 128 sets of the U-TLB, which gates the two tags to the inputs of the U-TLB tag comparator. The U-TLB tag itself is part of the virtual page number and is produced by concatenating 24 bits from the selected segment register with bits from the effective address, as shown in Figure 8.15.

At the same time, the four tags of the B-TLB are gated to the inputs of the B-TLB tag comparator. The B-TLB tag itself is the 15 most significant bits of the effective address. Where does the number 15 come from? The smallest block has 128 Kbytes, which requires 17 address bits. Hence, no more than the 15 upper bits of the 32-bit effective adddress are required to identify a block (obviously, the tag is shorter if the block is larger).

We summarize here the operations that take place in this first phase of the cache lookup:

1. The cache directory is accessed and the tags of the selected set are brought to the comparator inputs.

2. The U-TLB is accessed, the tags of the selected entry are brought to the U-TLB comparator inputs, and the corresponding RPNs are brought to the select logic.

3. A segment register is accessed and its contents are used to form the U-TLB tag, which goes to the other side of the U-TLB comparator.

4. The B-TLB is accessed, the tags are brought to the B-TLB comparator inputs, and the corresponding RPNs are brought to the select logic.

All four of these actions are done in parallel.

If there is a hit in the B-TLB, then the RPN is the one associated with the matching B-TLB tag. If there is a hit in the U-TLB, the RPN is the one associated with the matching U-TLB tag. Otherwise, there is a miss and the page tables must be accessed to update the U-TLB (of course, the page table lookup itself may end in a page fault).

Finally, if there is a B-TLB hit, a U-TLB hit, or both, the resulting RPN is compared with the cache tags. In case of a hit, all the information is available to access the cache arrays during the next clock cycle.

To simplify presentation, Figure 8.15 shows that the select logic produces an RPN, which is then compared with the cache tags. To save time, this order may be reversed, however. That is, "candidate" RPNs may be simultaneously compared with the cache tags, and the selection performed afterwards, when the results of accessing the U-TLB and B-TLB are known.

We have assumed so far that the cache is accessed for data. For instructions, a small, four-entry, fully associative, Instruction TLB (I-TLB) is also provided. Each entry translates the virtual address of one 4 Kbyte page (1024 instructions), so the entire I-TLB provides address translation for 4096 instructions. Due to the high locality of instructions, even this small I-TLB has a good hit ratio. The I-TLB is filled from the U-TLB, and, in case of a miss, the instruction fetch unit arbitrates for access to the U-TLB.

8.5 PowerPC 601 and POWER1 Implementations

The PowerPC 601 inherited most of the original POWER1 pipelined structure, and it is instructive to compare the 601 side by side with a multichip POWER1 (Figure 8.16). The following are the main differences in the structure of the pipelines.

- FXU decoding in the 601 is done in the same clock cycle (same pipeline stage) as dispatching. This was not feasible in POWER1, where dispatching involved chip crossing.

- In general, POWER1 has more buffering than the 601 (not shown in the figure).

- The 601 FPU pipeline is shorter, it does not include the predecoding and renaming stages because of chip area limitations (see Chapter 3 for more details on renaming).

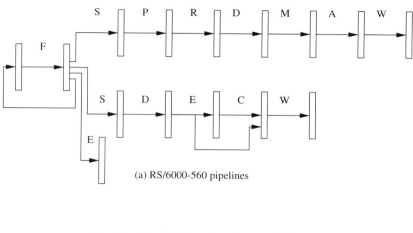

(a) RS/6000-560 pipelines

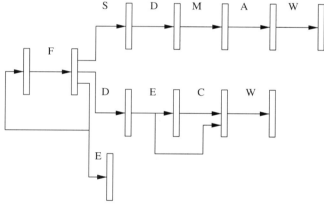

(b) PowerPC 601 pipelines

FIGURE 8.16 Pipeline structures.

While the PowerPC 601 does not implement floating-point register renaming, it does implement renaming for the Link and Count Registers (LR and CTR). The motivation for renaming is similar, but it involves two other units, the BU and FXU. Both units execute instructions that use or change the LR and CTR, and a resource dependence comes up whenever the BU (which is a shorter pipeline) changes either the LR or the CTR while it is still needed by another instruction in the FXU pipeline. It is clear that renaming the LR and CTR requires

Pipeline	Maximum rate (instructions per clock cycle)	
stage	PowerPC 601	POWER1
Fetch	8	4
Dispatch	3	4
FPU predecode	N/A	2
FPU rename	N/A	2
Other stages	1	1

FIGURE 8.17   **Instruction-processing rate.**

fewer resources than renaming the 32 double-length floating-point registers. Also, floating-point register renaming helps floating but not integer programs, while LR and CTR renaming improves both.

Figure 8.17 illustrates the POWER1 and 601 instruction-processing rates. While the 601 peak dispatching rate is lower (three instructions per clock cycle versus four in POWER1), in practice the difference is insignificant. The POWER1 reaches the peak rate if the four instructions at the top of the instruction buffer consist of a branch, a logical Condition Register instruction, and two integer or floating instructions (or one of each)—a mix that rarely occurs. However, the 601 may dispatch instructions out of order if the fixed-point instruction at the top of the buffer is interlocked, a situation that may come up more frequently.

One of the interesting differences between the 601 and POWER1 has to do with the way virtual address aliasing is handled. (See Section 5.4 for a discussion of aliases.) In POWER1, the problem is solved at the level of the architecture. The inverted page table implementation naturally enforces one-to-one virtual to physical address mappings; hence, two virtual addresses cannot simultaneously map to the same physical address.

In the PowerPC page table, aliases may occur, so the 601 uses an implementation-level solution. The set index field is entirely contained in the page offset field; cache lookup may be overlapped with virtual address translation because the set index field is not translated. The 8-way associativity was needed to implement a 32 Kbyte cache.

Code Example

Figure 8.18 shows POWER1 and 601 processing of a code example. The comparison may not be entirely "fair"; we look at single-precision data in the 601 and double-precision in POWER1. But we feel it is instructive to look at each processor running in the mode for which it is optimized. POWER1 performs all floating-point computations in double precision, and single precision actually may run slower because of the extra rounding instructions. The 601 is just the opposite: double-precision multiplication is slower, because it requires two passes

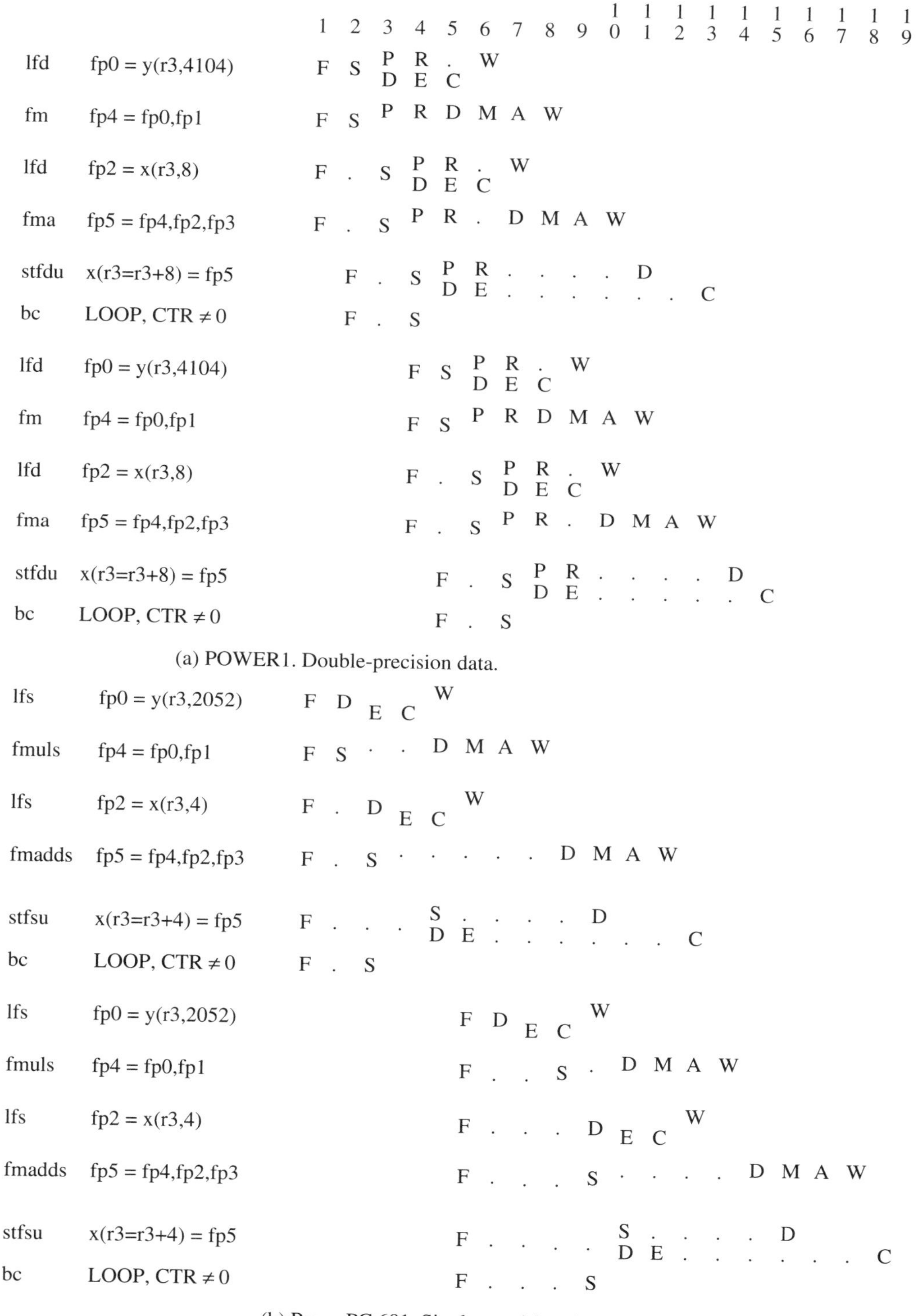

```
                                        1  1  1  1  1  1  1  1  1  1
                    1  2  3  4  5  6  7  8  9  0  1  2  3  4  5  6  7  8  9
lfd    fp0 = y(r3,4104)   F  S  P  R  .  W
                                D  E  C
fm     fp4 = fp0,fp1      F  S  P  R  D  M  A  W
lfd    fp2 = x(r3,8)      F  .  S  P  R  .  W
                                   D  E  C
fma    fp5 = fp4,fp2,fp3  F  .  S  P  R  .  D  M  A  W
stfdu  x(r3=r3+8) = fp5      F  .  S  P  R  .  .  .  .  D
                                      D  E  .  .  .  .  .  C
bc     LOOP, CTR ≠ 0        F  .  S
lfd    fp0 = y(r3,4104)           F  S  P  R  .  W
                                        D  E  C
fm     fp4 = fp0,fp1              F  S  P  R  D  M  A  W
lfd    fp2 = x(r3,8)              F  .  S  P  R  .  W
                                           D  E  C
fma    fp5 = fp4,fp2,fp3          F  .  S  P  R  .  D  M  A  W
stfdu  x(r3=r3+8) = fp5             F  .  S  P  R  .  .  .  .  D
                                            D  E  .  .  .  .  .  C
bc     LOOP, CTR ≠ 0               F  .  S
```

(a) POWER1. Double-precision data.

```
lfs    fp0 = y(r3,2052)   F  D  E  C  W
fmuls  fp4 = fp0,fp1      F  S  .  .  D  M  A  W
lfs    fp2 = x(r3,4)      F  .  D  E  C  W
fmadds fp5 = fp4,fp2,fp3  F  .  S  .  .  .  .  D  M  A  W
stfsu  x(r3=r3+4) = fp5   F  .  .  .  S  .  .  .  .  D
                                      D  E  .  .  .  .  .  .  C
bc     LOOP, CTR ≠ 0      F  .  S
lfs    fp0 = y(r3,2052)              F  D  E  C  W
fmuls  fp4 = fp0,fp1                 F  .  .  S  .  D  M  A  W
lfs    fp2 = x(r3,4)                 F  .  .  .  D  E  C  W
fmadds fp5 = fp4,fp2,fp3             F  .  .  S  .  .  .  D  M  A  W
stfsu  x(r3=r3+4) = fp5              F  .  .  .  S  .  .  .  .  D
                                              D  E  .  .  .  .  .  .  C
bc     LOOP, CTR ≠ 0                 F  .  .  S
```

(b) PowerPC 601. Single-precision data.

FIGURE 8.18   Code example from Figure 3.5 and Figure 8.7.

through the pipeline's multiply stage. (This, it could be argued, is also unfair; the PowerPC 601 is optimized for integer code, and this is a floating-point example.)

We have looked at this example before, in POWER1 (Figure 3.6) and in the PowerPC 601 (Figure 8.8); explanations of the timing diagrams can be found there. Comparing POWER1 with the 601, we see that the main difference has to do with the absence of bypass paths in the 601 floating arithmetic pipeline, as well as the lack of a register file write-through capability. A dependent arithmetic instruction must wait until the result is in its destination register. Bypass paths in POWER1 often reduce data dependence delays to a single clock cycle.

How significant is this in terms of performance? The three instructions that reach the 601 FPU pipe (`fmuls`, `fmadds`, and `stfsu`) flow through the POWER1 pipe in four clock cycles: three cycles for the `fm` and `fma`, taking into account one cycle delay due to the dependence, and one cycle to decode the store. It takes two extra cycles in the 601 to take care of the dependence between the arithmetic instructions. This estimate leads one to expect a ratio of roughly 1.5:1 in the floating performance of the two pipeline structures running this particular code example, assuming of course the same clock rate.

8.6   Summary and Conclusions

The overall structure of the PowerPC 601 is very much like its older sibling, POWER1. Being a single-chip implementation targeted at PC applications, however, it has some interesting differences.

A central feature is the unified cache. Studies (see [80]) have shown that a unified cache tends to gives better miss rates than a split cache of comparable size. A unified cache gives program-dependent flexibility in the way the cache is divided between instructions and data. In a processor with separate caches, this division is built into the hardware and may not be optimal for many programs.

Split caches are often used, however, because they provide higher bandwidth. Instructions and data can be accessed simultaneously. The bandwidth problem is overcome in the 601 by having a very wide (32-byte) access path to the cache. This width is possible because the cache is on-chip, so there are no pin limitation problems. The wide path can be used to fetch up to eight instructions or load the cache with a sector of memory data in a single cycle. A useful by-product of the wide path is that most unaligned data accesses can be done with no performance penalty.

A second significant feature of the 601 implementation is the emphasis on fixed-point performance (and a corresponding de-emphasis on floating point). There is no FPU register renaming and there are no bypasses for floating-point results. Several 64-bit floating-point instructions take multiple passes through the FPU execution unit. In a single-chip implementation, silicon real estate is at a premium, and engineering trade-offs must be made. In the 601, it is apparent that many of these trade-offs came at the expense of the FPU. In future implementations with denser logic technologies, we can expect that the FPU will return to the level of complexity it had with POWER1.

The de-emphasis on floating point in favor of fixed point probably reflects the personal computer application bias. In a typical PC workload, floating point is less important than it is in the typical workstation workload, where scientific and engineering applications are more common.

8.7 References

Because the PowerPC 601 is a new processor, there are few references. The Motorola 601 user's manual [62] is a useful reference, as are a series of papers that appeared in Compcon Spring 1993. The Compcon papers are Paap and Silha [68], which is an overview of the PowerPC architecture; Moore [61], a description of the 601 implementation; and Allen and Becker [2], a paper in which the focus is on multiprocessing capabilities of the 601.

POWERPC: SUPPORT FOR MULTIPROCESSING

9.1 Introduction

Personal computers and workstations are based on relatively simple system architectures, incorporating a single central processor. To provide higher performance, server-class systems are often based on shared-memory multiprocessors. The servers can provide high system throughput by running several independent jobs at once, or they can accelerate a single job by using parallel processing.

The POWER architecture has no special provisions for supporting shared-memory multiprocessor systems; it was designed for uniprocessor workstation and small server applications. Multiple-processor systems can be used in networked multicomputers, with each processor having its own address space. When used as a single computational entity, these multicomputer systems are often referred to as workstation "clusters." The RS/6000 approach of using multicomputer clusters is adequate for some server applications (for example, as file servers that require throughput), but multicomputers do not have the same flexibility as shared-memory systems, especially for parallel processing. Furthermore, the importance of multiprocessors will likely increase in the future as demands for performance become greater and hardware

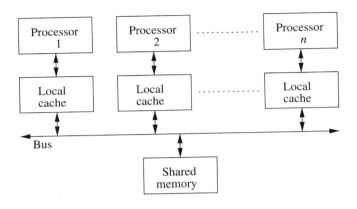

FIGURE 9.1   Single-bus shared-memory multiprocessor.

costs become lower. It is just a matter of time before single-user desktop systems begin using multiple processors.

PowerPC, intended as a long-term architecture designed to cover a broad spectrum of system applications, has a number of features for supporting shared-memory multiprocessing. Figure 9.1 is a block diagram illustrating the PowerPC 601 in a shared memory multiprocessor system. This chapter describes the different aspects of multiprocessing in the PowerPC 601. The discussion covers instructions to support process synchronization and coordination, as well as important aspects of the implementation, especially cache coherence.

9.2 Architectural Support for Multiprocessing

In a typical server, multiprocessing features support both system and user software. The operating system can run on any of the processors and is often "multithreaded," which means that more than one processor can be running operating system code at the same time. In a multithreaded operating system, features are required to support the sharing of important system tables, such as the page table. One processor might be running a thread that needs to make a change to shared memory, so it locks the page table, or a portion of it, before making the change. While locked, some of the page table may migrate into the processor's cache and be modified. When the processor is finished, the table is unlocked. Instructions to provide reliable locking are an important part of the multiprocessor architecture. Because other processors use the same table, cache coherence mechanisms are important to ensure an accurate global view of the page table.

User applications can also take advantage of multiple processors by running multiple

Iteration	Each iteration to a different processor	A block of 4 iterations to each processor
1	p1	p1
2	p2	p1
3	p1	p1
4	p2	p1
5	p1	p2
6	p2	p2
7	p1	p2
8	p2	p2

FIGURE 9.2   Static scheduling of a loop (eight iterations) onto two processors p1 and p2.

threads in parallel. To understand the synchronization and coordination features of the PowerPC architecture, consider the following loop from a user-level parallel application:

for (i = 1; i ≤ n; i++)
        x[i] = x[i] + y[i] * z[i];

Iterations of the loop are independent and may be executed in parallel; we assume the number of loop iterations, n, is large enough to make parallel processing worthwhile. The iterations of the loop are executed in parallel by assigning them to the available processors. There are a number of ways of doing this. The compiler can make the assignment either by giving consecutive iterations to different processors or by assigning a block of n/p iterations to each of the p processors (Figure 9.2). This static scheduling by the compiler requires little runtime coordination among the processors and may be the best choice if the processors have similar speeds and the number of processors is fixed throughout the runtime of the job. But in multiprogramming environments, the system is shared by a number of applications and the load on each processor varies dynamically, as may the number of available processors. Because of page faults and cache misses, the processors process individual loop iterations at different speeds, even though they apparently have similar amounts of work to do.

Rather than splitting the work equally at compile time, it may be better to assign less work to those processors that already have a higher load at runtime. This dynamic assignment of work to processors may be implemented by maintaining a global variable i to keep track of the next unassigned loop iteration. Work is assigned to the processors on "demand," using i. A processor that is done with its current assignment on behalf of this job may "grab" another loop iteration (or a block of iterations) by reading the value of i and incrementing it, so that the next processor demanding work will get the next iteration(s). This method requires two operations: fetch the value of a variable i, and add an increment value to it. The procedure will work using an ordinary load, a fixed-point add, and a store *provided* situations like the following never occur:

Processor 1	Processor 2
Fetch *i*	
	Fetch *i*
	Add 1 to *i*
Add 1 to *i*	

Here, both processors 1 and 2 get the same value of *i* and end up working on the same iteration of the loop; worse yet, the next iteration is skipped. Hence, the combined Fetch and Add operation must be performed *atomically*—while one processor is executing the Fetch and Add on *i*, no other processor may access *i*.

To implement an atomic Fetch and Add operation (as well as other synchronization primitives), the PowerPC architecture defines two instructions: load word and reserve indexed (lwarx) and store word conditional indexed (stwcx.).[1] (The 64-bit PowerPC instruction set also includes doubleword versions of these instructions, ldarx and stdcx., which are functionally equivalent, with the exception of the size of the referenced object.)

The lwarx instruction loads a variable and places a reservation on a block of memory addresses referred to as a *reservation granule*. The granule size is determined by the number of low-order bits of the real address that are ignored. The reservation granule is implementation-dependent, but the PowerPC architecture specifies that it should be a multiple of the *coherence granule;* in the 601, this is a cache sector. Recall that in the 601 a *sector* is half of a line and is the unit of transfer between the cache and main memory. A processor can hold no more than one reservation at any time. The reservation is lost if any of the following occurs:

1. The same processor that made the reservation executes another lwarx. The previous reservation is lost and a new one made.

2. The same processor that made the reservation executes a stwcx. instruction. The reservation is cleared even if the address of the stwcx. does not match the address of the lwarx.

3. Another processor executes a store on the same reservation granule. That is, by monitoring the bus, the processor can detect when another processor has performed a store to that reservation granule, and it clears the reservation. The data cache block set to zero (dcbz) instruction is treated as a store (all bytes of the block are set to zero), and has the same effect.

---

[1]The dot in the stwcx. mnemonic indicates that the instruction sets the condition register (field 0) to reflect whether the store operation was actually performed.

4. The processor is interrupted or trapped to supervisor state (away from the task that placed the reservation). The interrupt itself leaves the reservation intact, but the system software that services the interrupt may clear it.

The subsequent `stwcx.` is executed only if the reservation is intact; otherwise, `stwcx.` has no effect; it is treated as a no-op. The "eq" bit in Condition Register 0 is set if the store is successful. A conditional branch can then determine whether the atomic operation has completed or should be retried.

Using `lwarx` and `stwcx.`, the Fetch and Add operation may be implemented as follows.

```
                                # register r2 points to i
LOOP:   lwarx    r9 = i(r2)     # load i and reserve
        ai       r9 = r9,1      # increment i
        stwcx.   i(r2) = r9     # store new i conditionally
        bc       LOOP,cr0/eq=false  # branch if store failed
```

Example—Parallel Loop

To implement our earlier parallel loop example, we use the fetch and increment sequence given above, and add an additional comparison to ensure that $i \leq n$, the number of loop iterations. This code portions out a single iteration at a time; blocks of iterations are probably more efficient and can be implemented with code that is only slightly more complicated. Each processor performs the following:

```
                                # register r2 points to i
                                # register r3 contains n
LOOP:   lwarx    r9 = i(r2)     # load i and reserve
        cmp      cr0 = r9,r3    # compare i to n
        bc       EXIT,cr0/gt=true   # branch if i > n
        ai       r9 = r9,1      # increment i
        stwcx.   i(r2) = r9     # store new i conditionally
        bc       LOOP,cr0/eq=false  # branch if store failed
        execute iteration i of loop.
        b        LOOP           # go back to get more work to do
EXIT:   ...
```

Example—Table Locking

Let's now return to the problem of locking a table, modifying it, then unlocking it.

```
                                    # register r2 points to the table lock
LOOP:   lwarx    r9 = lock(r2)      # load lock and reserve
        cmp      cr0 = r9,1         # check to see if lock already set
        bc       LOOP,cr0/eq=true   # branch if lock already set
        addi     r9 = 1             # set the lock
        stwcx.   lock(r2) = r9      # store lock to memory
        bc       LOOP,cr0/eq=false  # try again if store failed
        perform modification to the table
        sync                        # make sure changes are visible
                                    # system-wide
        addi     r9 = 0             # clear the lock
        stwx     lock(r2) = r9      # store the lock to memory
EXIT:   . . .
```

Acquiring the lock is very similar to performing the Fetch and Add we did earlier. In this case, we check to see if the lock is already set; if so, we go back and try again. This is referred to as "spinning on the lock." If the lock is clear, the process sets the lock using a `stwcx.`, then checks to make sure the store went through; if not, it's back to spinning again. Once the lock is set, the process is free to modify the table; any other processor that checks the lock will find it set and have to wait. When the process is finished with the table, it can unlock it. First, it executes a `sync` instruction that halts instruction decoding until all stores are guaranteed to be visible throughout the system (more on this later.) To clear the lock, an ordinary store can be used; it is atomic in itself and does not have to be made so by a `stwcx./lwarx` pair.

9.3 Memory Ordering

In examples such as the ones above, it is natural to implicitly assume a well-behaved shared-memory model, that is, a model in which the memory references made by a processor are *performed* in shared memory in exactly the same sequence as the program specifies. By *perform,* we mean the result is globally visible to all the processors. Processors may run at different speeds so that the sequences of references from different processors may be interleaved in different ways, but all the references from the same processor are performed in order. This is commonly referred to as *sequential consistency.*

For example, assume the variables x and y are initially set to 0, and consider the following code sequence:

```
proc 0      proc 1
y=0         x=0
  ⋮           ⋮
x=1         y=1
a=y*2       b=x*2
```

With sequential consistency, it is possible for either a or b to be 0 when the code is finished, but it is not possible for both to be 0. One of them can be 0 if the two processors execute their code at different speeds. For example, if proc 1 executes b=x*2 before proc 0 executes x=1, then b will be 0. If this happens, a cannot be 0 by the following argument. With sequential consistency y=1 must be performed before b=x*2 and x=1 must be performed before a=y*2. Because b=x*2 yields zero, it must have been performed before x=1, so it follows that y=1 must have been performed before a=y*2, so a cannot be 0.

Although sequential consistency seems natural, it does not come naturally in many high-speed implementations. For example, the processors may have store buffers that allow loads to pass pending stores (we have already seen several examples in POWER1 and PowerPC 601 implementations). With store buffers, it is possible for both a and b to be 0. All it takes is for the x=1 and y=1 stores to be held up in a store buffer while the loads of x and y in a=y*2 and b=x*2 proceed.

We don't need a contrived example to find memory ordering problems, either. In our table lock example (ignoring the sync instruction for the moment), if the table update gets hung up in a buffer and the clear of the lock sails through, then another processor can get the lock and see a stale version of the table. Sequential consistency would prevent this from happening; the table update would have to be performed before the lock is cleared.

One could always enforce sequential consistency by making sure that loads and stores are always performed in strict program order. Unfortunately, performance would suffer. Recall the example in Figure 3.6 in which execution is able to proceed beyond pending stores so that the third loop iteration is already under way before the store at the end of the first iteration has been completed. Forcing all loads and stores to go in order would slow this loop considerably.

Furthermore, sequential consistency is not always needed for correctness during parallel processing. In our loop example, a processor assigned a block of loop iterations could use store buffering to improve performance. Loads and stores to x and y do not have to be in sequentially consistent because the loop iterations are independent.

These considerations lead to *weak ordering,* where all loads and stores have to be complete only at certain synchronization points. In the locked table example, this point would occur whenever the lock is cleared. In the loop example, memory ordering is typically enforced only after all the loop iterations are done—before another set of loops is performed on the same data (possibly by using a different assignment of iterations to processors). This form of ordering is referred to as *barrier synchronization.*

To enforce memory ordering only when it is needed, the PowerPC architecture has some explicit memory ordering instructions. In general, it is the responsibility of the application (either through the language, compiler directives, or the compiler itself) to place synchronization instructions as needed for correct program execution. The `sync` instruction delays all following instructions until all previous memory accesses have been performed. The `eieio` (enforce in-order execution of i/o) instruction performs a similar function but only waits for loads and stores to areas of memory where caching is inhibited (as would be the case for memory-mapped input/output).[2] In the 601, `sync` and `eieio` are actually implemented in the same way, because `eieio` was a late addition to the architecture. Consequently, the `eieio` is a little "stronger" than required. The `sync` instruction also waits for any exceptions to be reported by previous instructions; this makes it useful for enforcing precise interrupts.

In our locked table example, weak ordering is enforced by executing a `sync` instruction just prior to clearing the lock.

9.4   Cache Coherence

Memory ordering is a problem that exists independently of data caches. For example, the Cray supercomputers have special features to force memory ordering, and they have no data caches at all. Caches do have the potential to make the ordering problem worse, however, because they can obscure the "visibility" of stores to all the system processors. For example, consider the following sequence of events.

1. Processor 0 reads variable A; A is put into Processor 0's cache.

2. Processor 1 reads variable A; A is put into Processor 1's cache.

3. Processor 0 writes to variable A.

4. Processor 1 reads variable A; it uses its cached value.

The second time Processor 1 reads A, it gets a stale value (i.e., the value it originally read), not the value Processor 0 wrote, regardless of whether the caches are write-through or write-back. With a write-through cache, main memory is up-to-date, but the write still isn't visible to Processor 1.

Cache coherence mechanisms are intended to make updates to caches visible to the rest of the system, *as if* they had been done to a globally shared memory. That is, all memory operations are *performed* as soon as they are made to a processor's data cache. Like many recent processors, the PowerPC 601 supports cache coherence automatically in hardware.

A cache coherence scheme due to Goodman [26] is based on the concept of *snooping* or monitoring a shared-memory bus. By monitoring the bus, logic associated with a processor's local cache can determine that another processor executed a load or store to an address that is

---

[2]Ordinarily, we wouldn't have mentioned this instruction, but its mnemonic was too compelling.

currently in the first processor's cache (*snooping hit*). The activity on the bus effects the *state* of a line or sector. In the PowerPC, the coherence granule is the sector, which can be in any one of the following states: Modified, Exclusive, Shared, and Invalid.

- *Modified:* Main memory does not have an up-to-date copy of this sector (the cached copy of the sector is modified with respect to memory). No other cache has a copy of this sector.

- *Exclusive:* Main memory has an up-to-date copy of this sector. No other cache holds the sector (this cache has exclusive access to it).

- *Shared:* Main memory has an up-to-date copy of this sector. Other caches may also have an up-to-date copy.

- *Invalid:* This cache does not have a valid copy of the sector.

A cache coherence *protocol* defines the transitions between the states detected by the snooping logic on the shared bus, whether they are caused by load or store instructions executed by the processor or by read or write operations of other processors. Snooping protocols with the four states listed above are known as MESI, an acronym composed of the first letter of each state. The 601 implements a snooping cache coherence scheme using the MESI protocol. There are also three-state protocols that do not include the exclusive state, as well as five-state protocols that have an additional state (known as MOESI, the *O* being the fifth state called Owned).

The four MESI states are maintained separately for each cache sector. To support snooping, the cache directory has two ports. One port is used to perform lookup of load and store addresses. The second port is used by snooping logic. By operating both ports in parallel, snooping does not interfere with normal cache accesses made by the processor.

The 601 MESI cache coherence protocol is described in Figure 9.3. Let's first consider state transitions caused by load and store instructions made by the processor (part (a)). Any store causes a transition to the Modified state. If the previous state was Invalid or Shared, an invalidate operation must be broadcast on the bus to notify the other snooping caches. This is not necessary if the previous state was Exclusive, which implies that no other caches have a copy of this sector. Any load in the Invalid state is a miss. As a result of the miss, a cache sector is loaded and assigned the Exclusive state if no other caches have it; otherwise it is made Shared.

Now, we take the viewpoint of a processor snooping the bus for reads and writes by other processors. Consider the state diagram in Figure 9.3(b). All snooped writes on the bus that hit result in a transition to the Invalid state since the local copy of the sector is now out of date. Bus invalidate operations that hit have the same effect as writes. If the state is Exclusive and there is a snooping hit on a bus read operation, the state is changed to Shared, since now there is another cache that contains the same sector. If the state is Modified and there is a a snooping hit on a read, the local cache is the only one that has the valid data. A signal is broadcast

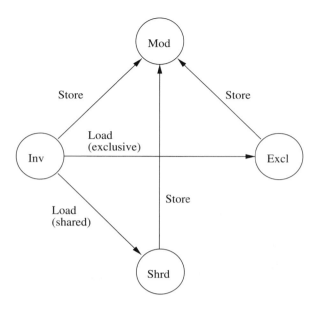

(a) Processor activities. Load (shared) means there are other caches that have copies of the loaded data. Load (exclusive) means this is the only copy.

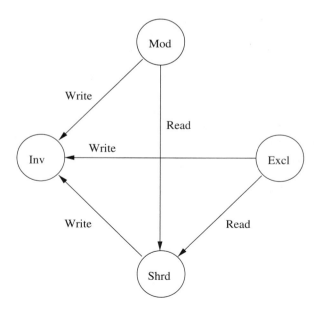

(b) Snooping activities. Read and Write are operations seen on the bus by the snooping logic.

FIGURE 9.3   601 MESI protocol.

| Cache 1 | | Cache 2 | | Memory |
Snooping	State	Snooping	State	transfer
	Inv		Inv	
	Inv → Excl			Read into cache 1

(a) Processor 1 executes a load instruction.

| Cache 1 | | Cache 2 | | Memory |
Snooping	State	Snooping	State	transfer
	Excl		Inv	
Read hit	Excl → Shrd		Inv → Shrd	Read into cache 2

(b) Processor 2 executes a load instruction.

| Cache 1 | | Cache 2 | | Memory |
Snooping	State	Snooping	State	transfer
	Shrd		Shrd	
	Shrd → Mod	Invalidate	Shrd → Inv	

(c) Processor 1 executes a store instruction.

| Cache 1 | | Cache 2 | | Memory |
Snooping	State	Snooping	State	transfer
	Mod		Inv	
Read hit	Mod		Inv	
	Mod → Shrd		Inv	Write from cache 1
	Shrd		Inv → Shrd	Read into cache 2

(d) Processor 2 executes a load instruction. It aborts the load and retries it after the modified sector is written from cache 1 into memory.

FIGURE 9.4   **Example—maintaining cache coherence in a two-processor system. The first line in each table is the initial state.**

on the bus to notify the requesting processor to abort its read operation. Next, the modified sector is written back to memory and the state is changed to Shared. Finally, the requesting processor retries the read, this time successfully.

The example in Figure 9.4 shows a sequence of state transitions in a two-processor system. All the references in cache 1 are to the same sector, and in cache 2 to a sector with the same address. Initially, the state of the sector is Invalid in both caches. A load instruction executed by processor 1 reads data from main memory and changes the state of the sector to Exclusive, since cache 1 is the only one that has valid data in this sector (part (a)). A load executed by processor 2 changes the sector state in both caches to Shared (part (b)). A subsequent store from processor 1 updates the data in the local cache and sets the state to Modified. It also broadcasts an invalidate signal on the bus; the snooping logic in processor 2 detects a hit and changes the state of the sector to Invalid (part (c)). Finally, the load instruction of processor 2 shows up on the bus as a read operation and leads to a snooping hit in processor 1. But the state is Modified, which indicates that the memory is stale. Consequently, the read bus operation is aborted, cache 1 writes the modified sector into memory, and changes the state to Shared. Now cache 2 retries a read operation (part (d)).

The 601 cache coherence protocol is implemented by means of snooping logic and a bus interface that provides the appropriate signals. A detailed description of the bus is in Chapter 10.

9.5 Higher-Level Caches

The PowerPC 601 has a single on-chip cache of 32 Kbytes, which is quite a large cache of this type. Even so, better performance can be attained with a larger cache; it just won't fit on a single chip. As a solution, the designers of the Hewlett Packard-PA implementations have built processors with no on-chip data cache, large off-chip caches, and very fast processor-to-cache interfaces. Another increasingly common alternative uses a relatively small on-chip cache and a larger off-chip cache, sometimes referred to as a "secondary" or "level 2" (L2) cache. Even when processor chips can support larger caches, it is likely that multiple levels of caches will continue to be used because larger caches lead to longer access times. Figure 9.5 illustrates a multiprocessor system with L2 caches. When the on-chip (L1) cache misses, the miss request is first serviced by the L2 cache. If the L2 cache also misses, then the sector is brought in from main memory and is placed in both the L1 and L2 caches.

With a view to implementations requiring larger caches, the PowerPC 601 designers have made provisions for supporting an L2 cache. The most important consideration is, once again, coherence. Maintaining coherence across multiple cache levels is simplified if *inclusion* is satisfied. That is, the contents of an upper-level cache (the L2 cache in our case) are made to always include the contents of lower-level caches (the on-chip cache). Addresses held in the L2 form a superset of those in the on-chip L1 cache. Thus, if snooped data are not in the L2 cache, there is no need to notify the L1 cache; it is guaranteed not to hold the data.

To support an inclusive L2 cache, the PowerPC implementation has pins that are used to tell the L2 cache which of the L1 cache's 8 associative lines has a sector replaced when a new sector is brought in. Also, when a sector is written to memory, a pin notifies the L2 cache whether or not a valid copy remains in the L1 cache.

To provide low-latency L2 accesses, provisions have been made for direct-mapped L2 caches that can anticipate a sector miss. A direct-mapped cache has the property that a given

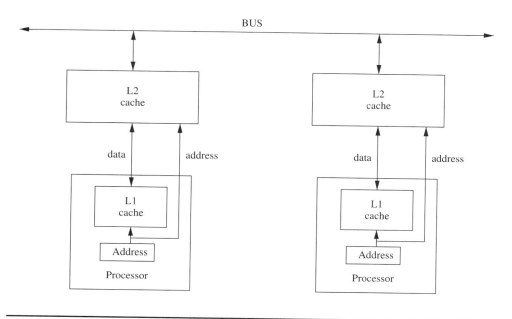

FIGURE 9.5   **Processors with L2 caches.**

piece of data can be in only one place if it is in the cache at all. Therefore, the processor can present an address to the L2 cache immediately after it is formed, and the L2 cache can start its data access in parallel both with the L1 access and with its own tag lookup and compare. In the event of an L1 miss, the data are delivered very quickly. Because the L2 cache can deliver data before it has even finished its tag check, there is a data retry function in the chip interface. If the L2 cache finds it has a miss after delivering data, it uses the data retry to flush the sector just loaded on the previous cycle.

9.6 Cache and Lookaside Buffer Management

Figure 9.6 lists synchronization, cache management, TLB management, and SLB management instructions. We have already discussed the `lwarx`, `stwcx.`, and `sync` instructions in the context of multiprocessing. In this section we focus on software management of the instruction and data caches, as well as two special-purpose caches, the TLB and SLB.

The effect of some cache management instructions depends on the coherence mode. Maintaining coherence involves bus traffic and memory updates. To reduce overhead, only

X-form

0	6	11	16	21	31
OPCD	RT	RA	RB	XO	/
	RS				

```
  lwarx    load word and reserve
* ldarx    load doubleword and reserve
  stwcx.   store word conditional
* stdcx.   store doubleword conditional
```

X-form

0	6	11	16	21	31
OPCD	//	RA	RB	XO	/

```
  icbi     instruction cache block invalidate
  dcbt     data cache block touch
  dcbtst   data cache block touch for store
  dcbf     data cache block flush
  dcbi     data cache block invalidate
  dcbz     data cache block set to zero
  dcbst    data cache block store
```

X-form

0	6	11	16	21	31
OPCD	//	//	RB	XO	/

```
* slbie    SLB invalidate entry
  tlbie    TLB invalidate entry
```

X-form

0	6	11	16	21	31
OPCD	//	//	//	XO	/

```
* slbia    SLB invalidate all
  tlbia    TLB invalidate all
  tlbsync  TLB synchronize
  sync     synchronize
  eieio    enforce in-order execution of I/O
```

XL-form

0	6	11	16	21	31
OPCD	//	//	//	XO	/

```
  isync    instruction synchronize
```

$$\text{Effective address} = \begin{cases} (RA) + (RB) & \text{if } RA \neq 0 \\ (RB) & \text{if } RA = 0 \end{cases}$$

FIGURE 9.6   **Synchronization and cache, TLB, and SLB management instructions.   64-bit PowerPC extensions are marked with ∗.**

shared data should be marked as requiring coherence. In the PowerPC, the resolution is at the page level. A bit (M) in the page table entry (Figure 7.27 and Figure 7.31) defines the coherence mode for all the cache lines contained in that page. In the rest of this discussion, "coherence is required" means that M = 1, and the hardware must enforce cache coherence. The cache management instructions are defined in terms of blocks—the unit of transfer between the cache and main memory. In the 601 implementation the unit of transfer is the sector, so all 601 cache management instructions operate on sectors.

The architecture provides two instructions to manage the instruction cache: `icbi` and `isync`. The first of these, `icbi`, invalidates the block containing the byte referred to by the effective address. If coherence is required, then the block is made invalid in all other processors that are also in coherence-required mode. If there is no instruction cache, `icbi` is a no-op. The 601 has no separate instruction cache and executes `icbi` as a no-op, without even validating the effective address.

The second instruction, `isync`, does not begin execution until all previous instructions have completed. Then it clears the instruction buffers and causes new instructions to be refetched from the cache or from memory if the cache block has been invalidated (by `icbi`). Unlike `sync`, `isync` has no effect on other caches in a multiprocessor system. The `icbi` and `isync` instructions would be useful in some situations when a processor self-modifies code, that is, if the processor stores new instructions into a region of memory that may be currently cached. These instructions will guarantee that the newly stored instructions are used, not the old ones.

The architecture also provides instructions to manage the data (or unified) cache. `Data cache block touch` (`dcbt`) is a software prefetching instruction. It is a hint that the cache block containing the byte referred by the effective address may soon be needed by a load instruction. The hardware, which does not guarantee that the block will be prefetched, must guarantee that the instruction will perform no operation if its execution would cause a protection or page fault exception. There is also a `data cache block touch for store` (`dcbtst`) instruction, which is very similar to `dcbt` but provides the information that the block will be needed by a store rather than load instruction. On the 601, `dcbt` and `dcbtst` have exactly the same effect.

The two instructions `data cache block flush` (`dcbf`) and `data cache block invalidate` (`dcbi`) flush or invalidate a block, respectively, while maintaining coherence if required. Both instructions invalidate a block if it is present in the cache of the processor executing the instruction. If coherence is required, this block is also invalidated in the caches of other processors. The only difference between the two instructions is that `dcbf` updates memory when necessary, while `dcbi` has no effect on it. If the block in the cache of the processor executing `dcbf` is modified, it is written back to memory. In coherence-required mode, execution of `dcbf` updates memory if there is a modified block with the address specified by the instruction anywhere in the system.

A block may be simply written back to memory with the `data cache block store` (`dcbst`) instruction. In coherence mode, this operation is performed on all the caches in the system; otherwise, its effect is limited to the local cache. The instruction is a no-op if the block(s) are unmodified.

We have seen that cache coherence must be enforced by the hardware when M = 1 (coherence required). So why does the architecture provide the dcbst and dcbf instructions? They can be used to write back or flush a cache block *earlier* than it would have been done by the hardware. Consider, for example, a graphics application. A frame buffer in main memory holds the graphics data and is used to refresh the screen. Frame buffer data may be cached (caching enabled) to allow fast access by the processor. The cached data must be periodically flushed to memory, so that changes will show up on the screen. The dcbst instruction could be used to update the frame buffer, but dcbf would also free up the cache block, which would be appropriate if the application can determine that the data are no longer required in the cache at this time.

Finally, the data cache block set to zero (dcbz) instruction clears the block containing the byte referred by the effective address. If the block is absent, a block containing all zeros is placed into the cache without fetching any data from main memory. This method is useful when a block is about to be completely overwritten, so that loading the data from memory first would be a waste of time and memory bandwidth.

Most cache management instructions are available at the user level, with the exception of dcbi, which is a privileged instruction. It was necessary to limit the use of dcbi to the system level in order to allow certain performance optimizations without compromising protection. Consider a process that requests a new page for the stack by invoking the C "malloc" routine. The operating system allocates a new page filled with zeros (as is required by C and some other environments). However, it is much faster to use the dcbz instruction to place in the cache blocks containing all zeros, rather than zero the page itself (which would require more expensive memory operations). The cache blocks are marked modified and are eventually written back to memory. Meanwhile, the page may still contain data of another process, to which it was allocated before the current process. If dcbi were available to the current process, that process could use it to mark a cache block as invalid. Then the next reference to the block would fetch data from the previous process into the cache.

TLB and SLB Management

A TLB is a type of cache; it holds the most recent address translations so they can be done quickly without reference to page tables. But because the TLB is a type of cache, it also brings with it a coherence problem. If a processor takes a page fault and the operating system decides to replace a page that mapped by the TLBs of other processors, then a translation held in any other TLB is stale; the page translation is no longer correct. One way to keep the TLBs coherent is to have the operating system interrupt all the other processors and invalidate the TLB entry. TLB entries must also be invalidated whenever a page table entry mapped by the TLB is changed, for example, if the protection attributes are changed.

In a system with software-managed TLBs, this problem can be simplified because the operating system can keep a table of the processors whose TLBs contain a given page translation and interrupt only those processors. The PowerPC 601 uses hardware TLB fills, so the operating system is likely to be unaware of which TLBs may hold stale translations. To reduce the overhead, the PowerPC has a special TLB invalidate entry (tlbie) instruction that broadcasts TLB address information over the bus, so that snooping hardware on each processor can automatically invalidate a TLB entry without having to interrupt the processor. In 64-bit PowerPC implementations, the SLB invalidate entry (slbie) instruction invalidates an entry in the SLB of the processor executing the instruction, but it has no effect on the contents of the SLBs in other processors. (32-bit implementations have segment registers; 64-bit implementations have a Segment Table and an SLB, as discussed in Section 7.5.)

The TLB invalidate all (tlbia) and SLB invalidate all (slbia) instructions are optional. The architecture specifies that an implementation may choose to perform these functions in a loop that invalidates separate TLB and SLB entries using the tlbie and slbie instructions. Indeed, the 601 does not implement the tlbia instruction. Of course, slbia is again applicable to 64-bit implementations only. Finally, the tlbsync instruction is also defined as optional and is not provided by the 601.

9.7 References

Goodman's paper [26] introduced the snooping cache coherence protocol. Many variations of this scheme have been proposed and implemented. Archibald and Baer [6] survey a number of coherence protocols. Wang and Baer [92] describe coherence in multilevel caches and the inclusion property. Dubois, Scheurich, and Briggs [21] discuss the concepts of sequential consistency, weak ordering, and synchronization in multiprocessors.

In the coherence method implemented in the Motorola 88110 (see Diefendorff and Allen [18]) a snooping hit to a modified sector is handled in two steps: the snooping cache writes the modified sector back to memory, and the other cache retries the read request. This *retry* protocol was apparently easier to implement than the alternative, the *intervention* protocol, in which the snooping cache supplies the modified sector directly to the cache that attempts the read request. The 601 inherited the 88110's cache coherence scheme and bus interface with some changes. Allen and Becker [2] describe multiprocessing facilities in the 601, including synchronization primitives, cache coherence, and the bus interface. The Motorola 601 manual [62] contains additional information and detailed timing diagrams describing bus transactions.

SYSTEM ORGANIZATION: MEMORY AND INPUT/OUTPUT

10.1 Introduction

So far, almost all our attention has been directed toward processors. The processor is only one of the major system elements, however. The other two—main memory and the input/output subsystem—and their interconnection to form a system are the subjects of this chapter. Throughout the chapter we will cover important aspects of all the types of systems in which POWER and PowerPC processors are likely to be found—from personal computers to large multicomputer clusters. The major characteristics of these system types were reviewed as part of the introduction in Section 1.6.

The POWER architecture, as implemented in POWER1, was initially developed for uniprocessor workstations, which resulted in certain design decisions that affected its usefulness for other types of systems. For example, the POWER architecture does not have important features (added in PowerPC) that would allow it to be easily used in a conventional shared-memory multiprocessor. Its first POWER1 implementation in the RS/6000 was a multichip design with emphasis on floating-point performance, making it rather ill suited for low-cost personal computer implementations. In contrast, the PowerPC architecture is intended for a very broad set of systems, from inexpensive PC-class systems to workstations to multiprocessor servers, and possibly even to massive parallel processing systems.

We will describe many aspects of system architecture and implementation, beginning with PCs and working our way up to large multicomputer clusters. We begin with "generic" PCs based on the PowerPC 601, focusing on the overall system structure and the buses that hold it together. Server-class PowerPC systems, implemented as shared-memory multiprocessors, are next in line. Several architectural aspects of shared-memory multiprocessors were covered in Chapter 9. In this chapter, we focus on the bus-based implementation of the multiprocessor architecture, discussing in some detail how cache coherence is actually implemented. Then, we turn to RS/6000 workstations, beginning with a description of the RS/6000 organization, followed by a description of its input/output and memory systems. Finally, we give an overview of the 9076 SP-1, a recently announced multicomputer cluster built of RS/6000s.

10.2 PowerPC Personal Computers

The PowerPC 601 will be used in personal computers made by a number of manufacturers, the two major ones being IBM and Apple. Naturally, there will be considerable diversity in these systems. Figure 10.1 is the block diagram for a low-cost PC built around a PowerPC 601. The system connects DRAM main memory, an expansion bus for I/O, and a 601 processor chip. Because of the drive to keep PC costs down, many of the "glue" chips being used to construct a system are being consolidated into fewer, more highly integrated chips. For example, the DRAM interface and the expansion bus control chips might be integrated. The expansion bus is one of a number of standard buses into which I/O controller cards can be inserted. The AT bus (ISA) is the most common, but EISA, NuBus, and, of course, IBM's Micro Channel are other possibilities. Later in this section we will describe the Micro Channel as an example of an expansion bus.

Although systems similar to Figure 10.1 are common today, a PowerPC is more likely to be used in a higher-performance PC, as shown in Figure 10.2.

The most striking feature in Figure 10.2 is the hierarchy of buses, made necessary by the considerable diversity of peripheral devices and the speed difference between the processor/memory and many of the peripherals. The major buses are the processor bus, a high-speed local bus, and an I/O expansion bus.

- The *processor bus* is sometimes referred to as the "pin bus" because it is defined by the protocol implemented at the processor chip's pins. The processor bus, connecting the processor and main memory, has the highest bandwidth of all the buses in the hierarchy.

- The *local bus* is a relative newcomer to the bus hierarchy. Local buses have appeared mainly because of the high-performance demands of video displays—the standard I/O expansion buses simply couldn't keep up. There are two main contenders as local bus standards: the VESA (video electronics standards association) Local bus (VL-bus), and

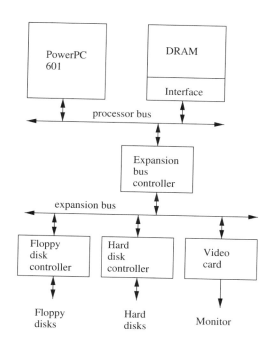

FIGURE 10.1 **Small PC system incorporating the PowerPC 601.**

the Intel-developed Peripheral Component Interconnect (PCI) bus. Because both IBM and Apple will be supporting the PCI bus in their systems, we will concentrate on it.

■ The *I/O expansion bus* is used to connect most I/O peripherals into the system. It consists of standard connector "slots" into which I/O controller cards can be inserted. By far the most popular of the standard expansion buses is the original IBM PC/AT bus, also called the Industry Standard Architecture (ISA) bus. At only 5 Mbytes/second, the ISA bus is inadequate for many of today's high-performance peripherals, however, higher performance expansion buses have been developed. These include the EISA (extended ISA) bus, and the IBM-developed Micro Channel. Because of its use in RS/6000 systems and in IBM PowerPC systems, we will discuss the Micro Channel in more detail.

Besides these three buses, there are also standard I/O interfaces intended for certain classes of peripherals. For example, we will discuss systems employing the SCSI (Small Computer Systems Interface), used primarily for storage devices.

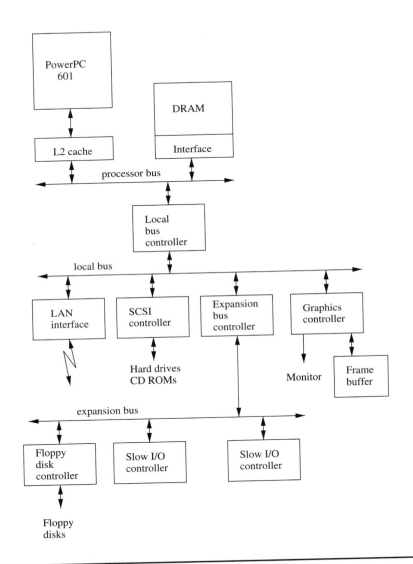

FIGURE 10.2   **High-end PC system incorporating the PowerPC 601.**

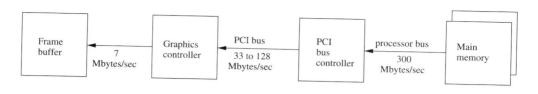

FIGURE 10.3 Data path for a video image traveling from main memory to a frame buffer.

Figure 10.3 illustrates the portion of the I/O hierarchy used to display television-quality video. Each image is transferred from a buffer in main memory, over the processor bus, the PCI bus, and finally from the graphics control to the video frame buffer. This path is typical of most I/O paths in that the bandwidths become successively lower as they go down the hierarchy. Meanwhile, the I/O hierarchy spreads out like a tree: at successively lower levels there are more and more of the lower-bandwidth paths to be fed.

PowerPC 601 processor bus

The 601 bus interface is an enhancement of the Motorola 88110 bus interface. The processor can be directly connected to the processor bus (Figure 10.1), or it may have an L2 cache interposed (Figure 10.2).

The bus itself consists of separate address and data buses that run largely independently. The bus is capable of "single-beat" transfers of 8 bytes, and "four-beat" transfers of 32 bytes. There are also some address-only cycles to support cache coherence. When running at maximum speed, the bus is capable of 320 Mbytes/second at 50 MHz.

The processor can talk to memory or the I/O controller with similar (but not identical) protocols. The T bit, held in the address segment registers (see Section 7.5), indicates whether the segment is a regular memory segment or maps to an I/O address.[1] An I/O segment is used to map load (store) data to (from) the bus interface residing on the processor bus. These loads and store are typically used to set up I/O transactions and to read status information. For I/O transactions, the bus signals are slightly different than for memory transactions, and, because many I/O devices are inherently serial, all I/O transfers are sequentially consistent—each must finish before the next begins.

Because its most interesting aspects are only apparent in multiprocessors, we will defer a detailed description of the PowerPC 601 processor bus until Section 10.3.

---

[1]We assume in this discussion that the T bit is used to distinguish between memory space and I/O space, as done by IBM software. Other PowerPC systems may choose to map both memory and I/O into the same address space with T = 0.

PCI bus

The PCI bus, developed by Intel, is initially defined to run at 33 MHz and is capable of interfacing up to 10 devices. PCI is defined for 32- or 64-bit data paths (32-bit required; 64-bit optional).

The data and address lines are multiplexed, which means that the same lines are used for both. Usually the lines first hold an address and are then switched to transfer data. Three types of transfers are supported: single-word, 4-word, and 100-word. With a 32-bit bus, single-word transfers can proceed at 33 Mbytes/second, 4-word at 76 Mbytes/second, and 100-word at 128 Mbytes/second.

A transfer on the bus takes place between a *master* and a *slave*. The master is capable of driving the control signals needed to perform the transfer. A slave is unable to control the bus but must be able to determine that it has been selected and to participate in the transfer by either receiving or supplying data.

Clearly, a bus master is a complex (and therefore likely to be expensive) device. Its usefulness depends on the environment. In DOS, which is a single-tasking operating system, the CPU does nothing while an I/O transfer is in progress, so it might as well do the transfer itself. Virtually nothing is gained by providing an add-in card with bus master capability. By contrast, in UNIX or Windows, both of which are multitasking environments, the CPU is free to run another process while the I/O transfer proceeds under the control of the bus master.

A *Direct Memory Access (DMA)* is a transfer performed between an I/O device and main memory without the intervention of the CPU (hence the term *direct*). A *DMA controller* is the logic that controls a DMA transfer. A bus master can itself act as a DMA controller by generating the appropriate control signals. A slave may participate in a DMA transfer if a separate controller drives the bus. DMA is not part of the PCI bus specification, but a device may be connected to the appropriate signals (interrupts, DMA controller) outside of the bus. Arbitration is also not part of the PCI bus and has to be provided separately.

Figure 10.4 shows a typical 4-word read cycle. It assumes that a master has gained access to the bus and activates `frame` for the duration of the transfer. (As with most PCI control signals, `frame` is active when it is at a low level.) The `command/byte enables` bus consists of 4 bits. During cycle 1, the command signals declare that there is valid information on the multiplexed address/data lines, identify this information as being an address, and indicate the direction of the transfer. The `byte enables` show which bytes of the data bus are valid while the data transfer takes place. The `device select` signal is activated by the device in response to recognizing its address. Finally, both devices participating in the transfer may pull up their respective ready signals to pace the transfer; this allows wait cycles to accommodate slower devices. The example illustrates two fast devices and the transfer taking place at the highest rate.

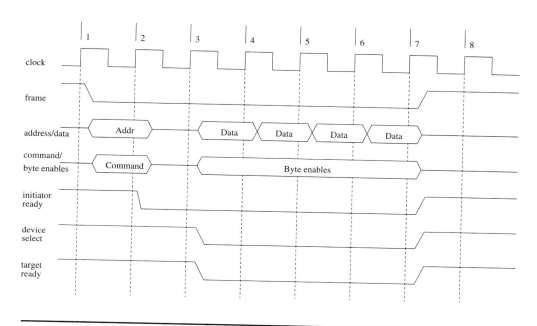

FIGURE 10.4 PCI bus signals for a 4-word read cycle. Control signals are active low.

Micro Channel

The Micro Channel (MCA) was designed by IBM to be a new PC standard bus. The original PC bus that came with the IBM XT had a rather limited 8-bit capability. Then, the AT was introduced with an expanded 16-bit bus that became a de facto standard (ISA). Finally, in 1987, IBM announced the Micro Channel, a technologically advanced bus engineered to support the I/O needs of desktop computers in the foreseeable future. A year later EISA (Extended ISA) arrived, this time from IBM competitors, as one might expect.

Compared with the AT bus, the Micro Channel provides significantly higher bandwidth primarily due to three factors: a 32-bit data bus; block transfers of data; and operation at a higher rate, due to better electrical characteristics.

The core of the MCA is a 32-bit address bus and a 32-bit data bus. The bus protocol allows the 32-bit address bus to be multiplexed (a feature implemented in certain high-end RS/6000 models), in which case 64-bit data transfers are feasible. 8-bit and 16-bit transfers are also supported for I/O cards that have a narrower data port.

The Micro Channel supports bus masters and DMA slaves. To gain access to the MCA, a master must *arbitrate* for the bus. Interestingly, a DMA slave cannot control the bus but can arbitrate for its ownership on behalf of the DMA controller. As a result of arbitration request(s) from one or more devices, the *Central Arbitration Control Point* (a function specified by the Micro Channel protocol) initiates an arbitration cycle.

The central arbiter does *not* determine which devices gain access to the bus as a result of the arbitration cycle. During this cycle every device involved in arbitration drives its own priority level on the arbitration bus. Every device must also monitor the bus to see if there are higher-priority requests; if so, the device must withdraw its own request and defer to the higher-priority device. Eventually, the arbitration bus will settle and the highest-priority request will be the only one remaining.

10.3 PowerPC Multiprocessor Systems

The PowerPC architecture is designed to accommodate shared-memory multiprocessor implementations. Figure 10.5 illustrates such an implementation. In the previous chapter, we discussed some higher-level aspects of multiprocessing: cache coherence and process synchronization. In this chapter, we look at a lower-level aspect, the processor interface.

Bus Overview

Jointly developed by IBM and Motorola, the PowerPC 601 borrows a processor design from a single-chip POWER design, the RSC, and the chip interface from the Motorola 88110 microprocessor. The 601 bus provides the communication path to main memory, as well as the means by which the local caches and memory are kept coherent in a shared-memory, shared-bus, multiprocessor system. The 601 bus interface is an enhancement of the Motorola 88110 bus interface; it includes support for second level caches in multiprocessors and pipelining of bus operations.

As is the case with many of the recent high-speed RISC microprocessors, the interface can be programmed to operate at some multiple of the internal clock period. For example, with an internal 20 ns clock period, the interface can operate at 20 ns, 40 ns, 60 ns, etc. This feature keeps manufacturing costs low by allowing looser electrical rules off-chip. That is, one can use a high-tech chip with a lower-cost circuit board. The on-chip data cache acts as a buffer, so performance is not reduced by as much as the slower interface might suggest. If the interface is operating at 50 MHz (20 ns), the interface is capable of sustaining a 320 MByte/second data rate (over one 32-bit word per clock period).

In addition to the 32-bit address bus, there is a separate 64-bit data bus. The two buses are largely independent, and a number of bus protocols can be supported. These include pipelined, nonpipelined, and split transaction buses.

The key feature that allows bus pipelining is separate arbitration for the address and data buses. Thus, a processor may acquire the address bus and transfer the address to memory, where it is latched. Then, the same processor or a different one may perform another address

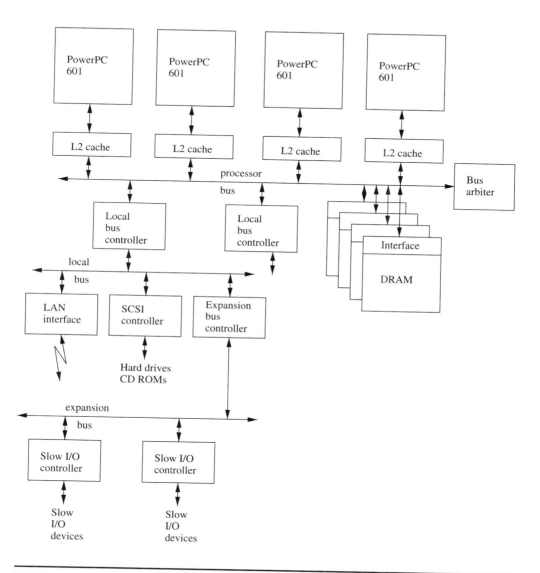

FIGURE 10.5   A PowerPC multiprocessor system.

transfer while the first operation is still pending. Finally, some arbitrary number of clock cycles later, the data bus is granted and the data transfer is performed.

Hence, the bus protocol supports split address and data transfers, but the extent to which this feature is used for pipelining depends on the processor and memory system implementation. The 601 allows pipelining of up to two requests from the same processor. Pipelining may also be used in a multiprocessor system for requests coming from different processors.

There are several types of bus operations. A *single-beat* operation performs an address transfer and a single data transfer. *Burst* operations perform an address transfer followed by multiple data transfers. An entire cache sector may be loaded (or stored) as a burst of four transfers on the 64-bit data bus (a total of 32 bytes). Burst operations are more efficient since the arbitration for the address and data buses, as well as the address transfer, are done only once for the entire operation. Finally, there are *address-only* bus operations, which are used to support the cache coherence protocol; for example, to send an invalidate signal along with the relevant cache sector address. The result is that all local caches with a matching address change the state of the sector to Invalid (see Section 9.4).

Signals

We briefly describe a subset of the bus signals that are used in examples in this section. A processor requests the address bus by activating the BusRequest (Address Bus Request) signal, which is connected to an external arbiter. The arbiter responds with BusGrant (Address Bus Grant).

However, even after BusGrant is asserted by the arbiter, the processor may not begin its address transfer until both signals AdrRetry (described below) and AdrBusBusy (Address Bus Busy) are inactive. AdrBusBusy asserted indicates that the previous bus owner has not completed its address transfer.

TransferStart is a dual-purpose signal. It indicates that there is a valid address on the address bus. It is also an arbitration signal that requests the data bus from the arbiter, which responds some time later by activating DataBusGrant.

AdrAck (Address Acknowledge) is returned by the memory when the address has been latched, indicating that the address bus may be released for another transfer. TransferAck (Transfer Acknowledge) is also asserted by the memory: during a read operation, when the data returned is placed on the data bus; during a write operation, when the data has been latched.

Global is used to distinguish between a bus operation that is of interest to all the processors in a multiprocessor (such as loads and stores of shared data) and operations that are local to a single processor.

SnoopRequest is an input signal that indicates there is a valid address on the address bus for the purpose of snooping. In most multiprocessor systems, the SnoopRequest input of each 601 should be tied to TransferStart. Snooping is done when both SnoopRequest and Global are active.

AdrShared	AdrRetry	Meaning	Action taken
Inactive	Inactive	No snooping hit	Mark exclusive
Active	Inactive	Snooping hit, unmodified sector	Mark shared
Inactive	Active	Collision	Retry read
Active	Active	Snooping hit, modified sector	Wait for write-back, then retry

FIGURE 10.6   **Signals used to maintain cache coherence.**

AdrRetry (Address Retry) tells the bus master that the bus operation should be aborted and retried later. This signal is used by a processor that detects a snooping hit to a sector in the Modified state. The current bus transaction should be aborted so the modified sector can be written back to memory.

When a new sector is read into the cache, it can be marked as either Shared or Exclusive. The distinction is made by the AdrShared (Address Shared) signal, which is asserted when one or more other caches in the systems contain the same sector.

These two signals, AdrRetry and AdrShared, are used to implement the MESI cache coherence protocol, as shown in Figure 10.6. A *collision* occurs when a processor initiates a bus transaction to a cache sector whose transfer is in progress. Following is an example of a scenario that leads to a collision. Processor1 begins a write transaction by asserting the Address, TransferStart, and AdrBusBusy signals. The memory latches the address and returns AdrAck. Processor1 deactivates AdrBusBusy allowing another processor (Processor2) to begin a bus operation. Processor2 requests and is granted the address bus and initiates the transfer of a sector that happens to have the same address. Processor1 detects a hit in its memory queue and asserts AdrRetry. Processor2 sees the AdrRetry active and aborts its transaction and retries later.

Collisions are a result of allowing split bus operations (that is, the address and data buses are granted and used separately), which is essential for pipelining. In contrast, so-called *tenured* buses do not permit split operations, and the address bus is held until the completion of the data transfer. Collisions may not occur, but bus bandwidth is wasted, as the address bus is idle for the duration of the data transfer.

A snooping hit to a modified sector is indicated by both AdrShared and AdrRetry being active. In this case, the initiating processor aborts the request and retries later, after the snooping processor writes the modified sector back to memory.

Example—Pipelining

Figure 10.7 illustrates pipelining of two transfer requests. In clock cycle 1, the processor requests the address bus by asserting BusRequest. Note that the control signals are active low. The arbiter responds in the next clock cycle by activating BusGrant and leaving the

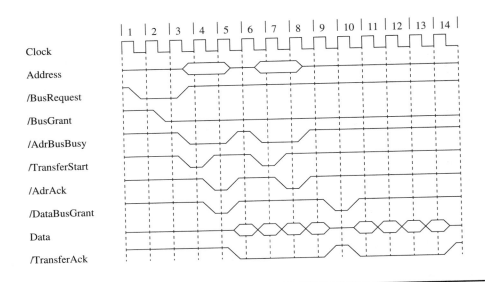

FIGURE 10.7   Pipelining two requests.

address bus granted to this processor for longer than needed for a single address transfer. The processor is *parked* on the bus, a feature that saves arbitration cycles if the bus is available and a processor has to perform multiple transfers. The bus ownership may be terminated by the arbiter at any time unless AdrBusBusy is asserted, which is done during clock cycles 4–5 and 7–8 in the example.

The first transfer begins in clock cycle 4 with the assertion of TransferStart. The processor maintains the address on the bus until the memory latches it as indicated by AdrAck in the next clock cycle. The external arbiter activates DataBusGrant, and the memory begins to return the data in clock cycle 6 (the timing may be different depending on the memory latency). The data transfer continues until a full sector is read, which takes four clock cycles on the 64-bit data bus. The memory asserts TransferAck to indicate that the data are valid on the bus.

The next address transfer is pipelined while the data transfer of the previous bus transaction is still in progress. The 601 allows pipelining of up to two requests from the same processor. Pipelining may also be performed on requests coming from different processors in a similar way, but there would be arbitration between the two transfers to change the bus ownership.

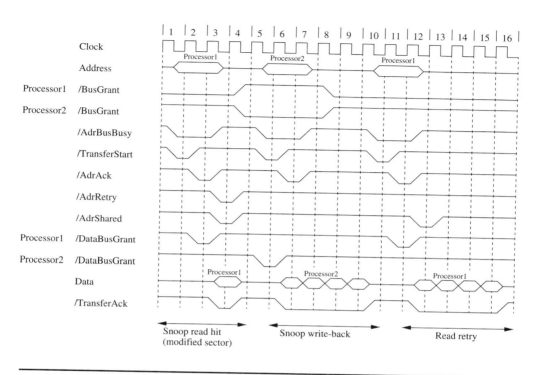

FIGURE 10.8   Snooping hit to a modified sector.

Example—Snooping

Figure 10.8 illustrates the timing diagram of a snooping hit. Processor1 owns the address bus and initiates a read operation by asserting the address and `TransferStart`. The memory returns `AdrAck` and actually begins the transfer. Meanwhile, Processor2 detects a snooping hit to a modified sector in its cache and indicates so by activating `AdrShared` and `AdrRetry`. In the 601 implementation, this response occurs within two clock cycles from the time there is a valid address on the bus. Processor1 aborts its transaction.

Processor2 requests the address bus, which is granted by the external arbiter, and writes the modified sector back to memory. It marks its sector as Shared. For simplicity, a few relevant signals (`BusRequest`, `Global`, `SnoopRequest`) were omitted from the diagram. `SnoopRequest` is not asserted during the write-back cycle. Now Processor1 retries its read operation, this time successfully. The `AdrShared` signal is asserted, indicating that there is at least one other cache that contains a valid copy of this sector. Processor1 marks the new sector Shared.

Models	220	350	560	980
Packaging	dt/ds	dt/ds	ds	rack
Clock rate (MHz)	33	42	50	62.5
Processor chips	1	3	3	3
DCU chips	none	2	4	4
Memory slots	8	2	8	8
Memory bus (bits)	64	64	128	128
I-Cache (Kbyte)	unified	8	8	32
D-Cache (Kbyte)	unified	32	64	64
Available MCA slots	2	4	7	8
64-bit MCA	no	no	no	yes
Optional second MCA	no	no	no	yes

FIGURE 10.9   Some RS/6000 models. "dt" is desktop, "ds" is deskside. Model 220 has a unified 8 Kbyte cache. MCA is Micro Channel.

10.4 RS/6000 Workstation Overview

POWER1 Systems

Unlike PowerPC systems, which are just now becoming available, RS/6000 systems based on POWER have been available for a few years. There is now a wide variety of systems; Figure 10.9 lists a small representative sample.

The systems shown begin with the 220, based on the single-chip predecessor to the 601. There is a series of workstations based on the RS/6000 chip set that use only 2 Data Cache Unit (DCU) chips, and a series of larger workstations, like the 560 that we have been using as our typical RS/6000 implementation. Finally, there are the 900-series rack-mounted server-class systems.

Figure 10.10 illustrates complete RS/6000 systems belonging to the 500-series and the 300-series. An interesting feature of the RS/6000 implementation is that it is intended to support different system configurations with the same chip set. Figure 10.10(a) illustrates one of the larger-scale systems on which we have focused throughout the book. In contrast, Figure 10.10(b) shows a smaller, less expensive system constructed of the same parts. This lower-cost system uses two DCU chips instead of four. Of course, bandwidths are lower because some important data paths are half as wide. And the data cache is smaller (each line is half as long). There are other simplifications within the processor: the FPU and FXU share the same data cache path, and the instruction cache is loaded via the SIO bus.

The RS/6000 systems consist of the processor, the main memory system, and the input/output system. A characterizing feature of the RS/6000 is the large number of wide data paths. Compared with other workstations, these provide very high system data bandwidth.

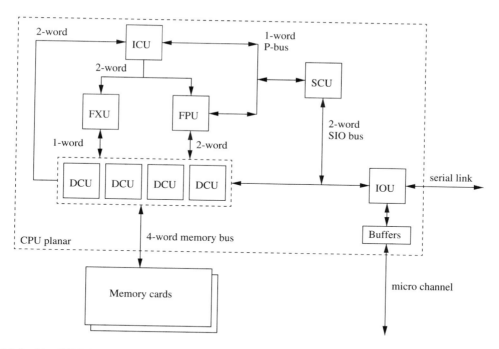

(a) 9-chip CPU. Memory cards must be installed in pairs to support the wide memory bus.

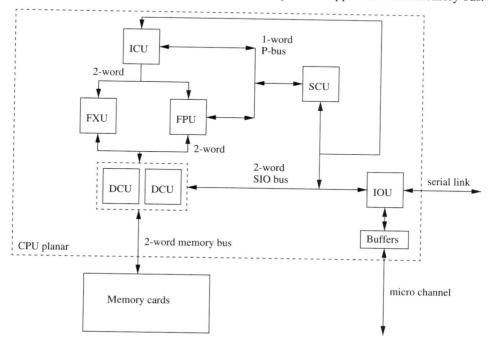

(b) Cost-reduced 7-chip CPU.

FIGURE 10.10 RS/6000 system.

This attention to system bandwidth reflects the RS/6000's IBM mainframe heritage. It also reflects the intention to provide good performance for commercial workloads (which tend to have higher I/O demands) as well as scientific and engineering workloads, which traditionally run on workstations.

The system-level data buses include:

1. A 4-word-wide bus (128 data bits) between main memory and the DCU (which holds the data cache memory).

2. A 2-word-wide bus between the DCU and the instruction cache.

3. A 2-word-wide System I/O bus (SIO) that interfaces to the I/O unit.

4. A 1-word-wide processor bus (P-bus) that is used for requesting cache line transfers and direct I/O operations from the processor.

The SCU is the "traffic cop" that manages all the traffic among the units connected by the above buses. It is the master for both the SIO and the main memory buses. When the processor needs a data transfer for a cache, either a data load or a write-back, it makes a transfer request to the SCU via the P-bus. The SCU then generates control signals to drive the memory system. When the processor issues an I/O load or store instruction, it is conveyed to the SCU via the P-bus, and then on to the SIO bus. The management of memory errors is also done by the SCU: it controls memory scrubbing (described in Section 10.5) and records memory errors detected in the DCU.

Note that through the SIO bus connects the I/O Unit (IOU) to the DCU, not to memory. Why would I/O pass through the Data Cache Unit? The cache itself is not used for I/O; the DCU chips, however, provide paths of different widths (as well as buffering in some cases) to the FPU, FXU, memory, I-cache, and IOU. The DCU is essentially a junction of buses; it may receive data from one of several sources and route it to its destination. This organization simplifies the interface of the main memory and allows the error detection and correction logic to be concentrated in one place, on the DCU chips.

POWER2 Systems

The two 500 series models shown in Figure 10.11 feature a POWER2 processor, a 32-Kbyte instruction cache, and a 256-Kbyte data cache. The rack-mounted model 990 has a higher clock rate and comes with a second Micro Channel bus that increases the number of available MCA slots to 15.

Figure 10.12 illustrates a complete POWER2 RS/6000 system. The 3-chip processor consists of the new ICU2, FXU2, and FPU2 chips and can execute up to four instructions per clock cycle. The four DCU2 chips (collectively called the Data Cache Unit or DCU) implement a 256-Kbyte data cache and an 8-word (32-byte) memory interface. The capacity of most other buses has been significantly increased relative to POWER1.

Models	58H	590	990
Packaging	ds	ds	rack
Clock rate (MHz)	55.5	66.6	71.5
Processor chips	3	3	3
DCU chips	4	4	4
Memory slots	8	8	8
Memory bus (bits)	256	256	256
I-Cache (Kbyte)	32	32	32
D-Cache (Kbyte)	256	256	256
Available MCA slots	7	7	15
64-bit MCA	no	yes	yes
MCA buses	1	1	2

FIGURE 10.11 Some POWER2 RS/6000 models. MCA is Micro Channel.

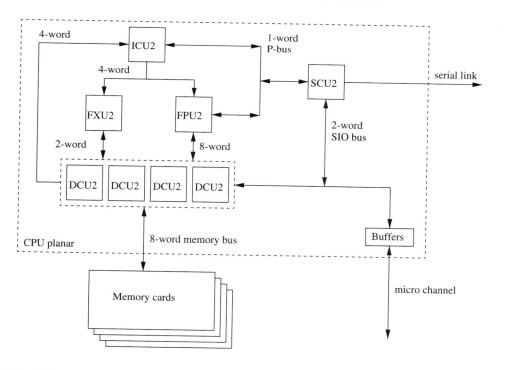

FIGURE 10.12 POWER2 RS/6000 system (8 chips). It takes four memory cards to support the wide memory bus.

The system-level data buses include:

1. An eight-word wide bus (256 data bits) between main memory and the DCU (which contains the data cache memory).

2. A four-word wide bus between the DCU and the instruction cache.

3. A two-word wide System I/O bus (SIO).

4. A one-word wide processor bus (P-bus) that is used for requesting cache line transfers and direct I/O operations from the processor.

The new SCU2 chip combines the functions of the POWER1 SCU and IOU chips. Therefore, the SCU2 chip manages all the traffic among the units connected by the above buses; it is the master for both the SIO and main memory buses; it implements the Micro Channel interface and buffers data in transit between an input/output device and memory.

10.5 RS/6000 Main Memory

Memory Components

The main memory of virtually every computer system being built today is constructed of DRAM (dynamic random-access memory) chips. DRAMs are designed to maximize the density of stored bits. The high storage density is achieved by storing each bit with a single transistor.

Because of the way it is stored, however, information in a DRAM is lost after some time, typically milliseconds. Hence the need to *refresh* the memory, or periodically read each bit and write it back.

Reads are destructive in a DRAM. That is, reading a bit removes it from its memory cell. Therefore, a read must be followed by a write in which the information just read is written back into memory. The memory cannot be accessed again until the write is finished. Hence, two important parameters for characterizing a DRAM are the *access time,* the time it takes to do a read, and the *cycle time,* the time before it can be accessed again.

Memory cells in a DRAM are organized in a two-dimensional matrix of rows and columns. A row is addressed with the upper half of the address (row address). The lower half is the column address. The row and column addresses are transferred into a DRAM in separate clock cycles using the same address lines. This *multiplexing* is done to cut the number of address pins into half. Fewer pins means smaller and less expensive packaging.

When a read is performed, the entire row is brought into a buffer; the column address is then used to select the proper column from the buffer. In some DRAMs, as long as the row address does not change, incrementing the column address causes references to be made to adjacent storage elements held in the buffer. This is called *page mode* access. Because successive accesses come from the row buffer, accessing a DRAM in page mode is fast.

SRAMs (static random-access memory) use multiple transistors per memory cell. They do not have to be refreshed, reads are nondestructive, and address pins are not multiplexed. Also, SRAMs are significantly faster than DRAMs but the cost per bit is also significantly higher. Their use, at least in PCs and workstations, is mainly for cache memories.

RS/6000 Memory Board

The DRAM chips are mounted on SIMMs (Single In-line Memory Modules), which offer a particularly dense way to package memory chips. As shown in Figure 10.13, a memory card consists of eight SIMMs, two data multiplexer chips, and a control chip. The control chip provides the control signals and takes care of the row/column addressing. The function of the data multiplexer chips is to make the connection between the selected DRAM data lines and the memory bus.

The interface of a memory card consists of two 40-bit buses and control lines. The 40-bit word includes 32 bits of data, 7 bits of error correction and detection code, and 1 spare bit. Hence, 20% of the memory capacity is dedicated to error handling.

The organization of the memory cards is identical, regardless of capacity: eight SIMMs and the three other chips as shown in Figure 10.13. Ten DRAMs per SIMM, as in the figure, with 1 Mbit DRAMs yield an 8 Mbyte memory card. Note that the capacity of the memory card is 10 Mbytes, of which 8 Mbytes are used for data and the rest to handle errors.

With a fixed number of eight SIMMs per memory card, how does one vary the memory capacity? Obviously, by varying the capacity of the SIMMs. Standard SIMMs are available that contain more than 10 DRAMs (the example shown in Figure 10.13), and the DRAMs themselves may have higher density (4 Mbit, for example).

Bit scattering

Each DRAM has a 4-bit data interface. As shown in Figure 10.14, each of these 4 bits is connected to a different word in the 4-word memory interface. DRAM DR0 supplies the bit 0 in each word, DR1 supplies bit 1, DR2 bit 2, and so on. Bits 0–31 are data, bits 32–38 are the error checking and correction code, and bit 39 is the spare bit.

Looking at it the other way around, every bit in a 40-bit word comes from a different DRAM. This *bit scattering* technique allows the memory to function despite the total failure of a single DRAM chip. The faulty DRAM provides a single erroneous bit in each word, which can be corrected by the error detection and correction logic.

As shown in Figure 10.14, it takes two memory cards to support the full 160-bit memory interface. Hence, memory cards in model 560 and other high-end RS/6000 models always come in pairs.

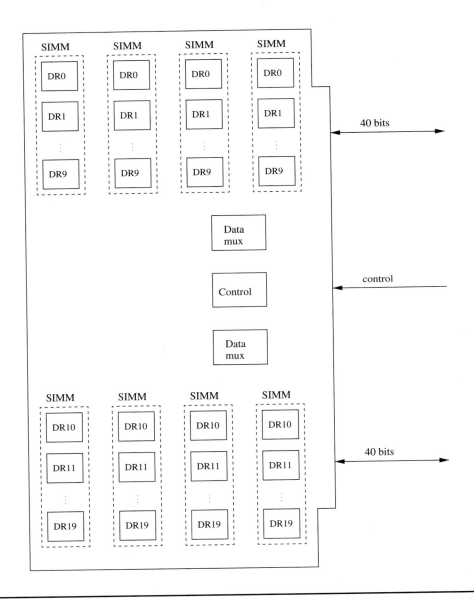

FIGURE 10.13 Memory card with 10 DRAMs per SIMM. SIMM is Single In-line Memory Module. DR is DRAM.

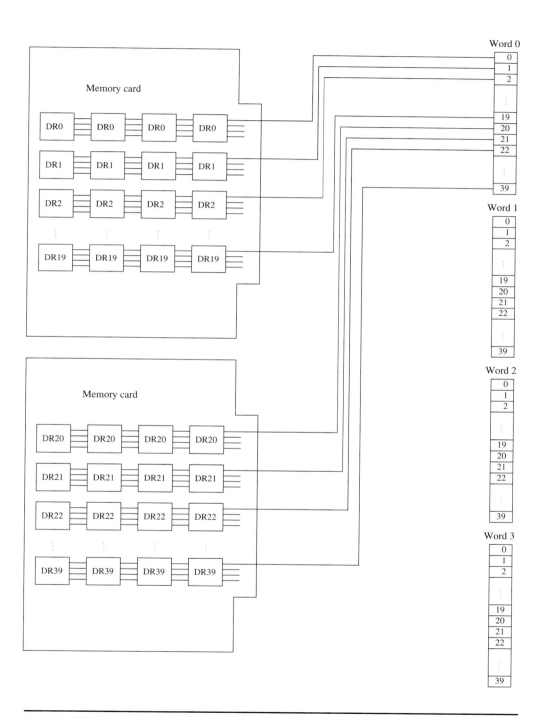

FIGURE 10.14 Bit scattering. DR is DRAM. The memory cards shown contain 80 DRAMs (10 DRAMs per SIMM).

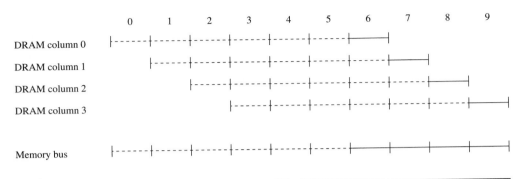

FIGURE 10.15 Timing in an interleaved memory. Clock cycles are numbered 0–9. Dashed lines indicate delay. Solid lines show data on the memory bus.

Memory Interleaving

It takes multiple clock cycles to access a DRAM for read or write. For example, a read operation consists of the following steps.

1. Set row address on address lines.

2. Set column address on address lines.

3. DRAM accesses the data internally.

4. DRAM places data on the bus.

The read takes place in the last step. The delay involved in the first three steps occurs each time the memory is accessed.

To provide higher memory bandwidth, that is, more data per cycle, memory is *interleaved*. The physical organization of a 4-way interleaved memory is shown in Figure 10.14. Each column of DRAMs supplies a full 160-bit quadword. By initiating the access of each DRAM column at consecutive clock cycles, one can get four consecutive quadwords returning from the memory after a certain delay.

The timing diagram is shown in Figure 10.15. DRAM column 0 is accessed in clock cycle 0, column 1 in clock cycle 1, and so on. After a delay of six clock cycles in this example, column 0 places its data on the memory bus on clock cycle 6, column 1 in clock cycle 7, and so on. The result is that the delay of six clock cycles is incurred only once, and four transfers are performed afterwards.

In POWER1, two memory cards operating in tandem provide four words, including error correction code and spare bits. In the instruction cache, the block size is 16 words. Hence, the 4-way interleaved memory is designed to supply a full instruction cache block in four clock cycles, after an initial delay of a few clock cycles. In the data cache, the block size is 32 words. The initial memory access delay occurs once; then the 32-word block is transferred in eight clock cycles. In POWER2, four memory cards may be accessed simultaneously to supply eight words. The instruction cache and data cache blocks are twice as long (32 and 64 words, respectively). As a result of doubling all the paths as well as the cache blocks, the access patterns for the instruction and data caches remain the same: D-1-1-1-1 for the instruction cache and D-1-1-1-1-1-1-1 for the data cache, where D is several delay clock cycles followed by a sequence of transfer clock cycles.

Memory Configuration

Physical memory is software configurable. That is, the address at which a memory module (called *bank*) is placed in the 32-bit physical address space is determined by software via a set of 16 memory configuration registers in the SCU. Each configuration register defines the size of the bank and its starting address. The 16 registers allow the system to be configured with a minimum of one bank and a maximum of 16.

Error Detection and Correction

Error handling is performed at two levels: transfers between the DCU and the processor chips, namely the ICU, FXU, and FPU; and transfers between the DCU and memory. In the first type of transfer, which is between chips on the processor board, single-bit errors are detected using a parity bit associated with each byte. The second type of transfer involves DRAMs on separate memory cards and more elaborate error detection and correction logic that is the subject of the rest of this section.

As we have seen, the memory interface consists of four 40-bit words. Each word has 32 data bits, 7 check bits, and 1 spare bit. The 7 check bits allow single-bit error correction and double-bit error detection, using a modified Hamming code. This Error Checking and Correction (ECC) code is produced by the ECC code generator and appended to every 32-bit data word prior to its storage in memory (Figure 10.16). The ECC code generator is located on the DCU chips.

In the other direction, when a word is read from memory, error detection logic on the DCU checks for errors and corrects single-bit errors. A parity generator adds 4 parity bits (one per byte) and the resulting 36-bit word is stored in a buffer. There are separate buffers on the DCU for the I-cache, D-cache, and System I/O (SIO). From the buffer, the 36-bit word is transferred to the I-cache, D-cache, or SIO bus.

When a D-cache miss occurs, to minimize the miss processing time, the requested word is sent to the requester (FXU or FPU) on the same cycle as it arrives from memory. A special path bypassing the error detection and correction logic and the buffer is provided in the DCU for this purpose. This provision makes the miss processing time one clock cycle shorter. If

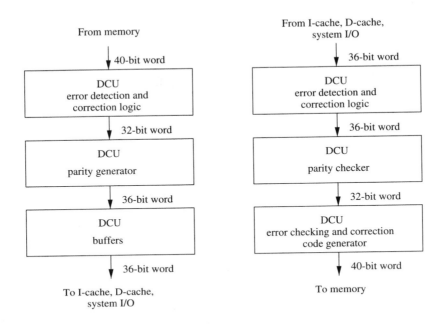

FIGURE 10.16 *Error detection and correction.*

an error is detected, a signal informs the requester that the data sent are invalid and must be discarded. Corrected data are sent in the following cycle, if the error is correctable.

Two types of errors may corrupt the data in memory: soft errors and hard errors. Soft failures are caused by a temporary change in a bit and can be corrected by restoring the bit to its original value. A *memory scrubbing* mechanism performs the following sequence:

1. Read word from memory to detect errors.

2. Write the corrected word back to memory.

3. Read again to check the corrected word.

The last step is necessary to ensure that the faulty bit is not stuck. The scrubbing sequence is controlled by software through three registers that determine the starting address, ending address, and scrub rate. Scrubbing has low priority for memory access and can be preempted by processor or input/output memory requests.

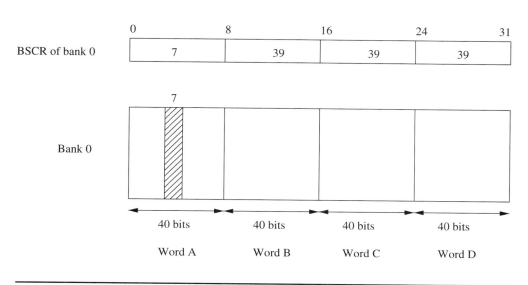

FIGURE 10.17 Bit steering. The 40 bits in a word are numbered 0–39. Bit 39 is the location of the spare bit. BSCR is the Bit Steering Configuration Register. The BSCR of bank 0 is programmed to steer the spare bit of word A into position 7 of word A. For words B, C, and D, the spare bit is steered to itself (position 39), which is the default when no replacement is necessary.

Bit Steering

Memory scrubbing cannot correct hard errors, in which a bit is permanently stuck to 0 or 1. Bit steering logic in the DCU can correct a hard error by replacing the faulty bit with the spare bit. The spare bit contained in a 40-bit word can be steered into the position of one of the remaining 39 bits. The steering information is the position of the faulty bit and is recorded in an 8-bit field (actually, 6 bits are sufficient) in a Bit Steering Configuration Register (BSCR). The 32-bit BSCR consists of four 8-bit fields; each field keeps track of the position of the faulty bit in one of the four 40-bit words in the 160-bit memory interface of a bank.

There are 16 bit steering configuration registers, one per bank. If steering is done, then replacement of the bit in the specified position with the spare bit is done in the entire bank. In the example in Figure 10.17, the BSCR associated with bank 0 specifies that bit 7 in word A is replaced with the spare bit. As shown, the replacement is done in the entire bank whether bit 7 is faulty or good. The bank shown in the figure spans two memory cards: one card supplies words A and B, and the second words C and D.

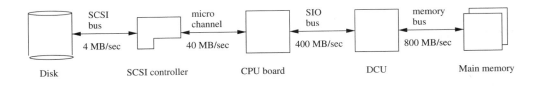

FIGURE 10.18 The path of a data transfer between a disk and main memory for a 50 MHz RS/6000 model 560.

10.6 RS/6000 Input/Output System

The I/O unit (IOU) is a separate chip in POWER1 and part of the SCU chip in POWER2. The main function of the I/O Unit (IOU) is to interface with the Micro Channel and SIO buses, and to provide buffering for data transfers. The chip also contains a serial link adapter (SLA), as well as a DMA controller to be used by simple I/O controllers not capable of driving the Micro Channel. The SLA can interface to optics cards which support fiber optic links.

Overview

As we discussed at the beginning of Chapter 5, secondary storage is a very important part of the memory hierarchy. Usually implemented as hard disk drives, secondary storage not only holds data and program files, it also provides backup storage for the virtual memory system.

In the RS/6000, disk drives (and tape units that have similar bandwidths) are connected to the system through the industry standard Small Computer System Interface (SCSI) bus (Figure 10.18). The SCSI bus connects to a SCSI controller that plugs into the Micro Channel. The controller is a printed circuit card[2] whose physical dimensions conform to those required by the Micro Channel. It typically hosts a microprocessor with some local ROM (I/O program) and RAM (data and buffering). The controller interfaces to two buses, SCSI and Micro Channel, and implements both bus protocols. It also functions as a buffer for "speed matching"; in a transfer from disk to memory, for example, it accumulates into a buffer data transferred on the SCSI bus at a relatively low speed (4 Mbytes/second). When the data in the buffer reach a certain level (determined by I/O parameters that control the transfer), the controller arbitrates for access onto the Micro Channel and, once access is granted, sends the data in a burst (data streaming) across the Micro Channel.

On the other end, the data reach the IOU on the CPU circuit board ("planar" in the IBM vernacular), where it is buffered again. The IOU supports 15 direct memory access (DMA)

---

[2] Some RS/6000 models have an integrated SCSI controller on the main board.

channels and has a separate buffer for each channel. The unusual number 15 has a simple explanation: the IOU itself is the 16th DMA controller, available to those controllers that cannot gain control and drive the Micro Channel themselves.

The concept of a *channel* in the I/O system is similar to that of a process in a multiprogramming environment. There may be multiple processes on a single physical processor. A process may run on the processor for a while, then it will be swapped out. Its state is saved and it may be restarted again some time later. In a very similar way, multiple DMA channels may share a single physical Micro Channel bus. A device capable of driving the bus may access the bus through any one of the 15 DMA channels. Its status is maintained in a channel status register, and the data are temporarily held in the buffer associated with that channel.

When sufficient data accumulate in the channel buffer (typically 64 bytes, the size of the buffer), it is transferred over the SIO bus to one final buffer in the DCU chips. The SIO bus is a 2-word (8-byte) bus operating at the processor clock rate; at 50 MHz its peak bandwidth is 400 Mbytes/second.

The sequence of buses from disk to memory shown in Figure 10.18 is actually a hierarchy of buses: those with relatively low bandwidth at the device end, and others with gradually increasing bandwidth as the main memory is approached. Using again the example in the figure, up to seven devices can connect through a single SCSI bus to a SCSI controller. Multiple controllers can plug into a Micro Channel bus, depending on the number of Micro Channel slots available in the specific RS/6000 model. Finally, a second Micro Channel bus is available in some RS/6000 models.

I/O Unit (IOU)

The IOU performs the following important functions:

- Buffers data transfers between the Micro Channel and SIO buses.

- Provides a DMA controller for DMA slaves.

- Implements a Central Arbitration Control Point as required by the Micro Channel protocol.

Another function that the IOU provides is *translation* of Micro Channel (MCA) addresses to main memory addresses.[3] While this concept resembles virtual to real address translation, the two should not be confused. We emphasize that *there are no virtual addresses in I/O transactions*. Rather, an I/O address asserted on the 32-bit Micro Channel address bus is translated by the IOU to a main memory address.

---

[3] In addition to main memory there is also *bus memory,* which is memory contained in an I/O card. We ignore bus memory in this discussion.

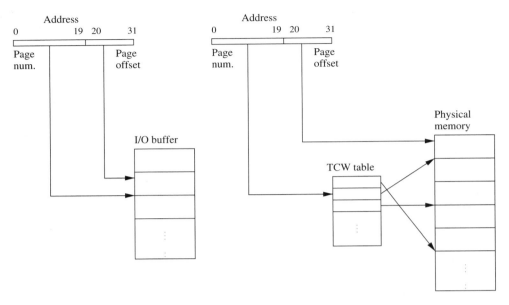

(a) The I/O device sees a contiguous
I/O buffer.

(b) The TCW table provides translation to
noncontiguous pages in physical memory.

FIGURE 10.19 A 32-bit address driven by a master on the Micro Channel address bus is translated by the IOU, using TCW tables, to a physical memory address.

Address translation provides a mechanism to map contiguous MCA addresses to noncontiguous physical pages scattered throughout the physical memory. This mechanism simplifies memory management; the page number in the 32-bit MCA address may be mapped to *any* physical page in main memory.

To understand how address translation is performed, consider the following example. Four pages are to be transferred from disk to main memory. The operating system sets up a map that consists of four entries, each entry specifying a physical page number in memory as well as some control information. Each entry is called a *Translation and Control Word (TCW)*. Returning to our example, the operating system then sets up four TCWs, each pointing to some physical memory page that was allocated for this I/O transfer. Thus, the I/O buffer consists of four pages, at noncontiguous memory locations in general (Figure 10.19).

To be specific, assume once again that the I/O device is a SCSI disk (Figure 10.18), and the transfer to be performed is reading four contiguous pages from disk into main memory. The CPU begins the transfer by providing the size of the transfer, the disk address of the first page, and the address of the I/O buffer. All this is done by running an I/O program that communicates these parameters to the SCSI controller and starts the transfer. From then on, the transfer is handled by the SCSI controller, which starts the disk and performs the transfer in the following steps:

- Receives data from the disk on the SCSI bus.

- Buffers the data. When sufficient data arrive, it arbitrates for the Micro Channel.

- When the Micro Channel is granted, it drives the address bus, as well as control signals, and provides the data on the data bus. The address is translated via the TCW table and tells the IOU where in main memory the data are going.

- For each block transferred, the SCSI controller increments the address by the size of the block.

When the transfer is complete, or an error occurs, the SCSI controller interrupts the CPU and provides status information.

So far we have described input/output performed by a SCSI controller, or a bus master in general. *A bus master is capable of driving the Micro Channel address bus*, an essential step in the above list. How does a DMA slave perform input/output? As pointed out above, *a DMA slave is not capable of driving the Micro Channel address bus*. Again, the goal is to set up a potentially long I/O transfer, by providing its size and memory address, and then have the transfer run to completion without intervention of the CPU.

DMA slaves use *tags* to perform input/output. A tag contains the size of a transfer, its *physical memory address* (not translated by TCW tables), control information, and a field that may point to another tag (Figure 10.20).

To perform a transfer via a DMA slave, the CPU sets up a chain of tags. Why a chain of tags and not a single tag? The reason, again, is to allow noncontiguous I/O buffers in main memory. Once the transfer is started, the IOU takes over and follows the linked list of tags. Each tag provides the size and memory address of the transfer. The DMA slave participates in the transfer but does not control it; a separate DMA controller drives the Micro Channel control lines. The data are buffered in the IOU.

10.7 RS/6000 Clustered Multicomputers

Multicomputer clusters provide a means for achieving scalable, cost-effective computing for many server applications. Although they cannot tackle some parallel processing tasks as well as a shared-memory multiprocessor, they are quite adequate for multithreaded service functions such as transaction processing, databases, and network file systems. For many problem domains, they are a suitable replacement for the traditional mainframes.

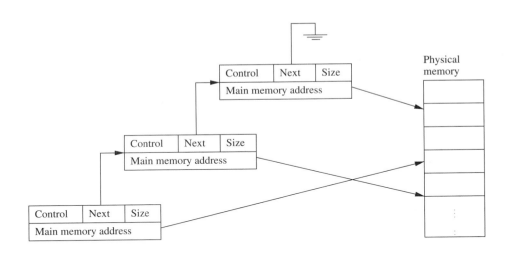

FIGURE 10.20 A DMA slave is not capable of driving Micro Channel addresses. The main memory address of the transfer, as well as its size, is provided by a linked list of tags.

One way to build clusters is to simply use a network of workstations (Figure 10.21). Clusters of this type can be used to connect workstations that are required for personal use but sit idle for some periods of time, say, overnight. Loosely coupled clusters of this type are useful to take advantage of compute cycles that would otherwise go unused. When connected to file servers, these workstation-based servers can be used to provide service to large networks of users.

Another type of cluster is built specifically for compute-intensive tasks. These are a little more experimental, but they provide an interesting example of the high computing horsepower that can be wrung out of workstation technology. Clusters of this type are at the top of the POWER/PowerPC computing hierarchy.

The IBM 9076 SP-1 (Scalable Processor) is shown in Figure 10.22. The SP-1 is scalable from 8 to 64 processors, placed in one to four hardware frames. Each frame can hold from 8 to 16 RS/6000 processors. The processors are high-end 62.5 MHz versions that can each provide up to 125 MFLOPS (Million Floating-Point Operations per Second). The largest system can provide as many as 8000 MFLOPS.

Each processor node contains not only the RS/6000 processor, but 64 to 256 Mbytes of memory and one or two disk drives. In a maximum 64-processor system, there can be 16 Gbytes of main memory.

An attached workstation acts as a single point of control for system management, admin-istration, monitoring, and control. The workstation and file servers to support the SP-1 are

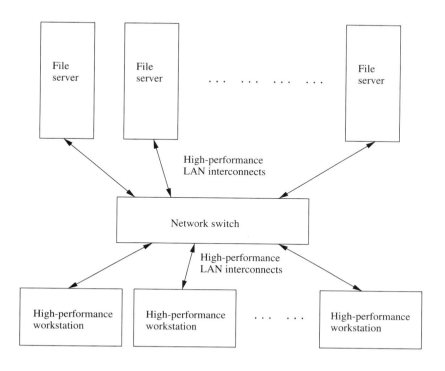

FIGURE 10.21　**A cluster based on high-performance workstations.**

connected into the frames via an Ethernet LAN. All files must come from the external file servers, as the node disks are used only for paging.

Unlike a shared-memory multiprocessor, each processor runs its own copy of the operating system. There is no mechanism for maintaining cache coherence between nodes, so processes can cooperate either by message passing, which seems to be the preferred method, or by using page faulting mechanisms to move pages of data from node to node.

Figure 10.23 shows the detail of a frame. Each RS/6000 node has an adapter that allows it to communicate with a high-performance switching network. The switch nodes are four by four crossbars with bidirectional links. Switch nodes in different frames are cross-connected, so that a node can communicate within its own frame or with different frames with equal ease. Four of the switch connections are used to tie into the external LAN for control and file service.

Messages pass through the switching network in a packet-switched manner. That is, each

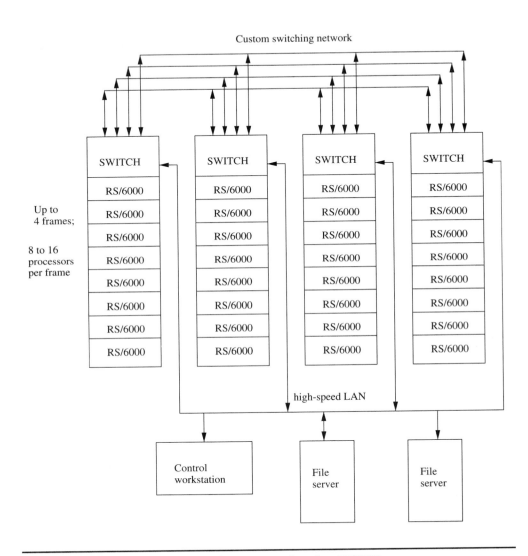

FIGURE 10.22 The IBM 9076 SP-1 Cluster system, based on RS/6000s.

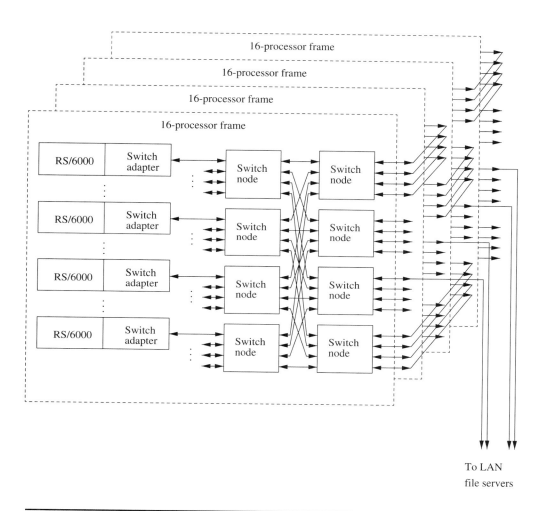

FIGURE 10.23 Detail of an SP-1 frame.

message contains routing information and works its way through the network independently of the others.

Each port into the switching network is one byte wide and can provide up to 40 Mbytes/second of bandwidth. The time it takes for a message to pass from one node to another is less than a microsecond in hardware. But software overhead is between one and two orders of magnitude higher, because passing a message requires that the operating system be called, in much the same way as an I/O request.

10.8 Summary

In this chapter, we have examined a range of system organizations using both POWER and PowerPC implementations. We considered PC-class systems composed of PowerPC 601s. The high-end versions of these systems use a hierarchy of I/O buses. These buses and their structure very much define the system characteristics (at least from a hardware perspective).

Multiprocessor server-class systems were studied at a high level in Chapter 8 where we discussed cache coherence and process synchronization. In this chapter, we looked at the low-level bus design used in the PowerPC 601. This bus is typical of the new processor buses, and it will likely be used in PowerPC systems beyond the 601.

The RS/6000 family of workstations has been available for several years, providing a good vehicle for us to look at memory systems and high-performance I/O systems.

We then illustrated the top of the computing "food chain" by highlighting the IBM 9076 SP-1, a system capable of 8000 MFLOPS with up to 16 Gbytes of memory. The SP-1, while somewhat experimental, may very well be a hint of the type of system that will eventually replace the traditional mainframe systems in centralized computing environments.

10.9 References

Hardell et al. [32] describe the DCU and its memory interface as well as error detection and correction. Nicholson et al. [64] discuss the RS/6000 Input/Output organization with focus on the IOU.

There is a wealth of information on the Micro Channel. Besides the IBM manual [43] and the architecture specification [59], a full issue of the *IBM Personal Systems Technical Journal* [45] is dedicated to it. See also Figueroa [22] for some timing diagrams and a local arbiter implementation. EISA and Micro Channel have been the target of many comparisons; see Marshall [57] for a recent one, including a discussion on bus fundamentals. The SCSI specification is available from ANSI [5].

POWERPC 601 AND ALPHA 21064: A TALE OF TWO RISCS

At this point many RISC purists will undoubtedly claim that this is not a RISC design.... This second-generation RISC design, representing a reasonable melding of RISC and CISC concepts, is likely to be the direction for many future RISC designs.

P. Hester, *RISC System/6000 Hardware Background and Philosophies*

We reapplied the principles of RISC to processor design to get maximum clock speed.

R. Sites, *RISC Enters a New Generation—An insider's look at the development of DEC's Alpha CPU*

11.1 Introduction

POWER1, POWER2, and PowerPC 601 are excellent examples of high-performance implementations that are tuned to an architecture. The fit is so good it's tempting to conclude this is the way RISC processors are "supposed" to be done. To provide a contrasting, but

	PowerPC	Alpha
Basic architecture	load/store	load/store
Instruction length	32-bit	32-bit
Byte/halfword load&store	yes	no
Condition codes	yes	no
Conditional moves	no	yes
Integer registers	32	32
Integer register size	32/64 bit	64 bit
Floating-point registers	32	32
Floating-register size	64 bit	64 bit
Floating-point format	IEEE	IEEE, VAX
	32-bit, 64-bit	32-bit, 64-bit
Virtual address	52–80 bit	43–64 bit
32/64 Mode bit	yes	no
Segmentation	yes	no
Page size	4 Kbytes	implementation specific

FIGURE 11.1   Summary of architectural characteristics.

equally valid, way of building RISC processors, we conclude the book with a discussion of an alternative RISC architecture and implementation. We compare the single-chip PowerPC 601 with the DEC Alpha architecture and its single-chip implementation, the 21064.

As we have seen, the PowerPC is focused on powerful instructions and a great deal of flexibility in the order in which instructions are processed. The Alpha 21064 depends on a very fast clock, with simple instructions and a more rigid implementation structure. Both PowerPC and Alpha are load/store architectures with 32-bit fixed-length instructions. They each have 32 integer and 32 floating-point registers. But there is little in common beyond these basic properties (Figure 11.1).

It is often more natural to begin the discussion of a processor with its architecture, then proceed to the way it is implemented; we've followed that order so far in this book. However, for our comparison in this chapter, we do the opposite. We first describe the major features of the Alpha 21064 implementation; then, we will be able to discuss the rationale for the architectural features and differences between it and the PowerPC 601.

To remain consistent with the rest of the book we use the same notation as in Figure 2.2. We label bits beginning with 0 at the most significant bit in the left-to-right direction as defined in PowerPC (and unlike Alpha). The reader should also be aware that our assembly language and pipeline naming differ from those used in DEC documentation. We use an assembly language similar to the one we have been using thus far for the IBM processors and label pipeline stages in a similar manner.

	PowerPC 601	Alpha 21064
Technology	0.6-micron CMOS	0.75-micron CMOS
Levels of metal	4	3
Die size	1.09 cm square	2.33 cm square
Transistor count	2.8 million	1.68 million
Total cache (instructions + data)	32 Kbyte	16 Kbyte
Package	304-pin QFP	431-pin PGA
Clock frequency	50 MHz, initially	150 to 200 MHz
Power dissipation	9 watts @ 50 MHz	30 watts @ 200 MHz

FIGURE 11.2 **Summary of implementation characteristics.**

11.2 Implementation Overview

Figure 11.2 compares the PowerPC 601 and Alpha 21064 chips. The 601 has a relatively small die size due to IBM's aggressive 0.6-micron CMOS technology with four levels of metal (a fifth metal layer is used for local interconnect). The 601 has a unified 32 Kbyte cache. The 21064 has split data and instruction caches, 8 Kbytes each. The 2:1 ratio in the cache sizes accounts to a large extent for the substantial difference in the transistor count.

Two striking differences appear in clock cycle and power dissipation. The Alpha is much faster but also runs much hotter. That a fast clock leads to more power is unsurprising: it is a well-known property of CMOS circuits. However, speed adds another variable to be considered in the fast clock versus complex pipe stages trade-off we discuss in this chapter. Even if a fast clock "wins" in performance, its higher power could lose applications, for example in portable personal computers.

21064 Pipelines

Figure 11.3 illustrates the 21064 pipeline complex. It is composed of three parallel pipelines: a fixed-point pipe, a floating-point pipe, and a load/store pipe. The pipelines are relatively deep, and the integer and load/store pipes are the same length. We describe the integer and load/store pipelines together.

1. *F, instruction Fetch:* the instruction cache is accessed and two instructions are fetched.

2. *S, Swap:* Two instructions are inspected to see if they require the integer or floating-point pipelines. The instructions are directed to the correct pipeline, sometimes swapping their positions. Branch instructions are predicted in this stage.

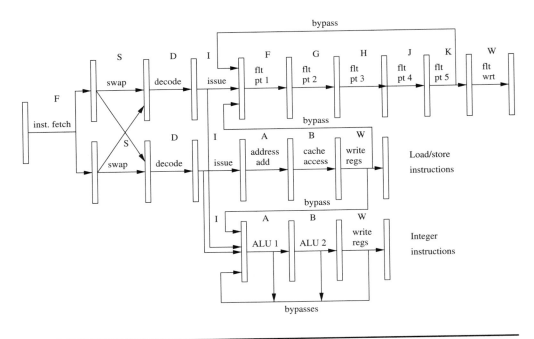

FIGURE 11.3   **The 21064 pipeline complex. Only a small subset of the bypasses is shown.**

3. *D, Decode:* Instructions are decoded in preparation for instruction issue—the opcode is inspected to determine the register and resource requirements of the instruction. Unlike in the IBM processors, registers are not read during the decode stage.

4. *I, Issue:* Instructions are issued and operands are read from the registers. Issue consists of checking register and resource dependences to determine if the instruction should begin execution or if it should be held back. After they have passed the issue stage, instructions are no longer blocked in the pipelines; they flow through to completion.

5. *A, ALU stage 1:* Integer adds, logicals, and short-length shifts are executed. Their results can be immediately bypassed back, so these appear to be single-cycle instructions. Longer-length shifts are initiated in this stage. Loads and stores do their effective address add in this stage.

6. *B, ALU stage 2:* Longer-length shifts complete in this stage; their results are bypassed back to ALU 1, so these are two-cycle instructions. For loads and stores, the data cache tags are read. Loads also read cache data.

7. *W, Write stage:* results are written into the register file. Cache hit/miss is determined. Store instructions that hit have their data stored in a buffer. The buffer contents will be written into the cache during a following cycle when there is no load.

The 21064 integer pipeline relies on a large number of bypasses for high performance. These are important in a deep pipeline to reduce apparent latencies. Figure 11.3 shows a few of the bypasses; there are a total of 38 separate bypass paths.

Referring again to Figure 11.3, floating-point instructions pass through F, S, D, and I stages just like the integer instructions. There are, then, five stages where floating-point multiply and add instructions are performed (stages F through K).[1] The floating-point divide takes 31 or 61 cycles, depending on single or double precision.

Dispatch Rules

Simultaneous dispatch rules are an important defining feature of superscalar architecture implementation. At this point we compare the dispatch rules of the PowerPC 601 and the Alpha 21064.

The dispatch rules in the 601 are quite simple. The architecture has three units, Integer (or Fixed-Point), Floating-Point, and Branch, and three instructions may issue simultaneously as long as each goes to a different unit. Integer operate instructions and all loads and stores go to the same pipeline (FXU), and only one instruction of this category may issue per clock cycle.

In the 21064, dispatch (in the 601-sense) occurs in the S pipeline stage. Instructions *issue* two stages later. In the 21064, issue significantly affects dispatch because instructions must issue in their original program order, and dispatch (i.e., the swap stage) helps to enforce this order. A pair of instructions belonging to the same aligned doubleword (quadword in DEC parlance) can simultaneously issue. Consecutive instructions in different doublewords may not dual-issue, and if two instructions in the same doubleword cannot simultaneously issue, the first in program sequence must issue first.

The 21064 implements separate integer and load/store pipelines, and several combinations of these instructions may be dual-issued (with the exception of integer operate / floating store, and floating operate / integer store).[2] The separate load/store unit requires an extra set of ports to both the integer and floating register files. The load/store ports are shared with the Branch Unit, which must have access to all the registers because the Alpha architecture has no condition codes and branches may depend on any integer or floating register. As a consequence, branches may not be simultaneously issued with any load or store instruction.

---

[1] There are two pipeline stages labeled F: instruction Fetch, and Floating-point stage 1. In both cases, F provides the easiest way to remember the pipeline stage, and the stages are so far apart that this shouldn't lead to any confusion in our diagrams.

[2] This exception is due to a conflict in instruction paths, not shown in Figure 11.3.

| | Integer ||| Floating ||| Branch |
	Load	Store	Operate	Load	Store	Operate	Branch
Integer load						×	×
Integer store						×	×
Integer operate						×	×
Floating load						×	×
Floating store						×	×
Floating operate	×	×	×	×	×		×
Branch	×	×	×	×	×	×	

(a) PowerPC 601. Three mutually compatible (marked with ×) instructions may issue simultaneously.

| | Integer ||| Floating ||| Branch ||
	Load	Store	Operate	Load	Store	Operate	Integer	Floating
Integer load			×			×		
Integer store			×					
Integer operate	×	×		×		×	×	
Floating load			×			×		
Floating store						×		
Floating operate	×		×	×	×			×
Integer branch			×					
Floating branch						×		

(b) Alpha 21064. Two compatible (marked with ×) instructions may issue simultaneously. Integer branches depend on an integer register, floating branches depend on a floating register.

FIGURE 11.4   Instruction Dispatch Rules.

Figure 11.4 summarizes the dispatch rules for both processors. In the PowerPC 601 table, two instructions may simultaneously issue if there is an X in the corresponding row/column of the table. For three instructions, all three pairs must have Xs. In the 21064 table, two instructions may simultaneously issue if there is an X in the table entry.

The ability of the 21064 to dual-issue a load and an integer operate instruction is a definite strength with respect to the 601. Many applications (not to mention the operating system) use very little floating point; the 21064 can still execute these codes with high efficiency.

	Integer registers		Floating registers	
	Read ports	Write ports	Read ports	Write ports
PowerPC 601	3	2	3	2
Alpha 21064	4	2	3	2

FIGURE 11.5   **Register file ports.**

For non-floating-point applications, the Floating-Point Unit of the 601 sits idle while integer instructions dispatch at the rate of only one per clock cycle.

Register Files

Quite different considerations in the two implementations led to register files that have almost the same number of ports (Figure 11.5). One write and two read ports are required to pipeline operate instructions. The 21064 provides an additional pair of read/write ports for load/store unit data. Branches share the load/store register ports, which brings the count up to 3R/2W for both integer and floating register files. One additional integer read port is needed to get the address value for stores, and it is also used for load addresses. The ability to do an integer store in parallel with an integer operate costs an extra integer read port. However, by not allowing a register plus register addressing mode, a register read port is saved.

Looking at the 601, beginning again with one write and two read ports for operate instructions, an additional integer read port is provided for single-cycle processing of store with index instructions, which read three registers (two for the effective address, one for the result). The extra integer write port allows the result of an operate instruction and data returned from the cache to be written in the same clock cycle. The same consideration accounts for two write ports in the floating register file. The three floating-point read ports are needed by the combined floating multiply-add instruction.

Data Caches

Yet another interesting contrast between the two implementations is the way the caches are implemented. Figure 11.6 shows the flow through the two data caches.

The 21064 uses separate instruction and data caches; the data cache is shown in Figure 11.6(a). These are small (8 Kbyte) direct-mapped data caches designed for very fast access times. The address add consumes one clock cycle. During the next clock cycle, the cache data and tag are simultaneously read; this is easily done with a direct-mapped cache where only one tag must be read, and the data, if present, can only be in one place. Simultaneously, the TLB is accessed. During the next clock cycle, the TLB address translation completes and the tag is compared with the upper address bits. A cache hit or miss is determined about halfway through this clock cycle. The data are always delivered to the registers

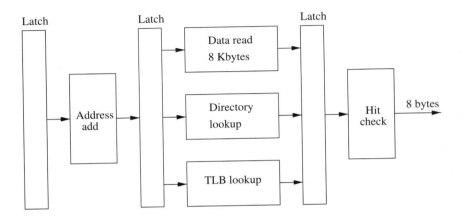

(a) Alpha 21064 cache access path.

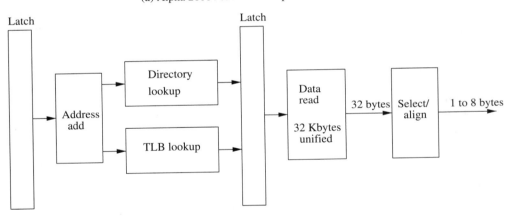

(b) PowerPC 601 cache access path.

FIGURE 11.6   The PowerPC 601 and Alpha 21064 cache access paths.

as an aligned 8-byte doubleword. Any alignment, byte selecting, etc. must be done with separate instructions.

In the PowerPC 601, the unified data/instruction cache is much larger, 32 Kbytes, and is 8-way set associative, so it can be expected to have a higher hit rate than the 21064. In Figure 11.6(b) we can clearly see how much more "work" the 601 does in a clock cycle compared with the 21064. It does an address add and the cache directory/TLB lookup in the same cycle (refer back to Figure 8.15). Then, during the next cycle, it accesses the 32-byte–wide data memory. During the same cycle, it selects and aligns the data field.

The 601 gets more done in fewer stages, but the 21064 has a clock cycle about a third to a fourth that of the 601's. When measured in nanoseconds, the two clock cycles in Figure 11.6(b) take much longer than the three cycles in Figure 11.6(a). To summarize, the 601 gains performance by having a larger cache, having a higher associativity, and doing data alignment automatically in hardware. The 21064 gains performance by having a very fast clock.

Example of Pipeline Flow

Figure 11.7 shows the same example that we used earlier for the POWER1 (Figure 3.6) and PowerPC 601 (Figure 8.8). Figure 11.8 is the Alpha pipeline flow for the example loop.

Just from looking at the "big picture," in-order issue and dual issue only for aligned instruction pairs are quite evident. The relatively long six-clock-period floating-point latency is also evident. We see that after the I stage, instructions never block.

Starting with the first two instructions, which cannot dual-issue because both are loads, we see the role the swap stage plays in ordering instructions for issue. The second instruction is held a cycle while the first moves ahead. The first dual issue occurs for the first addq mult pair. Because the mult is the first instruction in the doubleword, the addq must wait, even though the addq has no dependences holding it back. The sequence of dependent floating-point instructions paces instruction issue for most of the loop. Note that the floating store issues in anticipation of the floating-point result. It waits only four, not six, clock periods for the result, so that it reaches its write stage just in time to have the floating-point result bypassed to it.

Following the predicted branch at the end of the loop there is a bubble. Because other instructions in the pipeline are blocked, however, the bubble is "squashed" by the time the ldt following the branch is ready to issue.

Overall, the loop takes 16 clock periods per iteration in steady state. (The first ldt passes through I at time 4, and during the second iteration it issues at time 20.) In comparison, the PowerPC 601 (Figure 8.8)[3] takes only six clock periods, and POWER1 (Figure 3.6) takes even

---

[3]As before, we are using single-precision timing for the 601.

double x[512], y[512];

for (k = 0; k < 512; k++)
    x[k] = (r*x[k] + t*y[k]);

(a) C code.

```
                                    # r1 points to x
                                    # r2 points to y
                                    # r6 points to the end y
                                    # fp2 contains t
                                    # fp4 contains r
                                    # r5 contains the constant 1
LOOP:   ldt     fp3 = y(r2,0)       # load floating double
        ldt     fp1 = x(r1,0)       # load floating double
        mult    fp3 = fp3,fp2       # floating multiply double t*y
        addq    r2 = r2,8           # bump y pointer
        mult    fp1 = fp1,fp4       # floating multiply double, r*x
        subq    r4 = r2,r6          # subtract y end from current pointer
        addt    fp1 = fp3,fp1       # floating add double, r*x+t*z
        stt     x(r1,0) = fp1       # store floating double to x(k)
        addq    r1 = r1,8           # bump x pointer
        bne     r4,LOOP             # branch on r4 ne 0
```

(b) Assembly code.

FIGURE 11.7   **Alpha 21064 pipelined processing example.**

---

fewer: four clock periods. *But, don't forget,* the 21064 is running its clock three to four times faster.

The floating-point latencies are a major performance problem for the 21064 when it executes this type of code. Also, because of in-order issue, the loops don't "telescope" together like these in the 601—there is very little overlap among consecutive loop iterations. Figure 11.9 illustrates the telescoping phenomenon. In the figure, each parallelogram illustrates the general shape of the pipeline flow for a single loop iteration. In an in-order issue processor like the 21064, there is little overlap between loop iterations, and branch prediction is a major contributor to the small amount of overlap that occurs.

In an implementation like the PowerPC 601, however, the out-of-order dispatch, along with multiple buffers placed at key points, allows the loop iterations to be compressed, like a folding telescope. Furthermore, with a branch processor as in the 601, branch prediction is

	1	2	3	4	5	6	7	8	9	10	11	12	13	14	15	16	17	18	19	20	21	22
ldt fp3=y(r2,0)	F	S	D	I	A	B	W															
ldt fp1=x(r1,0)	F	.	S	D	I	A	B	W														
mult fp3=fp3,fp2			F	S	D	.	I	F	G	H	J	K	W									
addq r2=r2,8			F	S	D	.	I	A	B	W												
mult fp1=fp1,fp4				F	S	.	D	I	F	G	H	J	K	W								
subq r4=r2,r6				F	S	.	D	I	A	B	W											
addt fp1=fp3,fp1						F	.	S	D	.	.	.	.	.	.	I	F	G	H	J	K	W
stt x(r1,0)=fp1						F	.	S	D	.	.	.	.	.	.	.	.	I	A	B	W	
addq r1=r1,8							F	S	.	.	.	.	.	.	.	.	D	I	A	B	W	
bne r4,loop							F	S	.	.	.	.	.	.	.	.	D	I	A	.	.	
ldt fp3=y(r2,0)									F	.	.	.	.	.	.	.	.	S	D	I	A	B
ldt fp1=x(r1,0)									F	.	.	.	.	.	.	.	.	S	D	I	A	

FIGURE 11.8   21064 pipeline flow for loop example.

not needed to achieve this effect. The RS/6000, with register renaming, deeper buffers, and more bypass paths, achieves even more telescoping than the 601.

Software pipelining or loop unrolling (see Section 1.5) are likely to provide much better performance for a deeply pipelined implementation like the 21064. The DEC compilers unroll loops. Figure 11.10 shows the unrolled version of the same loop. The example loop is unrolled four times. To illustrate relative timing, the clock period at which instructions pass through the I stage is shown in the right-hand column.[4] Now, in steady state, four iterations take 23 clock periods, or about 6 clock periods per iteration, more than three times better than the rolled version. Also, the performance advantage of dual issue is now much more evident than with the rolled version.

Loop unrolling also improves the performance of the 601, as shown in Figure 11.11 (loop from Figure 8.7 unrolled four times). In the 601, after dispatching (which corresponds to issuing in Alpha) instructions may be held in a buffer or in the decode stage if the pipeline is blocked. Hence, we show FXU and FPU decode time, and BU execute time (which is the same cycle in which a branch is decoded).

We assume, as before, that the loop body is aligned in the cache sector. Eight instructions are fetched, and instruction fetching can continue to keep the instruction buffer full until time 2; after that, the cache is busy with load instructions. The instruction queue becomes empty and the pipeline is starved for instructions, but these cannot be fetched until time 9, when the

---

[4]This simplified timing notation is a by-product of in-order issue and no instruction blocking after the issue stage.

time

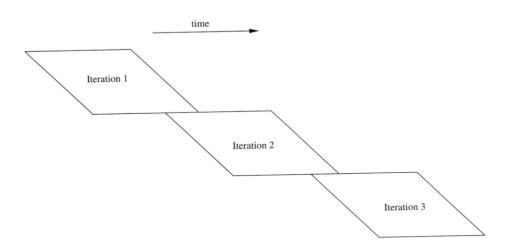

(a) General pipeline flow with a 21064-like implementation.

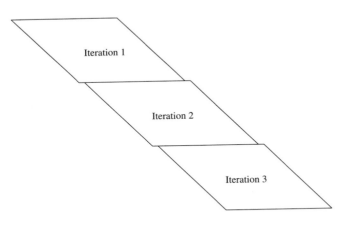

(b) "Telescoped" pipeline flow with a PowerPC-like implemenation.

FIGURE 11.9   Comparison of loop overlap in 21064-like and PowerPC 601–like implementations.

				Issue time
LOOP:	ldt	fp3 = y(r2,0)	# load y[k]	0
	ldt	fp1 = x(r1,0)	# load x[k]	1
	ldt	fp7 = y(r2,8)	# load y[k+1]	2
	ldt	fp5 = x(r1,8)	# load x[k+1]	3
	mult	fp3 = fp3,fp2	# t∗y[k]	4
	ldt	fp11 = y(r2,16)	# load y[k+2]	4
	mult	fp1 = fp1,fp4	# r∗x[k]	5
	ldt	fp9 = x(r1,16)	# load x[k+2]	5
	mult	fp7 = fp7,fp2	# t∗y[k+1]	6
	ldt	fp15 = y(r2,24)	# load y[k+3]	6
	mult	fp5 = fp5,fp4	# r∗x[k+1]	7
	ldt	fp13 = x(r1,24)	# load x[k+3]	7
	mult	fp11 = fp11,fp2	# t∗y[k+2]	8
	addq	r2 = r2,32	# bump y pointer	8
	mult	fp9 = fp9,fp4	# r∗x[k+2]	9
	subq	r4 = r2,r6	# remaining y size	9
	mult	fp15 = fp15,fp2	# t∗y[k+3]	10
	mult	fp13 = fp13,fp4	# r∗x[k+3]	11
	addt	fp1 = fp3,fp1	# r∗x[k]+t∗y[k]	12
	addt	fp5 = fp7,fp5	# r∗x[k+1]+t∗y[k+1]	13
	addt	fp9 = fp11,fp9	# r∗x[k+2]+t∗y[k+2]	15
	stt	x(r1,0) = fp1	# store x[k]	16
	addt	fp13= fp15,fp13	# r∗x[k+3]+t∗y[k+3]	17
	stt	x(r1,8) = fp5	# store x[k+1]	17
	stt	x(r1,16) = fp9	# store x[k+2]	19
	stt	x(r1,24) = fp13	# store x[k+3]	21
	addq	r1 = r1,32	# bump x pointer	22
	bne	r4,LOOP	# next loop	22
LOOP:	ldt	fp3 = y(r2,0)	# next iteration	23

FIGURE 11.10 Example loop, unrolled for the Alpha 21064.

				Instr. fetch time	FXU decode time	FPU decode time	BU exec. time
			# CTR = 128 (loop count/4)				
LOOP:	lfs	fp0 = y(r3,2052)	# load y[k]	0	1		
	lfs	fp4 = y(r3,2056)	# load y[k+1]	0	2		
	lfs	fp6 = y(r3,2060)	# load y[k+2]	0	3		
	fmuls	fp0 = fp0,fp1	# t*y[k]	0		4	
	lfs	fp8 = y(r3,2064)	# load y[k+3]	0	4		
	fmuls	fp4 = fp4,fp1	# t*y[k+1]	0		5	
	lfs	fp2 = x(r3,4)	# load x[k]	0	5		
	fmuls	fp6 = fp6,fp1	# t*y[k+2]	0		6	
	lfs	fp5 = x(r3,8)	# load x[k+1]	2	6		
	fmuls	fp8 = fp8,fp1	# t*y[k+3]	2		7	
	lfs	fp7 = x(r3,12)	# load x[k+2]	9	10		
	fmadds	fp0 = fp0,fp2,fp3	# r*x[k] + t*y[k]	9		11	
	lfs	fp9 = x(r3,16)	# load x[k+3]	9	11		
	fmadds	fp4 = fp4,fp5,fp3	# r*x[k+1] + t*y[k+1]	9		12	
	fmadds	fp6 = fp6,fp7,fp3	# r*x[k+2] + t*y[k+2]	9		13	
	fmadds	fp8 = fp8,fp9,fp3	# r*x[k+3] + t*y[k+3]	9		14	
	stfs	x(r3+4) = fp0	# store x[k]	10	14	15	
	stfs	x(r3+8) = fp4	# store x[k+1]	10	15	16	
	stfs	x(r3+12) = fp6	# store x[k+2]	10	16	17	
	stfsu	x(r3=r3+16) = fp8	# store x[k+3]	10	17	18	
	bc	LOOP,CTR≠0	# dec CTR, branch if CTR ≠ 0	11			15
LOOP:	lfs	fp0 = y(r3,2052)	# load y[k]	20	21		

FIGURE 11.11 Example loop, unrolled for the PowerPC 601. FXU instructions are dispatched and decoded in the same clock cycle.

cache finally becomes available. At this time the six remaining instructions of the cache sector are fetched (the first two were fetched at time 2).

The unrolled loop (four iterations) takes 20 clock cycles, which corresponds to 5 clock cycles per loop iteration (versus 6 clock cycles in the rolled version). The same unrolled loop[5] would take only 12 clock cycles (3 clock cycles per loop iteration) on POWER1, primarily because the split cache allows instruction fetching to proceed regardless of data references.

---

[5] Actually, unrolling it twice would be sufficient.

11.3   Architecture Comparison

Now we are ready to discuss the architectural differences of the PowerPC and Alpha. The discussion will focus on the "fit" between architecture and implementation.

Branch Instructions

There are significant differences in the way the two architectures handle branches. Figure 11.12 compares the format of conditional and unconditional branches. We discuss below other branch instructions whose format is not shown in the figure.

PowerPC implements branches with a special set of registers designed for that purpose. Conditional branches may test fields in the Condition Code Register and the contents of a special register, the Count Register. A single branch instruction may implement a loop-closing branch whose outcome depends on both the Count Register and a Condition Code value. Comparison instructions set fields of the Condition Code Register explicitly and most arithmetic and logical instructions may optionally set a condition field by using the record bit.

In Alpha, conditional branches test a general purpose register relative to zero or whether the register contents are odd or even.[6] Thus, results of other instructions can be tested as long as they are tested against zero (or odd/even). Comparison instructions leave their result in a general purpose register.

Certain control transfer instructions save the updated program counter to be used as a subroutine return address. These are special jump instructions in Alpha that save the return address in a general purpose register. In PowerPC, this is done in any branch by setting the Link (LK) bit to one, and saving the return address in the Link Register.

The Alpha also implements a set of conditional move instructions that move a value from one register to another, but only if a condition, similar to the branch condition, is satisfied. These conditional moves allow branches to be eliminated in many simple conditional code sequences. An example is shown in Figure 11.13. A simple if-then-else sequence is given in Figure 11.13(a). A conventional code sequence appears in Figure 11.13(b); the timing shown is for the best case path, assuming a correct prediction. Figure 11.13(c) uses a conditional move. While the load is being done, both shifts can be done (essentially) for free. The shift 4 is tentatively placed in register r3 to be stored to memory. If the test of a is true, then the conditional move to c replaces the value in r3 with the shift 2 results. The total time is not only shorter than the branch implementation (even in the best case), but it does not depend on branch prediction.

---

[6]The odd/even tests allows for compilers that use the low-order bit to denote "true" or "false" logical values.

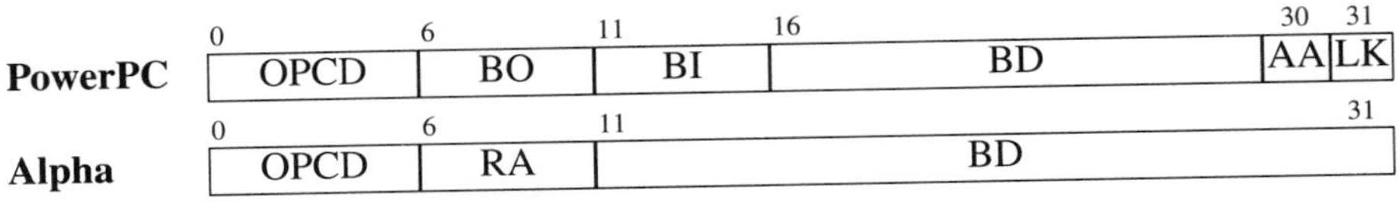

PowerPC Target address $= \begin{cases} PC + BD||00 & \text{if } AA = 0 \\ BD||00 & \text{if } AA = 1 \end{cases}$

Alpha Target address $= PC + BD||00$

(a) Conditional branches. Word addresses are concatenated with 00 to form byte addresses. BD is the branch displacement and is sign extended. PowerPC instruction fields have been defined in Chapter 7. In Alpha, RA designates the register tested to determine the branch outcome.

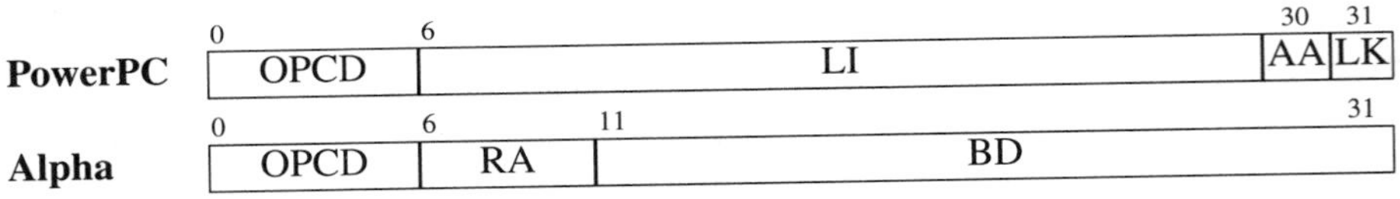

PowerPC Target address $= \begin{cases} PC + LI||00 & \text{if } AA = 0 \\ LI||00 & \text{if } AA = 1 \end{cases}$

Alpha Target address $= PC + BD||00$

(b) Unconditional branches. Word addresses are concatenated with 00 to form byte addresses. BD is the branch displacement and LI is a longer displacement (long immediate), both are sign extended. PowerPC instruction fields have been defined in Chapter 2. In Alpha, the updated program counter is written into register RA to be used as the return address if this is a subroutine call.

FIGURE 11.12 Branch instructions.

if (a == 1) c = b << 2;
else c = b << 4;

(a) C code.

				Issue time
			# initially, assume	
			# r1 contains b,	
			# r7 points to a,	
			# r8 points to c.	
	ldl	r2 = a(r7,0)	# load a from memory	0
	cmpeq	r5 = r2,1	# test a	3
	beq	r5,SHFT2	# branch if a==1	4
			# assume taken	
	sll	r3 = r1,4	# shift b << 4	
	br	STORE	# branch uncond	
SHFT2:	sll	r4 = r1,2	# shift b << 2	
STORE:	stl	r3 = c(r8,0)	# store c	6

(b) Assembly code with conditional branch.

			Issue time
		# initially, assume	
		# r1 contains b,	
		# r7 points to a,	
		# r8 points to c.	
ldl	r2 = a(r7,0)	# load a from memory	0
sll	r3 = r1,4	# shift b << 4	1
sll	r4 = r1,2	# shift b << 2	2
cmpeq	r5 = r2,1	# test a	3
cmov	r3 = r4,r5	# conditional move to c	4
stl	r3 = c(r8,0)	# store c	4

(c) Assembly code with conditional move.

FIGURE 11.13 Alpha 21064 conditional move example.

In general, branch target addresses are determined in the following ways:

■ *Adding a displacement to the program counter (PC relative).* This mode is found in both architectures.

■ *Absolute.* Available only in PowerPC, where the displacement is interpreted as an absolute address if the Absolute Address (AA) bit is set to one.

■ *Register indirect.* This mode is available in instructions not shown in Figure 11.12. These are the XL-form conditional branches in PowerPC (see Figure 2.16) and jump instructions in Alpha. The registers used for the branch target address are general purpose registers in Alpha and two special registers (Count Register and Link Register) in PowerPC.

Branch Prediction

Both processors predict branches in an effort to reduce pipeline bubbles. The PowerPC 601 uses a static branch prediction made by the compiler. Also, as a hedge against a wrong prediction, the 601 saves (for a while) the contents of the instruction buffer following a branch-taken prediction; these instructions on the not-taken path are available immediately if a misprediction is detected. The instruction buffer contents are kept until instructions from the taken path are delivered from memory.

The Alpha 21064 implements dynamic branch prediction with a 2048 entry table; one entry is associated with each instruction in the instruction cache. The prediction table is updated as a program runs, containing the outcome of the most recent execution of each branch. This predictor is based on the observation that most branches are decided the same way as on their previous execution. This observation is especially true for loop-closing branches.

This type of prediction does not always work well for subroutine returns, however. A subroutine may be called from a number of places, so the return jump is not necessarily the same on two consecutive executions. Alpha takes this into account by having special hardware for predicting the target address for return-from-subroutine jumps. The compiler places the lower 16 bits of the return address in a special field of the jump-to-subroutine instruction. When this instruction is executed, the return address is pushed on a four-entry prediction stack, so return addresses can be held for subroutines nested four deep. The stack is popped prior to returning from the subroutine and the return address is used to prefetch instructions from the cache.

Branch Processing

We are now ready to step through the pipeline flow for 21064 conditional branches (Figure 11.14).

```
        0   1   2   3   4   5   6   7   8   9   10  11  12  13
A       F   S   D   I   A   B   W
branch  F   .   S   D   I   A
B           F   S   D   I   A   B   W
C           F   .   S   D   I   A   B   W
```

(a) Instruction flow for correct branch prediction.

```
        0   1   2   3   4   5   6   7   8   9   10  11  12  13
A       F   S   D   I   A   B   W
branch  F   .   S   D   I   A
B           F   S   D   I   X   X   X
C           F   .   S   D   X   X   X   X
.
.
.
X                               F   S   D   I   A   B   W
Y                               F   .   S   D   I   A   B   W
```

(b) Instruction flow for incorrect branch prediction.

FIGURE 11.14 Timing for conditional branches in the Alpha 21064. X means instruction is flushed as a result of branch misprediction.

Figure 11.14(a) is one (of several) cases where the branch prediction is correct; Figure 11.14(b) is a case where the prediction is wrong. The swap stage of the pipeline examines instructions in pairs. After the branch instruction is detected and predicted, it takes one clock cycle to compute the target address and begin fetching, which may lead to a one-cycle bubble in the pipeline. The pipeline is designed to allow "squashing" of this bubble. That is, if the instruction ahead of the bubble blocks, and the instruction behind proceeds, the bubble is "squashed" between the two and is eliminated. In some cases, when there is a simultaneous dispatch conflict, as in Figure 11.14(a), the instruction preceding the branch must be split from it anyway. In this case, the branch instruction waits a cycle and naturally fills in the bubble (in effect, the branch fills its own bubble!). In other cases, if the pipeline stalls ahead of the branch, the bubble can be squashed by having an instruction behind the branch move up in the pipe (this happens in Figure 11.8). If the bubble is squashed, and the prediction is correct, the branch effectively becomes a zero-cycle branch.

Figure 11.14(b) shows the incorrect prediction case. The branch instruction has its registers read during issue stage. During the A stage, the register can be tested and the correctness of the prediction can be determined. This is done quickly enough that if there is a misprediction, the

Distance	Alpha 21064		PowerPC 601	
	Correct	Incorrect	Correct	Incorrect
0	0 to 1	4	0	2 or 1
1	0 to 1	4	0	1 or 0
≥2	0 to 1	4	0	0

FIGURE 11.15 Branch penalties for the Alpha 21064 and PowerPC 601. In the 601 the penalty may be one cycle shorter (1 instead of 2, for example), when the fetch cycle is saved in certain situations (see text).

instruction fetch stage can be notified while the branch is still in the A stage. Then, fetching the correct path can begin with the next cycle. As a result, four stages of the pipeline must be flushed when the prediction is found to be incorrect. For the jump-to-subroutine instruction, the penalty for a misprediction is five cycles.

For branches, the biggest architectural difference between the Alpha and the PowerPC is that the Alpha uses general purpose registers for testing and subroutine linkage. The PowerPC uses special-purpose registers held in the Branch Unit. Thus, the PowerPC can execute branch instructions in the Branch Unit immediately after instructions are fetched. In fact, the PowerPC looks back in the instruction buffer so that it can essentially execute, or at least predict, branches while they are being fetched. The Alpha 21064 implementation, in contrast, must treat branch instructions like the other instructions. They are decoded in the D pipeline stage, read registers in I, and "executed" in the A stage.

Figure 11.15 compares the approximate branch penalties for integer conditional branches (by far more common than floating-point branches). The penalties are expressed as a function of the number of instructions (distance) separating the condition—determining instruction (compare) and the branch; and the correctness of the prediction. The compare-to-branch instruction count is significant only in the 601, however. Instruction cache hits are assumed.

In the 21064, correctly predicted branches will usually take no clock cycles. They take one clock cycle when a bubble is created in the swap stage and is not later squashed. The 601 has a zero-cycle branch whenever there is enough time to finish the instruction that sets the condition code field prior to the branch and to fetch new instructions. This may take two clock cycles: execute the compare instruction, and fetch instructions from the branch target. This second clock cycle may be saved when a branch is mispredicted taken but is resolved before overwriting the instruction buffer; instructions may be dispatched from the buffer right after determining that the branch was not taken. With a two-instruction distance, the 601 has a zero-cycle branch even if it was mispredicted; the 21064 always depends on a prediction, regardless of the distance.

The PowerPC requires that fewer branches be predicted in the first place (Figure 11.16). In the 601, all loop-closing branches that use the CTR register do not have to be predicted; in

	Conditional branches (non-loop-closing)	Loop-closing branches	Subroutine returns
PowerPC 601	Static prediction	Always zero-cycle	Always zero-cycle
Alpha 21064	Dynamic prediction	Dynamic prediction	Stack prediction

FIGURE 11.16 Predictions methods versus branch type.

the Alpha these are ordinary conditional branches, although loop-closing branches are easily predictable. For a subroutine return, the return must read an integer register in Alpha, so these branches are predicted via the return stack. In the PowerPC, return jumps can be executed immediately in the Branch Unit; there is no need for prediction.

From both Figure 11.16 and Figure 11.15, we see that accurate branch prediction is much more critical in the 21064. Not only does the 21064 predict more of the branches, the penalties tend to be higher when it is wrong. For this reason, the 21064 has much more hardware dedicated to the task—history bits and the subroutine return stack. Furthermore, the Alpha architecture reduces the penalty for a misprediction by having branches that always test a register against zero; testing a register against another register would likely take an additional clock cycle.

Finally, we should point out that deeper pipelining in the 21064 makes clock cycle comparisons (as we have just done) unfair. Once again, remember that the 21064's clock is three to four times faster than the 601's.

It is sometimes suggested that the PowerPC method of using special-purpose registers for branches is a "mistake" because they present a potential bottleneck. We think not. These registers allow many branches to be executed quickly without prediction and are an important feature for supporting loop telescoping. (As discussed in Section 8.5, telescoping in the 601 is limited by the lack of store buffer in the FPU, which other implementations may choose to provide.)

Let us examine an implementation that uses general-purpose registers but executes branches in the instruction fetch unit (unlike PowerPC, which uses special-purpose registers for branches, and unlike the 21064, which uses general purpose registers but branches that go down the S, D, I, and A pipeline stages). Interlock problems arise involving the registers that are now read in two different pipeline stages: in the issue stage, as done normally, and in the fetch stage, to resolve branches right after fetching. Consider the way register dependences for most other instructions are resolved in the issue stage. If an instruction writes a register, it can set a register reservation bit that will hold a subsequent instruction that needs to read the register until the register is updated or a result bypass can be used.

If we use the same method in the instruction fetch stage, we must keep another set of register reservation bits (which means that all instructions must be at least partially decoded as part of the fetch process). We could decode all instructions before they are put into the instruction cache and keep them there in decoded form. Even if instructions are decoded in the fetch stage, it is possible to have more than one instruction that writes the same register in the pipeline at the same time. So instead of a reservation bit, there must be a reservation counter for each register, where the maximum count is the maximum number of instructions that can be in the pipeline between the fetch stage and the register write stage.

For example, consider the following short code sequence:

```
subl   r4 = r3,r5    # subtract, result to r4
addl   r4 = r4,r6    # add to r4
bgt    r4,LOOP       # branch on r4
```

The branch can't be evaluated until the `addl` is finished. So, as the `subl` and `addl` are passed up the pipeline from the fetch unit, a counter must be used to remember that *two* updates of r4 are needed before it is valid for testing by the branch. This counter can be decremented by the integer unit as the instructions modify register r4. When the count reaches zero, the branch can be evaluated.

Finally, it must be possible to read the registers in the fetch unit. For the conditional branch tests in Alpha, it is sufficient to keep "summaries" of all the registers to indicate only if they are zero and what their sign is. For fast execution of Jump to Subroutine, all the registers would have to be readable in the fetch unit. We see that it could be done, but the hardware complexity is greater than if it were designed into the architecture as in the PowerPC.

Memory Architecture and Instructions

Alpha is a 64-bit–only architecture. PowerPC has a mode bit, and implementations may come in either 32-bit or 64-bit versions, but all 64-bit versions must also have a 32-bit mode. The mode determines whether the condition codes are set by 32-bit or 64-bit operations.

Alpha defines a flat, or linear, virtual address space and a virtual address whose length is implementation-dependent within a specified range. PowerPC supports a system-wide segmented virtual address space in either 32-bit or 64-bit mode. Differences between the two modes affect the number of segments and their size, which also results in a difference in the virtual address space (52 bits versus 80 bits).

Flat virtual address spaces seem to be favored by software developers and architects today, although the very large segments available in PowerPC shouldn't present many problems.[7] The Alpha was defined as a 64-bit architecture from the start, so it was easy for developers to provide a flat virtual address space. The POWER architecture, in contrast, was defined

---

[7]The small 64K segments in the Intel 8086 architecture have given segmented memory a bad reputation, not deserved in our opinion. The 32-bit PowerPC has 256 Mbyte segments, 16 of which can be concatenated by placing consecutive Segment IDs in adjacent segment registers, to a maximum 4 Gbyte segment size. 64-bit PowerPC also has 256 Mbyte segments, 256 of which can be concatenated by placing consecutive Segment IDs in adjacent segment table entries, to a maximum 64 Gbyte segment size.

with 32-bit integer registers that were also used for addressing. This presented the POWER architects with a dilemma: either use a flat 32-bit virtual address space, which would likely be too small in the very near future, or encode a larger address in 32 bits. Such an encoding led to the segmented architecture inherited by PowerPC. Also, and perhaps more importantly, the single shared address space facilitates capability-based memory protection methods similar to those used in IBM's very successful AS/400 series of computer systems.

The Alpha architecture specification does not define a page table format. Because TLB misses are handled by trapping to system software, Alpha systems using different operating systems may have different page table formats. Two likely alternatives are VAX VMS and OSF/1 UNIX. A Privileged Architecture Library (PAL) provides an operating system–specific set of subroutines for memory management, context switching, and interrupts. The Alpha instruction set includes the following format for PAL instructions that are used to define operating system primitives.

```
0              6                                                    31
┌──────────────┬─────────────────────────────────────────────────────┐
│   Opcode     │                  PAL function                       │
└──────────────┴─────────────────────────────────────────────────────┘
```

The Call PAL instructions are like subroutine calls to special blocks instructions, whose location is determined by one of five different PAL opcodes. A PAL routine has access to privileged instructions but employs user mode address translation. While in the PAL routine, interrupts are disabled to assure the atomicity of privileged operations that take multiple instructions. For example, if an instruction turns off address mapping, an interrupt occurring before a later instruction can turn address mapping back on would not be good. The details of virtual address translation and page table format are considered a system software issue to be defined in the context of the particular operating system using PAL functions.

Figure 11.17 compares the format of memory instructions. The format of instructions using the displacement addressing mode is identical in PowerPC and Alpha. The effective address is calculated in the same way in both architectures, with the exception of the register that has the value 0, which is register 0 in PowerPC and register 31 in Alpha. There is no indexed addressing in Alpha. As pointed out earlier, this saves a register read port.

Another Alpha characteristic is that load and store instructions transfer only 32- or 64-bit data between a register and memory; there are no instructions that load or store 8-bit or 16-bit quantities. The Alpha architecture does include a set of instructions to extract and manipulate bytes from registers. This approach simplifies the cache interface that does not have to include byte-level shift-and-mask logic in the cache access path.

Figure 11.18 illustrates the core of an strcpy routine that moves a sequence of bytes from one area of memory to another; a byte of zeros terminates the string. Figure 2.10 shows a similar routine for the POWER architecture.

The ldq_u is a load unaligned instruction that ignores the low-order three bits of the address; in the example, it loads a word into r1, addressed by r4. The extract byte (extbl)

	0	6	11	16–31
Power	OPCD	RT	RA	D
Alpha	OPCD	RT	RA	D

Power Effective address $= \begin{cases} (RA) + D & \text{if } RA \neq 0 \\ D & \text{if } RA = 0 \end{cases}$

Alpha Effective address $= \begin{cases} (RA) + D & \text{if } RA \neq 31 \\ D & \text{if } RA = 31 \end{cases}$

(a) Load and store instruction format using register + displacement addressing. The displacement D is sign extended prior to addition. In Alpha, D is multiplied by 2^{16} if OPCD = LDAH. RT is the destination register.

	0	6	11	16	21	31
Power	OPCD	RT	RA	RB	EO	Rc

Power Effective address $= \begin{cases} (RA) + (RB) & \text{if } RA \neq 0 \\ (RB) & \text{if } RA = 0 \end{cases}$

Alpha Register + register addressing is not available.

(b) Load and store instruction format using register + register (indexed) addressing. RT is the destination register.

FIGURE 11.17 Memory instruction format.

instruction uses the same address, r4, but only uses the three low-order bits to select one of the eight bytes in r1. The byte is copied into r2. To move the byte to s, the sequence begins with another load unaligned to get the word containing the destination byte. The mask byte (`maskbl`) instruction uses the three low-order bits of r3 (the address of s) to zero out a byte in the just-loaded r5. Meanwhile, the insert byte (`insbl`) instruction moves the byte from t into the correct byte position, also using the three low-order bits of the address in r3. The `bis` performs a logical OR operation that merges the byte into the correct position, and the

```
                                      # A string is copied from t to s
                                      # r4 points to t
                                      # r3 points to s
LOOP:    ldq_u    r1 = t(r4,0)        # load t, unaligned
         extbl    r2 = r1,r4          # extract byte from r1 to r2
         ldq_u    r5 = s(r3,0)        # load s, unaligned
         maskbl   r5 = r5,r3          # zero corresponding byte in r5
         insbl    r6 = r2,r3          # insert byte into r6
         bis      r5 = r5,r6          # logical OR places byte in r5
         stq_u    s(r3,0) = r5        # store unaligned
         addq     r4 = r4,1           # bump the t pointer
         addq     r3 = r3,1           # bump the s pointer
         bne      r6,LOOP             # branch if nonzero byte
```

FIGURE 11.18 Alpha 21064 C strcpy function (null-terminated strings).

store unaligned (`stq_u`) instruction stores the word back into s. The t and s pointers are incremented, the byte is checked for zero, and the sequence starts again if the byte is nonzero.

Clearly the Alpha architects felt that the performance gained from shortening the cache load path is more important than the performance lost by having to use several instructions to do byte loads and stores, rather than one.

Regarding data alignment, the PowerPC 601 handles most unaligned data in hardware, occasionally requiring another cache access when data cross a cache sector boundary. The Alpha architecture handles unaligned data in one of two ways, depending on how often it is actually unaligned. If the data are usually aligned, aligned versions of loads and stores may be used. These will trap if an address should happen to be unaligned, and the trap handler takes care of the unaligned access. If the data are likely to be unaligned, then sequences of unaligned loads and stores can be combined with inserts, masks, and extracts to get the job done.

Operate Instructions

Figure 11.19 compares the formats of operate instructions that perform arithmetic, logical, compare, and shift operations. In PowerPC there are several other operate instruction formats in addition to those shown in the figure (see Figure 2.11).

The basic operations performed by both architectures are rather similar. One difference is the combined multiply-add in the PowerPC. This instruction requires three floating-point register read ports. The 21064 has three such ports, but uses one of them for stores so that

PowerPC

0	6	11	16		31
OPCD	RT	RA		SI	

Alpha

0	6	11	19 20	27	31
OPCD	RA	PI	1	EO	RT

(a) Register–immediate integer operate instructions. The immediate operand is a signed integer (SI) in PowerPC and a positive integer (PI) in Alpha. RA is the source register. RT is the destination register. EO is extended opcode.

PowerPC

0	6	11	16	21	31	
OPCD	RT	RA	RB	EO		Rc

Alpha

0	6	11	16	19 20	27	31
OPCD	RA	RB	unused	0	EO	RT

(b) Register–register integer operate instructions. RA and RB are the source registers. RT is the destination register. EO is extended opcode.

PowerPC

0	6	11	16	21	26	31	
OPCD	FRT	FRA	FRB	FRC	EO		Rc

Alpha

0	6	11	16	27	31
OPCD	FRA	FRB	EO		FRT

(c) Floating-point operate instructions. FRA and FRB are the source registers. PowerPC has a third source register FRC for the multiply-add. FRT is the destination register. EO is extended opcode.

FIGURE 11.19 Operate instruction formats.

a floating-point operate can be done simultaneously with a floating-point store; this can't be done in the 601.

The Alpha architecture does not have an integer divide instruction; it must be implemented in software. Leaving out integer divides, or doing them in clever ways to reduce hardware, seems to be fashionable in RISC architectures. However, iterative dividers are cheap, and one can expect that one by one the RISC architectures will succumb to divide instructions (as some already have).

The Alpha architecture has scaled integer adds and subtract that multiply one of the operands by 4 or 8, one of the few Alpha features that seems non-RISCy. These instructions are useful for address arithmetic in which indices of words or doubleword arrays are held as element offsets, then automatically converted to byte address values for address calculation using the scaled add/subtracts. The PowerPC has a richer set of indexing operations embedded in loads and stores as well as the update versions of memory instructions.

Imprecise Interrupts

Both architectures support high-performance implementations with multiple pipelines. In such an implementation, many instructions may be in the pipelines at any time, and precisely identifying an interrupt-causing instruction without limiting the machine's performance is difficult (see Section 4.4). Instead, an *imprecise* interrupt is signaled later, an arbitrary number of instructions after the interrupt-causing instruction.

A common problem occurs in the floating-point pipeline: it is usually longer than the integer pipe, so floating-point instructions finish late compared with instructions in the integer pipeline. When a floating-point interrupt is discovered, fixed-point instructions logically following the floating-point instruction may have already completed and modified a result register. An imprecise state at the time of the interrupt ensues. Allowing this to happen, however, leads to simpler implementations. Consequently, both Alpha and PowerPC allow imprecise floating-point interrupts in their normal operating mode.

With imprecise interrupts, user software cannot "patch" an excepting floating-point result and continue. Imprecise interrupts can also make program debugging more difficult. Consequently, both architectures have provisions for precise operation, but at degraded performance. In PowerPC, a bit in the Machine State Register may be set to make the machine enter a mode in which instructions are executed serially and interrupts are precise. PowerPC compilers may also provide a flag that inserts test code after each floating-point instruction that may cause an interrupt.

For implementing precise floating-point interrupts, Alpha has a "trap barrier" instruction that stalls instruction issuing until all prior instructions are executed without any interrupts. This instruction may be inserted after floating-point instructions to make floating-point interrupts precise. Of course, performance is degraded, because the degree of instruction overlap is greatly reduced.

11.4 Summary

The PowerPC 601 and Alpha 21064 follow two remarkably different philosophies for achieving high-performance implementations. The PowerPC uses independent pipelines, buffering, and out-of-order dispatching and does a lot of computation in each pipe stage. The 21064 has tightly coupled pipelines, little buffering, and in-order issuing and does relatively little work in each pipe stage, allowing it to have a very fast clock.

The PowerPC architecture leads to better branch handling and out-of-order dispatch, which can lead to more efficient use of the pipes and more overlap among loop iterations. The PowerPC's more complex instructions also get more work done with fewer instructions. The Alpha's simplicity, however, probably lends itself better to very high clock rate implementations. The Alpha can afford to execute more instructions if it can issue them faster and in parallel. The Alpha also has fewer restrictions on multiple instruction dispatches, especially when doing integer code.

The 601 gains performance by cleverness in the design; the 21064 gains performance by simplicity in the design. This trade-off is a classic one, and the fact that both philosophies still lead to viable processors is probably an indication that either choice is satisfactory as long as the implementation is done well.

11.5 References

The *Alpha Architecture Handbook* [19] defines the data formats and instruction set and includes guidelines for implementors of system software. An article by McLellan provides a good overview of the 21064, and two articles, Comerford [16] and Sites [79], describe the development of Alpha, the latter from the perspective of a co-architect. Dobberpuhl et al. [20] contains a description of the 21064 chip microarchitecture and a detailed section on the circuit implementation.

IEEE 754 FLOATING-POINT STANDARD

Approved in 1985, IEEE 754 has been adopted in virtually all PCs, workstations, and midrange systems, including all the RISC-based systems. There are some older proprietary architectures that were developed before the standard was adopted, but the manufacturers of many of those systems are now supporting, or planning to support, the IEEE standard in the future.

The standard has parts that are required and others that are optional. For example, it defines four precisions that specify the number of bits in each field of a floating-point number. Only the 32-bit format is required. Most systems implement in hardware both the 32-bit single precision and the optional 64-bit double precision.

A.1 Floating-Point Numbers

A floating-point number consists of three components: the sign S, exponent E, and fraction F (Figure A.1). S is the sign of the fraction, defined to be zero for positive numbers and one for negative numbers. Actual exponent values are obtained by subtracting a constant, called *bias,* from the exponent field E.

(a) Single precision.

(b) Double precision.

Precision	Exponent bits	Range of exponent E	Bias	Range of $E - $ bias
Single	8	1 to 254	127	-126 to $+127$
Double	11	1 to 2046	1023	-1022 to $+1023$

(c) Representation of exponents. The largest and smallest exponents, namely 0 and 255 in single precision, and 0 and 2047 in double precision, are treated as special values and their use is shown in Figure A.2.

FIGURE A.1   **Floating-point number format.**

When the exponent is in the range shown in Figure A.1(c), the value of the number is given by

$$2^{E-\text{bias}} \times 1.F$$

where $1.F$ is the *significand*. The "1" at the left of the binary point is a *hidden* bit and is not stored explicitly. As an example, in the single-precision floating-point number shown below, $S = 1$, $E = 129$, and $F = .75$. Hence these 32 bits represent the number $-1.75 \times 2^{129-127}$, which is -7.0.

1   10000001   11000000000000000000000

Normalization

Consider the following number:

0.00000101110011111010011011101 × 2^9

This number cannot be represented exactly in the single-precision floating-point format, which has only 23 bits to represent a fraction. The rightmost six bits do not fit in the space available.

Exponent E	Fraction F	Interpretation
0	$\neq 0$	Denormalized number
0	0	0
E_{max}	$\neq 0$	NaN
E_{max}	0	∞

FIGURE A.2   **Special exponent values. NaN is Not a Number. E_{max} is 255 in single-precision and 2047 in double-precision format.**

$0.\boxed{00000101110011111010011}\,011101 \times 2^9$

To use the available 23-bit space more efficiently, we can get rid of the zero bits on the left-hand side (called *leading zeros*) by shifting the fraction to the left. The exponent is adjusted to leave the value of the number unchanged. The result is a *normalized* number that has the property that the bit at the left-hand side of the binary point is always one. The number used in this example can be represented exactly in normalized format.

$1.\boxed{01110011111010011011101} \times 2^3$

While normalization does not guarantee exact representation of all numbers, it does improve precision by using space that is otherwise wasted on leading zeros. Hence, floating-point numbers are stored in registers and memory in normalized format whenever possible.

Denormalized Numbers and Non-Numerical Values

A floating-point number may be too small to be normalized. For example, the number 0.25×2^{-127} is represented in single-precision format as shown below.

0   00000000   01000000000000000000000

The exponent E is already zero and cannot be decremented. Denormalized floating-point numbers are represented by $E = 0$ and $F \neq 0$; there is no hidden one.

A few other special cases are represented using the minimum and maximum exponent values (Figure A.2). When $E \neq 0$, a fraction F of value 0 is not the number 0, due to the hidden one; rather, it is interpreted as a significand value of 1.0. The number 0 is represented by $E = 0$ and $F = 0$.

Other special cases occur when numbers are too large or too small to be represented in the specified format; these are shown as $+\infty$ or $-\infty$. Finally, certain operations are invalid. The result of such an operation has no arithmetic meaning and is encoded as NaN (*Not a Number*). An example is the attempt to divide zero by zero. NaNs are useful in error reporting to track down invalid operations.

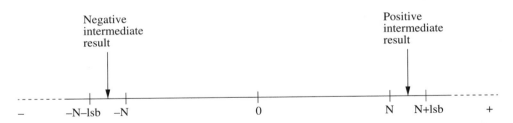

(a) An intermediate result is between two numbers that have exact representation in the
floating-point format.

Rounding mode	Rounded result if IR is positive		Rounded result if IR is negative	
Round to nearest	N	if IR < N + lsb/2	−N	if IR > −N − lsb/2
	N + lsb	if IR > N + lsb/2	−N − lsb	if IR < −N − lsb/2
	even	if IR = N + lsb/2	even	if IR = −N − lsb/2
Round toward 0	N		−N	
Round toward +∞	N + lsb		−N	
Round toward −∞	N		−N − lsb	

(b) The rounded result depends on the rounding mode. IR is the intermediate result. If the
mode is round to nearest, and the intermediate result is exactly halfway between the two
rounding values, the even value is chosen.

FIGURE A.3   **Rounding.**

Rounding

Arithmetic operations may produce intermediate results whose length, after normalization,
exceeds the length of the significand (24 bits in single precision, 53 bits in double precision).
Such a result must be rounded to fit in the floating-point format.

A positive intermediate result that cannot be represented exactly is between two numbers,
N and N + lsb. N is the result truncated to fit in the floating-point format, and lsb is the least-
significant bit of this format (Figure A.3(a)). Rounding consists of selecting one of the two
numbers, N or N + lsb, as an approximate representation of the intermediate result. Similarly,
a negative intermediate result is between −N and −N − lsb, and is rounded by choosing one
of these two numbers.

This choice depends on the rounding mode. The four rounding modes are: round to nearest, round toward zero, round toward +infinity, and round toward −infinity. Figure A.3(b) shows the rounded result for each mode.

A.2   Floating-Point Exceptions

Exceptions are used to report errors that occurred in the process of a floating-point computation or operations whose result cannot be represented accurately. Exceptions may be enabled or disabled by the user.

Here we discuss operations that may lead to one or more exceptions. We consider the following "problematic" cases:

- Result is Not a Number (NaN)

- Operations on infinities

- Division by zero

- Overflow

- Underflow

- Inexact result caused by rounding

Not a Number (NaN)

Certain operations are invalid and do not have a numerical result. Their result is encoded as NaN for the purpose of providing diagnostic information. The sign bit is ignored (the result is not a number, so it is neither negative nor positive), the exponent is set to its maximum value, and the fraction is not zero (Figure A.2). The leftmost bit of the fraction field is used to distinguish between quiet NaNs (bit set to one) and signaling NaNs (bit cleared to zero).

Quiet NaNs propagate through operations but do not signal an exception. Signaling NaNs propagate through operations and signal an exception if the Invalid Operation exception is enabled. There are two ways to get a quiet NaN.

1. As the result of an invalid operation when the Invalid Operation exception is disabled

2. As the result of any operation that uses a quiet NaN as an operand

There are two ways to get a signaling NaN.

1. As the result of an invalid operation when the Invalid Operation exception is enabled

2. As the result of any operation that uses a signaling NaN as an operand

Operation	Result	Exception
$\infty + \infty$	∞	no
$\infty \times \infty$	∞	no
$\infty - \infty$	invalid	yes
$\infty \times 0$	invalid	yes
$\infty \div \infty$	invalid	yes

FIGURE A.4   **Valid and invalid operations on infinities.**

Infinities

Infinities are numbers whose magnitude is too large to be represented exactly in the limited space specified by the floating-point number format. To encode infinities, the sign bit is used to distinguish between $+\infty$ and $-\infty$, the exponent is set to its maximum value, and the fraction is zero (Figure A.2).

Certain operations on infinities are valid (Figure A.4). These operations are easy to understand if we keep in mind that infinities are positive or negative numbers with large magnitude. The result of adding two large numbers is clearly a large number. Hence $\infty + \infty = \infty$. In contrast, the difference of two large numbers may not be large, and the operation $\infty - \infty$ is invalid. We have no way to determine if the result of the subtraction is a large number to be encoded as ∞, or a number small enough to fit in the floating-point format. In the latter case, of course, we wouldn't know the value of the result.

Division by Zero

The result of division by zero depends on the value of the dividend. An attempt to divide zero by zero is an invalid operation, the result is NaN, and an exception is flagged if the Invalid Operation exception is enabled.

The term *invalid operation* is used for operations that produce NaN. Division by zero of a nonzero dividend is considered a valid operation since it produces ∞, which is treated as a large number. The result cannot be represented exactly, however, and a Zero Divide exception is reported.

If the Zero Divide exception is enabled, the target register is not modified. Otherwise, if Zero Divide exception is disabled, the target register is set to ∞, the result of the operation. Zeros represented in an IEEE floating-point format have a sign, so the operation could be division by positive zero or division by negative zero. The result could be either $+\infty$ or $-\infty$, the sign is set according to the sign of the operands following the usual rules.

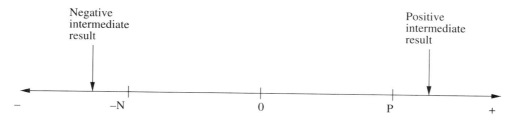

(a) Overflow occurs when an intermediate result is larger than N_{max} or smaller than $-N_{max}$. N_{max} is the largest magnitude (significand and exponent) that can be represented in the floating-point format.

Rounding mode	Result placed in FPR if IR is positive	Result placed in FPR if IR is negative
Round to nearest	$+\infty$	$-\infty$
Round to 0	N_{max}	$-N_{max}$
Round to $+\infty$	$+\infty$	$-N_{max}$
Round to $-\infty$	N_{max}	$-\infty$

(b) If Overflow exception is disabled and an Overflow occurs, the result depends on the rounding mode. IR is the intermediate result.

FIGURE A.5   **Overflow handling when Overflow exception is disabled.**

Overflow

Overflow is caused when a result has a magnitude that exceeds the magnitude defined by the largest significand and largest exponent in the floating-point format. If the Overflow exception is disabled, both the Overflow exception and Inexact exception bits are set. The result depends on the rounding mode as shown in Figure A.5.

If an Overflow exception is enabled, the Overflow exception is set to one. The intermediate result is adjusted by subtracting a constant (1536) from the exponent. (The discussion here refers to double-precision format.) This constant is chosen for the following reasons. Positive exponents are those larger than the bias, 1023. The value of $(E_{max} - E_{min}) \times 3/4$ is approximately in the middle of the positive exponent range, where $E_{max} = 2047$ and $E_{min} = 0$. The closest integer that also divides by 12 is 1536. Divisibility by 12 simplifies the computation of 2nd, 3rd, and 4th roots.

The result with the adjusted exponent is rounded and placed into the destination register.

This adjustment allows the correct result to be reconstructed even though the floating-point format does not have enough space to store it.

$$\text{Result} = 1.F \times 2^{E-\text{bias}} \times 2^{1536}$$

Underflow

Underflow occurs when an intermediate result is too small to be normalized. The exponent is already zero and cannot be decremented (see the example in Section A.1). If the Underflow exception is disabled, the Underflow exception is set to one, and the denormalized result is rounded and placed into the destination registers.

If the Underflow exception is enabled, the Underflow exception is set to one, and the intermediate result is adjusted by adding a constant (1536 for double precision) from the exponent. This constant is chosen for the same reasons as those discussed above for Overflow. The result with the adjusted exponent is rounded and placed into the destination register. This adjustment allows the correct result to be reconstructed even though the floating-point format does not have enough space to store it.

$$\text{Result} = 1.F \times 2^{E-\text{bias}} \div 2^{1536}$$

Inexact Exception

An Inexact exception occurs during rounding if the rounded result differs from the intermediate result. This simply indicates that the rounded number is an approximation of the intermediate result. An Inexact exception is also set if an Overflow occurs and the Overflow exception is disabled.

References

This appendix is a summary of the IEEE 754 standard. Of course, the authoritative document is the standard itself [41]. The article [14] describes some of the thought that went into making the standard, as well as some alternatives that were under consideration. Finally, the paper "What every computer scientist should know about floating-point arithmetic" [25] is just what its title suggests.

B POWER INSTRUCTION FORMATS

All instructions are 4 bytes long and are located on word boundaries. Thus, whenever instruction addresses are presented to the processing unit (as in branch instructions) the two low-order bits are ignored. Similarly, whenever the processing unit develops an instruction address, its two low-order bits are 0.

Bits 0 through 5 always specify the opcode. For XO-form instructions, an extended opcode is specified in bits 22 through 30. For all other X-form instructions, an extended opcode is specified in bits 21 through 30. For A-form instructions, an extended opcode is specified in bits 26 through 30.

The remaining bits contain one or more alternative fields for the different instruction formats.

D Form

0	6	11	16	
OPCD	RT	RA	D	
	RS		SI	
	FRT		UI	
	TO			
	BF			
	FRS			

B Form

0	6	11	16	30	31
OPCD	BO	BI	BD	AA	LK

I Form

0	6	30	31
OPCD	LI	AA	LK

SC Form

0	6	11	16	20	27	30	31
OPCD	///	///	FL1	LEV	FL2	SA	LK
				SV			

X Form

0	6	11	16	21	31
OPCD	RT	RA	RB	EO	Rc
	FRT	FRA	FRB		
	BF	BFA	SH		
	RS	SPR	NB		
	FRS		I		
	TO				
	BT				

XL Form

OPCD	BT	BA	BB	EO	LK
	BO	BI			

XFX Form

OPCD	RT	FXM	EO	Rc

XFL Form

OPCD	FLM	FRB	EO	Rc

XO Form

OPCD	RT	RA	RB	OE	EO′	Rc

A Form

OPCD	FRT	FRA	FRB	FRC	XO	Rc

A-form instructions are used for four-operand instructions. The operands, all floating-point registers, are specified by the FRT, FRA, FRB, FRC fields. The short extended opcode, XO, is in bits 26 through 30.

M Form

OPCD	RS	RA	RB	MB	ME	Rc
			SH			

Instruction Fields

AA (30) Absolute Address bit

> Bit Description
>
> 0 The immediate field represents an address relative to the current instruction address. For I-form branches, the effective address of the branch is the sum of the LI field sign-extended to 32 bits and the address of the branch instruction. For B-form branches, the effective address of the branch is the sum of the BD field sign-extended to 32 bits and the address of the branch instruction.
>
> 1 The immediate field represents an absolute address. For I-form branches, the effective address of the branch is the LI field sign-extended to 32 bits. For B-form branches, the effective address of the branch is the BD field sign-extended to 32 bits.

BA (11–15) Field used to specify a bit in the Condition register (CR) to be used as a source.

BB (16–20) Field used to specify a bit in the CR to be used as a source.

BD (16–29) Immediate field specifying a 14-bit signed two's complement branch displacement, which is concatenated on the right with b'00' and sign-extended to 32 bits.

BF (6–8) Field used to specify one of the CR compare result fields or one of the FPSCR fields as a target. If $i = BF(6–8)$, then field i refers to bits $i \times 4$ to $(i \times 4) + 3$ of the register.

BFA (11–13) Field used to specify one of the CR compare result fields, one of the FPSCR fields, or one of the XER fields as a source. If $j = BFA(11–13)$, then field j refers to bits $j \times 4$ to $(j \times 4) + 3$ of the register.

BI (11–15) Field used to specify the bit in the CR to be used as the condition of the branch.

BO (6–10) Field used to specify different options that can be used in conditional branch instructions. Following is the encoding for the BO field:

> BO Description
>
> 0000x Decrement the CTR, then branch if the decremented CTR $\neq$ 0 and condition is false.
>
> 0001x Decrement the CTR, then branch if the decremented CTR $=$ 0 and condition is false.
>
> 001xx Branch if condition is false.
>
> 0100x Decrement the CTR, then branch if the decremented CTR $\neq$ 0 and condition is true.

0101x Decrement the CTR, then branch if the decremented CTR = 0 and condition is true.

011xx Branch if condition is true.

1x00x Decrement the CTR, then branch if the decremented CTR ≠ 0.

1x01x Decrement the CTR, then branch if the decremented CTR = 0.

1x1xx Branch always.

BT (6–10) Field used to specify a bit in the CR as the target of the result of an instruction.

D (16–31) Immediate field specifying a 16-bit signed two's complement integer sign-extended to 32 bits.

EO (21–30) A 10-bit extended opcode used in X-form instructions.

EO′ (22–30) A 9-bit extended opcode used in XO-form instructions.

FL1 (16–19) A 4-bit field in the Supervisor Call (SVC) instruction.

FL2 (27–29) A 3-bit field in the SVC instruction.

FXM (12–19) Field mask, identifies which CR field is to be updated.

Bit	Description
12	CR Field 0 (bits 00–03)
13	CR Field 1 (bits 04–07)
14	CR Field 2 (bits 08–11)
15	CR Field 3 (bits 12–15)
16	CR Field 4 (bits 16–19)
17	CR Field 5 (bits 20–23)
18	CR Field 6 (bits 24–27)
19	CR Field 7 (bits 28–31)

FLM (7–14) Field mask, identifies which FPSCR field is to be updated.

Bit	Description
7	FPSCR Field 0 (bits 00–03)
8	FPSCR Field 1 (bits 04–07)
9	FPSCR Field 2 (bits 08–11)
10	FPSCR Field 3 (bits 12–15)

11 FPSCR Field 4 (bits 16–19)

12 FPSCR Field 5 (bits 20–23)

13 FPSCR Field 6 (bits 24–27)

14 FPSCR Field 7 (bits 28–31)

FRA (11–15) Field used to specify an FPR as a source of an operation.

FRB (16–20) Field used to specify an FPR as a source of an operation.

FRC (21–25) Field used to specify an FPR as a source of an operation.

FRS (6–10) Field used to specify an FPR as a source of an operation.

FRT (6–10) Field used to specify an FPR as the target of an operation.

I (16–19) Immediate field used as the data to be placed into a field in the FPSCR.

LEV (20–26) Immediate field in the SVC instruction that addresses the SVC routine by b'1' ‖ LEV ‖ b'00000' if SA = 0.

LI (6–29) Immediate field specifying a 24-bit signed two's complement integer that is concatenated on the right with b'00' and sign-extended to 32 bits.

LK (31) Link bit

Bit Description

0 Do not set the Link register.

1 Set the Link register. If the instruction is a branch, the address of the instruction following the branch instruction is placed into the Link register. If the instruction is an SVC, the address of the instruction following the SVC instruction is placed into the Link register.

MB (21–25) & ME (26–30) Fields used to specify a 32-bit string, consisting of either a substring of ones surrounded by zeros or a substring of zeros surrounded by ones.

MB (21–25) Index to start bit of substring of ones.

ME (26–30) Index to stop bit of substring of ones.

```
Let mstart = MB and mstop = ME.

If mstart < mstop + 1 then
    mask(mstart..mstop) = ones
    mask(all other) = zeros.
```

```
If mstart = mstop + 1 then
    mask(0-31) = ones.

If mstart > mstop + 1 then
    mask(mstop+1..mstart-1) = zeros
    mask(all other) = ones.
```

NB (16–20) Field used to specify the number of bytes to move in a load or store string immediate.

OPCD (0–5) The basic opcode field of the instruction.

OE (21) Used for extended arithmetic to inhibit setting of OV and SO in XER.

RA (11-15) Field used to specify a GPR to be used as a source or as a target.

RB (16–20) Field used to specify a GPR to be used as a source.

Rc (31) Record bit.

Setting	Description
0	Do not set the Condition register.
1	Set the Condition register to reflect the result of the operation.

For fixed-point instructions, CR bits (0–3) are set to reflect the result as a signed quantity. The result as an unsigned quantity or a bit string can be deduced from the EQ bit.

For floating-point instructions, CR bits (4–7) are set to reflect Floating-Point Exception, Floating-Point Enabled Exception, Floating-Point Invalid Operation Exception, and Floating-Point Overflow Exception.

RS (6–10) Field used to specify a GPR to be used as a source.

RT (6–10) Field used to specify a GPR to be used as a target.

SA (30) SVC Absolute.

Setting	Description
0	SVC routine at address '1' ‖ LEV ‖ b'00000'.
1	SVC routine at address x'1FE0'.

SH (16–20) Field used to specify a shift amount.

SI (16–31) Immediate field used to specify a 16-bit signed integer.

SPR (11–15) Special Purpose register.

SPR	Special Purpose Register
00000 (00)	MQ
00001 (01)	XER
00100 (04)	from RTCU
00101 (05)	from RTCL
00110 (06)	from DEC
01000 (08)	LR
01001 (09)	CTR
10100 (20)	to RTCU
10101 (21)	to RTCL
10110 (22)	to DEC
11010 (26)	SRR0
11011 (27)	SRR1

TO (6–10) TO bit ANDed with condition.

TO bit	ANDed with Condition
6	Compares less than
7	Compares greater than
8	Compares equal
9	Compares logically less than
10	Compares logically greater than

UI (16–31) Immediate field used to specify a 16-bit unsigned integer.

XO (26–30) A 5-bit extended opcode used by A-form instructions.

**P O W E R   I N S T R U C T I O N
S E T
S O R T E D   B Y   M N E M O N I C** *

Refer to *Assembler Language Reference for IBM AIX Version 3 for RISC System/6000* (SC23-2197) for information on a specific instruction.

Mnemonic	Instruction	Format	Primary opcode	Extended opcode
a[o][.]	Add	XO	31	10
abs[o][.]	Absolute	XO	31	360
ae[o][.]	Add Extended	XO	31	138
ai	Add Immediate	D	12	
ai.	Add Immediate and Record	D	13	
ame[o][.]	Add to Minus One Extended	XO	31	234
and[.]	AND	X	31	28
andc[.]	AND with Complement	X	31	60
andil.	AND Immediate Lower	D	28	
andiu.	AND Immediate Upper	D	29	
aze[o][.]	Add to Zero Extended	XO	31	202

*Reprinted with permission of International Business Machines, Inc. from *RISC System/6000, POWERstation and POWERserver, Hardware Technical Reference, General Information*, Second Edition, 1992.

Mnemonic	Instruction	Format	Primary opcode	Extended opcode
b[l][a]	Branch	I	18	
bc[l][a]	Branch Conditional	B	16	
bcc[l]	Branch Conditional to Count Register	XL	19	528
bcr[l]	Branch Conditional Register	XL	19	16
cal	Compute Address Lower	D	14	
cau	Compute Address Upper	D	15	
cax[o][.]	Compute Address	XO	31	266
clcs	Cache Line Compute Size	X	31	531
clf	Cache Line Flush	X	31	118
cli	Cache Line Invalidate	X	31	502
cmp	Compare	X	31	0
cmpi	Compare Immediate	D	11	
cmpl	Compare Logical	X	31	32
cmpli	Compare Logical Immediate	D	10	
cntlz[.]	Count Leading Zeros	X	31	26
crand	Condition Register AND	XL	19	257
crandc	Condition Register AND with Complement	XL	19	129
creqv	Condition Register Equivalent	XL	19	289
crnand	Condition Register NAND	XL	19	225
crnor	Condition Register NOR	XL	19	33
cror	Condition Register OR	XL	19	449
crorc	Condition Register OR with Complement	XL	19	417
crxor	Condition Register XOR	XL	19	193
dclst	Data Cache Line Store	X	31	630
dclz	Data Cache Line Set to Zero	X	31	1014
dcs	Data Cache Synchronize	X	31	598
div[o][.]	Divide	XO	31	331
divs[o][.]	Divide Short	XO	31	363
doz[o][.]	Difference or Zero	XO	31	264
dozi	Difference or Zero Immediate	D	09	
eqv[.]	Equivalent	X	31	284
exts[.]	Extend Sign	X	31	922
fa[.]	Floating Add	A	63	21
fabs[.]	Floating Absolute Value	X	63	264
fcmpo	Floating Compare Ordered	X	63	32
fcmpu	Floating Compare Unordered	X	63	0

Mnemonic	Instruction	Format	Primary opcode	Extended opcode
fd[.]	Floating Divide	A	63	8
fm[.]	Floating Multiply	A	63	5
fma[.]	Floating Multiply Add	A	63	29
fmr[.]	Floating Move Register	X	63	72
fms[.]	Floating Multiply Subtract	A	63	28
fnabs[.]	Floating Negative Absolute Value	X	63	136
fneg[.]	Floating Negate	X	63	40
fnma[.]	Floating Negative Multiply Add	A	63	31
fnms[.]	Floating Negative Multiply Subtract	A	63	30
frsp[.]	Floating Round to Single Precision	X	63	12
fs[.]	Floating Subtract	A	63	20
ics	Instruction Cache Synchronize	XL	19	150
l	Load	D	32	
lbrx	Load Byte Reverse Indexed	X	31	534
lbz	Load Byte and Zero	D	34	
lbzu	Load Byte and Zero with Update	D	35	
lbzux	Load Byte and Zero with Update Indexed	X	31	119
lbzx	Load Byte and Zero Indexed	X	31	87
lfd	Load Floating-Point Double	D	50	
lfdu	Load Floating-Point Double with Update	D	51	
lfdux	Load Floating-Point Double with Update Indexed	X	31	631
lfdx	Load Floating-Point Double Indexed	X	31	599
lfs	Load Floating-Point Single	D	48	
lfsu	Load Floating-Point Single with Update	D	49	
lfsux	Load Floating-Point Single with Update Indexed	X	31	567
lfsx	Load Floating-Point Single Indexed	X	31	535
lha	Load Half Algebraic	D	42	
lhau	Load Half Algebraic with Update	D	43	
lhaux	Load Half Algebraic with Update Indexed	X	31	375
lhax	Load Half Algebraic Indexed	X	31	343
lhbrx	Load Half Byte Reverse Indexed	X	31	790
lhz	Load Half and Zero	D	40	

Mnemonic	Instruction	Format	Primary opcode	Extended opcode
lhzu	Load Half and Zero with Update	D	41	
lhzux	Load Half and Zero with Update Indexed	X	31	311
lhzx	Load Half and Zero Indexed	X	31	279
lm	Load Multiple	D	46	
lscbx[.]	Load String and Compare Byte Indexed	X	31	277
lsi	Load String Immediate	X	31	597
lsx	Load String Indexed	X	31	533
lu	Load with Update	D	33	
lux	Load with Update Indexed	X	31	55
lx	Load Indexed	X	31	23
maskg[.]	Mask Generate	X	31	29
maskir[.]	Mask Insert from Register	X	31	541
mcrf	Move Condition Register Field	XL	19	0
mcrfs	Move to Condition Register from FPSCR	X	63	64
mcrxr	Move to Condition Register from XER	X	31	512
mfcr	Move from Condition Register	X	31	19
mffs[.]	Move from FPSCR	X	63	583
mfmsr	Move from Machine State Register	X	31	83
mfspr	Move from Special Purpose Register	X	31	339
mfsr	Move from Segment Register	X	31	595
mfsri	Move from Segment Register Indirect	X	31	627
mtcrf	Move to Condition Register Fields	XFX	31	144
mtfsb0[.]	Move to FPSCR bit 0	X	63	70
mtfsb1[.]	Move to FPSCR bit 1	X	63	38
mtfsf[.]	Move to FPSCR Fields	XFL	63	711
mtfsfi[.]	Move to FPSCR Field Immediate	X	63	134
mtmsr	Move to Machine State Register	X	31	146
mtspr	Move to Special Purpose Register	X	31	467
mtsr	Move to Segment Register	X	31	210
mtsri	Move to Segment Register Indirect	X	31	242
mul[o][.]	Multiply	XO	31	107
muli	Multiply Immediate	D	07	
muls[o][.]	Multiply Short	XO	31	235

Mnemonic	Instruction	Format	Primary opcode	Extended opcode
nabs[o][.]	Negative Absolute	XO	31	488
nand[.]	NAND	X	31	476
neg[o][.]	Negate	XO	31	104
nor[.]	NOR	X	31	124
or[.]	OR	X	31	444
orc[.]	OR with Complement	X	31	412
oril	OR Immediate Lower	D	24	
oriu	OR Immediate Upper	D	25	
rac[.]	Real Address Compute	X	31	818
rfi	Return from Interrupt	XL	19	50
rfsvc	Return from SVC	XL	19	82
rlimi[.]	Rotate Left Immediate Then Mask Insert	M	20	
rlinm[.]	Rotate Left Immediate Then AND with Mask	M	21	
rlmi[.]	Rotate Left Then Mask Insert	M	22	
rlnm[.]	Rotate Left Then AND with Mask	M	23	
rrib[.]	Rotate Right and Insert Bit	X	31	537
sf[o][.]	Subtract from	XO	31	8
sfe[o][.]	Subtract from Extended	XO	31	36
sfi	Subtract from Immediate	D	08	
sfme[o][.]	Subtract from Minus One Extended	XO	31	232
sfze[o][.]	Subtract from Zero Extended	XO	31	200
sl[.]	Shift Left	X	31	24
sle[.]	Shift Left Extended	X	31	153
sleq[.]	Shift Left Extended with MQ	X	31	217
sliq[.]	Shift Left Immediate with MQ	X	31	184
slliq[.]	Shift Left Long Immediate with MQ	X	31	248
sllq[.]	Shift Left Long with MQ	X	31	216
slq[.]	Shift Left with MQ	X	31	152
sr[.]	Shift Right	X	31	536
sra[.]	Shift Right Algebraic	X	31	792
srai[.]	Shift Right Algebraic Immediate	X	31	824
sraiq[.]	Shift Right Algebraic Immediate with MQ	X	31	952
sraq[.]	Shift Right Algebraic with MQ	X	31	920
sre[.]	Shift Right Extended	X	31	665
srea[.]	Shift Right Extended Algebraic	X	31	921
sreq[.]	Shift Right Extended with MQ	X	31	729
sriq[.]	Shift Right Immediate with MQ	X	31	696
srliq[.]	Shift Right Long Immediate with MQ	X	31	760
srlq[.]	Shift Right Long with MQ	X	31	728

Mnemonic	Instruction	Format	Primary opcode	Extended opcode
srq[.]	Shift Right with MQ	X	31	664
st	Store	D	36	
stb	Store Byte	D	38	
stbrx	Store Byte Reverse Indexed	X	31	662
stbu	Store Byte with Update	D	39	
stbux	Store Byte with Update Indexed	X	31	247
stbx	Store Byte Indexed	X	31	215
stfd	Store Floating-Point Double	D	54	
stfdu	Store Floating-Point Double with Update	D	55	
stfdux	Store Floating-Point Double with Update Indexed	X	31	759
stfdx	Store Floating-Point Double Indexed	X	31	727
stfs	Store Floating-Point Single	D	52	
stfsu	Store Floating-Point Single with Update	D	53	
stfsux	Store Floating-Point Single with Update Indexed	X	31	695
stfsx	Store Floating-Point Single Indexed	X	31	663
sth	Store Half	D	44	
sthbrx	Store Half Byte Reverse Indexed	X	31	918
sthu	Store Half with Update	D	45	
sthux	Store Half with Update Indexed	X	31	439
sthx	Store Half Indexed	X	31	407
stm	Store Multiple	D	47	
stsi	Store String Immediate	X	31	725
stsx	Store String Indexed	X	31	661
stu	Store with Update	D	37	
stux	Store with Update Indexed	X	31	183
stx	Store Indexed	X	31	151
svc[l][a]	Supervisor Call	SC	17	
t	Trap	X	31	4
ti	Trap Immediate	D	03	
tlbi	TLB Invalidate Entry	X	31	306
xor[.]	XOR	X	31	316
xoril	XOR Immediate Lower	D	26	
xoriu	XOR Immediate Upper	D	27	

POWERPC INSTRUCTION FORMATS [*]

D.1 Instruction Formats

All instructions are four bytes long and word-aligned. Thus, whenever instruction addresses are presented to the processor (as in *Branch* instructions) the two low-order bits are ignored. Similarly, whenever the processor develops an instruction address, its two low-order bits are zero.

Bits 0:5 always specify the opcode (OPCD, below). Many instructions also have an extended opcode (XO, below). The remaining bits of the instruction contain one or more fields as shown below for the different instruction formats.

The format diagrams given below show horizontally all valid combinations of instruction fields. The diagrams include instruction fields that are used only by instructions defined in Book II, "PowerPC Virtual Environment Architecture," or in Book III, "PowerPC Operating Environment Architecture." See those Books for the definitions of such fields.

---

[*] Reprinted with permission of International Business Machines, Inc. from *The PowerPC Architecture: A Specification for a New Family of RISC Processors*, Second Edition, Morgan Kaufmann Publishers, 1994. Note that cross-references to specific page numbers in this appendix refer to *The PowerPC Architecture* text.

In some cases an instruction field is reserved, or must contain a particular value. If a reserved field does not have all bits set to 0, or if a field that must contain a particular value does not contain that value, the instruction form is invalid and the results are as described in Section 1.9.2, "Invalid Instruction Forms," on page 25.

Split Field Notation

In some cases an instruction field occupies more than one contiguous sequence of bits or occupies one contiguous sequence of bits that are used in permuted order. Such a field is called a "split field." In the format diagrams given below and in the individual instruction layouts, the name of a split field is shown in small letters, once for each of the contiguous sequences. In the RTL description of an instruction having a split field, and in certain other places where individual bits of a split field are identified, the name of the field in small letters represents the concatenation of the sequences from left to right. In all other places, the name of the field is capitalized and represents the concatenation of the sequences in some order, which need not be left to right, as described for each affected instruction.

I-Form

OPCD	LI	AA	LK
0	6	30	31

FIGURE D.1 I instruction format.

B-Form

OPCD	BO	BI	BD	AA	LK
0	6	11	16	30	31

FIGURE D.2 B instruction format.

SC-Form

OPCD	///	///	///	1	/
0	6	11	16	30	31

FIGURE D.3 SC instruction format.

D-Form

OPCD	RT		RA	D
OPCD	RT		RA	SI
OPCD	RS		RA	D
OPCD	RS		RA	UI
OPCD	BF	/ L	RA	SI
OPCD	BF	/ L	RA	UI
OPCD	TO		RA	SI
OPCD	FRT		RA	D
OPCD	FRS		RA	D

0   6   11   16   31

FIGURE D.4 D instruction format.

DS-Form

OPCD	RT	RA	DS	XO
OPCD	RS	RA	DS	XO

0   6   11   16   30 31

FIGURE D.5 DS instruction format (64-bit implementations only).

X-Form

OPCD	RT		RA	RB		XO		/
OPCD	RT		RA	NB		XO		/
OPCD	RT	/	SR	///		XO		/
OPCD	RT		///	RB		XO		/
OPCD	RT		///	///		XO		/
OPCD	RS		RA	RB		XO		Rc
OPCD	RS		RA	RB		XO		1
OPCD	RS		RA	RB		XO		/
OPCD	RS		RA	NB		XO		/
OPCD	RS		RA	SH		XO		Rc
OPCD	RS		RA	///		XO		Rc
OPCD	RS	/	SR	///		XO		/
OPCD	RS		///	RB		XO		/
OPCD	RS		///	///		XO		/
OPCD	BF	/ L	RA	RB		XO		/
OPCD	BF	//	FRA	FRB		XO		/
OPCD	BF	//	BFA //	///		XO		/
OPCD	BF	//	///	U	/	XO		Rc
OPCD	BF	//	///	///		XO		/
OPCD	TO		RA	RB		XO		/
OPCD	FRT		RA	RB		XO		/
OPCD	FRT		///	FRB		XO		Rc
OPCD	FRT		///	///		XO		Rc
OPCD	FRS		RA	RB		XO		/
OPCD	BT		///	///		XO		Rc
OPCD	///		RA	RB		XO		/
OPCD	///		///	RB		XO		/
OPCD	///		///	///		XO		/

0   6   11   16   21   31

FIGURE D.6 X instruction format .

XL-Form

OPCD	BT		BA		BB		XO	/
OPCD	BO		BI		///		XO	LK
OPCD	BF	//	BFA	//	///		XO	/
OPCD	///		///		///		XO	/

0   6   11   16   21   31

FIGURE D.7 XL instruction format.

XFX-Form

OPCD	RT		spr		XO	/
OPCD	RT		tbr		XO	/
OPCD	RT	/	FXM	/	XO	/
OPCD	RS		spr		XO	/

0   6   11   21   31

FIGURE D.8 XFX instruction format.

XFL-Form

OPCD	/	FLM	/	FRB	XO	Rc

0   6 7   15 16   21   31

FIGURE D.9 XFL instruction format.

XS-Form

OPCD	RS	RA	sh	XO	sh	Rc

0   6   11   16   21   30 31

FIGURE D.10 XS instruction format (64-bit implementations only).

XO-Form

OPCD	RT	RA	RB	OE	XO	Rc
OPCD	RT	RA	RB	/	XO	Rc
OPCD	RT	RA	///	OE	XO	Rc

0   6   11   16   21 22   31

FIGURE D.11 XO instruction format.

A-Form

OPCD	FRT	FRA	FRB	FRC	XO	Rc
OPCD	FRT	FRA	FRB	///	XO	Rc
OPCD	FRT	FRA	///	FRC	XO	Rc
OPCD	FRT	///	FRB	FRC	XO	Rc

0   6   11   16   21   26   31

FIGURE D.12 A instruction format.

M-Form

OPCD	RS	RA	RB	MB	ME	Rc
OPCD	RS	RA	SH	MB	ME	Rc

0   6   11   16   21   26   31

FIGURE D.13 M instruction format.

MD-Form

OPCD	RS	RA	sh	mb	XO	Rc	Rc
OPCD	RS	RA	sh	me	XO	Rc	Rc

0   6   11   16   21   27   30 31

FIGURE D.14 MD instruction format (64-bit implementations only).

MDS-Form

OPCD	RS	RA	RB	mb	XO	Rc
OPCD	RS	RA	RB	me	XO	Rc

0   6   11   16   21   27   31

FIGURE D.15 MDS instruction format (64-bit implementations only).

Instruction Fields

AA (30)
   Absolute Address bit.

   0 The immediate field represents an address relative to the current instruction address. For I-form branches the effective address of the branch target is the sum of the LI field sign-extended to 64 bits and the address of the branch instruction. For B-form branches the effective address of the branch target is the sum of the BD field sign-extended to 64 bits and the address of the branch instruction.

   1 The immediate field represents an absolute address. For I-form branches the effective address of the branch target is the LI field sign-extended to 64 bits. For B-form branches the effective address of the branch target is the BD field sign-extended to 64 bits.

BA (11:15)
   Field used to specify a bit in the CR to be used as a source.

BB (16:20)
   Field used to specify a bit in the CR to be used as a source.

BD (16:29)
   Immediate field specifying a 14-bit signed two's complement branch displacement which is concatenated on the right with 0b00 and sign-extended to 64 bits.

BF (6:8)
   Field used to specify one of the CR fields or one of the FPSCR fields to be used as a target.

BFA (11:13)
   Field used to specify one of the CR fields or one of the FPSCR fields to be used as a source.

BI (11:15)
   Field used to specify a bit in the CR to be used as the condition of a *Branch Conditional* instruction.

BO (6:10)
   Field used to specify options for the *Branch Conditional* instructions. The encoding is described in Section 2.4, "Branch Processor Instructions," on page 35.

BT (6:10)
Field used to specify a bit in the CR or in the FPSCR to be used as a target.

D (16:31)
Immediate field specifying a 16-bit signed two's complement integer which is sign-extended to 64 bits.

DS (16:29)
Immediate field specifying a 14-bit signed two's complement integer which is concatenated on the right with 0b00 and sign-extended to 64 bits. This field is defined in 64-bit implementations only.

FLM (7:14)
Field mask used to identify the FPSCR fields that are to be updated by the *mtfsf* instruction.

FRA (11:15)
Field used to specify an FPR to be used as a source.

FRB (16:20)
Field used to specify an FPR to be used as a source.

FRC (21:25)
Field used to specify an FPR to be used as a source.

FRS (6:10)
Field used to specify an FPR to be used as a source.

FRT (6:10)
Field used to specify an FPR to be used as a target.

FXM (12:19)
Field mask used to identify the CR fields that are to be updated by the *mtcrf* instruction.

L (10)
Field used to specify whether a Fixed-Point *Compare* instruction is to compare 64-bit numbers or 32-bit numbers. This field is defined in 64-bit implementations only.

LI (6:29)
Immediate field specifying a 24-bit signed two's complement integer which is concatenated on the right with 0b00 and sign-extended to 64 bits.

LK (31)
LINK bit.
0 Do not set the Link Register.
1 Set the Link Register. If the instruction is a *Branch* instruction, the address of the instruction following the *Branch* instruction is placed into the Link Register.

MB (21:25) and ME (26:30)
Fields used in M-form instructions to specify a 64-bit mask consisting of 1-bits from bit

MB+32 through bit ME+32 inclusive and 0-bits elsewhere, as described in Section 3.3.13, "Fixed-Point Rotate and Shift Instructions," on page 115.

MB (21:26)

Field used in MD-form and MDS-form instructions to specify the first 1-bit of a 64-bit mask, as described in Section 3.3.13, "Fixed-Point Rotate and Shift Instructions," on page 115. This field is defined in 64-bit implementations only.

ME (21:26)

Field used in MD-form and MDS-form instructions to specify the last 1-bit of a 64-bit mask, as described in Section 3.3.13, "Fixed-Point Rotate and Shift Instructions," on page 115. This field is defined in 64-bit implementations only.

NB (16:20)

Field used to specify the number of bytes to move in an immediate string load or store.

OPCD (0:5)

Primary opcode field.

OE (21)

Used for extended arithmetic to enable setting OV and SO in the XER.

RA (11:15)

Field used to specify a GPR to be used as a source or as a target.

RB (16:20)

Field used to specify a GPR to be used as a source.

Rc (31)

RECORD bit.

0   Do not alter the Condition Register.

1   Set Condition Register Field 0 or Field 1 as described in Section 2.3.1, "Condition Register," on page 32.

RS (6:10)

Field used to specify a GPR to be used as a source.

RT (6:10)

Field used to specify a GPR to be used as a target.

SH (16:20, or 16:20 and 30)

Field used to specify a shift amount. Location 16:20 and 30 pertains to 64-bit implementations only.

SI (16:31)

Immediate field used to specify a 16-bit signed integer.

SPR (11:20)

Field used to specify a Special Purpose Register for the *mtspr* and *mfspr* instructions. The encoding is described in Section 3.3.14, "Move To/From System Register Instructions," on page 128.

SR (12:15)

See Book III, Section 1.5.1, "Instruction Fields," on page 379.

TBR (11:20)

See Book II, Section 4.1, "Time Base Instructions," on page 352.

TO (6:10)

Field used to specify the conditions on which to trap. The encoding is described in Section 3.3.11, "Fixed-Point Trap Instructions," on page 101.

U (16:19)

Immediate field used as the data to be placed into a field in the FPSCR.

UI (16:31)

Immediate field used to specify a 16-bit unsigned integer.

XO (21:29, 21:30, 22:30, 26:30, 27:29, 27:30, or 30:31)

Extended opcode field. Locations 21:29, 27:29, 27:30, and 30:31 pertain to 64-bit implementations only.

**POWERPC
INSTRUCTION SET
SORTED BY MNEMONIC**[†]

This appendix lists all the instructions in the PowerPC Architecture in order by mnemonic.

Form	Opcode		Mode Dep.[1]	Page	Mnemonic	Instruction
	Primary	Extended				
XO	31	266	SR	83	add[o][.]	Add
XO	31	10	SR	85	addc[o][.]	Add Carrying
XO	31	138	SR	86	adde[o][.]	Add Extended
D	14			82	addi	Add Immediate

[†] Reprinted with permission of International Business Machines, Inc. from *The PowerPC Architecture: A Specification for a New Family of RISC Processors*, Second Edition, Morgan Kaufmann Publishers, 1994. Note that cross-references to specific page numbers in this appendix refer to *The PowerPC Architecture* text.

Form	Opcode		Mode Dep.[1]	Page	Mnemonic	Instruction
	Primary	Extended				
D	12		SR	84	addic	Add Immediate Carrying
D	13		SR	84	addic.	Add Immediate Carrying and Record
D	15			82	addis	Add Immediate Shifted
XO	31	234	SR	87	addme[o][.]	Add to Minus One Extended
XO	31	202	SR	88	addze[o][.]	Add to Zero Extended
X	31	28	SR	109	and[.]	AND
X	31	60	SR	111	andc[.]	AND with Complement
D	28		SR	106	andi.	AND Immediate
D	29		SR	106	andis.	AND Immediate Shifted
I	18			38	b[l][a]	Branch
B	16		CT	38	bc[l][a]	Branch Conditional
XL	19	528	CT	40	bcctr[l]	Branch Conditional to Count Register
XL	19	16	CT	39	bclr[l]	Branch Conditional to Link Register
X	31	0		99	cmp	Compare
D	11			99	cmpi	Compare Immediate
X	31	32		101	cmpl	Compare Logical
D	10			100	cmpli	Compare Logical Immediate
X	31	58	(SR)	114	cntlzd[.]	Count Leading Zeros Doubleword
X	31	26	SR	114	cntlzw[.]	Count Leading Zeros Word
XL	19	257		42	crand	Condition Register AND
XL	19	129		45	crandc	Condition Register AND with Complement
XL	19	289		44	creqv	Condition Register Equivalent
XL	19	225		43	crnand	Condition Register NAND
XL	19	33		44	crnor	Condition Register NOR

Form	Opcode Primary	Opcode Extended	Mode Dep.[1]	Page	Mnemonic	Instruction
XL	19	449		42	cror	Condition Register OR
XL	19	417		45	crorc	Condition Register OR with Complement
XL	19	193		43	crxor	Condition Register XOR
X	31	86		349 (II)	dcbf	Data Cache Block Flush
X	31	470		439 (III)	dcbi	Data Cache Block Invalidate
X	31	54		348 (II)	dcbst	Data Cache Block Store
X	31	278		346 (II)	dcbt	Data Cache Block Touch
X	31	246		347 (II)	dcbtst	Data Cache Block Touch for Store
X	31	1014		347 (II)	dcbz	Data Cache Block set to Zero
XO	31	489	(SR)	94	divd[o][.]	Divide Doubleword
XO	31	457	(SR)	96	divdu[o][.]	Divide Doubleword Unsigned
XO	31	491	SR	95	divw[o][.]	Divide Word
XO	31	459	SR	97	divwu[o][.]	Divide Word Unsigned
X	31	310		491 (III)	eciwx	External Control In Word Indexed
X	31	438		492 (III)	ecowx	External Control Out Word Indexed
X	31	854		350 (III)	eieio	Enforce In-order Execution of I/O
X	31	284	SR	111	eqv[.]	Equivalent
X	31	954	SR	112	extsb[.]	Extend Sign Byte
X	31	922	SR	113	extsh[.]	Extend Sign Halfword
X	31	986	(SR)	113	extsw[.]	Extend Sign Word
X	63	264		178	fabs[.]	Floating Absolute Value
A	63	21		179	fadd[.]	Floating Add
A	59	21		179	fadds[.]	Floating Add Single
X	63	846	()	190	fcfid[.]	Floating Convert From Integer Doubleword

Form	Opcode Primary	Opcode Extended	Mode Dep.[1]	Page	Mnemonic	Instruction
X	63	32		192	fcmpo	Floating Compare Ordered
X	63	0		191	fcmpu	Floating Compare Unordered
X	63	814	()	187	fctid[.]	Floating Convert To Integer Doubleword
X	63	815	()	188	fctidz[.]	Floating Convert To Integer Doubleword with round toward Zero
X	63	14		189	fctiw[.]	Floating Convert To Integer Word
X	63	15		190	fctiwz[.]	Floating Convert To Integer Word with round toward Zero
A	63	18		182	fdiv[.]	Floating Divide
A	59	18		182	fdivs[.]	Floating Divide Single
A	63	29		183	fmadd[.]	Floating Multiply-Add
A	59	29		183	fmadds[.]	Floating Multiply-Add Single
X	63	72		178	fmr[.]	Floating Move Register
A	63	28		184	fmsub[.]	Floating Multiply-Subtract
A	59	28		184	fmsubs[.]	Floating Multiply-Subtract Single
A	63	25		181	fmul[.]	Floating Multiply
A	59	25		181	fmuls[.]	Floating Multiply Single
X	63	136		179	fnabs[.]	Floating Negative Absolute Value
X	63	40		178	fneg[.]	Floating Negate
A	63	31		185	fnmadd[.]	Floating Negative Multiply-Add
A	59	31		185	fnmadds[.]	Floating Negative Multiply-Add Single
A	63	30		186	fnmsub[.]	Floating Negative Multiply-Subtract
A	59	30		186	fnmsubs[.]	Floating Negative Multiply-Subtract Single
A	59	24		200	fres[.]	Floating Reciprocal Estimate Single
X	63	12		187	frsp[.]	Floating Round to Single-Precision

Form	Opcode		Mode Dep.[1]	Page	Mnemonic	Instruction
	Primary	Extended				
A	63	26		201	frsqrte[.]	Floating Reciprocal Square Root Estimate
A	63	23		202	fsel[.]	Floating Select
A	63	22		198	fsqrt[.]	Floating Square Root
A	59	22		198	fsqrts[.]	Floating Square Root Single
A	63	20		180	fsub[.]	Floating Subtract
A	59	20		180	fsubs[.]	Floating Subtract Single
X	31	982		345 (II)	icbi	Instruction Cache Block Invalidate
XL	19	150		346 (II)	isync	Instruction Synchronize
D	34			50	lbz	Load Byte and Zero
D	35			50	lbzu	Load Byte and Zero with Update
X	31	119		51	lbzux	Load Byte and Zero with Update Indexed
X	31	87		50	lbzx	Load Byte and Zero Indexed
DS	58	0	()	59	ld	Load Doubleword
X	31	84	()	77	ldarx	Load Doubleword And Reserve Indexed
DS	58	1	()	60	ldu	Load Doubleword with Update
X	31	53	()	60	ldux	Load Doubleword with Update Indexed
X	31	21	()	59	ldx	Load Doubleword Indexed
D	50			171	lfd	Load Floating-Point Double
D	51			172	lfdu	Load Floating-Point Double with Update
X	31	631		172	lfdux	Load Floating-Point Double with Update Indexed
X	31	599		172	lfdx	Load Floating-Point Double Indexed
D	48			169	lfs	Load Floating-Point Single
D	49			170	lfsu	Load Floating-Point Single with Update
X	31	567		171	lfsux	Load Floating-Point Single with Update Indexed

Form	Opcode Primary	Opcode Extended	Mode Dep.[1]	Page	Mnemonic	Instruction
X	31	535		170	lfsx	Load Floating-Point Single Indexed
D	42			54	lha	Load Halfword Algebraic
D	43			54	lhau	Load Halfword Algebraic with Update
X	31	375		55	lhaux	Load Halfword Algebraic with Update Indexed
X	31	343		54	lhax	Load Halfword Algebraic Indexed
X	31	790		68	lhbrx	Load Halfword Byte-Reverse Indexed
D	40			52	lhz	Load Halfword and Zero
D	41			53	lhzu	Load Halfword and Zero with Update
X	31	311		53	lhzux	Load Halfword and Zero with Update Indexed
X	31	279		52	lhzx	Load Halfword and Zero Indexed
D	46			71	lmw	Load Multiple Word
X	31	597		73	lswi	Load String Word Immediate
X	31	533		74	lswx	Load String Word Indexed
DS	58	2	()	57	lwa	Load Word Algebraic
X	31	20		77	lwarx	Load Word And Reserve Indexed
X	31	373	()	58	lwaux	Load Word Algebraic with Update Indexed
X	31	341	()	58	lwax	Load Word Algebraic Indexed
X	31	534		69	lwbrx	Load Word Byte-Reverse Indexed
D	32			55	lwz	Load Word and Zero
D	33			56	lwzu	Load Word and Zero with Update
X	31	55		57	lwzux	Load Word and Zero with Update Indexed
X	31	23		56	lwzx	Load Word and Zero Indexed
XL	19	0		45	mcrf	Move Condition Register Field
X	63	64		194	mcrfs	Move to Condition Register from FPSCR

Form	Opcode		Mode Dep.[1]	Page	Mnemonic	Instruction
	Primary	Extended				
X	31	512		131	mcrxr	Move to Condition Register from XER
X	31	19		132	mfcr	Move From Condition Register
X	63	583		194	mffs[.]	Move From FPSCR
X	31	83		389 (III)	mfmsr	Move From Machine State Register
XFX	31	339		130	mfspr	Move From Special Purpose Register (also see Book III, page 387)
X	31	595	{}	441 (III)	mfsr	Move From Segment Register
X	31	659	{}	442 (III)	mfsrin	Move From Segment Register Indirect
XFX	31	371		352 (II)	mftb	Move From Time Base
XFX	31	144		131	mtcrf	Move To Condition Register Fields
X	63	70		195	mtfsb0[.]	Move To FPSCR Bit 0
X	63	38		196	mtfsb1[.]	Move To FPSCR Bit 1
XFL	63	711		195	mtfsf[.]	Move To FPSCR Fields
X	63	134		194	mtfsfi[.]	Move To FPSCR Field Immediate
X	31	146		389 (III)	mtmsr	Move To Machine State Register
XFX	31	467		129	mtspr	Move To Special Purpose Register (also see Book III, page 384)
X	31	210	{}	440 (III)	mtsr	Move To Segment Register
X	31	242	{}	441 (III)	mtsrin	Move To Segment Register Indirect
XO	31	73	(SR)	91	mulhd[.]	Multiply High Doubleword
XO	31	9	(SR)	92	mulhdu[.]	Multiply High Doubleword Unsigned
XO	31	75	SR	92	mulhw[.]	Multiply High Word
XO	31	11	SR	93	mulhwu[.]	Multiply High Word Unsigned
XO	31	233	(SR)	90	mulld[o][.]	Multiply Low Doubleword
D	7			90	mulli	Multiply Low Immediate
XO	31	235	SR	91	mullw[o][.]	Multiply Low Word

Form	Opcode Primary	Opcode Extended	Mode Dep.[1]	Page	Mnemonic	Instruction
X	31	476	SR	110	nand[.]	NAND
XO	31	104	SR	89	neg[o][.]	Negate
X	31	124	SR	110	nor[.]	NOR
X	31	444	SR	109	or[.]	OR
X	31	412	SR	112	orc[.]	OR with Complement
D	24			107	ori	OR Immediate
D	25			107	oris	OR Immediate Shifted
XL	19	50		379 (III)	rfi	Return From Interrupt
MDS	30	8	(SR)	119	rldcl[.]	Rotate Left Doubleword then Clear Left
MDS	30	9	(SR)	120	rldcr[.]	Rotate Left Doubleword then Clear Right
MD	30	2	(SR)	118	rldic[.]	Rotate Left Doubleword Immediate then Clear
MD	30	0	(SR)	116	rldicl[.]	Rotate Left Doubleword Immediate then Clear Left
MD	30	1	(SR)	117	rldicr[.]	Rotate Left Doubleword Immediate then Clear Right
MD	30	3	(SR)	121	rldimi[.]	Rotate Left Doubleword Immediate then Mask Insert
M	20		SR	122	rlwimi[.]	Rotate Left Word Immediate then Mask Insert
M	21		SR	119	rlwinm[.]	Rotate Left Word Immediate then AND with Mask
M	23		SR	121	rlwnm[.]	Rotate Left Word then AND with Mask
SC	17			41	sc	System Call (also see Book III, page 378)
X	31	498	()	444 (III)	slbia	SLB Invalidate All
X	31	434	()	443 (III)	slbie	SLB Invalidate Entry
X	31	27	(SR)	123	sld[.]	Shift Left Doubleword
X	31	24	SR	124	slw[.]	Shift Left Word
X	31	794	(SR)	127	srad[.]	Shift Right Algebraic Doubleword

Form	Opcode		Mode Dep.[1]	Page	Mnemonic	Instruction
	Primary	Extended				
XS	31	413	(SR)	126	sradi[.]	Shift Right Algebraic Doubleword Immediate
X	31	792	SR	128	sraw[.]	Shift Right Algebraic Word
X	31	824	SR	126	srawi[.]	Shift Right Algebraic Word Immediate
X	31	539	(SR)	124	srd[.]	Shift Right Doubleword
X	31	536	SR	125	srw[.]	Shift Right Word
D	38			61	stb	Store Byte
D	39			62	stbu	Store Byte with Update
X	31	247		62	stbux	Store Byte with Update Indexed
X	31	215		61	stbx	Store Byte Indexed
DS	62	0	()	66	std	Store Doubleword
X	31	214	()	79	stdcx.	Store Doubleword Conditional Indexed
DS	62	1	()	67	stdu	Store Doubleword with Update
X	31	181	()	68	stdux	Store Doubleword with Update Indexed
X	31	149	()	67	stdx	Store Doubleword Indexed
D	54			176	stfd	Store Floating-Point Double
D	55			177	stfdu	Store Floating-Point Double with Update
X	31	759		177	stfdux	Store Floating-Point Double with Update Indexed
X	31	727		176	stfdx	Store Floating-Point Double Indexed
X	31	983		198	stfiwx	Store Floating-Point as Integer Word Indexed
D	52			174	stfs	Store Floating-Point Single
D	53			175	stfsu	Store Floating-Point Single with Update
X	31	695		175	stfsux	Store Floating-Point Single with Update Indexed
X	31	663		175	stfsx	Store Floating-Point Single Indexed
D	44			63	sth	Store Halfword

| Form | Opcode | | Mode Dep.[1] | Page | Mnemonic | Instruction |
	Primary	Extended				
X	31	918		69	sthbrx	Store Halfword Byte-Reverse Indexed
D	45			63	sthu	Store Halfword with Update
X	31	439		64	sthux	Store Halfword with Update Indexed
X	31	407		63	sthx	Store Halfword Indexed
D	47			72	stmw	Store Multiple Word
X	31	725		75	stswi	Store String Word Immediate
X	31	661		76	stswx	Store String Word Indexed
D	36			64	stw	Store Word
X	31	662		70	stwbrx	Store Word Byte-Reverse Indexed
X	31	150		78	stwcx.	Store Word Conditional Indexed
D	37			65	stwu	Store Word with Update
X	31	183		66	stwux	Store Word with Update Indexed
X	31	151		65	stwx	Store Word Indexed
XO	31	40	SR	83	subf[o][.]	Subtract From
XO	31	8	SR	86	subfc[o][.]	Subtract From Carrying
XO	31	136	SR	87	subfe[o][.]	Subtract From Extended
D	8		SR	85	subfic	Subtract From Immediate Carrying
XO	31	232	SR	88	subfme[o][.]	Subtract From Minus One Extended
XO	31	200	SR	89	subfze[o][.]	Subtract From Zero Extended
X	31	598		80	sync	Synchronize
X	31	68	()	104	td	Trap Doubleword
D	2		()	102	tdi	Trap Doubleword Immediate
X	31	370		445 (III)	tlbia	TLB Invalidate All
X	31	306		444 (III)	tlbie	TLB Invalidate Entry

Form	Opcode		Mode Dep.[1]	Page	Mnemonic	Instruction
	Primary	Extended				
X	31	566		445 (III)	tlbsync	TLB Synchronize
X	31	4		105	tw	Trap Word
D	3			103	twi	Trap Word Immediate
X	31	316	SR	110	xor[.]	XOR
D	26			108	xori	XOR Immediate
D	27			108	xoris	XOR Immediate Shifted

[1]Key to Mode Dependency Column

The entry is shown in parentheses () if the instruction is defined only for 64-bit implementations.

The entry is shown in braces {} if the instruction is defined only for 32-bit implementations.

blank   The instruction has no mode dependence, except that if the instruction refers to storage when in 32-bit mode, only the low-order 32 bits of the 64-bit effective address are used to address storage. Storage reference instructions include loads, stores, branch instructions, etc.

CT   If the instruction tests the Count Register, it tests the low-order 32 bits when in 32-bit mode and all 64 bits when in 64-bit mode.

SR   The instruction's primary function is mode-independent, but the setting of status registers (such as XER and CR0) is mode-dependent.

CROSS-REFERENCE FOR CHANGED POWER MNEMONICS†

For PowerPC Architecture

The following table lists the POWER instruction mnemonics that have been changed in the PowerPC Architecture, sorted by POWER mnemonic.

To determine the PowerPC mnemonic for one of these POWER mnemonics, find the POWER mnemonic in the second column of the table: the remainder of the line gives the PowerPC mnemonic and the page on which the instruction is described, as well as the instruction names.

POWER mnemonics that have not changed are not listed. POWER instruction names that are the same in PowerPC are not repeated: i.e., for these, the last column of the table is blank.

---

† Reprinted with permission of International Business Machines, Inc. from *The PowerPC Architecture: A Specification for a New Family of RISC Processors*, Second Edition, Morgan Kaufmann Publishers, 1994. Note that cross-references to specific page numbers in this appendix refer to *The PowerPC Architecture* text.

Page	POWER Mnemonic	POWER Instruction	PowerPC Mnemonic	PowerPC Instruction
85	a[o][.]	Add	addc[o][.]	Add Carrying
86	ae[o][.]	Add Extended	adde[o][.]	
84	ai	Add Immediate	addic	Add Immediate Carrying
84	ai.	Add Immediate and Record	addic.	Add Immediate Carrying and Record
87	ame[o][.]	Add To Minus One Extended	addme[o][.]	Add to Minus One Extended
106	andil.	AND Immediate Lower	andi.	AND Immediate
106	andiu.	AND Immediate Upper	andis.	AND Immediate Shifted
88	aze[o][.]	Add To Zero Extended	addze[o][.]	Add to Zero Extended
40	bcc[l]	Branch Conditional to Count Register	bcctr[l]	
39	bcr[l]	Branch Conditional to Link Register	bclr[l]	
82	cal	Compute Address Lower	addi	Add Immediate
82	cau	Compute Address Upper	addis	Add Immediate Shifted
83	cax[o][.]	Compute Address	add[o][.]	Add
114	cntlz[.]	Count Leading Zeros	cntlzw[.]	Count Leading Zeros Word
353 (II)	dclz	Data Cache Line Set to Zero	dcbz	Data Cache Block set to Zero
80	dcs	Data Cache Synchronize	sync	Synchronize
113	exts[.]	Extend Sign	extsh[.]	Extend Sign Halfword
179	fa[.]	Floating Add	fadd[.]	
182	fd[.]	Floating Divide	fdiv[.]	
181	fm[.]	Floating Multiply	fmul[.]	
183	fma[.]	Floating Multiply-Add	fmadd[.]	
184	fms[.]	Floating Multiply-Subtract	fmsub[.]	
185	fnma[.]	Floating Negative Multiply-Add	fnmadd[.]	
186	fnms[.]	Floating Negative Multiply-Subtract	fnmsub[.]	

Page	POWER		PowerPC	
	Mnemonic	Instruction	Mnemonic	Instruction
180	fs[.]	Floating Subtract	fsub[.]	
352 (II)	ics	Instruction Cache Synchronize	isync	Instruction Synchronize
55	l	Load	lwz	Load Word and Zero
69	lbrx	Load Byte-Reverse Indexed	lwbrx	Load Word Byte-Reverse Indexed
71	lm	Load Multiple	lmw	Load Multiple Word
73	lsi	Load String Immediate	lswi	Load String Word Immediate
74	lsx	Load String Indexed	lswx	Load String Word Indexed
56	lu	Load with Update	lwzu	Load Word and Zero with Update
57	lux	Load with Update Indexed	lwzux	Load Word and Zero with Update Indexed
56	lx	Load Indexed	lwzx	Load Word and Zero Indexed
450 (III)	mtsri	Move To Segment Register Indirect	mtsrin	
90	muli	Multiply Immediate	mulli	Multiply Low Immediate
91	muls[o][.]	Multiply Short	mullw[o][.]	Multiply Low Word
107	oril	OR Immediate Lower	ori	OR Immediate
107	oriu	OR Immediate Upper	oris	OR Immediate Shifted
122	rlimi[.]	Rotate Left Immediate Then Mask Insert	rlwimi[.]	Rotate Left Word Immediate then Mask Insert
119	rlinm[.]	Rotate Left Immediate Then AND With Mask	rlwinm[.]	Rotate Left Word Immediate then AND with Mask
121	rlnm[.]	Rotate Left Then AND With Mask	rlwnm[.]	Rotate Left Word then AND with Mask
86	sf[o][.]	Subtract From	subfc[o][.]	Subtract From Carrying
87	sfe[o][.]	Subtract From Extended	subfe[o][.]	
85	sfi	Subtract From Immediate	subfic	Subtract From Immediate Carrying
88	sfme[o][.]	Subtract From Minus One Extended	subfme[o][.]	
89	sfze[o][.]	Subtract From Zero Extended	subfze[o][.]	

Page	POWER		PowerPC	
	Mnemonic	Instruction	Mnemonic	Instruction
124	sl[.]	Shift Left	slw[.]	Shift Left Word
125	sr[.]	Shift Right	srw[.]	Shift Right Word
128	sra[.]	Shift Right Algebraic	sraw[.]	Shift Right Algebraic Word
126	srai[.]	Shift Right Algebraic Immediate	srawi[.]	Shift Right Algebraic Word Immediate
64	st	Store	stw	Store Word
70	stbrx	Store Byte-Reverse Indexed	stwbrx	Store Word Byte-Reverse Indexed
72	stm	Store Multiple	stmw	Store Multiple Word
75	stsi	Store String Immediate	stswi	Store String Word Immediate
76	stsx	Store String Indexed	stswx	Store String Word Indexed
65	stu	Store with Update	stwu	Store Word with Update
66	stux	Store with Update Indexed	stwux	Store Word with Update Indexed
65	stx	Store Indexed	stwx	Store Word Indexed
41	svca	Supervisor Call	sc	System Call (see also Book III, page 378)
105	t	Trap	tw	Trap Word
103	ti	Trap Immediate	twi	Trap Word Immediate
454 (III)	tlbi	TLB Invalidate Entry	tlbie	
108	xoril	XOR Immediate Lower	xori	XOR Immediate
108	xoriu	XOR Immediate Upper	xoris	XOR Immediate Shifted

For Virtual Environment Architecture

The following table lists the POWER instruction mnemonics that have been changed in the PowerPC Virtual Environment Architecture, sorted by POWER mnemonic.

To determine the PowerPC mnemonic for one of these POWER mnemonics, find the POWER mnemonic in the second column of the table: the remainder of the line gives the PowerPC mnemonic and the page on which the instruction is described, as well as the instruction names.

POWER mnemonics that have not changed are not listed.

Page	POWER		PowerPC	
	Mnemonic	Instruction	Mnemonic	Instruction
347	dclz	Data Cache Line Set to Zero	dcbz	Data Cache Block set to Zero
346	ics	Instruction Cache Synchronize	isync	Instruction Synchronize

For POWERPC Operating Environment Architecture

The following table lists the POWER instruction mnemonics that have been changed in the PowerPC Operating Environment Architecture, sorted by POWER mnemonic.

To determine the PowerPC mnemonic for one of these POWER mnemonics, find the POWER mnemonic in the second column of the table: the remainder of the line gives the PowerPC mnemonic and the page on which the instruction is described, as well as the instruction names.

POWER mnemonics that have not changed are not listed. POWER instruction names that are the same in PowerPC are not repeated: i.e., for these, the last column of the table is blank.

Page	POWER		PowerPC	
	Mnemonic	Instruction	Mnemonic	Instruction
441	mtsri	Move To Segment Register Indirect	mtsrin	
378	svca	Supervisor Call	sc	System Call
444	tlbi	TLB Invalidate Entry	tlbie	

BIBLIOGRAPHY

[1] Acosta, R. D., J. Kjelstrup, and H. C. Torng. Sept. 1986. An instruction issuing approach to enhancing performance in multiple functional unit processors. *IEEE Transactions on Computers*. C–35(9):815–828.

[2] Allen, M. S., and M. C. Becker. Feb. 1993. Multiprocessing aspects of the PowerPC 601. In *Proceedings of the IEEE Compcon 1993*. San Francisco. 117–126.

[3] Alpert, D., and D. Avnon. 1993. Architecture of the pentium processor. *IEEE Micro*. 13(3):11–21.

[4] Anderson, D. W., F. J. Sparacio, and R. M. Tomasulo. Jan. 1967. The IBM System/360 Model 91: machine philosophy and instruction-handling. *IBM Journal*. 11:8–24.

[5] ANSI. 1986. *ANSI X3.131–1986 SCSI–I Specification*. 1430 Broadway, New York, NY 10018.

[6] Archibald, J., and J.-L. Baer. Nov. 1986. Cache coherence protocols: Evaluation using a multiprocessor simulation model. *ACM Transactions on Computer Systems*. 4(4):273–298.

[7] Bakoglu, H. B., and T. Whiteside. 1990. RISC System/6000 Hardware Overview. In *IBM RISC System/6000 Technology*. Publication number SA23–2619. Austin, Texas: International Business Machines Corporation.

[8] Bhandarkar, D., and D. W. Clark. Apr. 1991. Performance from architecture: comparing a RISC and a CISC with similar hardware organization. In *Proceedings 4th International Conference on Architectural Support for Programming Languages and Operating Systems (ASPLOS-IV)*. Santa Clara, Calif. 310–319.

[9] Bloch, E. 1959. The engineering design of the Stretch computer. In *Proceedings of the Eastern Joint Computer Conference*. 48–58.

[10] Bucholz, W. 1962. *Planning a computer system: Project Stretch*. New York: McGraw-Hill.

[11] Case, B. Dec. 26, 1991. RS/6000 architecture fine-tuned for PowerPC. *Microprocessor Report*. 5(24):9–12.

[12] Case, B. Oct. 28, 1992. IBM delivers first PowerPC microprocessor. *Microprocessor Report*. 6(14):6–10.

[13] Cocke, J., and V. Markstein. Jan. 1990. The evolution of RISC technology at IBM. *IBM Journal of Research and Development*. 34(1):4–11.

[14] Cody, W. J. Mar. 1981. Analysis of proposals for the floating-point standard. *IEEE Computer*. 14(3):63–68.

[15] Cohen, D. Oct. 1981. On holy wars and a plea for peace. *IEEE Computer*. 14(10):48–54.

[16] Comerford, R. July 1992. How DEC developed ALPHA. *IEEE Spectrum*. 29(7):26–31.

[17] Cragon, H. G. 1992. *Branch Strategy Taxonomy and Performance Models*. Los Alamitos, Calif.: IEEE Computer Society Press.

[18] Diefendorff, K., and M. Allen. 1992. Organization of the Motorola 88110 superscalar RISC microprocessor. *IEEE Micro*. 12(2):40–63.

[19] Digital Equipment Corporation. 1992. *Alpha Architecture Handbook*.

[20] Dobberpuhl, D., et al. Nov. 1992. A 200-MHz 64-bit dual-issue CMOS microprocessor. *IEEE J. of Solid State Circuits*. 27(11):1555–1567.

[21] Dubois, M., C. Scheurich, and F. A. Briggs. Feb. 1988. Synchronization, coherence, and event ordering in multiprocessors. *Computer*. 21(2):9–22.

[22] Figueroa, J. Dec. 1987. Designer's guide to the Micro Channel: implementing DMA and arbitration. *Microprocessor Report*. 1(4):8–11.

[23] Flynn, M. J., C. L. Mitchell, and J. M. Mulder. Sept. 1987. And now a case for more complex instruction sets. *IEEE Computer*. 20(9):71–83.

[24] Franklin, M., and G. S. Sohi. May 1992. The expandable split window paradigm for exploiting fine-grain parallelism. In *Proceedings 19th International Symposium on Computer Architecture*. Gold Coast, Australia. 58–67.

[25] Goldberg, G. Mar. 1991. What every computer scientist should know about floating-point arithmetic. *ACM Computing Surveys*. 23(1):5–48.

[26] Goodman, J. R. June 1983. Using cache memory to reduce processor-memory traffic. In *Proceedings 10th Annual International Symposium on Computer Architecture*. Stockholm. 124–131.

[27] Grohoski, G. F. Jan. 1990. Machine organization of the IBM RISC System/6000 processor. *IBM Journal of Research and Development*. 34(1):37–58.

[28] Grohoski, G. F., J. A. Kahle, L. E. Thatcher, and C. R. Moore. 1990. Branch and Fixed-Point Instruction Execution Units. In *IBM RISC System/6000 Technology*. Publication number SA23–2619. Austin, Texas: International Business Machines Corporation.

[29] Gwennap, L. Oct. 4, 1993. IBM Regains Performance Lead with POWER2. *Microprocessor Report*. 7(13):1–10.

[30] Gwennap, L. Aug. 23, 1993. TFP Designed for Tremendous Floating Point. *Microprocessor Report*. 7(11):9–13.

[31] Hall, C. B., and K. O'Brien. Apr. 1991. Performance characteristics of architectural features of the IBM RISC System/6000. In *Proceedings 4th International Conference on Architectural Support for Programming Languages and Operating Systems (ASPLOS-IV)*. Santa Clara, Calif. 303–309.

[32] Hardell, W. R., D. A. Hicks, L. C. Howell, W. E. Maule, R. Montoye, and D. Tuttle. 1990. Data cache and storage control units. In *IBM RISC System/6000 Technology*. Publication number SA23–2619. Austin, Texas: International Business Machines Corporation.

[33] Hayes, J. P. 1988. *Computer Architecture and Organization*. 2d ed. New York: McGraw-Hill.

[34] Hennessy, J. Dec. 1984. VLSI processor architecture. *IEEE Transactions on Computers*. C–33(11):1221–1246.

[35] Hennessy, J., N. Jouppi, F. Baskett, T. R. Gross, and J. Gill. Mar. 1982. Hardware/software tradeoffs for increased performance. In *Proceedings Symposium on Architectural Support for Programming Languages and Operating Systems (ASPLOS)*. Palo Alto, Calif. 2–11.

[36] Hester, P. D. 1990. RISC System/6000 Hardware Background and Philosophies. In *IBM RISC System/6000 Technology*. Publication number SA23–2619. Austin, Texas: International Business Machines Corporation.

[37] Hill, M. D. Dec. 1988. A case for direct-mapped caches. *Computer*. 21(12):25–40.

[38] Hokenek, E., and R. K. Montoye. Jan. 1990. Leading-zero anticipator (LZA) in the IBM RISC System/6000 floating-point execution unit. *IBM Journal Research and Development*. 34:71–77.

[39] Hwang, K., and F. A. Briggs. 1984. *Computer Architecture and Parallel Processing*. New York: McGraw-Hill.

[40] Hwu, W. W., and Y. N. Patt. Dec. 1987. Checkpoint repair for high-performance out-of-order execution machines. *IEEE Transactions on Computers*. C–36(12):1496–1514.

[41] IEEE, Inc. Aug. 1985. *IEEE Standard for Binary Floating-Point Arithmetic*. ANSI/IEEE Std 754–1985. New York.

[42] International Business Machines Corporation. 1994. *The PowerPC Architecture: Specifications for a New family of RISC Processors*. San Francisco: Morgan Kaufmann Publishers.

[43] International Business Machines Corporation. 1989. *IBM RISC System/6000 Hardware Technical Reference Micro Channel Architecture*. Publication number SA23–2647.

[44] International Business Machines Corporation. 1989. *IBM RISC System/6000 POWERstation and POWERserver Hardware Technical Reference—General Information Manual*. Publication number SA23–2643.

[45] International Business Machines Corporation. 1989. *IBM Personal Systems Technical Journal*. Issue 4.

[46] Johnson, M. 1991. *Superscalar Microprocessor Design*. Englewood Cliffs, N.J.: Prentice-Hall.

[47] Jouppi, N. P., and D. W. Wall. Apr. 1989. Available instruction-level parallelism for superscalar and superpipelined machines. In *Proceedings 3rd International Conference on Architectural Support for Programming Languages and Operating Systems (ASPLOS-III)*. Boston. 272–282.

[48] Kessler, R. E., R. Jooss, A. Lebeck, and M. D. Hill. May 1989. Inexpensive implementations of set-associativity. In *Proceedings 16th Annual International Symposium on Computer Architecture*. Jerusalem, Israel. 131–139.

[49] Kogge, P. M. 1981. *The architecture of pipeline computers*. New York: Hemisphere Publishing.

[50] Kunkel, S. R., and J. E. Smith. June 1986. Optimal pipelining in supercomputers. In *Proceedings 13th Annual International Symposium on Computer Architecture*. Tokyo. 404–414.

[51] Lam, M. June 1988. Software pipelining: An effective scheduling technique for VLIW machines. In *Proceedings SIGPLAN Conference on Programming Language Design and Implementation*. Atlanta, Ga. 318–328.

[52] Lam, M. S., and R. P. Wilson. May 1992. Limits of control flow on parallelism. In *Proceedings 19th Annual International Symposium on Computer Architecture*. Gold Coast, Australia. 46–57.

[53] Lee, J. K. F., and A. J. Smith. Jan. 1984. Branch prediction strategies and branch target buffer design. *Computer.* 17(1):6–22.

[54] Lilja, D. J. July 1988. Reducing the branch penalty in pipelined processors. *Computer.* 21:47–55.

[55] Malik, N., R. J. Eickemeyer, and S. Vassiliadis. Dec. 1992. Interlock collapsing alu for increased instruction-level parallelism. In *Proceedings 25th Annual International Symposium on Microarchitecture.* Portland, Oreg. 149–157.

[56] Markstein, P. W. Jan. 1990. Computation of elementary functions on the IBM RISC System/6000 processor. *IBM Journal of Research and Development.* 34(1):111–119.

[57] Marshall, T. Mar. 1992. System bus or system bottleneck? *Byte.* 131–138.

[58] McFarling, S., and J. Hennessy. June 1986. Reducing the cost of branches. In *Proceedings 13th Annual International Symposium on Computer Architecture.* Tokyo. 396–403.

[59] Micro Channel Developers Association. 1992. *Micro Channel Architecture Specification revision 2.0.* 2280 North Bechelli Lane, Suite B, Redding, Calif. 96002.

[60] Montoye, R. K., E. Hokenek, and S. L. Runyon. Jan. 1990. Design of the IBM RISC System/6000 floating-point execution unit. *IBM Journal Research and Development.* 34:59–70.

[61] Moore, C. R. Feb. 1993. The PowerPC 601 microprocessor. In *Proceedings of the IEEE Compcon 1993.* San Francisco. 109–116.

[62] Motorola Inc. 1992. *PowerPC 601 RISC Microprocessor User's Manual.* Publication number MPC601UM/AD.

[63] Myers, G. J. 1982. *Advances in Computer Architecture.* 2d ed. New York: John Wiley.

[64] Nicholson, J., et al. 1990. RISC System/6000 I/O structure. In *IBM RISC System/6000 Technology.* Austin, Texas: International Business Machines Corporation. Publication number SA23–2619.

[65] Nicolau, A., and J. A. Fisher. Nov. 1984. Measuring the parallelism available for Very Long Instruction Word architectures. *IEEE Transactions on Computers.* C–33(11):968–976.

[66] Oehler, R. R., and R. D. Groves. Jan. 1990. IBM RISC System/6000 processor architecture. *IBM Journal of Research and Development.* 34(1):23–36.

[67] Olsson, B., R. Montoye, P. Markstein, and M. Nguyen Phu. 1990. RISC System/6000 Floating-Point Unit. In *IBM RISC System/6000 Technology*. Austin, Texas: International Business Machines Corporation. Publication number SA23–2619.

[68] Paap, G., and E. Silha. Feb. 1993. PowerPC: A performance architecture. In *Proceedings of the IEEE Compcon 1993*. San Francisco. 104–108.

[69] Patt, Y. N., W. Hwu, and M. C. Shebanow. Dec. 1985. HPS, a new microarchitecture: rationale and introduction. In *Proceedings 18th International Microprogramming Workshop*. Asilomar, Calif.

[70] Patterson, D. A. Jan. 1985. Reduced instruction set computers. *Communications of the ACM*. 28(1):8–21.

[71] Patterson, D. A., and J. L. Hennessy. 1990. *Computer Architecture: A Quantitative Approach*. San Mateo, Calif.: Morgan Kaufmann Publishers.

[72] Patterson, D. A., and C. Sequin. Sept. 1982. A VLSI RISC. *Computer*. 15(9).

[73] Przybylski, S. May 1990. The performance impact of block sizes and fetch strategies. In *Proceedings 17th Annual International Symposium on Computer Architecture*. Seattle. 160–169.

[74] Przybylski, S., M. Horowitz, and J. Hennessy. May 1988. Performance tradeoffs in cache design. In *Proceedings 15th Annual International Symposium on Computer Architecture*. Honolulu. 290–298.

[75] Radin, G. Mar. 1982. The 801 minicomputer. In *Proceedings International Symposium on Architectural Support for Programming Languages and Operating Systems*. Palo Alto, Calif. 39–47.

[76] Riseman, E. M., and C. C. Foster. Dec. 1972. The inhibition of potential parallelism by conditional jumps. *IEEE Transactions on Computers*. C–21(12):1405–1411.

[77] Schneck, P. B. 1987. *Supercomputer architecture*. Norwell, Mass.: Kluwer Academic Publishers.

[78] Simmons, M. L., and H. J. Wasserman. Nov. 1990. Performance evaluation of the IBM RISC System/6000: comparison of an optimized scalar processor with two vector processors. In *Proceedings Supercomputing '90 Conference*. New York.

[79] Sites, R. L. Aug. 1992. RISC enters a new generation. *Byte*. 141–148.

[80] Smith, A. J. Sept. 1982. Cache memories. *ACM Computing Surveys*. 14:473–530.

[81] Smith, A. J. Sept. 1987. Line (block) size choices for CPU cache memories. *IEEE Transactions on Computers.* C–36(9):1063–1075.

[82] Smith, J. E. May 1981. A study of branch prediction strategies. In *Proceedings of the 8th Annual Symposium on Computer Architecture.* Minneapolis. 135–148.

[83] Smith, J. E. July 1989. Dynamic instruction scheduling and the Astronautics ZS–1. *Computer.* 22(7):21–35.

[84] Smith, J. E., and A. R. Pleszkun. May 1988. Implementing precise interrupts in pipelined processors. *IEEE Transactions on Computers.* C-37(5):562–573.

[85] Smith, M. D., M. Johnson, and M. A. Horowitz. Apr. 1989. Limits on multiple instruction issue. In *Proceedings 3rd International Conference on Architectural Support for Programming Languages and Operating Systems (ASPLOS-III).* Boston. 290–302.

[86] Sohi, G. S. Mar. 1990. Instruction issue logic for high-performance, interruptible, multiple functional unit, pipelined computers. *IEEE Transactions on Computers.* 39(3):349–359.

[87] Stephens, C., et al. May 1991. Instruction level profiling and evaluation of the IBM RS/6000. In *Proceedings 18th Annual International Symposium on Computer Architecture.* Toronto. 180–189.

[88] Stone, H. S. 1990. *High-performance computer architecture.* 2d ed. Reading, Mass.: Addison-Wesley.

[89] Tjaden, G. S., and M. J. Flynn. Oct. 1970. Detection and parallel execution of parallel instructions. *IEEE Transactions on Computers.* C–19(10):889–895.

[90] Tomasulo, R. M. Jan. 1967. An efficient algorithm for exploiting multiple arithmetic units. *IBM Journal.* 11:25–33.

[91] Wall, D. W. Apr. 1991. Limits of instruction-level parallelism. In *Proceedings 4th International Conference on Architectural Support for Programming Languages and Operating Systems (ASPLOS-IV).* Santa Clara, Calif. 176–188.

[92] Wang, E.-H., and J.-L. Baer. May 1988. On the inclusion property for multi-level cache hierarchies. In *Proceedings 15th International Symposium on Computer Architecture.* Honolulu. 73–80.

[93] Weiss, S., and J. E. Smith. Oct. 1987. A study of scalar compilation techniques for pipelined supercomputers. In *Proceedings 2nd International Conference on Architectural Support for Programming Languages and Operating Systems (ASPLOS-II).* Palo Alto, Calif. 105–109.

[94] Wulf, W. A. May 1992. Evaluation of the WM architecture. In *Proceedings 19th Annual International Symposium on Computer Architecture*. Gold Coast, Australia. 382–390.

INDEX